Complete Book of

HOME IMPROVEMENT

Complete Book of

HOME

A Popular Science Book

IMPROVEMENT

Darrell and Frances Huff

Illustrated by Gerald and Carolyn Kinsey
and Bray-Schaible Design Inc.

POPULAR SCIENCE PUBLISHING COMPANY · HARPER & ROW

NEW YORK · LONDON

Library of Congress Catalog Card Number: 74-134231

Designed by Jeff Fitschen

Manufactured in the United States of America

To Paul Corey

Contents

APPENDIX

INDEX

Complete Book of

HOME IMPROVEMENT

Introduction

The Pleasures of Home Improvement

If you find this book tinged here and there with overenthusiasm, please forgive. The enthusiasm arises naturally, out of a conviction about the things with which this book deals. We think that making such substantial home improvements is just about the finest and most productive of spare-time activities.

For the body, there's good exercise in it; and for the soul, the satisfactions of doing, and of having done, something creative and enduring.

Family relationships may benefit as well, and generation gaps narrow. Share with a youngster the pleasures of paneling a wall of his room, or of building a hobby corner into it, and he'll never again take either his room or you quite so unthinkingly for granted.

The economic benefits are equally impressive. They begin with the physical improvement in the quality of your living that a better house brings. But there's more: When you make improvements in your home, you add to its value. To the extent that you do the work yourself, you can expect to add two or three dollars of value for every dollar you lay out. On some of the activities in this book, the ratio is more like one to ten.

1

Improving the home you own is a personal answer to the menace of inflation. The improvements increase the real value of your home, and inflation gives the dollar value an extra boost. Up go the net worth of your family and its financial stability.

All these factors no doubt are reasons why you, as a home-improver, are part of a big industry. The best figures to be had say that it comes to twelve billion dollars a year. Since the estimated one-third of this that is spent on do-it-yourself improvements produces double or triple value, the worth of each year's home improvements actually must come to far more.

This, you will note, is not a remodeling book. It is meant to be a treasury of techniques and ideas from which you can select to produce a total result as small or as large as you wish.

Whatever you do, do it your way. Even if your home is nondescript or impersonal to begin with, you can slowly impose upon it a touch of your own style. Even if you don't think you have one, you'll find one developing as you go.

Darrell and Frances Huff
Carmel, California

PART I

IMPROVE YOUR FLOORS

1

Planning for New and Better Floors

Which of the many modern tile and sheet materials will do the most for your room?

Floors set the keynote for a room—in fact, for the whole house. One decorator calls the floor a "fifth wall" and suggests that floors are the place to start a thorough renovation of any home in need of a fresh, interesting, and practical new look. What's more, some of the new flooring materials are meant to be used on walls, too. This gives flooring a greater importance than it's ever before had for the homeowner.

In the not-too-distant past, the choice was limited. Either the floor was covered with traditional hardwood, splintery softwood, or some kind of carpet. Most of these floor coverings were not only expensive but required constant care and frequent refinishing. Some were delicate, more to look at than walk or run upon.

No longer. The most elegant floors today are as practical and easy to care for as the kitchen sink. Some kinds can be washed, square by square, in that sink. Fine wood floors come with prefinished surfaces that defy scratching. Hardwood flooring is available in many colors, shades, patterns, and finishes. It is resistant to wear and scratches, and can be put down by the homeowner. All the difficult part is done before you get it—the sanding, finishing, and waxing.

Installation in many instances is so easy you can put down

a complete floor and be using it the same day. Some prefinished floors are guaranteed not to chip, mar, or scratch and to last the lifetime of the house.

Variety? You can have random-width planks, parquet squares, ranch planks with beveled edges and walnut pegs, or the more traditional narrow strip flooring. Pieces are even pre-drilled so pegs and screws can be easily installed.

One of the newest products (offered by Bruce*) is Old English, a plank floor with texture. The broad, random-width floor planks are finished with a charcoal-gray stain and then wire-brushed to bring out the texture of the original wood grain, giving the look of a floor that has taken on a patina over a hundred years of wear.

No matter what kind of old floor you now have—concrete, wood, asphalt tile, or solid subfloor—you can get a good job on your new floor. Special mastics are recommended by each manufacturer for his own products, adapted to fit your situation.

There is a new self-stick laminated block flooring (also a Bruce product) which has strips of pressure-sensitive tape on the back. Peel away and place the block in position.

You may want a change from wood. Yours may be an older home with a worn floor that has layers of old varnish, cracks, or dents that cannot be removed with any amount of work. Yet you may not want to undertake the difficult job of removing the floor that is thoroughly nailed down. Carpet squares can be the solution to this problem. They will go a long way toward hiding imperfections without requiring removal of the old floor.

Changes in family situation or size may necessitate a change in flooring. Then the squares of carpet can easily be removed to another room. Worn ones can be shifted to inconspicuous areas to hide cigarette burns or permanent food stains.

Some soft flooring materials do not require binding and will not ravel when trimmed with ordinary scissors or sharp knife. Much of today's roll carpeting comes with a self-back, can be glued down if you wish. If the carpet has no self-pad, adding a hair or foam pad will add a luxurious feel plus years of life to the wear of the carpet.

Resilient floor tile is another easy material for the homeowner to install. But if the old floor is even slightly rough, damaged, or dented, don't make the mistake of thinking the new floor will hide these imperfections. It may when you put it down, but only for a short time, and then your beautiful new floor will take on the shape of those same old bumps and hollows. This is no fault

* Manufacturers' full names and addresses are given in the Appendix.

of the flooring. The fault will be yours. You will need a subfloor of underlayment. This is not expensive or difficult to install. It can be of ¼″ hardboard, particle board, or plywood. There is even a new underlayment with a layer of styrofoam to provide flooring insulation.

What kind of flooring tile should you buy? You can now get three basic types of tile—asphalt, vinyl asbestos, and pure vinyl. There are also cork, rubber, and pure marble tile, but they are not as easy to use in all situations nor are they as inexpensive and versatile as the first three.

Tile patterns resemble anything from ancient Roman mosaic to Greek marble. Some have colored chips floating at random or in patterns. There are stained-glass effects which cannot be detected as plastic until you touch them. Manufactured tile in vinyl imitate glass, marble, slate, stone, and brick so perfectly that they cannot be readily spotted as not the real thing. In use they wear better and stay beautiful longer without the care needed by their genuine counterparts. They do not need to be waxed.

For example, one new type of vinyl-asbestos tile is a duplicate of intricately carved antique Spanish tile, but the cost is only about 35 cents a square foot. For 70 cents a square foot you can buy a diagonally striped tile that permits you to create an individually designed custom floor just by changing the positions of the tile until they please you. You can have a diamond pattern, chevron design, zigzag, or whatever you can think up.

Or how about a vinyl tile that the Congoleum Company promises will never need wax? It's called Shinyl Vinyl, has been floor-tested for several years and only a gentle wiping with mild detergent keeps the new surface glowing. Soon other flooring products will be wearing this same shining surface.

Asphalt tile, lowest priced, is fast losing out to the much-superior vinyl-asbestos, which shares its virtue of being safely usable below grade where there may be dampness.

Exotic and dramatic vinyls can run as high as several dollars per square foot, but most types are in a moderate price range. They are available in both tile and sheets, but the large sheets are more difficult for the inexperienced homeowner to lay.

Proceed in choosing a new floor by considering all the materials and the areas of recommended use. What kind of family do you have? Pets and small children do not go well with fragile materials or non-cleanable delicate shades. Teenagers are big eaters and they spill soft drinks. Are there careless smokers in your household? Is the new flooring going into a room where the present floor is cold or damp? Are there a lot of angles and cutouts which may waste wide widths of flooring but use material efficiently if it comes in squares or sections? Do you plan to rent your house, or will the flooring be used solely by a couple of careful adults in their retirement years?

Your choice should definitely be guided as much by the who as the where. One householder, who eventually laid a large, expensive slate floor, first tested a sample of slate material by spilling a bottle of permanent ink and a cup of oil on the sample and letting it sit for twenty-four hours. When no stain remained after the ink and oil were wiped up, he was sure his four children couldn't think of anything that would damage slate.

Thus slate, often thought of only for a roof or entryway, makes an excellent indoor floor. It isn't soft, but it is no harder than many other materials and requires no maintenance beyond an optional annual treatment with a slate sealer. It mops or sweeps easily. Scratches can be removed with water, and it cannot be worn out in any human lifetime.

Laying a slate floor is well within the capacity of any determined householder. Yet it is extremely expensive to have it put down by a trained craftsman. You can lay slate in ordinary mortar, the usual practice over a concrete slab, letting the same mortar form the grouting between the pieces of slate.* Or you can put it down with ceramic-tile adhesive, which has the advantage of adhering well to wood or other surfaces and of adding very little thickness. Grouting is then done with portland-cement mortar.

Whatever type of floor you choose, consider the overall effect you wish to achieve. A different flooring, no matter how luxurious, in every room will make your home seem chopped and cluttered. It may be a good decision to do all the living area in one material, and all the hard-use rooms in another. Visit model homes for ideas. The small samples you see in a store can be as deceiving as choosing paint for a house by relying on a 1″ square sample of the color.

Contractors usually stick to the same carpet throughout a model house in order to create an illusion of generous space. You can do this, too. They know that a neutral color, or a tweed mixture, shows less traffic and soil than a dark color. Light colors also give a feeling of spaciousness.

If hardwood floors are used, then color and variety can be achieved by using scatter rugs. If stone, slate, or brick is chosen, then softness can be brought in with extra-luxurious, colorful area

* How to do this is shown photographically and described in detail in the author's book, *How to Work with Concrete and Masonry,* published by Popular Science Publishing Co., Inc., and Harper & Row.

rugs. It is far more economical to use the same material in large amounts than to work with a half-dozen types.

Today's floor coverings are so practical and easy to use that updating any floor is the easiest and least expensive way to make a major change in your home.

How do you go about it? Laying a wood floor? Pouring a seamless plastic floor? Working with floor tile? Doing a job with large sheets of material? The chapters that follow will give you step-by-step information that lets you save money by doing the work yourself.

2

Which Wood Flooring?

Strip, plank, or block? Oak, maple, or hemlock? How to buy the best for the purpose and spend the least

What kind of wood floor would you like? Name it and most likely you can have it. With so many kinds of wood offered in so many dimensions, patterns, shades and colors there is almost no end to the effects you can obtain.

Your basic choice is among three general types. *Strip* flooring is narrow boards. *Plank* flooring is wide boards, usually containing contrasting pegs. *Block* gives a parquet effect, most often in squares.

With that choice made, you'll go on to pick a kind of wood and perhaps a kind of grain in that wood. You will also have a choice of stain. Flooring today not only comes in its natural colors but in other shades such as deep forest green, charcoal, or blue. You may also have a choice of grade, which boils down to how much you are willing to pay for absence of knots and other defects. You'll also have to consider thickness and type of pattern, matters having little to do with final appearance and depending mostly on what floor situation you are starting with.

And then there is your final choice: some kinds come either unfinished or prefinished. The unfinished kinds call for more work, of course, and the prefinished for more outlay of money. New types of really durable factory finish cannot be duplicated by the home craftsman, so there is much to be said for choosing a factory sanded and finished material.

STRIP FLOORING. This is the most usual kind, the type you may already have if you own an older home. It's what people usually mean when they say simply "hardwood floors." In popularity it's losing ground to block and plank types.

The most common strip flooring is oak boards tongued and grooved on edges and ends, $25/32$" thick and $2\frac{1}{4}$" wide. Or it may be $1\frac{1}{2}$", 2", or $3\frac{1}{4}$" wide. A popular variation calls for alternate strips of $2\frac{1}{4}$" and $3\frac{1}{4}$" widths.

All these dimensions are actual and do not include the width of the tongue.

If you are laying a new floor over a sound old one you'll very likely prefer to use thinner flooring—$\frac{3}{8}$" or $\frac{1}{2}$". These won't raise the floor level so much and they'll save you money.

T&g strip flooring is made in these dimensions in white and red oak and in beech, birch, hard maple, and pecan, less often in other woods. You'll also find hemlock, an excellent softwood flooring, in $25/32$" x $2\frac{1}{4}$".

This kind of strip flooring is laid by blind or "secret" nailing—diagonally through the tongues. It is face nailed only along edges where molding will cover.

Less often used in square-edge strip flooring, which you simply butt together and face nail. Nail heads are then set and holes filled before finishing. Oak square-edge strips are commonly made in $5/16$" thickness, $1\frac{1}{2}$" or 2" wide. In maple, birch, beech, and pecan it is usually $25/32$" thick, $2\frac{1}{2}$" and $3\frac{1}{2}$" wide.

Some makers offer strip flooring in prefinished form. As soon as it's nailed it's ready to use.

PLANK FLOORING. You're seeing more and more of this type in new homes, particularly those of ranch style. It ordinarily consists of much wider boards and usually contains pegs (small, round pieces of wood placed in the planks as described later).

As with strip, the most usual type is tongued and grooved on edges and ends, although some varieties are not end matched and others are square-edged all round. Usual thickness is $25/32$" or $13/16$" or, in a veneered type, $\frac{7}{8}$". Widths run all the way from 3" to 9" and it is unusual width of the boards, usually laid random, that gives plank floors so much of their charm.

You can vary the width used within a strip by butting one length of 3", say, and one of 5" against the end of an 8" strip.

Most plank flooring is blind-nailed like strip, but it needs more than that to hold it securely because so many of the boards are so wide. Usual method is to put one or two screws near the ends of the boards and additional screws or face nails at intervals of about 30″ between. Screw holes are counterbored and heads covered by pegs made for this purpose. It is customary to use contrasting pegs (walnut with oak flooring) at the ends of the boards and matching pegs elsewhere.

A popular variation is really strip flooring, prefinished and laid in alternate $2\frac{1}{4}$″ and $3\frac{1}{4}$″ strips with blind nailing alone. Since it contains round walnut plugs that resemble actual functioning dowels or pegs, it looks very much like traditional plank floor.

Also unusual and quite different is a plank effect laid in mastic without any nailing, in much the same manner as asphalt tile. It can be fastened to almost any sound subsurface—wood, plywood, concrete, terrazzo, old asphalt tile. Thus it permits a plank floor laid directly over a concrete slab without sleepers.

This flooring is made of $\frac{3}{16}$″ oak, prefinished blond or medium, is 9″ wide and comes in assorted lengths 4′ to 8′. Almost invisible slits every half inch, top and bottom, reduce any problems of expansion and contraction and also let the flooring conform to slight irregularities of subfloor.

BLOCK OR PARQUET. Fine parquetry is mighty expensive and has always been associated with public buildings or ballrooms in mansions rather than small houses. Modern block types, however, are within the cost range of other flooring and can be installed by the home craftsman.

The basic type is 9″ square and $\frac{1}{2}$″ or $\frac{25}{32}$″ thick. One company now makes squares 19″ x 19″, available in ten kinds of wood. The joints are square with no dirt-catching beveled edges.

Usual kinds are tongued and grooved and may be laid in mastic over concrete or nailed to a wood subfloor or old floor. Bruce has recently come out with a self-stick parquet square.

Also made for laying over concrete (including slab floors containing radiant heating) are *laminated* oak blocks $\frac{1}{2}$″ thick. The three plies increase stability and make membrane waterproofing unnecessary in the slab unless there is hydrostatic pressure. No expansion spaces or joints are needed.

A new development brought on by the increasing use of radiant floor heat is 8″-square tiles of $\frac{5}{16}$″ gothic oak, each tile being made up of four strips. The strips cut down the expansion problem and the oak itself—long considered a fine cabinet wood— has the great advantage of expanding only one fourth as much as plain oak under changes in humidity. Gothic oak is also offered in foot-square tiles consisting of four 6″ squares flexibly cemented together.

Still another handsome parquet type is a basketweave pattern of foot-square blocks composed of 2″ x 4″ and 2″ x 2″ pieces. These ¼″-thick units are made in gothic, blond and medium oak, walnut, mahogany, and teak. Like all the other special types described above, this kind comes prefinished.

Most hardwood floors are oak, made of the nine varieties classed as white oak or the eleven called red oak. Red oak has a pinkish cast rather than brownish and finishes to more of a reddish brown. Red oak is somewhat more uniform in color and may be slightly easier to finish. One gives as good a floor as the other.

In oak you have a further choice between plain- and quarter-sawed. The latter gives a prominent figure that you may not prefer.

Next in popularity is hard maple. It is harder than oak and will take heavier wear, a quality of more interest in gymnasiums than homes. The grain and figure are, of course, much less conspicuous than with oak and there are no pores to fill in finishing.

Birch and beech make a very hard floor, much like maple. Pecan is harder and darker in color than any other wood commonly used for flooring.

Hemlock, though technically a softwood, makes a floor that can be both handsome and durable at relatively low cost. One maker calls it the "hard softwood" and offers it in the tongue-and-grooved and end-matched pattern that is most popular in oak strip flooring.

All the woods mentioned here are widely used in production of strip flooring. You may not be able to find plank types in anything except oak, although walnut and teak and many veneers are used. Block floors are mainly offered in oak too.

Whether you choose strip, plank, or block flooring, you can find both unfinished and prefinished types. You'll have a choice of light and dark shades, as well as colors.

FINISHES. If you have sanding equipment available (and rental sanders are offered almost everywhere), you can save a good deal of money by doing your own finishing. You'll earn the money, of course.

Prefinished flooring permits you to use the floor as soon as it is laid and insures a good and lasting finish. Some of the new plastic finishes are extremely durable, will not yellow, do not need frequent refinishing, may last the life of the floor.

Prefinished flooring also permits you to avoid the dust and mess made in an occupied house by a sander.

If you do decide on unfinished flooring, keep in mind that most manufacturers now recommend penetrating sealers rather than the older stain-and-varnish treatment or shellac or lacquer. Penetrating sealers look good longer, can easily be refinished or touched up in worn spots, don't chip or scratch. Principal objection is that sealers give a good deal less shine to the floor. Not everyone will consider this a drawback.

ECONOMIZING. Buying something less than the choicest grade offers the best opportunity to save money on a flooring job. Any grade will give a good, sound floor. Higher grades simply are freer of knots, streaks, sapwood, variations in color, and small manufacturing defects that have little to do with strength and durability. Higher grades often include pieces that are somewhat longer.

It is worth considering also that lower grades are preferred by some people because of the informality, interest, and character given to a floor by these natural defects.

Another chance to save money is in buying the very cheapest grade to be found and then cutting out serious defects. This produces shorter pieces and makes more work but it also gives a fine floor at a considerable saving.

Starting in each case with the finest—and most costly— variety, the grades of quarter-sawed oak are clear, sap clear, select; of plain-sawed, clear, select, No. 1 common, No. 2 common.

Beech, birch, and maple are graded first, second, third. So is pecan, which is also made in a fourth grade. In prefinished oak flooring, grades are prime, standard & better, standard, tavern. Prefinished beech and pecan are normally offered only in one grade, tavern & better.

Many special floorings are offered in only a single thickness but the standard varieties in widest use often come in a choice of several.

Thinner flooring is naturally cheaper. And it will do as well, if applied over an old floor or a thoroughly sound subfloor.

If the subfloor is doubtful, it is wise to use one of the thicker types, usually about $25/_{32}''$. If your floor is to be put down over screeds (sleepers) on concrete, or directly onto joists without any subfloor, use flooring at least $25/_{32}''$ thick.

ADHESIVES, NAILS, ETC. Along with the flooring of your choice you'll probably buy what it takes to put it down. Mastic is no problem: just buy the adhesive made or recommended by the manufacturer of the flooring you are using.

Best bets in nails for strip flooring are usually suggested by the manufacturer. Don't try to economize on nails; the answer to squeaky floors is plenty of nails, and the best time to do the nailing is when the floor goes down.

Square-edge flooring calls for $1\frac{1}{8}''$ barbed-wire flooring brads with No. 16 heads. Put two nails every $7''$.

For plank floors buy enough nails to blind-nail in the same manner as for strip flooring. You'll also need $1\frac{1}{4}''$ No. 12 flathead wood screws for the ends of the pieces and about every $30''$ between. Some of the newer and more expensive plank floors come with pre-drilled screw holes.

Unless you are flooring a room in which the old molding can be salvaged, you'll need something to finish off the edges. Commonly this is a base mold, in any width you like, plus a shoe mold. Shoe mold is like quarter-round (and you can substitute a quarter-round if you like) except for being longer one way than the other.

Fancy base molds are still made but the plain ones are more in use these days. Most are simple rectangles in cross-section except for having hollowed backs for better fit and the upper corner rounded. An interesting variation has the diagonally opposite corners rounded—permitting you to reverse the molding if one side or edge should be damaged.

Also offered in some places are special base molds to be used without a shoe mold.

One last pointer: Have your flooring delivered several days before you'll be ready to lay it. You'll get a smoother, tighter floor if the material can be kept for four or five days in the house where it is to be used. Stack it loosely in a room heated to about 70 degrees so that its moisture content can become the same as that of the house. Don't store it or lay it in a damp house—one that has just been plastered, for instance.

A good wood floor can be a lifetime proposition, so it's worthwhile to select it carefully and handle it right.

Wood-Block Floors

You can now put oak or pecan prefinished blocks over old floors, even asphalt tile

Dingy old floors depress a room and make for a lot of upkeep. Any you have in your house now can be transformed with pre-finished wood blocks that are pleasant to walk on and easy to maintain.

Today's improved adhesives make it possible to install oak or pecan blocks over any sound surface that is dry and reasonably smooth. The nature of the blocks themselves makes it easy.

The blocks are factory-finished 9″ squares (one company makes a 19″ square) of laminated oak or pecan, with tongue-and-groove joints. They can safely be installed directly over wooden floors or subfloors or on concrete that remains dry year round. A new slab should have thirty days to cure first.

In at least one line, that made by E. L. Bruce Co., you have a choice of regular and self-stick tiles. Just strip off protective paper and put down the tiles on a suitable surface. The plain tiles go down with mastic, spread with a notched trowel.

Start by taking up the shoe mold at the baseboard. Then prepare the old floor. Here's how:

Asphalt tile. Scrub thoroughly to remove all the old wax. Remove any loose tiles and level the space with the latex patching cement that flooring dealers sell.

Concrete. Grind down any high spots with a coarse abrasive stone. Fill low spots with patching cement. Sweep carefully, then prime. If dampness may be present in on-grade concrete, spread a thin layer of mastic (100 square feet per gallon) plus a layer of two-mil polyethylene film. Bring the film up behind the baseboards if possible. Then spread mastic for block flooring.

Painted concrete. Scrub it clean. Scrape or sand off any loose paint. Spread mastic and lay one block. Check it for adhesion in the morning. If it sticks—go ahead. If it comes up, try other types of mastic or remove the paint entirely.

Plywood. Be sure it's nailed down tight, usually at 4″ intervals along edges and 8″ throughout. Check for high spots and sand them down. Scuff-sand any painted areas.

Wood floors. Scrub away the old wax. If floorboards are warped, cover with a well-nailed underlayment of hardboard or ¼″ plywood.

Establish a guide line across the center of the room. Lay down a single row of blocks from the center point to the wall, starting with the first block centered on the center point. If you end up with less than a half block at the wall, start with a joint at the center point and you will get a larger block along the wall. You'll have less waste and the border tiles will be an even width.

HOW TO LAY A WOOD-BLOCK FLOOR

1. Before laying wood blocks over an old floor, level any low spots with latex patching cement. Then sand or grind down high spots and bumps.

2. Recement any loose tile. Pry up broken tile and fill holes with floor-leveling compound (left). Before laying blocks on painted floor, be sure to clean it thoroughly with solvent or wax-remover (right). Blocks will not adhere to a surface that is dirty, oily, or waxed.

3. Use a brush primer on any area of bare concrete to assure a good bond when the block is cemented.

4. If you're applying parquet blocks to an old wooden floor, be sure it is smooth and solidly nailed. Over a wooden subfloor, as shown here, put down sheets of underlayment. When subfloor is tongue-and-groove material or 5/8" or thicker plywood, the underlayment is usually not necessary.

17

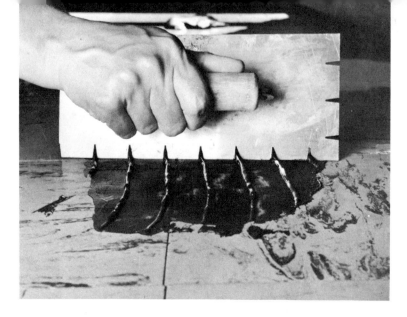

5. Spread the adhesive with a specially notched trowel obtained from block supplier or made from an ordinary finishing trowel. Notches are $\frac{5}{32}''$ wide, $\frac{7}{16}''$ deep, $1''$ apart. Hold trowel almost vertical to make heavy ridges of adhesive, as shown here.

6. With room temperature above 50 degrees and maximum ventilation, spread cement to cover about 55 square feet per gallon. Have all fans, pilot lights, stoves, motors, and other sources of fire or sparks shut off. Let adhesive dry at least twenty minutes. To test adhesive, press a corner of a block into it. Unless some adheres, as shown here, adhesive is too dry and must be scraped up and new coating given to the surface.

7. Mastic should be troweled on about two hours before laying the blocks. Snap blocks into place as shown, with a minimum of sliding.

6.

7.

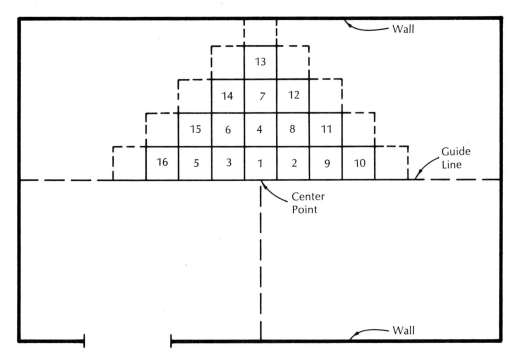

8. Diagram indicates method of establishing center point and procedure for laying blocks on one side of the guide line first, then on the other. Follow the numbers.

You can buy a notched mastic trowel, but you can make one from an inexpensive plasterer's trowel. File V notches on $\frac{1}{2}''$ center, making them $\frac{3}{16}''$ wide and $\frac{1}{4}''$ deep.

Be sure the room is well ventilated, then spread mastic over all the area to one side of the guide line. Lay blocks from center of guide line towards the walls. Use mineral spirits to remove any mastic that sneaks onto the surface of the blocks.

Fit blocks around obstacles and up to walls as closely as possible. Except in very large rooms, no expansion strips or spaces at the walls are needed. To shape the blocks, use any woodworking tools. A band saw is especially useful.

Complete the job by installing oak nosing strip wherever needed to overcome any difference in elevation at doorways. Replace the old shoe mold or install a new one at the walls. Both nosing and shoe mold are offered in prefinished oak.

Laminated hardwood blocks are in the same cost range as cork or solid vinyl.

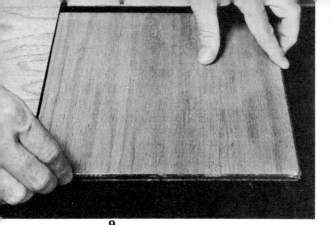

9.

10.

9. Lay the blocks in a straight line, checking occasionally to be sure they line up properly. Press each block down firmly and slide it slightly into position to break the film that forms on the surface of the adhesive. Don't slide too far or adhesive may be forced up through the joint.

10. If an occasional block refuses to slide fully into place, tap it in lightly with a hammer or mallet. You can do this most easily by using a scrap block of flooring. You will lay most blocks while kneeling on a section just laid. If this section tends to skid slightly, use a platform of plywood about 24" x 30" to work from.

11. Laminated block flooring needs no allowance for expansion. It should be placed tightly from wall to wall so it can't slip and open up cracks between blocks. Tighten it up by driving in wedges wherever there are gaps, as here. Wedges can be made from scraps of the blocks themselves. When you add the trim or replace the old molding you'll cover them.

12. A few of these headless, hardened steel nails will come in handy. Get them from the flooring supplier. You can use them to lock flooring edges after first prying pieces tightly together with a pinch bar, as shown here. If any area in the finished floor squeaks slightly, it's an indication of a depression in the old floor. Use hardened nails to fasten it down, even to concrete.

11.

12.

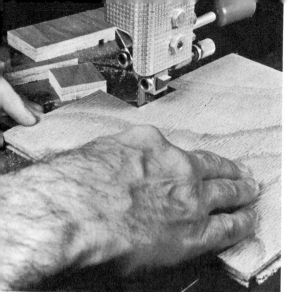

13.

14.

13. Blocks that go around the edges of the room will probably have to be cut to fit. A handsaw will do the work, but a power saw is faster. A jigsaw is handiest for odd-shaped pieces.

14. Apply pressure to the blocks as soon as you've finished an area. Six feet are better than two, but, lacking several daughters, you can borrow a floor roller from your dealer. To remove handling marks and make your floor look its best, finish the job with a light paste-waxing and polish it.

15. You'll find your block floor is as pleasant to use as to look at. It will require little mainenance, thanks to the factory finish. Dry-mop—don't wash—it, or you may remove the attractive brand-new look which should stay for years.

4

How to Pour a Floor

Seamless floors are now a do-it-yourself product with a multitude of home-improvement uses

The intriguing pour-and-scatter process of laminating a floor has slipped from the professional applicator's grasp into yours and mine.

Ten years ago it didn't exist, and today more than a billion square feet of plastic have revolutionized the flooring and home-renovating business. There are a number of interesting combinations of clear acrylic, epoxy, or urethane plastic which, combined with colorful plastic chips, produce a three-dimensional effect—and add a realm of possibilities to the home-improvement field for do-it-yourselfers.

As a flooring it is seamless, durable, decorative, resistant to most liquid spills found in a home, and almost maintenance-free. Since you pour and roll it into place, you can bring it right up to a bathtub and even all the way up a wall and across the ceiling if you want to.

It is excellent for kitchen counters, indoor and outdoor tabletops, bathtub surrounds, and even for coating a whole shower or cast-in-place tub—walls, base and all.

It promises to be a remodeler's standby, since it can be applied over any sound old surface, including plywood and concrete and all the usual resilient floorings such as asphalt tile. Major exception: it is not recommended for application over cork.

New concrete should not be coated until it has had thirty days to cure, and all smooth concrete should be acid-etched.

Smooth metals should be etched, and the hard surface of ceramic tile should be abraded to roughen it slightly.

Although seamless flooring is a new product for house-holders, it has been thoroughly tested over several years of professional application. At applied prices of one to several dollars a square foot, its use has necessarily been limited. But when you do the job yourself and have only material cost to consider, you can have a seamless floor for somewhere around 50 cents a square foot.

The product you see in the photographs is Flecto Seamless*. It is sold in retail stores in the form of kits to cover from 25 square feet up in any of 10 color combinations. These vary from a soft beige effect called parchment to brilliant yellows and greens.

The various other seamless-floor systems now available to do-it-yourselfers differ from this one chemically and in packaging —and somewhat in procedures, in color effects offered, and in where they may be used successfully.

Flecto can be used outdoors as well as inside since its plastic is an acrylic and will not yellow when exposed to sunlight. Some brands use urethane plastic in one formulation for the chip coat and another for the finish glaze. A special exterior grade is often available.

Urethane tends to take on a yellowish tone if exposed to much sun. One way to lessen this effect is to stick to shades of yellow, brown, or red which hide the yellowing effect. Avoid shades of blue and green. Acrylics, although they do not yellow, are not as durable as the urethane plastics and require refinishing more frequently. Gloss life of a urethane plastic can be as long as five years, whereas a plastic with an acrylic topping may need to be reglazed twice a year.

The seamless-floor product called Dur-A-Flex is the most unlike the others. It begins with an epoxy base coat, white or tinted, into which the color chips are sown, eliminating a separate chip coat. An optional sealer coat may be used over the chips for better leveling. This pretty much eliminates sanding and also reduces the amount of glaze required for finishing. A catalyst that comes with the clear urethane can be used to speed curing.

STEP 1—SURFACE PREPARATION. In using Flecto Seamless, as with almost any finishing, the first step is surface preparation. Clean the old surface to remove such things as dirt, grease, wax, and loose paint. Unless the floor is thoroughly cleaned, the base coat might lift and all other coats would lift with it. Nail down anything that is loose, and fill all cracks.

* See Appendix for manufacturer's address.

If you are dealing with a poor surface, such as rough sub-floor in new construction, install underlayment. Plywood is good for this, and so is hardboard. On the basis of consultation with an experienced professional applicator of seamless floors, it is suggested that you use particleboard for the same reason he does—it is smooth, easy to handle, and cheap.

Nail the underlayment thoroughly, leaving a slight gap between sheets. Use galvanized nails to avoid rust spots from action of the water-base first coat. Disguise all the joints with a good crack-filler, using this also between underlayment and wall unless molding will cover. Sand the filler level.

Instead of providing a new surface, sealing an old one may be what is called for. Some manufacturers, including Flecto, offer a sealer to be applied over any floor that might produce asphalt or color bleeding. If you're in doubt, the maker suggests, use it. Or you can proceed with the next two steps on a small test area, watching for evidence of bleeding. Rust stains from nails may not show up for twelve hours or so.

STEP 2—BASE COAT. A roller applies it nicely, with help from a paintbrush in corners and tight spots. This is a water-soluble paint —making for easy cleaning of brush and roller—but once it has dried, water won't touch it. Apply a full wet coat of this base, which is white in most of the color combinations offered in Flecto kits. Give it two or three hours to dry. Better wash your brush, hands, and any spills immediately. They won't come off so easily in an hour or so.

STEP 3—PLASTIC COAT. Apply a coat of laminating plastic to an area not larger than about 16 square feet. This, too, should be a full wet coat and a short-nap paint roller handles it nicely. Disposable rollers are best, because the plastic cannot be cleaned out easily.

Observe all safety precautions advised for flammable products. This means that when working with the laminating plastic you should provide ample ventilation and have no fires or pilot lights in the area. Even devices that may produce sparks when starting, such as electric refrigerators, should be disconnected temporarily. And, of course, no smoking!

Although most seamless-surface materials are far less hazardous than some common paint and adhesive products, it is wise to treat them with respect. Inhale fumes as little as possible. And if you are particularly sensitive, or if you are working in an area hard to ventilate well—such as a shower—use a chemical mask or goggles.

1.   **2.**

1. Seamless flooring can be applied directly to a solid old floor that is sound, smooth, and level. With floors that are in bad condition, or with wood subfloors—especially strip or block floors—simplest way to provide a good base is by putting down underlayment. Particle board is shown here. Since none of the seamless systems will bridge cracks, you must fill gaps between underlayment sheets or tile. When crack-filler has dried, sand it smooth. Any hollows or bumps you leave will show when floor is completed. They may not show up for weeks after you finish the job.

2. A roller is quickest for applying the base coat, and a long handle eases big jobs and saves your knees. Where there is danger of color, nail, or asphalt bleeding, as when covering floor tiles, precede base coat with a sealer coat applied in the same way.

3. Roll on a coat of clear laminating plastic, covering about 16 square feet to begin with, and then immediately scatter, sow, or pitch color chips. Let them sift from a height of 2 feet or so till they cover the wet plastic completely and uniformly. If you should miss a few spots the patching can be done inconspicuously when you put on a second coat of plastic.

4. Continue to roll on clear plastic in areas about 2' by 8', covering each area with chips before proceeding to the next. Try to stop chips slightly short of the end of the plastic coat each time.

5. After chip-coating the whole floor, allow several hours for drying. Then sweep off excess flakes with a clean broom. Sweep gently, and save the flakes for use next time. Now give the floor another hour or two to dry thoroughly.

6. Give the whole floor another full wetcoat of laminating plastic to lock in the flakes. Although the floor will usually be dry enough to walk on after about three hours, it should be permitted to dry at least overnight before sanding.

3.

4.

5.

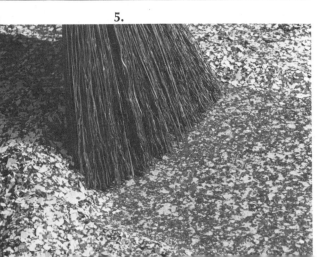

6.

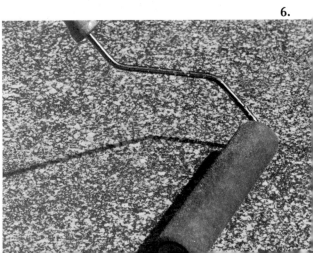

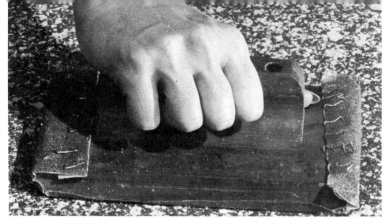

7. Sand the whole floor lightly with a medium-grit paper. Moderate pressure is sufficient. All you are doing is removing any rough spots produced by flakes standing on edge. Use a damp cloth or a vacuum cleaner to get rid of sanding dust.

8. Apply a final coat of the same clear plastic. This provides the wearing surface and adds to the lustre and to the three-dimensional effect. Areas of hard use can have another coat or two.

9. Dappled sunlight playing on family-room floor of Flecto Seamless flooring picks out flecks of white and parchment in the clear acrylic to give effect of depth.

27

STEP 4—SEED WITH CHIPS. Take handfuls of the colored chips included in the kit and toss them over the wet surface. You can do this standing up, pitching them as you would a baseball and letting them sift down like snowflakes. Sow them generously till the surface is well covered; you'll sweep up the excess to use later.

Continue across the floor, rolling on the liquid plastic and seeding with chips. You can sweep off the excess chips with a clean broom after the chip coat has dried for one to two hours. If you find bare spots where chips have failed to cover, brush on a little plastic and toss on some chips.

STEP 5—SECOND COAT. After another couple of hours, apply a second full wet coat of the clear laminating plastic, right over the flakes this time. Your roller will pick up bits of flakes but will then deposit them again, with no harm done. This coat locks in the color flakes. Let it dry at least overnight. It should not feel tacky to the touch. It will pick up threads, lint, or bits from your broom until it is thoroughly dry.

STEP 6—SAND THE SURFACE. A sanding block helps. Garnet paper in 80 grit is about right. After sanding, use a cloth or a vacuum cleaner to take up the dust.

STEP 7—FINAL COAT. Apply a final coat of the clear laminating plastic. You can use a roller this time too, and a brush in any tight corners, or you can take a tip from the pro. He says he can get a quicker job with less chance of bubbles by dumping the plastic onto the floor and spreading it with a trowel.

You'll find that this works fine. It is especially good for small areas to which you want to give a heavy coat for maximum protection, such as a sink counter or a tabletop. But don't make the mistake of using an old cement-finishing trowel that has spots of rust on it. The rust will leave stains. You'll have to wipe them up and start over.

If you want more depth to your floor, or if you want it to wear even longer in a place having a lot of traffic, you can add another plastic coat after several hours.

Or you can wait until some future year when signs of wear show up. Then clean the floor and spread on another coat of plastic. Easy renewal is another of the big virtues of this process. Renewing it only partially in a few areas will match up well with areas that have not received wear or damage.

Maintenance of a seamless floor has been found to take no more than half the time required for most conventional surfaces.

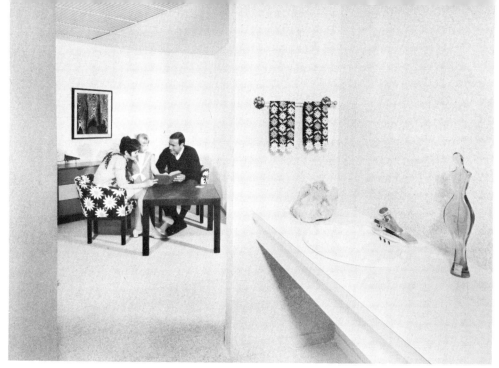

Seamless goes anywhere. Here it goes up the baseboard and onto the walls, is as appropriate for bath as for game room, lends itself to gay decorative accents, and provides a housewife with an easily cleaned surface.

No waxing or buffing is required. Spots come off with a little ammonia in water. Sweep or damp-mop it.

A seamless floor is not the perfect answer to all floor problems. Some manufacturers do not recommend their product for use on outdoor decks or floors below grade where there may be moisture seeping up from underneath. Nor is it as soft under foot as cushioned vinyl, cork, or rubber. But it is more resilient than slate, brick, or tile, and if you put it down over a cushioned floor that is old you will, of course, retain the cushioning of the old floor.

A seamless floor does eliminate the old problem of cracks that catch dirt. It is attractive and can be dramatically beautiful, depending upon the artistic eye of the homeowner who can choose the colors and design his own patterns.

5

How to Lay Resilient Floor Tile

Whether your tile is vinyl-asbestos, pure vinyl, asphalt, or cork, here are the steps in using it

Floor tile is the all-purpose cure for an old floor, especially for the do-it-yourselfer who wants an installation job that doesn't require a lot of skill. Resilient floor tile is not difficult to lay—*if* you have a smooth floor surface to begin with and *if* you use the recommended adhesive and follow the directions that come with your tile.

Price range for the various kinds of resilient tile can be from as little as 10 cents a square foot to several dollars, depending on whether you pick up a small lot of discontinued colors or patterns at a sale or whether you want a floor in the best vinyl with an elaborately embossed pattern in stained-glass colors. But the laying job is much the same regardless of cost of the material.

No matter how expensive the tile, it won't adhere evenly and permanently unless the old floor is free of wax and grease.

The floor must also be free of grit and bumps. Imperfections from the floor beneath will not show up at first, but they will within a few months, and then there is no way to get rid of them. It's a rare floor that is so perfect you can lay a new floor directly on top of it. In this series of photographs the experts show you how to do a good job.

STEPS IN LAYING RESILIENT FLOOR TILE

1. Make sure old floor is smooth and free of wax, paint, varnish, grease, and oil. Holes or cracks in subfloors should be filled with crack filler. Plane down high spots and renail loose boards of wood floors.

2. Where wood subfloor is only a single layer, or double-layer floor boards are in bad condition, the old floor should be covered with underlayment hardboard. You can also use particle board or plywood underneath.

3. Nail underlayment with coated or ring-groove nails every 4″ along edges and over entire face of the panels. On this type of underlayment the handyman helpers are green dots printed every 4″ as a nailing guide. You could rent a nailing machine to ease and speed up this part of the job.

4. Find the center point of each of the two end walls of the room. Connect these two points with a chalk line down middle of room.

5. Locate the center of this line. Use a carpenter's square, as shown here, and draw a perpendicular line. Or place a tile with one edge on center of line to establish the perpendicular.

6. Along this perpendicular line, strike another chalk line extending to both of the side walls.

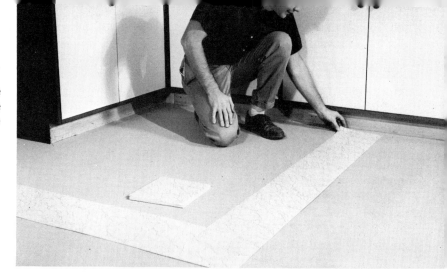

7. Along chalk lines, lay one test row of uncemented tile from the center point to one side wall and end wall.

8. Measure distance between the wall and the last tile. If the distance is less than 2″ or more than 8″, move the center line parallel to that wall 4½″ closer to the wall.

9. If the distance between the last tile in the previous step is less than 2″ or more than 8″, move the center line parallel to that wall 4½″ closer to the wall. Strike a new center line.

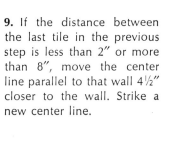

10. By moving the center line closer to the wall, additional space is gained that eliminates the need of installing border tiles that are too narrow. Since the line is moved 4½", half the size of one tile, the border tile remains uniform around the entire room.

11. Spread a coat of brushing-grade cement over one quarter of the room. Do not cover the chalk lines. For the new embossed vinyl-asbestos tiles, the adhesive should be troweled on. A brush can be used for regular vinyl-asbestos tile.

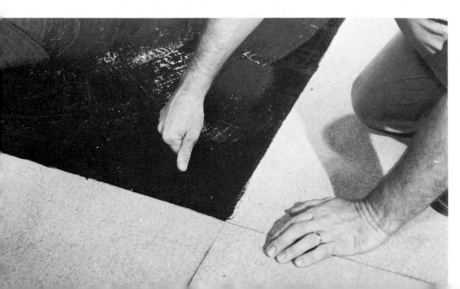

12. Allow cement to dry about fifteen minutes. Then test the cement for proper tackiness by touching lightly with the thumb. It should feel tacky but should not stick to the thumb. If it sticks to the thumb, allow more drying time.

13. Starting at the center, place tiles in cement, making sure that the first tiles are flush with the chalk lines and each tile is butted against the adjoining tiles. Do not slide tiles into place.

14. To fit border tiles, place a loose tile exactly over the last tile in the row. Then take another tile and place it on top of loose tile. Butt second tile against the wall and mark first tile with a pencil along the edge of second tile. With ordinary scissors cut tile along the pencil mark.

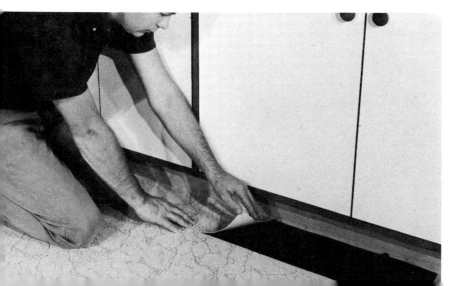

15. The cut portion of the first tile will fit exactly onto the border space. Repeat this procedure until the border area is completely covered. Each quarter of the room should be rolled with a smooth roller when done.

35

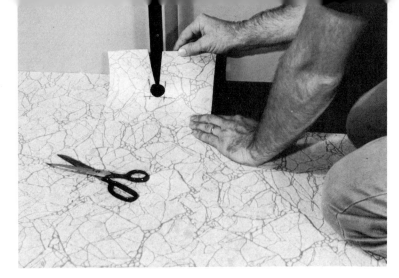

16. To fit around pipes or other obstructions, first make a paper pattern to fit the space exactly. Then trace the outline into the tile and cut with scissors.

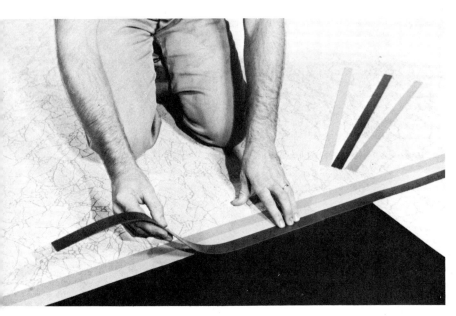

17. Plain colors in vinyl-asbestos strips can be used to create an unusual custom design. Several colors will give an interesting accent.

18. Final step is installation of a vinyl cove base. This is an optional extra that eliminates the dirt-catching crack at the edge. Color can be matching or contrasting.

6

How to Lay Sheet Vinyl

Loose-lay method and new 12′-wide material make this a do-it-yourself job at last

If you like to do a floor job yourself, you've probably installed at least one resilient floor in your home. Most likely it was a tile floor.

Until now, tile flooring was the only material easy enough for the homeowner to use. Sheet flooring, so desirable because it goes down in a hurry and has no seams, was just too complicated for an inexperienced person to install expertly. A professional had to be hired to do the job.

No longer!

You can now obtain 12′-wide cushioned vinyl flooring that goes down quickly at any grade level without the use of adhesives. Armstrong Cork Company produces it under the name of Castilian. It is laid over concrete, plywood, hardboard—or even an old resilient floor—and is finished with a quarter-round moulding or vinyl cove base around the edge of the room.

The extra width of this material—double that of ordinary sheet vinyl flooring—reduces the number of seams in the finished job. In small rooms there are no seams at all. In an average 12′ x 15′ kitchen, for example, it produces a totally uninterrupted floor surface with no seams to attract or hold dirt and moisture. There is no crack to be damaged or broken in use.

In rooms that are wider than 12′, making a seam necessary, it is best to apply a 4″ band of adhesive along the seam line.

Of course, the new 12'-wide flooring can still be installed by conventional methods, using adhesive over the entire subfloor.

This new sheet-vinyl flooring is produced by rotogravure technique. Its printed design is covered by a tough layer of clear vinyl which needs little maintenance. Its special core of resilient foam makes it comfortable and quiet underfoot. The backing is moistureproof asbestos which makes the flooring suitable for usually damp areas such as garages, porches, and basements.

Asbestos backing also gives dimensional stability to prevent the flooring from creeping or buckling when loose-laid. This eliminates the necessity of retrimming when the floor is finished.

Almost no subfloor preparation is required. Vinyl sheeting is simply rough-cut from the roll to the approximate dimensions of the room, then is laid in place on the floor and finish-trimmed with a sharp linoleum knife. Doorways can be finished off with a strip of threshold metal.

Cost? About $4.50 a square yard. From start to finish the job should take only a few hours. The floor is then ready for immediate use.

Begin your installation by inspecting the existing floor or other base for roughness, nail heads, and high edges. Pound down any old nails. Smooth out rough spots. Since you will be putting your new floor down directly over the old one without the use of lining felt, be especially careful to sweep the floor thoroughly.

The photographs and captions lead you through the steps that follow this preparation and cleanup.

Tips for a Better Job: When a seam is necessary, to get a perfect fit the edges of the adjacent pieces should be overlapped. Using a sharp linoleum knife or straight blade knife and a straightedge as a guide, cut through both pieces. Hold knife in vertical position. Before cutting seams, place a piece of scrap material under seam to protect the knife point. When adhesive is used at seams, flooring underneath should be lightly sanded where adhesive is to be applied.

STEPS IN LAYING SHEET VINYL

1. After smoothing the floor wherever it needs it, remove the present base of quarter-round molding by slipping the edge of a wrecking bar or claw hammer under it. Carefully raise it to loosen nails.

2. Measure room to determine maximum length and width. For irregularly shaped rooms, several measurements may need to be taken to avoid excessive waste of material.

1.

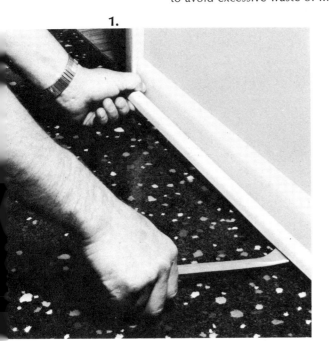

2.

3. Transfer room measurements onto your sheet of flooring material by snapping chalk line. Make flooring 3″ wider and longer than room to be fitted. Measurement and cutting should be done in a large room where flooring can be unrolled.

39

4.

5.

4. Use a heavy shears or sharp linoleum knife to trim waste material. Always cut flooring with the face up for clean, even edge.

5. Select longest, straightest wall of room as a starting point. Line straight edge of flooring up to this wall and allow the material to flash up other three walls. In this kitchen, flooring material has been precut to fit around protruding cabinets.

6. Press flooring material firmly into place and trim off remaining waste with notched blade knife or heavy scissors. Allow $\frac{1}{32}''$ clearance along all walls.

7. At doorway facings where resilient flooring meets hardwood, dispense with $\frac{1}{32}''$ clearance and trim vinyl flush with the wood. Edge of floor should be either cemented or capped with threshold.

8. Final step in the job is to replace quarter-round. Temporarily slip a piece of scrap flooring between the quarter-round and the flooring. Moulding should be nailed into the base, not to the floor. Furniture and heavy objects should be fitted with protectors or cups.

6.

7.

8.

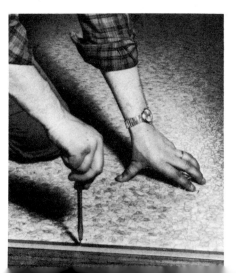

7

Using the Carpet
That Goes Anywhere

**Some kinds go outdoors as well as in, others come in squares
that can be taken up instantly for moving or washing**

Carpets tough enough to use outdoors make it feasible now to have
soft floors in kitchens, laundries, bathrooms, and porches.

For all these uses, except ones where actual flooding frequently occurs, a newer version is even more versatile: self-stick
shag carpet squares.

Besides being useful in rooms you might previously have
hesitated to carpet, these carpet tiles can be put down anywhere,
then picked up and moved as the mood or need arises. They can be
cleaned with a broom or vacuum or in the kitchen sink. They are
made of synthetic materials that should wear for years and never
fade.

Removable-reusable carpet, available in every imaginable
color and pattern, can be put down and taken up without leaving
any stain or mark on the floor beneath (especially important if
you are renting). The adhesive which gives it just enough "stick"
to keep it from sliding around stays with the carpet square itself,
even when you hold it under the faucet to rinse off cigarette ashes
or scrub away a stain with brush and detergent.

Traffic patterns, burns, ink spills, pet accidents are disasters
when one huge carpet covers a room. There's just no answer but to
take it all up and buy a whole new carpet. No longer. The answer
is to use tiles that can be shifted around or replaced one at a time.

Tiles that have suffered wear or minor disasters can still be used by concealing them under furniture or in a closet, and the still new-looking squares can come out from under the bed to lengthen floor newness by years.

If you use several colors and design your own random or conventional patterned floor, and you get tired of the whole effect, you can change it anytime you feel like it. In children's or teen-age rooms each occupant can work out a suitable color scheme that meets his own taste. At any time he can change the carpet-squares arrangement or swap with a sibling. A two-color job could be arranged to add another color or two when the first effect is no longer pleasing or enough squares need replacing to warrant the purchase of some extras.

Carpet squares are good for areas which take really hard wear, such as the recreation room. Often it is located in a basement or half of the garage with cold, hard floor underfoot. The resilient backing on tiles insulates and also provides bounciness from the foam backing.

If a large number of squares become marred or stained and no one wants them in the house, they still have a life to live. Move them to the workshop or give the dog a floor he never dreamed of. One man plans to carpet his garage so he can work on the car in comfort—if his wife ever gives up the ones she put in the bedroom. Squares resist chemical stains like ammonia, chlorine, and iodine, so there's no reason why they can't spend their old age in the dirtiest areas of the home, often the ones that need them most.

Divide room into quarters with a chalk line and carpenter's T-square. Then the self-stick tiles will be perfectly aligned. Patterned tiles like these not only conceal small stains but seam lines as well, giving the effect of wall-to-wall carpeting.

Until recently most types of carpet couldn't be cut by a non-professional because the raw edges had to be machine-bound to keep them from fraying and shedding. These synthetic squares can be cut with a craft knife or scissors, or even a sharp paper cutter. They stay neat, lie flat, fit together perfectly, and most of them come in the 12″ square size which are easy to handle but not so small it takes ages to put them down.

Americans are great movers, as well as do-it-yourselfers. These squares fit right back into their original boxes, if you move, because pairs of tiles fit back to back without affecting the adhesive. The new owner or tenant can't complain because you've put no wear on the original floor and have left it clean. Whether you move to a place with rooms that are larger or smaller you can use the ones you own and buy a few more or stow away the extras for replacements.

You might try this suggestion from the Ozite people: put carpet tile on the walls and ceilings to provide warmth and sound deadening. This might be especially useful in an apartment where walls are not thick enough to keep voices and bathroom or kitchen sounds from traveling. A downstairs powder room is another place that could use the durability and privacy-effect of carpet squares as a complete lining.

With the trend toward using carpet in kitchen and bath some homeowners are wary of putting a soft surface in front of a toilet, lavatory, sink, or range. These self-stick squares, some of which come in elaborate patterns, designs that resemble paisley or tapestry, do not reveal every tiny spot or stain. Really vulnerable areas are not large and a few tiles as replacements are inexpensive.

Women are famous for their urge to decorate and do it often. Now they can do it by rearranging the flooring, and they can do it themselves without waiting for a tired man to lend his back or give up his weekend golf.

What colors can you get? The usual ones, ranging from charcoal gray to brilliant red and orange. Some are tweed mixtures. One company* has a line of pastels that go by the name of Orange Ice, Alice Blue, Limeade, Lemon Drop, Taffy, and Peppermint. Light colors, just as in other flooring materials, are the best choice for a family with children and pets. They do not show dust marks from feet, lint, pet hair, or food crumbs. Since most synthetic floor materials are somewhat electrostatic, this tendency to attract lint will be less noticeable in the lighter shades or patterned effects.

Just out are a new line of carpet squares with long shag for the people who want texture. A woman can handle the whole carpeting job with these squares that are all nylon face tufted into a

* Consult Appendix for names and addresses of manufacturers.

Four shades of foam-rubber-backed self-stick carpet tiles in a random pattern go on the floor and up the wall to do a double job. They make the room decorative and at the same time quiet playroom sounds. Bedroom nearby has room-size seamless indoor-outdoor carpet. Both are scrubbable, but tiles are for indoors only.

44

Surprisingly, this floor covering is tile—18″ squares of luxurious
nylon shag carpeting with which anyone can do a wall-to-wall installation. They're self-stick, made by Ozite.

polypropylene back with a white, high-density, foam-rubber cushion and self-stick bonding system. Squares come in an 18″ size.

This is probably only the beginning of a carpet revolution. With shag tiles there are possibilities of doing a room in stripes, squares, mod patterns, or with a large monogram. As with indoor-outdoor carpet, this can be cut with a scissors and will not ravel. It's available in eight colors, costs about $9 a square yard. Since there is no extra cost for installation or a pad, or any waste, the cost is quite a bit less than for conventional carpet at the same price per square yard.

These are the squares of shag carpeting. They have foam backing, cost about the same as similar roll carpet, can be moved or replaced a square at a time, require conventional rug cleaning. Seams are invisible.

Regular indoor-outdoor carpeting is still first choice for exterior use and most demanding interior conditions. This nylon needlebond carpet goes well in both kitchen and dining areas. Patterned or tweed types are more practical than plain in rooms where food accidents occur. This romantic pattern helps the antique Tiffany lamp and old-fashioned look of the kitchen blend with the modern plastic dining set.

You can give any floor a custom touch—even a pattern as complex as this. Basis is indoor-outdoor carpet, since this method cuts with a sharp knife and doesn't need a bound edge. One method of insetting calls for cutting a pattern from a piece of thin hardboard, then using this as a guide. For a simpler method, follow the four steps beginning on the opposite page.

Carpet manufacturers predict that creativity is going to become an important part of do-it-yourself carpet laying.

Once only the rich could afford monograms or inlays in their floors. But with these all-purpose carpets, either in squares or the seamless roomsize materials, any artistically inclined man, woman, or child can think up a design, cut it with a sharp knife and put it down. Carpets that don't have self-stick backing can be put down with double-faced tape.

Educators feel that we give our children too little opportunity to use their artistic interests on projects that have meaning. Here they can experiment with original ideas in room decorating and get attractive, usable results. Easy-to-work-with carpet, wonderful colors, and such simple tools as scissors and ruler are all that are needed.

HOW TO CUT PATTERNS IN CARPET

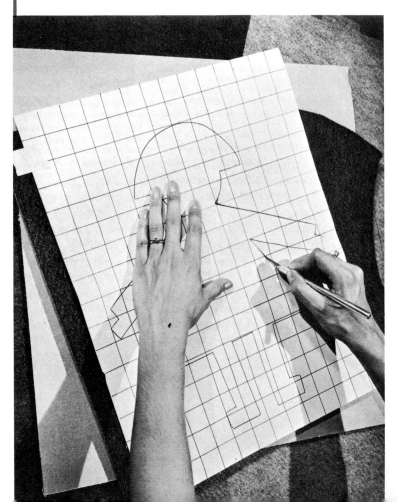

1. Tape a pattern securely to a piece of carpet and cut out the inset. Designs are offered in a free portfolio by Armstrong, but you can think up one of your own. Draw it freehand or use squared paper as shown here.

2. Place inset on your carpeted floor and cut around it. Scraps or carpet samples in assorted colors, often available in stores at sale time, make economical insets for patterns.

3. Remove the piece of carpet from the floor. You can use the cutout as a custom design somewhere else. Press your inset down on double-faced carpet tape (available at carpet dealers or variety stores) that you have applied to the bare spot. If you're working with self-stick material, of course you won't need the tape.

49

4. Although this design job was done on an area size indoor-out-door carpet, you could do a similar job with the tiles. A mistake would be less disastrous, so this might be the best starting place for a child. One miscut tile could be thrown away, or small scraps could be arranged in a square to form a pattern. With the self-stick backing it would be easy to experiment.

Experimenting with the new Ozite shag carpet tiles, the author did this floor job in an afternoon. Full tiles go down in a few seconds, but those along one wall almost invariably have to be cut to fit. In this room there was a hearth to fit around as well, a far simpler job with tile than with any other form of carpeting. As demonstrated by young Chris Kinsey, son of the artists who did the drawings for this book, the tiles come up without leaving a mark.

PART II

IMPROVE
YOUR
WALLS

8

Planning New Walls

Panel with plastic-finished panels, murals, real wood, polyurethane that looks like wood, antique boards from the side of a barn

One of the best ways to wave the remodeling wand is by paneling a room, one wall, or part of a wall. There are hundreds of types of paneling materials to help you transform a drab, dingy wall and the room itself into an area of charm and warmth without spending much money or hiring workmen to do the job.

No matter how cracked and ugly the plaster or how many layers of thick, peeling wallpaper on your present walls, you can cover them with paneling. Even if your problem is so serious a one as moisture, there are a few types of paneling which can be used safely in high humidity or moisture areas. Most paneling will hide imperfections and still not require you to go through tedious preparation before you can get to the real job.

Today's mastics stick forever, squeeze from a handy carton, make it feasible to glue panels directly to any solid, even wall.

How much of a craftsman need you be? Elementary carpentry skills and the ability to read and carefully follow instructions that come with the panels are all it takes.

Since your own time is worth money, start by window-shopping the samples, pictures, leaflets, actual materials, and demonstrations at your building-material dealers, hardware stores, lumberyards. Lumberyards customarily display complete 4′ x 8′ panels so you can see, feel, and judge the appearance and quality of a large area of the material before you have the dealer place your order. There are so many types of paneling on the market that most dealers will not carry them in stock.

Usually you can borrow a panel to take home and try for effect or to match up with other materials in the room. It's difficult to judge and easy to make a mistake if you select solely on the basis of a small sample under difficult lighting in a show room.

What's available?

Well, there are plastic-coated panels in a marble finish that doubles for real marble and is recommended as durable even in moisture areas. They come in black veined with gold, beige and gold, pink, pale green. Marlite is their name.

For variety—or to make up for lack of a view—you can have paneling with a mural: a seascape, foreign view, South Pacific island, windswept trees on the Pacific Coast. One pictorial panel, called Ponta Roma, is a reproduction of an historic engraving by artist Gian Battista Piranesi. If your room has colonial furniture, you might want a panel depicting life in early America. These panels are washable and colors are permanent.

One panel type duplicates Chantilly lace. A most practical kind is Peg Board, which creates storage and shelf space on the walls. You can buy hooks and hanging accessories.

There are also plastic-finished panels that you can't tell from wood. Some have woodgrain patterns but are in unusual stains—deep green, red, or blue.

Vinyl-shield wall panel will take a lot of rough treatment. It comes in hickory, pecan, walnut, oak, teak, and a textured finish, costs about $20 to panel an 8' x 12' wall. Georgia-Pacific makes this one.

Should you find a bargain buy in unmatched or damaged panels, there's a self-adhesive burlap, $20 for an 8-yard roll, to turn them into matching decorator paneling. For small jobs the easiest way to buy this burlap is in 18" widths in hardware, variety, and department stores, where it is found with other self-adhesive roll materials.

If you want to separate rooms but not keep out light, there are translucent, glasslike panels that duplicate Venetian handmade glass or stained glass. Masonite makes a Florentine type in olive green, clear, and amber. There is a Spanish design also which comes in amber, smoke, ruby red, and blue. One unusual type, called Basque, looks leaded and has a backlighting effect.

When light filters through these panels, the effect is one of diffused glow, but the delicate look is deceiving. These panels will not crack or break under a hard blow, and they do not require polishing. If you don't need a solid paneling there's one called filigree which can be painted with brush, spray, or roller to match the rest of the room.

The majority of today's paneling varieties are not solid wood. Wood grains are usually veneer on plywood. Some are photographed wood prints that have been applied to large sheets of hardboard.

In spite of the tough plastic-coated surfaces and elaborate patterns and textures, panels are in the price range of any remodeler. Some cost only 50 cents a square foot. During lumberyard sales, after inventory especially, closeouts and overstock or discontinued panels can be purchased at a bargain price.

Do not, however, be guided by price alone. Some panels are suitable only for a living room. Others work fine in kitchen or bath. One kind shows dents, scratches, can't take moisture.

The following are the main types and what they can be expected to do:

SOLID WOOD PANELS. You can't beat the real thing for beauty. If you're weary of imitations and can afford the most expensive, you can buy wood paneling of walnut, oak, birch, cherry, elm, ash, teak, rosewood. Or you can have such unusual shades as tawny oak, antique birch, platinum birch, cinnamon cherry, Mediterranean Oak. Many real wood panels are available in other than their natural colors. Mediterranean Oak (Weyerhaeuser's Forestglo line) is an unusual green.

Solid wood panels are expensive compared to the imitations, but they are boards up to $3/4''$ thick. Softwood panels are less expensive. Both are available with matching moldings, finished or unfinished, can be touched up with a matching Putty Stik when scratched or dented.

Even a rare wood with a very high price tag is not prohibitively costly if used on only one wall and may be well worth using to transform a shabby setting into a luxurious one.

PLYWOOD PANELS. Here again you'll get real wood, but it will be veneer on a plywood base. You have the same range of wood varieties that you do in solid-wood panels. In addition to veneered panels, there are also printed types. Wood grains are authentic in appearance and color, but these panels will not take the hard knocks nor will they be easily repairable, because their grain is only paper-thin.

Most panels come in 4' widths and up to 10' high. They are often grooved. If your rooms are of an unusual height, or you want a matched-wood job, you can get a custom job with shades and grain matching from one panel to the next.

Many materials once thought suitable only for exterior use have now come into the house in the form of barn, or rough-sawn, paneling. Redwood, with its rich, warm color, has become especially popular. Redwood will darken or bleach with age, depending upon the amount of exposure to light, but you can get it prefinished with a sealer. Or you can seal it with a product such as Cabot's Stain Wax and retain the original color forever. Stain Wax will also repel moisture, so you'll get no water spotting if you are using your redwood paneling in the kitchen or dining room.

Don't overlook used boards, especially if your remodeling job includes tearing down an old shed or garage. Boards weathered for half a century now sell at a premium price, and many an old barn is becoming a wall in a luxury living room. Companies that demolish old houses and barns have weathered boards for sale. Finding just the right kind adds to the interest of the job. Most built-in shelves in the author's own home came from redwood boards that had weathered to a silver gray as siding on an old garage that stood on the property. The boards could also have paneled a wall. Don't treat old boards as firewood. If they are solid and unwarped, they are antiqued panels!

HARDBOARD PANELS. Are they wood? Yes, but in a special way. These panels are made from wood fiber that has been ground, heat treated, compressed, and turned into sheets that are denser and stronger than wood and suitable to become many types of paneling material.

Some are covered with plastics that resemble fabric, stone, leather, or marble. They will never stain, cannot easily be dented, will wash, and no one yet knows how long they will last—probably for a lifetime if not abused. Panels coated with melamine-plastic are best in bathrooms and kitchens, where they not only resist moisture but where soil is heavy and cleaning means scrubbing.

One company has a wall system of panels that go up with clips and have slotted seams into which you put brackets to hold bookshelves, hooks, and even a desk or dressing table. Shelves and furniture accessories can be moved at any time, leaving no holes or marks on the panels.

PEG BOARD. Once available only in unpainted brown, Peg Board now comes in bright colors as well as a neutral monk's cloth print, or with a hard melamine finish, especially good in moisture areas. Devices that make the panels useful for storing tools or household equipment fasten easily. There's a tool, resembling a pliers, that turns any small jar with a lid into a storage container that hangs on Peg Board.

Peg Board comes in sheets up to 8′ high and in thicknesses from ⅛″ to ¼″.

INSULATED PANELS. Some panels have built-in insulation. When remodeling a cold area, such as basement or garage, added insulation is almost an essential.

Polyurethane paneling has its own insulation, equal to a fairly heavy layer of fiberglass or mineral wool. The panels come in woodgrain with knots and axmarks that duplicate fine old weathered paneling.

9

Cover a Wall with Wood

How to choose it, how to make a panel, how to finish it, put it up, clean it

When you panel with wood—real boards—you have a choice of as many kinds as there are trees in the forest. The effect you get depends upon the kind of wood, the width of the boards, the type of joint treatment, how you put up the boards, how you finish them —and how much of the room you choose to cover. Paneling a single wall is often the best way to give a room new life.

Softwood is a good choice. If you're going to paint it, one may do as well as another. But for stain or natural finishes, the original color and grain of the wood are highly important.

Typical of light-colored woods used for paneling are the pines and spruces and white fir. Douglas fir is a bit darker. Darkest of the softwoods commonly used for paneling are redwood and the cedars.

Some woods are offered in pecky or knotty grades. In most, the appearance will be determined by how much you want to pay —or how little you can pay and still get a satisfying look. Clear grades cost several times as much as grades that permit large knots or sap markings. Yet often they aren't as interesting or as suitable for a room that needs to look cozy or woodsy. One popular cabin material actually has huge insect holes and tracks that many homeowners find suited to the atmosphere of a room in a vacation home.

There is one exception worth noting to the rule that hardwoods come high. That is Philippine mahogany. It costs little more than fine grades of softwoods. With a clear-lacquer finish it has a cinnamon shade. It takes well to wax finishes, too.

Among softwoods, pine is the all-time, all-over favorite. Redwood, rather similar to pine in texture and working qualities, has made its way from the West Coast to popularity nationally. You'll see it most often in homes of ranch style or modern architecture.

JOINTS. Paneling, whether bought out of stock or made for the job, usually meets in a V-joint produced by beveled edges. This gives a pleasant pattern and, at the same time, conceals any slight slips in workmanship or any shrinkage coming from using lumber that is not as well dried as it should be. V-joint lumber may be either tongue-and-groove or shiplap, the latter usually having a broader and deeper bevel.

To emphasize the pattern in a V-joint wall, use narrower boards. Or buy one of the types of standard paneling having Vs plowed at intervals in the face of wide boards.

Tongue-and-groove lumber is also produced with no bevel

Strong vertical lines in this California redwood paneling blend well with modern furnishings. This paneling resembles board-on-board but is more economical. One side is smooth, the other saw-textured. You can apply it to show either side or a combination of the two.

When your t&g redwood is 1″ x 4″, 1″ x 6″, or possibly 1″ x 8″, you can put it up solely with blind-nailing. Then there will be no nail holes to fill or to see. For both harmony and economy in redoing a room, use the same paneling lumber for built-ins.

and gives a plain, flush wall. Some t&g has a bevel on just one side, permitting its use either way. Softwood flooring, such as hemlock, makes fine paneling of the flush type.

Other good-looking joints are shown in the photographs. Plain boards may be butted together and the joints concealed by battens. For an unusual effect use back-battens.

Of all these the V-joint is far and away the most often seen and you can't go wrong in using it.

HORIZONTAL OR VERTICAL? Most paneling is put on vertically. Doing so usually eliminates end joints and also avoids the dust-catching annoyance of horizontal joints.

Horizontal lines, however, make a room look larger and this may be important to your project. It is often possible to nail horizontal paneling directly to studs (in new construction) or through plaster or old wallboard to studs. Vertical paneling nearly always requires furring strips unless you are using adhesive.

Most horizontal paneling uses V-joints. Others are likely to give a barnlike effect or to catch too much dust.

If you have a good eye for line you may find a wall that will look striking when paneled diagonally. This treatment will also add strength if that is needed.

MAKING PANELS. If you can find ready-made paneling or ship-lap or t&g that is what you want, there is no great saving in buying boards instead and jointing them. T&g redwood, for example, commonly sells for about one cent a square foot more than similar plain boards.

If, however, you have the power tools called for and can't find paneling to your taste and pocketbook, you may save by shopping around for the right boards and going on from there. And if you have some special effect in mind you'll have to make the paneling yourself or pay to have it milled to order.

A good example of make-it-yourself paneling that cannot be duplicated on the market is back-battened rough redwood. This is made of thin batten strips behind narrow rabbets cut in 1″ red-wood rough boards. Used in a big, informal room, this material can give a beautiful panel look that nothing else can equal. When the rough boards are lightly hand-sanded, and perhaps varnished, to make them fairly smooth to the touch, they will make a fine, rugged wall.

Trim is a simple matter with a wood-paneled wall. For horizontal paneling it consists of matching quarter-round at the ceiling line and at the floor. This works well also with vertical paneling of the flush variety.

Quarter-round is not very satisfactory when the wall has vertical V-joints. Most desirable is a horizontal strip placed first at the floor line, with the paneling butted against it. A narrow strip, such as 1″ x 2″ lumber, is attractive. Then quarter-round may be placed against the strip, if desired, and against the paneling at the ceiling.

FINISHING. Wood paneling can be painted, using the usual two coats of flat or semigloss wall paint. It can also be painted and

Photo left

The clean, light look in this paneling is produced by West Coast hemlock with a natural finish. One quick way to get this effect is by wiping on either clear Stain Wax or a mixture of clear and white. Test various mixes first.

Photo right

For all its warm, elegant look, this redwood paneling, called La Honda, costs no more than many kinds of wallpaper. The fact that it is only ⅜″ thick keeps down the cost without affecting the appearance of the wall.

then scraped which will show up the grain, yet give some color and conceal most imperfections. There is not much point to using wood on a wall if it is to be concealed under paint.

Perhaps the best-looking finish for wood paneling is none at all. Pine, for instance, mellows handsomely if left untreated. But this is feasible only for areas out of reach of sticky fingers, so it often cannot be done. Wood once stained with grease and moisture is difficult, if not impossible, to clean.

Next best thing for a natural look is water-clear lacquer or wallpaper lacquer. A single coat may be enough, but two coats will give better and more lasting protection. Lacquer has the additional advantage of drying quickly, permitting a second coat in an hour or two, and the odor goes out of the room in a short time. When a whole room is paneled, this matter of odor and fumes can be not only annoying but dangerous. Always provide as much ventilation as possible.

Distinctive hallway storage unit uses rough-sawn redwood boards to contrast with smooth translucent Filon shoji. Good finishing choice is black Stain Wax for shoji frame, mix of about 10 parts clear to one of white Stain Wax for redwood.

Clear wood-sealers, shellac, or flat varnishes also give natural finishes. A variation is a coat of boiled linseed oil followed by one of white shellac, then waxed.

For results lighter in color than the natural wood, a white-pigmented sealer may be used. This is brushed on, allowed to penetrate for a few minutes, then gently wiped with a soft cloth. A little raw umber or other pigment may be added to white sealer for a variation in tint.

For drastic bleaching, commercial wood bleach should be used. Light bleaching can be done with household bleaches such as Clorox.

Also used to bleach is a saturated solution of oxalic acid crystals in boiling water. Apply it hot. Let it dry. Remove any bloom that appears with alcohol. Sandpaper. Finish with one coat of water-clear lacquer and buff lightly with fine steel wool.

Any paint store offers a stock of standard wood stains that may be used to add color to paneling. Stain may be followed by a protective coat of shellac, lacquer, or flat varnish. There are many attractive one-coat sealer stains, such as Color Rez. For color with the soft glow of wax, use Cabot's Stain Wax. It comes in clear, white, or many shades.

You can make up finishes in any shade you like by mixing colors-in-oil with a suitable carrier. For transparent effects, mix the color with boiled linseed oil and thin with turpentine. For a softer and more opaque result—especially good if the wood has too violent grain—mix the color with enamel undercoater and thin with linseed oil.

For finishes of this type, the color can be just about anything you like. Most unusual is one of the brown pigments with just a little ultramarine blue. Protect with white shellac, lacquer, or flat varnish, plus wax. Or just use wax.

When to finish is almost as important as how. The general rule for any two-coat finish on wood paneling is to apply the first coat before putting the paneling onto the wall. This gets the finish into the joints where otherwise a streak of raw wood might show up in case the panels should shrink or move. It also protects the wood from fingermarks during installation.

Second and any other coats may then be applied after the paneling job is completed.

In addition to the general methods just described, there are many special finishes used on paneling. Here are some simple and attractive ones.

Clear pumpkin brown. Use this on pine or other light-colored wood. Mix burnt sienna in boiled linseed oil. Thin with turpentine. Add a trace of ultramarine blue. Apply one coat and sandpaper lightly when dry.

Seal with a thin coat of white shellac. Finish with two applications of paste wax.

Honey Brown. Follow same procedure as for clear pumpkin brown, but use more ultramarine blue. Add enough to change color from red brown to yellow brown.

Antique tawny brown. Use light oak oil stain. Follow with well-thinned coat of flat gray paint wiped off while wet. Wax.

This finish goes especially well with blue and yellow furnishings.

Two-tone brown over gold. Tint white undercoater with dark chrome yellow and add three times as much boiled linseed oil as you have undercoater. For each gallon of mixture add one pint of turpentine. Brush on and let dry for twenty-four hours.

Apply a coat of dark oak stain reduced 20 percent with boiled linseed oil. Highlights may be had by wiping stain in some places or by buffing with 2/0 steel wool when dry.

Cover with thin coat of white shellac, followed by flat varnish or clear lacquer.

Driftwood gray. Mix raw umber with white undercoater and add a small amount of chrome green. Thin slightly with turpentine, and apply with brush or cloth. Wipe off with cloth, depth of color depending upon how soon wiping is done.

May be sealed with shellac or lacquer or simply waxed.

Gray acid stain. Sponge wood with water to raise gray. Sand smooth when dry. Apply stain made by leaving common nails in vinegar for at least 24 hours. Wipe off surplus stain. Sand when dry.

Apply wash coat of thinned white shellac. Sand. Use paste wax.

FURRING. These are narrow strips of lumber, usually 1″ x 2″s, which are fastened to the wall. They are the nailing strips to which the paneling is then fastened.

Furring is normally required whenever paneling is placed vertically. It is needed also for horizontal paneling if the wall is masonry, if it shows any signs of dampness, or if it is not flat and even.

Horizontal paneling may be nailed directly to the studs in new construction or if the interior wall has been removed to expose the studs. It may be nailed directly over an old dry wall or plaster wall if it is level. Nailing should be through the wall and into the studs after you have found their location by pounding and verified by driving in a long, thin nail. You can usually assume that, once you have located a stud, others will be spaced away from it on 16″ centers.

Space your furring strips about every 2′—horizontally for vertical paneling. If there is to be a wood base for the paneling to butt against, insert an extra strip just above the one at the floor line, so that the joint between the base and the ends of the panel boards will fall on it. You may need to do something similar at the ceiling, depending on what trim method you are using. If there is no trim at either end, you will need no extra furring. Nails holding the furring should go into the studs hidden in the wall.

Paneling seen here is only ⅜" thick for economy, comes kiln-dried in protective cardboard package. Widths offered are 4", 6", 8". Accompanying photos show how to put up such a wall with narrow paneling.

HOW TO INSTALL NARROW-WIDTH PANELING

1. Start by nailing up furring strips of 1" x 2" pine or fir. For hard masonry wall, use adhesive to fasten furring. Furring may often be omitted if wall is sound and level.

2. To bring furring strips to dead level where wall is out of flat, wedge with bits of wood or hardboard. Stack panels for a few days in the room where they are to be used.

1.

2.

For horizontal paneling, furring strips should go right over the studs, one for each stud.

If yours is a masonry wall you have a different fastening problem. This is easily solved in the case of lightweight concrete blocks: simply nail the furring right to them.

If the masonry wall will not take nails and contains no nailing course or fasteners, you'll have to work out a way. You can drill holes (with power drill use a carbide-tipped masonry drill; by hand use a star drill) and insert plugs made to take nails or screws.

If your masonry wall offers any moisture problem, you'd better tackle it before paneling over it. Use hot coal-tar pitch or an asphaltum solution sold for this purpose. As an additional precaution, back prime the paneling. If the moisture problem is a slight one, back priming alone may be enough. Use primer paint, aluminum paint, or shellac.

3. Thin panels may be put up either with nails or panel adhesive. Apply adhesive in dabs to the wall as shown here or in continuous beads along all furring strips.

4. When using mastic or panel adhesive, it may be applied to backs of panels or to wall or furring. Advantage of adhesive over nails is timesaving, no holes.

3.

4.

5. If you are using tongue-and-groove boards and they are not over 8" wide, you can use nails instead of adhesive and still have no holes to fill. Blind nail as here, and set.

NOW PANEL IT. Nailing procedure depends, of course, on the kind of paneling you are using.

With tongue-and-groove boards all nailing can be blind. When the boards are up the job is done, except for completing the finishing.

Most other paneling must be face-nailed. Use finishing nails, set them below the surface, and fill the holes. Mendwood, Plastic Wood, or wood putty is often available in color to match most kinds of paneling, or the neutral shade can be tinted.

Wood paneling ordinarily requires little care. It can be dusted with a vacuum cleaner or soft cloth. But don't use an oily cloth; it will leave the paneling in fine condition to collect dust. Waxing may leave streaks that can't be polished out.

When your paneling needs washing, go over it with a cloth or sponge dipped into soapy water and wrung out. Then wipe dry.

Scratches or small damage can usually be camouflaged with crayon or colored wax. Or use a bit of the original finishing material.

Wood paneling that has been well finished will last almost forever with little attention. When you panel with wood you are making a permanent investment in the beauty of your home.

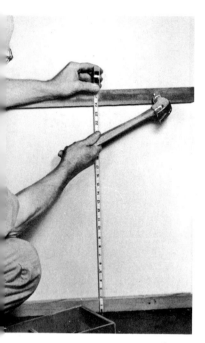

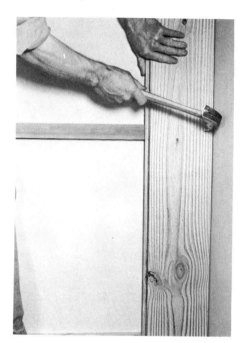

1. 2. 3.

The three steps to very strong glue-and-nail installation of vertical paneling are demonstrated here. The wood is pine that has been sandblasted, stained, and varnished. **1.** Nail 1" x 2" furring strips stoutly to the wall, spaced on 2' centers. **2.** Place first board at corner and face-nail it near grooved edge, then toenail through tongue. **3.** Spread glue on each furring strip before paneling is placed, to produce added strength and discourage warping. Nailing is with finishing nails, which must be set.

10

Paneling:
The Bigger the Quicker

**Factory-finished big sheets—plywood or woodgrained—
transform your home with instant walls**

For quick and permanent transformation of a dingy wall, pre-finished big-sheet paneling is hard to beat. As soon as the panels are up the room is ready to use. There's no laborious finishing to do, no dropcloth to fuss with, no cracks to fill, no waiting for the solvent smell to fade away.

With the growth of interest in prefinished wood and wood-grain panels, your choice of materials and tones becomes wider all the time.

Just one manufacturer, Weyerhaeuser, gives you these choices, each in many different woodgrains and color tones:

Forestglo $\frac{1}{4}''$ V-grooved plywood;

Craftwall $\frac{7}{16}''$ V-grooved wood-core veneer board;

Muralwood $\frac{1}{4}''$ prefinished woodgrained hardboard;

Woodhue $\frac{1}{4}''$ prefinished woodgrained flakeboard.

Even when you're after a special effect you can't find in factory-finished panels, you can get some of the advantages by doing your own prefinishing of plywood panels before you put them up. You'll find this feasible with saw-textured redwood ply-wood, for example, one of the few varieties not offered with a factory finish.

By using a wax finish you'll be able to protect rough red-wood against finger marks without changing its natural appearance.

The method works well also with smooth plywood and plywood doors.

We use wax in the form of Cabot's Stain Wax, sold by paint and building-materials dealers. Since the unpigmented type, like all clear finishing materials, tends to darken wood, we mix it with white-pigmented Stain Wax.

Use about eight parts of natural Stain Wax to one of white, but you should start by testing these proportions on a scrap and then modifying them if necessary. Just mop the Stain Wax on with a rag or brush, then wipe off after about ten minutes. At first the pigment, such as white, will look too white, but this disappears and becomes a natural effect with a white tone that counteracts the tendency of some woods, redwood especially, to take on a yellowish cast as it ages. With rough plywood, skip the wiping.

CONDITIONING. Big-sheet paneling materials usually should be allowed to stabilize in moisture content before application. If humidity is average, stand the panels on their sides around the room for a couple of days before installing them. This won't be necessary if both panels and room are quite dry.

If room is damp, hardboard panels such as Muralwood should be given two weeks to take on similar humidity. You can speed up the process with these panels by scrubbing warm water into the backs of the panels with a clean broom and then stacking them back to back for two days or until used. Use sticks between pairs of panels.

If the room is very damp, from wet plaster or concrete, it is better to delay paneling till room dries. Continuously damp or leaky basements are risky places in which to use any big-sheet paneling.

WALL PREPARATION. In new construction or remodeling, you can panel directly to studs if they are straight and dry. If the paneling is ¼″ plywood, however, this won't give you a very solid wall or much of a sound barrier, so it's better to put a base material first, such as ½″ gypsum board or plywood. Apply this so the joints won't coincide with those in the paneling.

As a precaution against dampness, do not apply paneling directly to masonry walls. Provide a moisture barrier over furring strips. With concrete nails or anchor devices or adhesives, fasten the furring to the wall, shimming where necessary. Attach 4-mil polyethylene sheeting to the furring as a vapor barrier. If you have any joints in your plastic sheeting, overlap 3″. Provide ventilation back of the paneling by leaving occasional gaps of about an inch in the horizontal furring strips near the floor and the ceiling.

Here, in a revealing pair of before-and-after photographs, is evidence of how much you can accomplish by paneling just one wall. Furniture, walls, floors remain unchanged—but what a difference in the whole feel of the room!

One of the things you get when you pay the price of better-quality plywood paneling is the "mismatch" featured in this Weldwood prefinished cherry. Surface veneers are separate strips so grain varies as with solid wood paneling.

To achieve this Oriental effect when you panel, choose a quiet-grain wood such as pine. Cut panels to 2' width or less, depending upon framing. Cover framing with plywood strips (left). Stain or paint them black before putting up paneling.

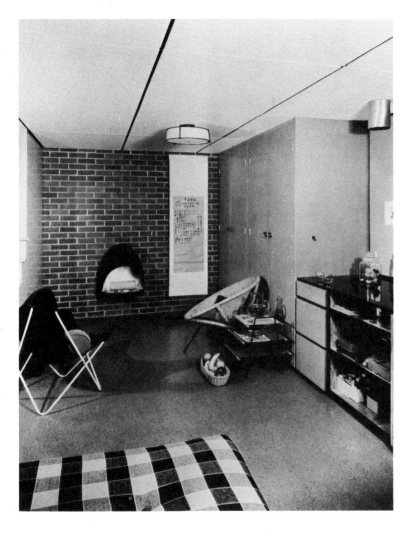

Resin-overlaid fir plywood is the workhorse material here. Ceiling panels are painted, giving the smooth finish this material is known for; closet walls are left natural. Brick curtain wall holds an enameled metal fireplace similar to those shown in a later chapter, while concealing both its chimney and a furnace. Chapter 4 gives details on how to pour a Flecto Seamless floor like this one.

Furring strips are the cheap and effective remedy for any wall, whether solid or bare studs, that isn't plumb and level. Walls in older homes are particularly in need of furring strips.

Use dry 1″ x 2″ lumber, applying it every 48″ vertically and every 12″ to 16″ horizontally. With heavier panels such as ⅜″ rough redwood or ⁷⁄₁₆″ Craftwall, you can safely stretch the horizontal spacing to 24″.

Nice thing about furring is that it lets you provide a perfectly plane surface for paneling. Just shim out the furring strips where necessary. Or rasp out a bit of wood if you encounter a high spot in a rough wall.

HOW TO MEASURE A ROOM FOR PANELING

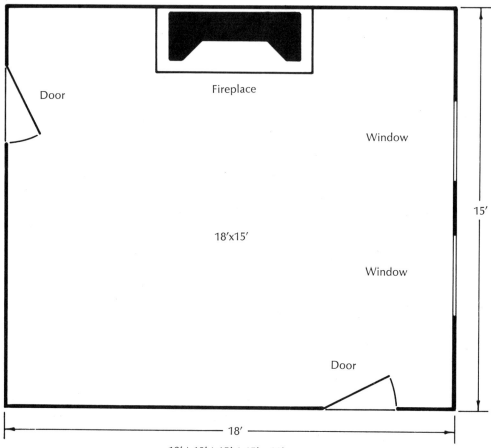

Door

Fireplace

Window

18'x15'

Window

Door

15'

18'

18'+18'+15'+15'=66'

CONVERSION TABLE
Measuring for
Room Paneling

Perimeter	Panels Needed
20'	5
24'	6
28'	7
32'	8
60'	15
64'	16
68'	17
72'	18
92'	23

1. Figure the *perimeter* of the room you want to panel.

2. Next *convert* perimeter into the number of panels you'll need. The conversion table below tells how. For instance, our room diagram has a perimeter of 66'. Our table indicates that 17 panels are required (when perimeter falls between figures, use the next higher number). *Note:* If ceiling height is more than 8', do not use conversion table; consult your dealer.

3. *Deduct* for areas such as doors, windows, fireplaces, etc. For estimating purposes, deduct ⅔ panel for a door; ½ panel for a window or fireplace.

4. *Subtract* your total deductions from the number of panels originally determined. Round off the remainder to the next higher number. Our example shows 17 panels minus 3½ panels for doors, windows and a fireplace, or a net of 13½ panels. Therefore we need 14 panels.

Photo left

When paneling over a typical sheetrock wall, first drive nails to locate studs beneath. Measure 16" from one located stud to find next one.

Photo right

Mark location of studs, then nail up furring strips as seen in next photograph. Usual material for furring is 1" x 2" fir or pine.

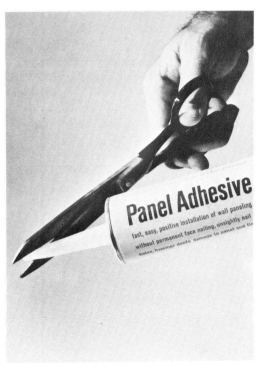

Panel Adhesive
fast, easy, positive installation of wall paneling
without permanent face nailing, unsightly nail
holes, hammer dents, damage to panel and fi...

Photo left

Trim panels to size if necessary. If electric-box cutouts are made with power saber saw, make cut from back of panel. Here handsaw is used from front of panel.

Photo right

For prefinished paneling, use of panel adhesive instead of nails will give neater job. Cut off nozzle at angle.

FITTING. If the corner wall where you begin is uneven or out of plumb, you'll want to scribe the first panel to fit in. Place the panel against the corner and use a level to make sure it's straight up and down. Then mark with dividers and cut to this line.

Ordinarily you will place panels so they clear floor by perhaps ¼″, using molding to cover the gap. You can do the same thing at the ceiling, with cove molding, or you can fit the panel to the ceiling—scribing if necessary.

To cut around windows, doors and built-ins, mark from behind if you can. Otherwise measure and mark. Remember the old carpenter's maxim that says if you measure once you may have to cut twice—but if you measure twice you'll have to cut only once.

Sometimes you can avoid the measuring methods for cutouts for electrical outlets and switches. Chalk the box and press panel against it to mark. When paneling directly to an old wall, you can bring switches and receptacles to the new surface by shimming under the holding screws with bits of the paneling. Be sure electricity is off first.

For handsawing use a fine-tooth crosscut saw, cutting with panels face up. A plywood blade is best with a circular saw. With saber saw or portable circular saw, or when crosscutting, use a fine-tooth crosscut saw. Keep good side of panel up when cutting with a handsaw, table saw, or with a radial saw in crosscut position. That is, the saw should cut into the face side of the panel to prevent splintering. When making cutouts for electric boxes, the rule can be disregarded since a cover plate will extend over the cut edges. Touch up cut edges with a plane or sanding block.

STICKY STUFF. Installation by adhesive is becoming the rule with prefinished panels to avoid spoiling the unblemished surface with nail holes.

Panel adhesives, which come in tubes to fit calking guns, vary considerably. Some grab quickly, rather in the manner of contact cement. Others require some nailing for temporary support. With any of them, it is best to do at least some auxiliary nailing in places that won't show.

In general, you should squeeze out adhesive in a continuous bead where panel edges will go, and in dotted lines on intermediate bearings or at 12″ intervals on a solid wall.

Using contact cement—the liquid kind—is slower. It is also trickier, since once you've placed the panel you won't be able to shift it a bit. However, it does a first-class job with most kinds of paneling. The makers of the hardboard-based Muralwood woodgrain paneling do not recommend the use of either contact or tileboard cement with it.

Nailless alternative to panel adhesive is contact cement. Coat furring strips and back of panel in matching pattern.

Contact cement may not work well on a rough wall, such as most plastered ones. And if there is any paint or wallpaper on the wall, it should be removed first. After using paint remover, clean away any trace of wax with painter's naphtha.

Fumes from some kinds of contact cement are highly flammable, even explosive, so observe any safety warnings on the container. Contact-cement fires have been started by such small things as a forgotten pilot light or spark from a refrigerator starting up.

On a solid wall, brush contact cement in roughly a 2″ stripe where panel edges will come and in horizontal stripes every 12″. With exposed studs or furring, coat the whole surface. Paint matching stripes on back of panel.

When cement is dry, place panel precisely. Begin with the edge and swing the rest of panel carefully into place.

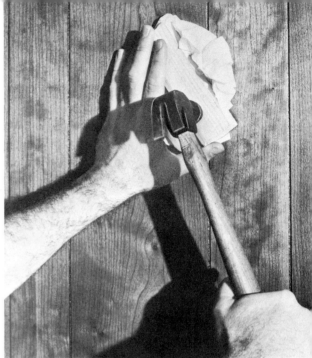

Photo left
No nails will be needed with contact cement, possibly one or two at top with panel adhesive. Press panel down firmly.

Photo right
Use a rubber mallet or a hammer and padded block to make firm contact with adhesive, either contact cement or panel type.

NAILING. Begin nailing at one edge and work toward the other—or begin at the middle and work both ways. Nailing both edges first can lead to buckling. Finishing nail should be driven not quite flush, then set, and holes filled. Dealers selling prefinished paneling can usually supply matching Putty Stik for filling holes.

When installing $\frac{1}{4}''$ plywood without adhesive, use 4d finishing nails every 8″ around edges and every foot on intervening framing or furring. Nail in the grooves where possible. When paneling directly on a plaster or gypsum board wall, use 6d (2″) finishing nails.

Same rules go for $\frac{7}{16}''$ paneling, such as Craftwall, except that wider spacing is all right. Space nails 12″ around edges, 16″ elsewhere.

Recommended nails for woodgrained hardboard and flakeboard panels are .058″-diameter ring-grooved hardboard nails, in color matching the groove. Nail every 6″ around edges, 8″ else-where—and never closer than ¼″ to panel edge. When paneling directly over gypsum board or plaster, 6d galvanized casing nails are best.

TRIM. Details for handling casing and trim in typical situations are solved by buying prefinished moldings of suitable dimensions and matching finish from your paneling dealer. You can also get un-finished moldings and save money by finishing them yourself before you put them up.

Makers of prefinished paneling sometimes offer kits for this purpose. These are also useful for finishing slab doors or built-ins to match the new paneling.

The usual finishing schedule is this:
1. Sand with 3/0 (fine) paper.
2. Apply filler-stain prescribed for the paneling.
3. Brush on sealer coat.
4. Follow with two coats of clear finish, sanding with 7/0 (very fine) paper between coats.

MAINTENANCE. The better grades of prefinished plywood panel-ing have a fine-furniture finish. You can clean and preserve them with a wax-based furniture polish.

Remove crayon, pencil, and grease marks by rubbing lightly with the grain. Sometimes an ordinary pencil or art gum eraser will do the job. For a stubborn stain use a little Bon Ami household cleaner on a damp cloth.

Paint spots are best removed with solvent or thinner suited to the type of paint.

Woodgrained panels can be cleaned with a damp cloth. For washing use a mild household detergent. Rinse with a damp cloth, taking care not to soak panels. Liquid waxes with cleaning ingredients are also fine for removing smudges. Attack stubborn stains with a cloth and naphtha, thinner, or lighter fluid.

To conceal heads of any nails after setting them be-low the surface, use Putty Stik, made in colors to match most wood.

These four photographs demonstrate how the techniques shown in the other pictures can be used to modernize a room. An unwanted and unattractive archway vanishes, adding substantially to the working size of the living room, while the paneling gives new warmth.

WHO SELLS PANELING? Almost all lumberyards, building-material dealers, some discount houses, and a few hardware and department stores. Don't overlook the want-ad section of your local paper. Contractors sometimes have unused or leftover lots which you can get at a bargain price. You can write directly to any of the companies listed in the Appendix for further information.

How to Work With Hardboards

Treat them right and they'll give you new eye-catching glamour in color and texture along with their durability and outstanding economy

Hardboard, that dull-brown workhorse of building and shop materials, has changed so much that you can look at it today and not even recognize it.

In taking on new form, size, color and texture, it has multiplied its usefulness inside the home and out. There are few build-it, make-it, or fix-it jobs you should undertake without giving some kind of hardboard at least careful consideration.

That's why the trade tricks of working with hardboard have become essential for anyone with a spark of do-it-yourself in his soul. Like any other material, hardboard has its own requirements to be observed for lasting results.

Although hardboard has floor and ceiling uses, covered in detail in other chapters, it is primarily a wall material.

It can make a plain wall, for papering or painting.

It can form a prefinished decorative wall, in its patterned and embossed forms.

As Peg Board, predrilled with small holes, it can be a working wall.

The photographs will suggest many of these uses for your home.

Hardboard today can be blonde, brown, or very brunette. It can be smooth on one side or both, dense, normal, comparatively airy, or even lacelike filigree with intricate cutouts. It can be striated for pattern, grooved like siding, textured like leather, prefinished with stain, baked enamel, or just a prime coat . . . all this when you buy it.

You can get it as tongued-and-grooved planks. You can buy sheets as thin as $\frac{1}{8}''$ or as thick as $\frac{3}{4}''$—at which point it becomes a sturdy structural material for cabinetwork. Some types come in sheets as big as 4' x 16', permitting you to cover a long wall and have only a single joint.

In the higher price brackets you can get it prefinished to look like delicately veined marble, or fine oak or walnut that has been finished and rubbed by hand.

Photo left
Realistic woodgrain Royalcote hardboard is stiff enough to make a good wall when applied directly to studs.

Photo right
When hardboard paneling like this, or plywood paneling, is V-grooved at intervals, the joint between sheets vanishes.

HOW TO CONDITION IT. Working effectively with hardboard is a matter, first, of selecting the type to fit your job. Application, as with any product, should follow these principles: the right nails properly spaced; correct mastic if you're putting it up with adhesive; effective joint treatment; and spacing between sheets where called for.

Conditioning is the most important of all. Troubleshooters for the hardboard industry have found that slipups in this one matter are behind nearly all complaints and failures. You can avoid them.

The reason for conditioning is that, like wood, hardboard swells when its humidity increases, shrinks when it dries. Unlike wood, it does this equally in both directions, in proportion to the dimension. In extreme conditions a 4' panel will expand about $3/_{16}$". The result *can* be warping or buckling, a disaster after a lot of hard work on a remodeling job.

The way to condition a hardboard for normal interior use is merely to let it stand at least twenty-four hours in the room where it will be used. Panels should be taken from their carton or wrapping and stood separately about the room.

Additional treatment is needed if the hadboard is to be installed where humidity is great or fluctuating. This means all exteriors and also kitchens, bathrooms, laundries, and basements. For such use the hardboard should be conditioned with water.

To condition panels with water, scrub each panel on the back or textured side with cold water, using a broom or brush. Then stack the panels back to back. Cover the pile to keep the moisture in. Use a tarpaulin, heavy paper, treated paper dropcloth, a sheet of polyethylene plastic, or even old newspapers. Let the water soak in and equalize for twenty-four to forty-eight hours. Then the hardboard will be ready to nail into place.

WORKING RULES. Cut hardboard just as you would lumber or plywood, with a hand or power saw. Work with the good face of the material upward when cutting with a handsaw or a stationary power saw—either table or radial type. When you cut it with a portable electric saw, however, cut with the good face of the hardboard down for smoothest results.

Any circular-saw blade suitable for crosscutting will do, but a fine-toothed variety of the kind recommended for plywood is best. If you have a carbide-toothed saw, by all means use it— especially on the tempered hardboards.

Here's a trick worth knowing when you're cutting large panels by hand. Lean two 2' x 4's against the wall and clamp the

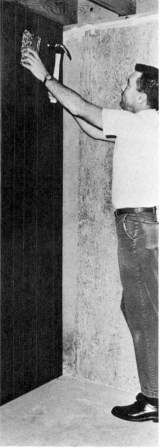

Photo left

When faced with a masonry wall that won't take nails, use panel adhesive to apply furring as well.

Photo right

Marlite's clip system makes paneling very fast to put up and removable to boot. Woodgrain surface is plastic coated.

hardboard sheet to each of them at the top. Then you'll be able to saw right down without the saw binding or the material breaking for lack of support.

For drilling, a twist drill is better than an auger bit. You'll get less rupture of the finished surface.

Almost all types of fasteners may be used: nails, wood screws, bolts, toggle bolts, rivets, even staples. Most stapling, however, will call for a gun that takes long staples; best is the big type of nailing stapler that you hit with a mallet.

Adhesives are often called for. For cabinetwork, any wood glue is satisfactory. For applying large sheets, however, you will want an inexpensive mastic such as waterproof linoleum cement or tileboard adhesive. Spread the adhesive evenly, taking care to keep it off the face of the hardboard. On a wall, brace the panel temporarily in place or use a few nails.

The most common hardboard is plain standard panels—⅛″ thick if over solid backing, preferably ¼″ when put onto studs or furring. Studs should be on centers of 16″ or less.

For horizontal paneling the furring strips should be placed on 8″ centers. For panels placed vertically, space furring strips about 10″ up to shoulder height. Above that 16″ is all right. Strips must back up all joints between the panels, of course.

Joints are the principal problem in using ordinary panels. One solution is to put narrow wood molding between the hardboard sheets. Another is to cover the joints with small battens.

A V-joint is a simpler and often more attractive answer. Create this by beveling the edges of sheets (with sandpaper on a block of wood) before putting them up.

The big sheets in which hardboard is now available—4′ wide and up to 16′ long—permit still another solution. Apply the panels horizontally and there will be only one joint on any wall not more than 16′ in length. Place a chair molding at this single joint.

Cutaway view shows typical wood trim for woodgrain hardboard paneling. Quarter-round molding at base is traditional but not needed.

Tongue-and-groove hardboard eliminates the joint problem —and also the one of concealing nail heads. This material is made in planks 16" wide and 8 ' long in an attractive light color that can be stained or left natural. The joints formed by the tongue-and-groove planks are smooth and pleasant, and all nailing is in the grooves and does not show.

Almost equally good at solving problems are the striated and the grooved hardboards made originally for exterior siding. The grooved type shows no joints when applied. The striations in the other variety make it difficult to see where sheets meet; and they also cause nail heads to sink from view.

Smooth hardboard may be finished like wood: prime coat, unless you are using a pre-primed hardboard, and one or two coats of any wall paint.

Textured hardboard—either leather pattern or striated—can be given a matching two-tone finish. Easiest way is to brush on one coat of paint, then wipe it gently from the surface. This exposes the natural color of the hardboard against a background of the paint hue.

For more elaborate effects, first paint the textured hardboard and let the paint dry. Then put on a second coat of glazing liquid or of paint—preferably the same color as the first coat but darker in hue. Wipe this with a cloth so that it remains only in the depressions.

The new blonde shades of hardboard offer additional possibilities. One is simply to do nothing. If you wish to protect the surface and still retain the light color, use a sealer before applying lacquer or varnish. This may be either a white resin sealer (white Rez or white Firzite) or a clear sanding sealer.

To introduce color without obscuring the grain of these light boards, use a wiping finish. Make it by adding some color in oil (sometimes called tube color) to white enamel undercoater or white resin sealer. Mix the color—blue, green, red, umber, whatever you like—thoroughly with the sealer, then brush it on. After about two minutes, wipe it off gently with a clean cloth.

If the surface will get hard use, protect it with clear varnish or lacquer.

Stains similar to these may be bought ready mixed in some soft shades of gray, green, and brown under the name Color Rez.

PREFINISHED HARDBOARD. One of the newest offerings in hardboard is tempered panels that have been prefinished in a light neutral-tan shade called sandalwood. The color goes into the panel so that scratches will show very little. You can still change the tone

Plastic-finished hardboard panels of Marlite are resistant to bathroom moisture, almost maintenance-free, easy to put up over existing walls. On these walls you see natural-textured travertine marble paneling. On the outer wall and double sink area, wormy chestnut textured paneling gives the dark warmth of wood. Even the tile-look around the sunken tub is hardboard paneling. Lacking a window with a view, the builder decided to put a plastic-surfaced washable mural of Ponta Roma above planter.

with wiping stain if you wish, but the only treatment ordinarily needed is a light waxing for protection.

In a higher price group are hardboards that come with a baked enamel finish in many pastel shades. These may be bought in tile or plank form (tongue-and-groove edges in both cases) in dull finish or in 4' x 8' sheets in high-gloss finish.

Prefinished hardboard is available nationally under the name Marlite.

PROJECTS WITH HARDBOARD. If you take a tip from furniture manufacturers you will begin to make much more use of hardboards in your shop projects. The new light colors make them much more attractive where paint is not to be used—and make them easier to paint too, particularly in the light colors.

Use tempered hardboard over wood framing for cabinets, cupboards, and other built-ins, fastening it with glue and nails.

1. If your basement looks like this, it's not unusual. Many new homes make no use of such valuable space. With hardboard the transformation to a usable recreation room can be quick and inexpensive.

2. The cluttered catch-all basement is now a relaxation and entertainment center. The ceiling was lowered to give adequate lighting as well as coziness. Walls and stairway were faced with Royalcote English Walnut, a prefinished hardboard. These panels go up with either adhesive or nails, can be wiped clean with a damp cloth.

The prefinished hardboards are particularly useful for surfaces that will show and those that will get hard wear. The woodgrains or high-gloss colors are a durable choice for table and cabinet tops.

Less expensive and striking are the light colors and also black in unfinished tempered hardboard.

Any form of tempered hardboard is good for renewing the top of a table or your shop workbench to give it a harder surface than it had originally.

Balanced hardboard is another one of the newer developments that can be useful to the do-it-yourselfer. In one form this is hardboard having two smooth sides, making it suitable for such things as doors.

For large doors—particularly large sliding ones—you can get thicker hardboards with both sides smooth. Usual thicknesses are $3/8''$, $1/2''$, $5/8''$, and $3/4''$. In this form it can be used for cabinet construction and doors—much as if it were lumber or plywood.

It can be cut, routed, and rabbeted like lumber. Its screw-holding power is greater than that of fir plywood or pine lumber, and it is remarkably warp-resistant. When screws or nails are to go into the edge of the sheet, drill pilot holes first.

A minister paneled this wall with cherry woodgrain hardboard, used scraps to make the matching woodbox. Molding at floor is vinyl-clad. The insulated metal fireplace, made by Vega, comes as a complete prefabricated unit.

Even what looks like leather may be hardboard, as in the case of this Masonite paneling. It comes in four colors —brown, tan, green, white —and seems especially appropriate when used in a den, as here. Damp-wiping will clean it.

BENDING HARDBOARD. Ability to take a sweeping curve smoothly is one of the useful qualities of hardboard in many wall and furniture applications.

Ordinarily such a curve will be on a permanent supporting frame, and the hardboard can be bent into position and fastened with glue and nails or screws. If the curve is extreme, dampen the hardboard first just as you would to condition it for use in humid conditions.

If the hardboard is to remain unsupported, you can give it a permanent curve after it has had a water treatment, as described earlier in this chapter, by fastening it to a form and letting it dry in that position. There will be some springback, of course, so you make the form in a curve somewhat more exaggerated than you require.

The extent to which hardboard can be bent varies somewhat from brand to brand. But for ⅛″ material it runs from a minimum radius of about 4″ to 8″.

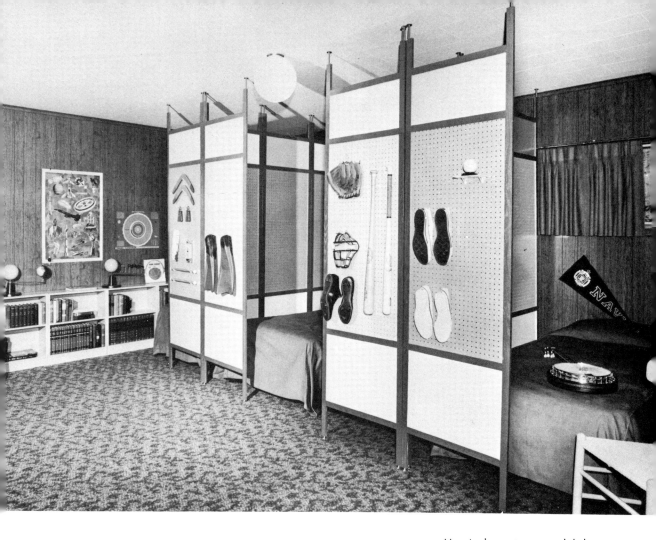

Here's how to remodel by dividing. This large room for two boys was made more useful by splitting it into sleeping cubicles and an activity room. Dividers are Peg Board, walls are Royalcote Pecan—all hardboard.

HARDBOARD AS AN UNDERLAYMENT. When standard hardboard has been shaved to a precise $7/32''$ or $1/4''$ thick it is sold in $3' \times 4'$ and $4' \times 4'$ sheets as underlayment. It is used over wood floors or subfloors to provide a flat, smooth surface for linoleum, rubber, asphalt, and other tiles as well as the new pour-on plastic floors.

It should be put down only on floors that have been properly leveled and made solid by additional nails where needed. Over a subfloor, apply a layer of building paper (vapor-barrier paper if the subfloor is over an unheated crawl space in a climate having an average January temperature below 45 degrees).

Spacing to allow for expansion should be $1/8''$ between underlayment and wall and $1/16''$ between sheets. A nail is a suitable spacer. Begin nailing at the center of the panel. Use $1''$ or $1\frac{1}{4}''$ barbed box nails, ring nails or drive-screw underlay nails. Space them $6''$ apart over the entire area and not closer to the edge of the panel than $3/8''$.

Since underlayment is the same material it may be used in place of standard hardboard if it is easier to obtain in the sizes wanted.

If you are interested in saving money and are paneling a wall or backing cabinets where maximum strength is not important, keep an eye out for lighter density boards.

These are sold under such trade names as Thriftwood, Panelwood, and Hardlite; the usual generic name is panel board. They have the same appearance and smooth surface as ordinary hardboard. But because they are lighter they have almost twice as great insulating value—and the price is less.

But all hardboard is a bargain today. It's a uniform, dependable, strong material. In the new patterns and colors it's a workhorse with glamour.

12

Rough Stuff For Paneling

Exterior woods come indoors to give the remodeler a natural, rugged material that is homey, economical, and durable

Rough wood, once thought suitable only for the exterior of a house, has come inside for the home handyman to use when he wants walls that conceal scuffing, scratching, scarring, and denting.

Wood panels with a rough texture can take the activities of children and pets just as they take rough weather when they are used outdoors.

Most of them are available under such names as Roughtex, Cedar-Sawn, Planktex, FactriSawn, Trendtex, Ruf-Sawn, Cedar-Etched, Knotty Cedar, Pecky Cypress, Wormy Chestnut, Rusticwood.

Increased demand for wall paneling with rough texture has come as a surprise to manufacturers, too. It started with architects and builders who wanted unusual custom effects in expensive new homes. Now these textured woods are easier and cheaper to buy. You have a choice of etched, saw-textured and pecky surfaces. All three come in boards, plywood, and hardboard panels. The cost is about the same in all three categories, 20 to 30 cents a square foot for most plywoods and thin lumber.

Figure on spending about $100 for a fair-sized room, and about $35 for one full-height wall 12' long.

PLYWOOD. Available in rough-textured panels, 4' wide and 8' to 10' long, plywood goes up fast. Here are some of the types:

California redwood comes in a band-saw pattern. Simpson makes it and calls it Ruf-Sawn.

Cedar or fir, made by U.S. Plywood in a rough-sawn texture, is called Roughtex.

Planktex, another rough redwood, has tiny saw grooves at 8" intervals to produce a board-to-board effect. This one is a U.S. Plywood product.

Dullness and monotony vanish from even the simplest of modern home designs when the surfaces have texture. Walls of t&g rough redwood go nicely with slate floors.

Rough-paneled wall like this might be matched boards or grooved plywood, actually is hardboard. Seamless floor, another major step in this basement conversion, was not laid but poured.

Cedar etched panels, brushed to give a texture of weathered wood, are made by Evans. Wide but shallow grooves in the Western red cedar produce a subtle shadow line at intervals of 2″, 4″, 6″, or 8″ as you choose. You can also get the panels without grooves, in both saw-textured and etched surfaces.

All these types are about ⅜″ thick. If you search through types that are still being used for exterior siding you can get panels ⅝″ thick.

SOLID WOOD also comes in rough-faced versions. You can even get a saw-textured redwood that is smooth on one side, rough on the other. Georgia Pacific makes this one.

Where tongue-and-groove boards give you butt joints or V

Texture in this wall comes from V-grooves as well as the striations milled into the redwood paneling. Color is produced by mixing sapwood and heartwood.

Texture 1-11 plywood has a rough surface as well as plowed grooves. If it is used as an exterior material for a house, it may be continued inside as well, to give continuity as well as added textural interest.

grooves, channel patterns produce wide joints that look like reverse-batten siding.

Board-and-batten is especially good in such remodeling jobs as turning a garage, basement, or attic into a recreation area. Informality of activity seems to call for walls that not only look tough but which are tough enough to take ping pong, hobbies, carpentry, games. You can get board-and-batten in a pattern called TrendTex, made by Potlatch Forests. It comes in rough-sawn pine prefinished to a weathered gray and also in a rough-faced pine plywood.

MAN-MADE PANELS. Rough printed surfaces on hardboard fool the eye and are easier on the budget than real wood. Pecky Teak, a Masonite textured hardboard, is one type.

In a somewhat different category, but still an imitator of nature, is the travertine marble panel with fissured veins and marble colors. This comes in a 4′ x 4′ sheet.

INSTALLATION. No nails are necessary for these rough-textured panel materials. They can be put up with adhesives, available in easy-squeeze cartridges. Instructions call for a continuous bead applied to wall where edges of panels will go and intermittent stippling of adhesive on other bearings.

How good is adhesive? Testers at U.S. Plywood did a sample installation by traditional nailing methods, then duplicated the job with adhesive. Panels went up in about half the time, and there were no nail holes to fill.

Convert smooth trim material to match rough paneling by sanding with *very coarse* belt or etching with wire brush.

Produce rough-sawn surface on paneling or trim by pulling boards through band saw *backwards* against the teeth.

BUYING GUIDE: ROUGH-WOOD PANELING

PATTERN	NAME	LUMBER	DIMENSIONS	WHO MAKES IT
TONGUE-AND-GROOVE	Saw-textured paneling-siding	Redwood	1″ x 6″, 8″, 10″	Georgia-Pacific
	3-Way Rustic, one side smooth, one side FactriSawn		1″ x 6″, 8″, 10″, 12″	Simpson
	Noyo Thrift FactriSawn one side		Thin: ⅜″ x 6″, 8″	Union
	G-P cypress paneling (pecky)	Cypress	1″ x 4″, 6″, 8″, 10″	Georgia-Pacific
	Rough-sawn cypress paneling		Various widths in t&g and shiplap	
	End-matched pecky cypress		1″ x 6″, 8″, 10″, 12″	Townsend
	Rough-sawn hardwood paneling	Wattled walnut, colonial cherry, colonial red oak	End-matched, ½″ x 4″, 5″, 6″, 7″ 8″ (oak 4″, 5″, and 6″ only)	
	Rough-sawn Douglas fir, Ponderosa pine, Idaho white pine	Western softwoods	Usually 1″ x 4″ to 1″ x 12″ (also in 2″ thickness)	Members of Western Wood Products Assn.
	Cedar flush or V-joint paneling siding	Western red cedar	1″ x 4″, 5″, 6″	Members of Western Red Cedar Assn.
BOARD-AND-BATTEN	FactriSawn board-and-batten	Redwood	12″ boards, matching battens	Members of Calif. Redwood Assn.
	Cedar board-and-batten	Western red cedar	1″ x 12″ boards, 1″ x 3″ battens	Members of Western Red Cedar Assn.
	TrendTex board-and-batten	Prestained white pine	1″ x 12″ boards, 1″ x 3″ battens	Potlatch
BOARD-ON-BOARD	Santa Rosa FactriSawn	Redwood	Alternating ½″ and 1″ boards, 6″, 8″, 10″, or 12″ wide	Members of Calif. Redwood Assn.
	TrendTex board-on-board weathered gray	Prestained white pine	1″ x 6″ boards	Potlatch

ROUGH-WOOD PANELING (Cont'd.)

CHANNEL RUSTIC	Channel cedar	Western red cedar	1" x 8" and 1" x 10"	Members of Western Red Cedar Assn.
	FactriSawn Channel rustic	Redwood	1" x 6" to 1" x 12"	Members of Calif. Redwood Assn.

BUYING GUIDE: TEXTURED-PLYWOOD PANELING

TEXTURE	NAME AND WOOD	GROOVE PATTERN	WHO MAKES IT
BRUSHED (ETCHED)	Cedar-etched	⅜" grooves on 2", 4", 6", or 8" centers; also ungrooved	Evans Products
	Rusticwood brushed redwood	⅜" grooves 4" or 8" o.c.; or alternating 4" and 12" o.c.	Simpson
NATURAL PERFORA-TIONS	Copper-inlaid vintage fir	½" strips of copper 4" o.c.	Georgia-Pacific
EITHER SAWN OR ABRADED	Ivy League fir or cedar	Wide, shallow grooves 4", 8", or 16" o.c.	U.S. Plywood
STRIATED	Striated fir	All-over planed pattern	Georgia-Pacific and U.S. Plywood
ROUGH-SAWN	Cedar-sawn	⅜" grooves on 2", 4", 6", or 8" centers; also made without grooves	Evans Products
	Planktex rough-sawn fir or redwood	Narrow grooves on 8" centers for plank effect	U.S. Plywood
	Rough-sawn fir	Kerfed 4" or 8" on center	Georgia-Pacific
	Roughtex cedar or fir	Saw texture aligned across face; no grooves	U.S. Plywood
	Ruf-sawn redwood	Ungrooved	Simpson
	TrendTex pine	Ungrooved; prestained weathered gray	Potlatch

13

Ways With Wallcoverings

Don't call it wallpaper—walls now wear washable vinyl, polyethylene fiber, metal, cork, velour, flocking . . . you name it

Remodel with wallpaper? Of course. But the wallcovering you use today in the manner of yesterday's wallpaper very likely will not be paper at all. It may have the surface of silk or of a coarse fiber. It may be grasscloth, cork, silver, or gold foil, a rare tapestry, embroidery, or animal skin. It may even be a mural that brings to your home an exotic view from anywhere in or out of this world.

Even the simplest wallpaper is no longer an oatmeal-hued, difficult-to-apply, horridly practical stuff that your family has selected by a series of compromises from a big book of similar samples. At the least it is likely to be prepasted, pretrimmed, strippable, and scrubbable. It may be vinyl-coated or made with strong polyethylene that looks extremely delicate but is so tough it can live in a steamy bathroom and keep its new look.

Photographs of a variety of modern patterns are included in this chapter to give you at least a hint of what is available in wallcoverings today.

You can update any room by changing one or more walls, and it won't take you more than a few hours. There's no messy cleanup job either, if you choose the kinds that have adhesive on the back.

Using the new wall materials means easier housekeeping. Many clean with a damp cloth and mild soap and water. Even some of those delicately flocked types that look like velvet or hand-embroidered fabrics can actually be scrubbed with a brush and won't show water spots from bathroom splashes. Some wallcoverings are now heavy and flexible enough to serve as structural reinforcement on plaster surfaces where there are cracks. Manufacturers of vinyl wall coverings say they will level out rough areas and hide small hairline cracks.

They resist quick temperature changes as well as moisture, and yet you can still peel off the old wallcovering and put on the new without steaming, soaking, and scraping.

If you change your mind some year and want the paper off, just peel it. Most papers strip off so neatly and thoroughly that paint can be applied to the surface with ease.

HOW TO USE THEM. You can bring variety to a room paneled in wood by doing a single section of the wall in a colorful textured fabric. It can accent a window, odd corner, section over a fireplace. It can form a backdrop for a bed. It can go up the wall, behind the bed and onto the ceiling to form a canopy effect. A tapestry or velvet covering can add an exotic note. It can turn a formal room into an informal one, or vice versa. It can accent a door, a mirror, an archway. It can hide an offensive structural feature. It can be used vertically to make a room look higher, or horizontally to make a room look wider.

Wallcoverings on screens and dividers make them a part of the room, instead of accessories. A high ceiling can be lowered with a dark or bold design. A small print confuses the eye and hides undesirable features. A bold, bright print can cheer up a dark room and liven up the occupants. A quiet, soft covering can bring calm and restfulness.

The effectiveness of wallcovering color and design should not be underestimated. One writer demonstrated this when he based his plot on a character who drove a woman mad by covering the walls of her bedroom with material that horrified and frightened her purely by color and design.

Color creates mood. You can make a shaded unsunny room warm and cheerful with textured wall coverings in red, orange, or yellow. Blues, greens, and pale lavenders make a room cool and quiet. With wallcoverings that are so strippable you can move them about, it would be quite feasible to have winter and summer wallcoverings for the same room. Just switch the feeling of warmth with reds in winter to the feeling of cool with pale blues and greens in summer.

Some colors make people feel happy and energetic. Others

A handprinted wallcovering (United Wallpaper) is shown here in black flocking. It is also available in gold flocking on white or may be custom ordered in any combination of colors.

Brilliant plaid would be a good choice for a den or a boy's room. It's prepasted and strippable.

You may never own one of these cars, but you can still enjoy looking at them on the walls.

Let your teenager have his collection of road signs on the wall instead of getting them from the roads. "The End," from United-DeSoto, has red-and-black designs on a white background.

Bathroom or recreation room might be the place for these life-size footprints on an amusing wall covering from United-DeSoto.

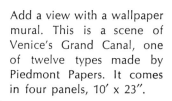

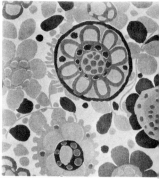

The wet look, called "Kicky," features floating, oddly contoured shapes in orange, yellow, white, green, chartreuse, pink, blue, green combinations on black or white.

Add a view with a wallpaper mural. This is a scene of Venice's Grand Canal, one of twelve types made by Piedmont Papers. It comes in four panels, 10' x 23".

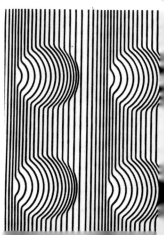

Space Age eyeshaking wall-covering might be best for a small area. It comes in black and white or orange and gold combinations.

Prepasted, vinyl-coated, strippable material portrays show biz in pink, orange, lime, black and white, purple, or marine blue.

Stylized bouquets of fresh field flowers in gay colors make this a bright, cheerful wallcovering. Called Scottsdale, from United Wallpaper.

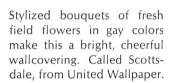

Good things to eat are featured in handsome colors on this prepasted strippable wall material, appropriate for kitchen or breakfast area.

Patriotic design in red, white, and blue is naturally titled "Old Glory" by United-De-Soto. The pattern is a part of the Bravo series.

make them congenial and sleepy. Patterns also affect the way people react. These are things to consider when you choose a wallcovering. You can give your home the kind of mood you want by your choice of colors or patterns on the walls.

WHAT ABOUT COST? Most wallcoverings are not expensive in the long run now that they are so durable and cleanable. Unusual and exotic wallcoverings, however, can be extremely expensive, up to thousands of dollars for a roll if you want an antique Oriental paper or cloth hanging for just one wall of a room.

Honey-smooth, skin leather with the soft, peachy feel of suede is expensive. Cobra skin and unusual colors in leather are costly. But high price alone need not rule out the use of such materials. They can be employed in small amounts to highlight just one wall, or a part of a wall, and to serve as a keynote for decoration of a whole room.

105

You might paint three walls of a room, or panel them with wood, and enliven the fourth with a strippable covering featuring the occupant's hobby—sport cars for a boy, authentic ship plans on a blueprint-colored vinyl for a yachtsman, scenes from a favorite far-off place for a traveler.

You can take the term wallcovering less than literally. Do the floor of a family room or nursery in a catchy dirt-concealing pattern, using something vinyl-coated for washability and strippable for instant change. Or cover panels of a room divider or sliding door to contrast with or match the walls of the room.

STRIPPABLE is the magic word for do-it-yourselfers. It means that the material can be removed for replacement merely by prying up a corner and pulling off the whole strip in one piece. It also means that the covering is so strong you can hang a strip upside down or crooked, peel it off and put it back on correctly.

Strippable really means that the wallcovering material is stronger than the paste you put it up with. This quality is built into Wallweave, a stout cotton fabric resembling canvas, made by Piedmont Papers. It is also a natural feature of pure vinyl coverings, including Varlar made by United-DeSoto, and Tyvek, a polyethylene-fiber material by Du Pont.

What's new is the addition of this strippable characteristic to conventional wallpapers. It's done by using as the base stock International Paper Company's I-Peal. This combination of synthetic and wood fibers and resins is strong wet or dry.

WASHABLE, meaning any paper with a waterproof shiny coating. In the old days, washing had to be done carefully and could not be repeated many times. Now there are many types of materials that can not only be washed but actually scrubbed—a few with a scouring pad. Washability can now be found in many elegant wall coverings that have the texture of velvet, velour, or tapestry.

United Wallpaper puts out a delicate-looking flocked material which can be washed. It has one fine feature. It diminishes sound transmission. The denser the flocking, of course, the better the sound barrier.

Flockings are the most elegant innovation in wallcoverings. There are four-color flocks on pearlescent backgrounds, flock op-art designs, flocks that feel like velvet, and a whole zoo of animal papers you can "feel"—flocked zebra, leopard, and tiger. These would be fine for a den, recreation room, or children's area.

The cloth covering called Wallweave has been given

Wallpaper can go on the floor as well as the wall. Use a kind that is vinyl-coated for quick cleaning and strippable when change is required.

Simulated animal hide in a zebra pattern gives a safari look to this room. It's available from United Wallpaper in tiger and leopard, too, and is washable.

washability by chemical means—and fire resistance as well—without taking on a trace of coated look.

A traditional favorite in textured wall material is grasscloth. This is now offered in coated form where it may be exposed to moisture, as in a bathroom.

EXTRUDED VINYL can be embossed in such a variety of patterns that it has given rise to a whole new family of wallcoverings. Price is still high on these.

Less expensive versions for the home are now coming out

Photo left
Small-pattern design with matching border, called "Tiber" by Van Luit, give a mosaic look to the walls of this room. It's vinyl and comes in four jewel-tone colors.

Photo right
Actual blueprints have been transferred to this wallcovering to complete the nautical scheme in this study. It's a Van Luit vinyl.

Vinyl wallcoverings not only go on the walls but on room accessories as well. No scrap of material need be wasted.

with do-it-yourself instructions in each roll. They go up with a special vinyl adhesive. Patterns include burlap, woodgrain, travertine, grass cloth, and several fibers.

One extruded vinyl called Vicrwall, has a surface of Du Pont Tedlar, so stainproof it is described as resistant to the harshest cleaning agents, ballpoint pens, iodine, blood, tar, or lipstick. Among its many patterns are leathers, oriental fabrics, woodgrains, and stonelike surfaces of amazing depth.

PREPASTED MATERIALS come in two types. One is a descendant of old-fashioned wallpaper. But the patterns are brighter and the material may be either paper that is vinyl-coated or actual vinyl wallcloth.

These coatings are pretrimmed in most cases. They go up without the use of wallpaper paste after being passed through a waterbox filled with warm water.

The other family of prepasted coverings is found on display racks in hardware and variety stores. This type has a pressure-sensitive adhesive protected by backing paper. You can buy it by the inch, foot, or as much as you like. It goes up dry, with no

Prepasted wallcovering is easy to hang by rolling it loosely through waterbox half filled with warm water. Immerse material one minute before applying to wall.

dipping or pasting, after the backing is removed. It's especially convenient for small areas but does not stick too well to some surfaces. Test it on a small area first.

This quick form of material is coming out in more elaborate designs all the time. You can get it in velvet, flock, velour, microthin cork, foil, burlap, lace. It is available only in narrow widths.

ADHESIVES. Traditional inexpensive wheat paste is still being used on fabric or paperlike coverings. Waterproof materials such as vinyl-coated, vinyl cloth, and extruded vinyls require a special vinyl paste. The type is packaged and recommended by the maker of the wallcovering.

A conventional alternative for either type is a liquid all-purpose wall adhesive that gets you out of the messy job of mixing. Although this costs several times as much as a floury paste, you'll still be spending only a couple of dollars for adhesive for a good-sized wall.

110

You're not likely to be faced with any serious decision in choosing an adhesive. Wallcovering makers are quite specific in their recommendations, because using the wrong adhesive could mean failure for the whole job, regardless of the quality of material used. Dealers stock the appropriate adhesives.

TIPS ON HANGING. Whatever your choice of materials, know before you start whether you are working with prepasted, strippable, plastic, or paper. The thicker the covering the better it will hide wall imperfections. If you aren't sure, start the job in a small, inconspicuous area.

The wall needs to be in good condition. Remove picture hangers, nails, switch plates, molding, and trim strips. Old wallpaper which is peeling, or heavy layers of paper, will have to be removed by steaming or scraping.

Large cracks and holes need to be filled with plaster or spackling compound and then sanded smooth, when dry.

You'll get a better job if you put on a coat of thin glue

Photo left
A big table is essential to a good job when using non-prepasted wallcovering. A sheet of plywood, or a door on level supports, will do.

Photo right
Keep table clean of paste, or you'll have adhesive on the surface side of the paper. A large brush speeds up the job.

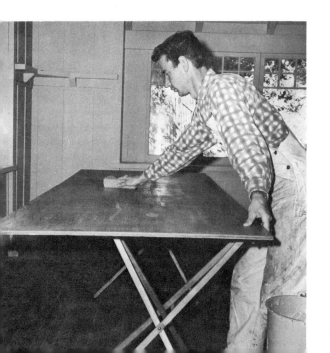

sizing first. This is a powder, available at your dealer, that you mix with water. It goes on quickly and dries rapidly.

The art of hanging wallcoverings has been refined and simplified over the years. The basic steps follow.

Start with a Vertical Line

Starting right of doorway (or fireplace if it's the focal point of a room), measure less than width of wallcovering. Then take a cord or string the same height as wall. Rub cord with chalk and with a tack attach one end near ceiling at point measured. To other end, attach a weight or plumb bob. Let it drop freely. Now, hold "plumb" at baseboard and snap cord against the wall. The vertically straight mark left by the chalk is your starting point. Position the right hand side of first strip along this line.

Measure and Cut Wallcovering to Size

On a flat working surface or table, unroll wallcovering, pattern side up. Pull it gently but firmly across the edge of the table to remove curl. Using scissors, cut strips the height of the wall plus an extra 6" at ceiling and another 6" at baseboard for matching and trimming. Match pattern of each succeeding strip exactly at the right hand side of the preceding strip. (A flock wallcovering should be cut one strip at a time.)

To Hang Prepasted Wallcoverings

Half fill waterbox (purchasable from dealer) with warm water and place against baseboard near chalked plumb line. Set ladder next to it. Taking one strip at a time, roll loosely, pattern side in. Thread a small piece under the wire guide and immerse for about a minute. Hold top of strip and pull up gently from waterbox, stepping up on ladder at same time. Apply top of strip about 2" or 3" above ceiling line, smoothing against wall with a clean cellulose sponge.

Keeping right hand edge of paper along plumb line, work your way down to baseboard. Smooth down all wrinkles from strip in a down and out motion. Move waterbox under area where next strip will go. Slide the next strip flush along first strip so pattern matches

and edges meet. Do not overlap seam. Repeat smoothing procedure. Then trim excess of both strips at ceiling and baseboard with razor.

To Hang Unpasted Wallcoverings

Using a wide brush, apply paste sparingly and evenly to one half of the strip first. Start from center and work paste toward ends, leaving an inch or so at edges free of paste. Fold pasted half toward the center, paste to paste, without creasing. Now paste remaining half of strip in same manner and fold so ends of strip meet at the center.

Carry strip to marked plumb line area. Holding the unpasted top edge with one hand, pull pasted fold apart with other. Start strip about 2″ or 3″ above top of wall and line up right edge flush with chalked plumb line. With a dry brush, or cloth, smooth strip into place. Check to see that there are no wrinkles. Then proceed with lower half of strip in the same way. Follow same procedure for remaining strips. Make sure pattern matches and edges meet. Do not overlap seams. Trim excess at ceiling and baseboard with razor before adhesive dries.

To Hang Flocked Wallcoverings

Wall surface must be smooth and clean. Remove old paper, especially metallics. For finest results, use a lining paper base (see your dealer for more information). Then prepare a perfectly smooth, medium thick, non-staining paste, straining out lumps and grit. Cut and paste one strip at a time, allowing paste to soak just long enough to "relax" sheet, and to prevent distortion of flock. When trimming, place straight edge on the selvage, not on body of sheet, to avoid creasing flock. Use a soft, natural-bristle smoothing brush. Avoid overbrushing. Set seams by tapping with brush. Never use a hard roller on flock. Keep paste off surface; if paste does get on flock surface, remove immediately with damp sponge or wet cloth. Clean lint and dust from flocks with soft-brush attachment of vacuum cleaner.

Corner Strategy

Whether inside or outside (concave or convex), corners may not be perfectly straight, so extend your wallcovering around the corners at least a half inch. The next strip should overlap in the corner, but hang it only after snapping another plumb line to insure vertical hanging on the new wall.

Around Lighting Fixtures

Before applying wallcovering to a wall or a ceiling, lower all lighting fixtures and remove electrical switch plates. Cut an area slightly smaller than the ceiling mount of the fixture—*after* the whole strip has been applied or pasted to the wall or ceiling. If the lighting fixture is too large or difficult to lower, cut a big "X" in the wallcovering before the strip is hung, slide over fixture, smooth strip into place, and then trim edges with razor blade.

Hint

Remove excess paste or possible finger marks with a sponge wrung damp in clean water. Do this as you go along, strip by strip.

Save any leftover paper to use for possible repair jobs later on. If you need to patch, don't cut a neat square with a scissors. Tear an irregular piece and glue it to the wall. Wipe the patch with a sponge, wrung dry. The repair will be almost invisible.

HOW MUCH WALLCOVERING YOU WILL NEED

Find the approximate size of your room on the chart. Look at the two bottom rows to find out how many standard single rolls of wallcovering and how much border material you will need. Figures here are generous enough to allow for ceilings up to 9' high. With wallcoverings it is important to buy plenty to begin with, arranging to return excess. If you run short you may have to buy from a new run in which colors are not a perfect match for your original purchase

LONG HALLS	3' x 11'	3' x 14'	3' x 18'	3' x 23'			
		4' x 13'	4' x 17'	4' x 22'	4' x 25'		
			5' x 16'	5' x 21'	5' x 24'	6' x 30'	
REGULAR ROOM SIZES	6' x 8'	6' x 12'					
	7' x 7'	7' x 11'	7' x 14'				
		8' x 10'	8' x 13'	8' x 18'			
		9' x 9'	9' x 12'	9' x 17'	9' x 21'		
			10' x 12'	10' x 16'	10' x 20'	10' x 24'	
				11' x 15'	11' x 19'	11' x 23'	11' x 28'
				12' x 14'	12' x 18'	12' x 22'	12' x 26'
					13' x 17'	13' x 21'	13' x 25'
					14' x 16'	14' x 20'	14' x 24'
SINGLE ROLLS OF SIDEWALL	6	8	10	12	14	16	18
YARDS OF BORDER	12	16	16	20	24	24	28

14

How To Improve
Your Ceiling

Make a room look higher, lower, brighter, darker by changing the ceiling—and improve it functionally, too

Old-fashioned homes with ceilings that are too high or too dark can be remodeled by changing the type and height of the ceiling. A plain ceiling can be given a paneled look, recessed lighting, and even authentic-looking hand-hewn beams, if you choose.

The need to remodel a ceiling is often a part of updating an attic, garage, or porch into a livable room. These areas usually have no ceilings and are in need of insulation and lighting as well as a finished look.

If an existing ceiling is still usable but merely dirty or dull, then a good wallcovering can do the job. Choice of pattern or color can fool the eye into thinking the ceiling is higher or lower. Bringing wall material down from the ceiling a few inches may be all that is really needed to create a feeling of coziness.

Or you can get a paneled look on the ceiling. There's a type of random-plank material that gets away from the too-familiar commercial look produced by 12″ x 12″ tiles. There's also a woodgrained random-plank ceiling material that comes in boards of varying widths and in 4′ lengths. Planks look like wood, are available in an antiqued finish, and can be staggered to give a rustic effect.

If you want to change a room into one with a more modern

feel, then there are woodgrained tiles that come with a heavily beveled edge that gives the ceiling a sculptured look.

Another big help to the remodeler is a suspended ceiling that has a decorative wood-panel appearance when risers are set into place on top of the grid runners that support the ceiling.

Woodridge Gridrisers (Armstrong Cork Company) give a recessed look to the usual suspended ceiling. Formerly, ceiling panels rested on runners. Now, with this riser method, hanger wires are attached to ceiling joists and the metal runners of the suspension system are fastened to the wires.

Next, risers are put in place, and the ceiling panels are laid in position. The old ceiling concealed above is still easily accessible if it is necessary to get at wiring or pipes.

A new ceiling for a 12′ x 15′ room costs under a hundred dollars with this system.

Should you want to panel the old ceiling with the more usual 12″ x 12″ tile, you may be confronted by another problem.

Give a new look to an old ceiling with Wood Grain, a tile made in 4′ t&g boards of varying widths. For a random-plank effect, install boards in alternating widths with joints staggered.

Light fixtures already there are not going to fit in with the new ceiling. Replacing these fixtures can be more expensive than the ceiling itself.

This problem can be solved with a specially designed ceiling light fixture called Tilemate. It comes in the same size as the tile, takes the place of a single 12″ x 12″ tile, and drops right in.

If you already have a perfectly acceptable ceiling but still want a change without doing much work or spending a lot of money, there's a newcomer in the ceiling field that is easy on the back and eye. It's called Lite Beam, a polyurethane material, which has all the appearance of a real hand-hewn wood material, but none of the weight or cost.

A few of these beams in a basement or recreation room will give the look of an Old English barn or tavern to an existing ceiling that has no distinction.

The photographs show how to go about using these new materials and methods.

Avoid the look of conventional ceiling tile by using this type, made with a broadened beveled edge. This pattern, called Brunswick, is made by Armstrong.

Photo left
Another way to renew a ceiling is with one of the wallcoverings described in the preceding chapter. Professionals here demonstrate the art of handling wallpaper at ceiling level.

Photo right
When papering a ceiling, iron out any bubbles and wrinkles with a small hand roller before paste dries. Small-patterned paper like this shows any flaws of technique less than a plainer paper would.

HOW TO PUT BEAMS ON YOUR CEILING

1. Polyurethane Lite Beams have a hand-hewn look that makes them almost impossible to tell from real wood, are easily handsawed.

119

2. Adhesive is used to install the beams. The precut 2″ center groove makes it possible to apply the beams over a wood strip.

3. Since a beam 8″ wide weighs only 1 pound to the lineal foot, it is easy for one person to fasten in place.

4. An interesting beamed effect like this is possible with the polyurethane type in rooms where weight of wood beams rules them out.

5. Close-up shows texture of polyurethane wall paneling made in 4' x 8' sheets to m a t c h beams. Paneling, shown also in the previous photograph, is ultralight, fire-retardant, has insulating value of 2" of fiberglass.

Suspended ceiling combines acoustical efficiency with modern appearance. Also important to a basement remodeling like this is the fact that any panels can be lifted out for access to plumbing or wiring concealed above. Lighting comes from translucent panels with fluorescent fixtures, installed as shown elsewhere.

1. To install a suspended ceiling, begin by determining the height you prefer. Mark by snapping chalk line around perimeter of room.

2. Attach molding to wall at chalk-line height. Use concrete stub nails for a masonry wall, ordinary 6d nails for wood or plaster.

3. Locate position of first ceiling runner by measuring room to find width of border panel, as when installing ordinary ceiling tile. Using temporary reference string as guide, align runner in position and install first screw eye.

4. Install second reference string perpendicular to the first approximately 1⅛" above molding and work out across the room, attaching hanger wires at 4' intervals. Bend each wire at point where it intersects reference string. This will insure that all runners hang at exactly the same height.

5. Install first ceiling runner by resting one end on wall molding and fastening other end to bent wire. Twist several times to secure loose end. Then work back along runner, fastening hanger wires every 4' to provide additional support.

6. Continue this procedure across the room until all runners are installed. Odd lengths of runner, when needed, may be cut with aviation snips and spliced into the system.

7. Install 4' cross tees between main runners at 24" intervals. Simply insert end tab of cross tee into runner slot and push to lock.

8. With suspension system now complete, lay ceiling panels into grid. Tilt panel slightly upwards, s l i d e through opening, and rest on grid flanges.

1. Many suspended - ceiling systems have matching translucent lighting panels. This one has Gridmate, a fluorescent fixture, as well. First step in installing it is attaching mounting brackets to grid flanges.

2. Now attach fixture by sliding the two tabs at each end through the slots in the mounting bracket. Bend tabs to lock fixture into place. You can use any of three pairs of slots, to adjust height of fixture.

3. Attach the reflector panels to the top of the fixture. To avoid the slightly chilly effect produced by ordinary cold-white fluorescent tubes, the kind most commonly sold, shop around till you find warm white.

4. With the fixture connected to power source and switch, and tubes inserted, slip the diffusing panel into the grid. Panels come in a variety of types, including plain, louvered, eggcrate.

PART III

MODERNIZE YOUR DOORS

15

How To Update Your Doors

Ideas for entrancing entrances—new doors as well as ways to make old ones better than new

Doors have gone dramatic and artistic. Single entrance doors have become double doors. Normal-height doors have been changed for doors that are 14′ or 16′ feet high. Ordinary doors are wearing carvings and antiquing.

Your doors can do this too, with your help. The entire appearance of the house can be substantially changed by taking out a weatherbeaten or merely uninteresting door and replacing it with a new one. Often the first thing a professional remodeler does is invest in a really handsome pair of doors for an old house. He knows he'll get his money back just by putting up a good front door.

You can now buy a door wrapped in vinyl that can't be distinguished from wood. You can have one of metal that will look better with age and last forever. You can get a fiberglass-plastic door.

Or, more economically yet, you can take that plain old solid door you already own and transform it. This chapter will tell you how to do it.

You can take someone else's ideas for door decor or you can invent your own with unusual hardware, interesting finishes, and hobby materials such as copper foil.

If the door now in use is still serviceable, but ugly, try out some of the new antiquing materials that come in spray cans or as brush-on or rub-on types with either oil or water-based pigment. Antiquing goes well on plastic panels, medallions, and edging that can't be distinguished from wood once the door is antiqued.

A door can also update hall or entryway lighting when it transmits light instead of barring it. Plastics in stained-glass colors, doors made entirely of plastic with materials sandwiched between layers of different color and design, and doors updated with patterned glass or plastic in the upper half can all serve to bring cathedral light into what has been a dismal entrance.

HAND-CARVED DOORS. Imports from Mexico are well made and less expensive than any carved in the United States. You'll find these Mexican doors at import shops, which also offer unusual door knobs and hardware imported from Mexico and Asia.

Another source of carved doors is a wrecking company in a big city. There you may discover a unique one, perhaps one or a pair of double doors that originally came from Europe. The price will be high. Watch also when an old home is being wrecked in your own area. If you show up during the initial stages, you may get a rare buy.

PLASTICS. Today plastics are so beautiful and durable and come in such compelling colors, either plain or copies of stained glass, that you can use them to produce doors of great beauty and permanence.

Good plastics are virtually unbreakable, so they are an excellent safety factor compared to a wooden door that can be kicked in or smashed. Consider also the possibility of adding a few squares or a panel of plastic in the door you now have. Or keep the door you have, antique or paint it, and complement it with a panel of plastic, door height, next to it. Light will come through and brighten the entrance as thoroughly as if you'd changed the door itself.

With a translucent white panel of Filon you can create a changing pattern of light effects by placing ferns, bamboo, pine, or philodendron outdoors to throw a shadow pattern that seems to be a part of the plastic.

One company, Cardenas Glass Laminators in Tacoma, Washington, will work with you or your architect or builder to design a custom door of reinforced polyester bonded to core material without use of any glues or adhesives. These doors are sealed to provide insulation against heat and cold, have low sound

Solid-core door that darkened this entryway was replaced with "Interplay," plastic door designed by Kenton T. Pies for Cardenas Division of Architectural Designs, Inc. The authors fitted the door and installed an attractive modern lock. Door is yellow and green, and the panel next to it is a translucent white plastic that lets in additional light.

transmission, no condensation on the interior, no warping or noise because of extreme temperature variation, and no upkeep or maintenance. If you have no confidence in your own artistic ability to design the perfect door, you can still work with this company, offering your own ideas and requirements, and their artists will produce a door for your home.

A less-expensive procedure is to use a stock door design from the same company. All of their doors bring light and art into the home. Your building materials dealer may have them on display or can get one. Shown in the photograph is a Cardenas door made in yellow and green shades with a pebble finish. Like a painting, it has a title, "Interplay"; and an artist-designer, Kenton T. Pies.

Other stock doors in the same line come in shoji style, Aztec pattern, small circles that duplicate rings or slices of natural bamboo, and diamonds in brilliant harlequin style.

Plastic doors have a number of advantages in addition to

their beauty. No burglar is going to kick one in. A tremendous blow with a weapon won't easily crack this material. A door in a pebble finish won't be scratched by kicks or by an impetuous family dog. It won't show soil, but you should give it an occasional wipe with a damp cloth dipped in mild detergent just for sanitary reasons. The new look will remain indefinitely.

Are plastics cold? Not as cold as glass. If there are two layers of plastic with space between, the double core is good insulation against heat or cold. Plastics are pleasant to the touch and do not get moisture drips as glass may do.

In addition to doors, matching plastic panels are offered by many dealers, so they can be incorporated into the home in other ways, such as for room dividers. Panels are easily trimmed or fitted with a circular power saw or handsaw and plane.

Double-core plastic panels can also be used to form an entire wall. When set in mastic, in frames, they are strong enough for an exterior wall and give a custom touch to an ordinary house.

The cost of many of these plastics is not low, but then any art work is expensive if it's well done; and here you not only get art but utility and new decor as well.

CHANGE ALL THE DOORS. Door changes throughout the house can do more than just give you new doors. You can add spare ones without actually increasing room dimensions if you replace ordinary doors with folding, sliding, or cafe doors. Sliding doors need no clearance. They make possible new room arrangements and eliminate a hazard from a door that blocks free passage.

Louvered doors give ventilation. Changing solid closet doors to louvered ones brings in air but not light, so clothes do not fade yet still get proper ventilation. In a warm, humid climate, changing over to a louvered door will bring in breeze without loss of privacy.

A house that has too much open planning may be a candidate for new door arrangements. A pair of cafe doors will close off a view of a room, such as the kitchen, without making quarters too confined.

In a too-small room a changeover from a solid wood door to a mirrored one creates spaciousness without real structural change. The new self-stick mirror squares can be used on a closet or bathroom door.

You might substitute strings of beads for a solid door or a spot where there was no door. They are decorative and fool the eye without blocking air or light. Department stores and mail-order houses, as well as some import shops, sell beads as full door panels or by the yard, so you can make up your own size and color combination. A door panel costs about $10 for the 30″ x 78″ size.

For the most unusual collection of doors, door panels, shojis, grilles, carved wooden insets, authentic hand-leaded, stained-glass doors, there is one company that can supply every kind of door in the world or the ingredients for creating them. The ultimate in a door offered in solid jade with a price tag of $25,000. For the do-it-yourselfer there are endless possibilities in considerably lower price ranges that offer a challenge to ingenuity and creativity.

In many remodeling jobs, just changing, adding, or redoing the existing doors is sufficient to create an entirely new home appearance without touching any other feature of the house. Mobile-home owners have found this out, too, and are updating their factory homes by giving them unusual individualized doors.

DOUBLE-DUTY DOOR. The odds are that somewhere in your home there is a door that is not working as hard as it could. With a handful of dowels and a little lumber, you can turn it into a magazine rack. In a bathroom it could be a towel rack.

Basically the rack is a wood frame with several crossbars to support the magazines and dowels to keep them from falling over. Cover the back of the frame with plywood, hardboard, or lumber and it becomes a door. Or you can add the rack to your present door.

Begin by making the frame. If it is to be fastened to a door you already have, make it just enough smaller than the door to keep it from hitting the knob or door casing. If it is to replace an old door, make it the same size as the door.

Cut two pieces of 2″ x 2″ and one of 2″ x 4″ as long as your frame is to be wide. (Purpose of the 2″ x 4″ is to provide plenty of wood at the point where you may wish to put the door-knob or other kind of hardware.)

Cut 14 dowels—the ½″ or ⅝″ kind, available in lumber-yards or hardware stores—to a length just 1″ longer than the cross-pieces. How all these pieces will fit together is shown in the diagram.

Now mark the two long 2″ x 2″s as shown at the left of the diagram, beginning at the bottom of the door. Draw lines across the inner edge at 20″, 37¾″, 56″, 69″ to show where the cross-pieces will go. Center marks at the other points indicated, and drill a hole ½″ deep at each. Make the holes the same diameter as the dowels you are using.

Now assemble the frame. First fasten all the crosspieces

PLAN FOR BUILDING THE
DOUBLE-DUTY DOOR

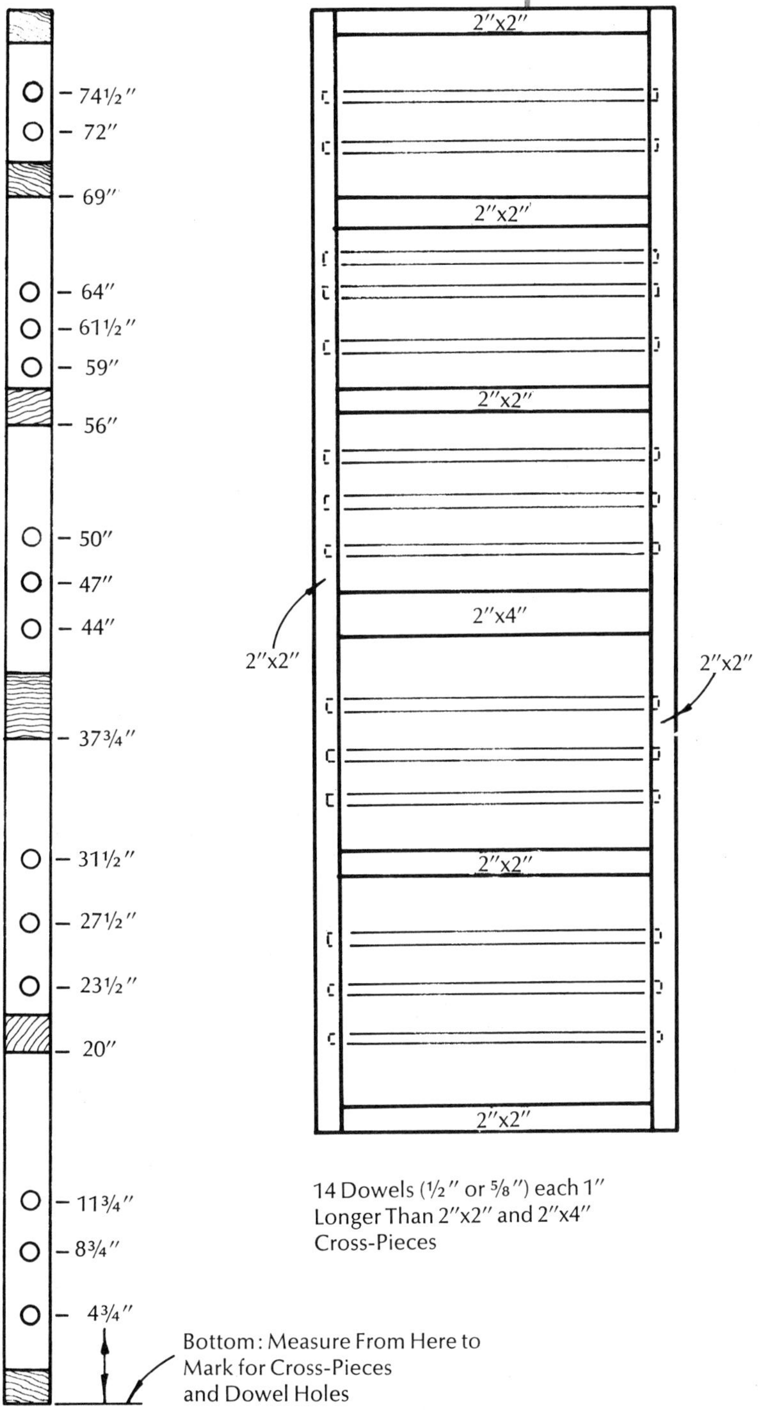

- 74½"
- 72"
- 69"

- 64"
- 61½"
- 59"
- 56"

- 50"
- 47"
- 44"

- 37¾"

- 31½"

- 27½"

- 23½"

- 20"

- 11¾"

- 8¾"

- 4¾"

2"x2"

2"x2"

2"x2"

2"x2"

2"x4"

2"x2"

2"x2"

2"x2"

2"x2"

14 Dowels (½" or ⅝") each 1"
Longer Than 2"x2" and 2"x4"
Cross-Pieces

Bottom: Measure From Here to
Mark for Cross-Pieces
and Dowel Holes

to one of the long uprights, using glue and a pair of 2″ or longer flathead wood screws in each. (For a neater-looking door edge, countersink the screw heads well below the surface and fill the holes with wood filler.)

Drop a little glue into each of the holes you have drilled, and push in a dowel. Now fasten on the other long 2″ x 2″ in the same manner. That completes the frame and rack.

If you are using an old door, take it down by pulling the long hinge pins. Use three screws along each side and one at the top and one at bottom to fasten the rack to the door. Paint or stain. Stain Wax, rubbed on, is a good choice, too, because it gives color and a water-repellent finish at the same time.

If your new rack is also to form the entire door, back it with lumber and hardboard or plywood, using glue and screws.

DUTCH DOOR. For exterior locations, either at the front entrance or at an exit to a garden or a patio, consider either of the low-cost do-it-yourself ideas offered in the photographs.

One of these is turning an ordinary wooden door, however ancient or shabby, into a copper-clad stunner. The other idea is to make a Dutch door.

The inviting charm, convenience, and flexibility of the Dutch door need not be reserved to houses of period design. The modern versions shown go well with today's architecture.

In one kind of Dutch door, the first one shown, the upper section is glazed—for light and view at any season. And the glazing is by the back-putty-and-stop method that gives permanent results and calls for no previous experience. The chapter on building a window wall describes and pictures the method of glazing.

If your door is to go where privacy is a problem or the view is uninviting, you may wish to substitute plastic for glass. You might use either a plain translucent type, such as Filon, in white or color, or one of the patterned varieties. Some resemble antique stained glass.

To make the lower half of the door, begin by building a frame of 1″ to 1¼″ pine or redwood ¼″ narrower than the opening and about 36″ high. It should consist of the six pieces shown in the diagram.

The top piece has a rabbet to form a lip where the door halves meet. If you don't have tools to make a rabbet like this, glue on a strip instead.

Complete the lower door by fastening ¼″ exterior-grade plywood on both sides. Use waterproof glue and finishing nails.

Note that one of your pieces of plywood must be cut shorter than the other by the width of the rabbet or ledge.

The upper door is made of four pieces of 2″ x 4″ pine or redwood with lap joints at the corners. The actual thickness of this lumber will determine how thick the stock should be for the frame of the lower door, since both doors should be of the same thickness when completed.

Before assembling the upper door, rabbet the pieces to a width and depth of ½″ to take the glass or plastic. Do this rabbeting on the front—exterior—side of the door. Put this frame together with waterproof glue and nails, and rabbet the front of the lower edge to match the bottom door.

Again, if you are not equipped to cut a rabbet, you can assemble the frame and then nail on strips to produce a similar result. This is equivalent to the method shown in the window-wall chapter.

Cut four stops. These are strips of wood ½″ square that you will use to hold in the glass. Make top and bottom ones first, then side ones to fit between them.

It is easier to put finish on the door at this point rather than after hanging it. But you should make cuts for the hinges and

DUTCH DOOR

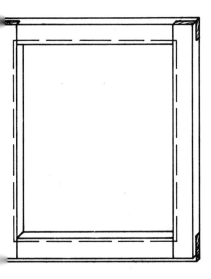
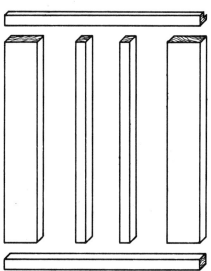

Modern version of Dutch door built by a do-it-yourselfer. Upper part is redwood, stained to retain its natural color. Bottom section is lacquered bright yellow to accent the white house with its natural-redwood door frame.

a lock now and do a trial hanging for exact fit. The usual hardware is a pair of butt hinges for each door half, a bolt to hold the two sections together, and a standard lock with knobs, mounted near the top of the lower door. You might want to consider some of the ideas in the chapter on locks in choosing equipment for this door.

Treat the Dutch door as a unit in hanging it, so that the whole thing will swing freely.

With the door back down again for finishing, set all nails and fill the holes. Complete any sanding needed.

Your choice of finish will naturally be determined by surroundings. The door you see in the photograph has its lower section painted yellow for contrast with the rather unexciting white paint around it. Redwood upper section has a natural finish to harmonize with natural-redwood trim of the house.

Now for the final step: glazing. Have a piece of double-strength window glass cut slightly smaller than the opening, just enough smaller to fit it easily.

Take it out, and apply putty all around to form a bed for the glass. Use soft putty, or glazing compound, or add a few drops of linseed oil to soften it. Bed the glass firmly against it. Set the wood stops in place and nail them to the frame, keeping the nails parallel to the glass to avoid danger of cracking.

The photographs show two other Dutch doors, both using panels of translucent plastic to add a safety factor and still bring light into the house.

The design of one of these doors is based on a painting by the artist Piet Mondrian. The panels are in red, white, and yellow.

You can design your own door-painting, or adapt a door from a real painting, and use colors to harmonize with your own home. One big advantage of this door is that it can be seen and admired as well from the outside as from inside. It is especially beautiful at night when interior light makes it readily visible to the outdoors.

A door like this also transmits warmth when sun hits it. Plants placed around or near it will benefit. In a household where there are small children or pets, the closed lower half keeps them indoors, or out, and yet the open upper half lets in air. Neither children nor pets can easily damage the plastic inserts. Ordinary scratches and bangs won't show, and dirt can be wiped off with a damp cloth. This door is framed in Philippine mahogany with clear Stain Wax rubbed on the surface. This finish repels water and

Drawing left

This Dutch door gives a stained-glass effect when light comes through its red, yellow, and white panels. Appropriately enough, it is in the manner of the Dutch painter, Piet Mondrian. Panels are small enough so they can be made of scraps of plastic left over from other jobs or available at low cost in shops that sell craft or building materials. Narrow strips of wood glued around the frame on the outside hold the panels in place. Plastic inserts cannot be easily damaged.

Photo right

Another way to make a Dutch door: Buy an ordinary solid-core door. This one is birch. Cut it in half. Saw rectangles out of both halves and replace with panels of white or colored fiberglass plastic so light will filter through. Trim plastic panels on both sides with small strips of wood. Finish off door halves with additional strips of wood, at top of lower door and bottom of upper so they lap.

fingermarks and does not obscure the grain of the wood. An occasional rewiping with Stain Wax will maintain the new appearance indefinitely.

COPPER DOOR. Charming and welcoming though Dutch doors are, you may prefer the ultimate in solidity for the appearance of your home's main entrance. A sure way to accomplish this is to trade that drab old front door you have now for one clad in antiqued copper.

And for all its durability and costly—even ancient—look, a metal clad door is absurdly inexpensive when you make it yourself.

You can bring off the whole job for as little as $12, assuming that you use your existing door as the basis and that your covering material is Coppertone Foil. This is actually aluminum, copper colored on one side, made in a lightweight gauge for tooling, and sold by dealers in craft materials.

Real copper will be more expensive, the cost depending upon the thickness you use and where you buy it. Tooling foil is what to look for, in any case. Being thin and soft, it is both economical and easy to glue and tool.

Real copper will give you a wider choice of effects. Produce them by treating the finished door with chemicals obtained from craft shops. You can get a weathered green to black surface, or an iridescent effect, by rubbing on such materials as sulphur, salt, lemon, vinegar, or a combination of these materials. No two doors will ever look alike or weather in the same way. Commercial copper polish will, of course, retain the bright original surface.

With Coppertone Foil, you use a pigment rather than a chemical treatment. You antique it by brushing on any flat paint, most often slating black, then wiping most of it off after it has become tacky.

For a look of mixed copper and silver, antiqued, try a brand-new idea. Wipe the paint lightly with a rag that has a little lacquer thinner on it. This will take off not only much of the dark paint but also some of the copper-colored coating on the aluminum. The result has to be seen to be believed.

Test your treatment first, of course, on a scrap of the foil, glued to wood and hammered.

If yours is a slab door, it may need no preliminary treatment. If it's a panel door you will have to fill the depressions with scraps of plywood, lumber, and filler to turn it into a flush door.

If you're buying a new door for the purpose, shop for one that has been marked down because of damage, or try a wrecker for a second-hand one at a great saving. For the door in the photograph, at a patio entrance, a solid-core flush door at $5 was used. It had been rejected for imperfections in the cores.

Begin by taking off hinges and locks. If the surface has finish on it, test with some of the adhesive you are using, to be sure it doesn't lift too much for satisfactory adhesion. If it does, you may have to remove some of the old finish.

Tooling foil, applied with contact cement and hammered and antiqued, makes this ruggedly handsome patio entrance. It looks like a solid copper door. A few yards away, its twin is the front door of the house.

Standard contact cement makes a good adhesive for this job. Use it outdoors if possible and *well away from any fire, including pilot lights.*

Cut the foil with a scissors or a knife and straight-edge. Coat the door and the back of the foil with the contact cement. When this is dry, place the foil and press it down—but be careful: this cement grabs and won't let you shift the foil around.

Lap the strips of foil by any convenient amount—from ¼ to an inch or so. When your door is all covered, replace the hardware.

Tooling is done by beating the surface with a ball-peen or mechanic's hammer, making thousands of little dents. Then comes the antiquing, which finishes the job.

If you find the tooling tedious, that and the antiquing can be done at leisure after you have rehung the door.

You might, as was done with the door in the photograph, let everybody who comes along—family and guests alike—have a part in tooling your door. Hang a ball-peen hammer conveniently near it and invite passers-through to stop and take a few dozen whacks.

Thus the task will be no chore at all—and everyone around can feel that he has had a part in making your entryway one of the handsomest in town.

FIX THE DOORS YOU ALREADY HAVE

Not only old doors, but new ones as well, frequently need adjustments or repairs to keep them from whistling, squeaking, banging, or refusing to close and open properly. Here are a few remedies for doors that need doctoring, not replacing:

SQUEAKING DOOR: A few drops of light oil on each hinge. Then move the door back and forth several times. This will usually cure the squeak immediately. Wipe off excess oil.

WHISTLING DOOR: Listen closely when the whistle is blasting. Usually you will find that wind is coming in under the door. Weatherstripping on the bottom may be all it needs. Sometimes an all-round weatherstrip job is necessary.

DOOR WON'T STAY OPEN: Take the screws out of the bottom hinge and insert a piece of cardboard beneath the hinge. Tighten the screws.

DOOR WON'T STAY CLOSED: A cardboard shim placed under the upper hinge will usually solve this problem caused because the door is leaning down.

DOOR WON'T LATCH CORRECTLY: Trouble may be with the strike plate rather than the door. Examine plate. If there is a shiny spot on the strike plate, you know where the worn spot is. File the opening of the strike plate larger at the spots where wear is indicated.

DOOR SCRAPES FLOOR: Sanding, not planing, is the safest thing to try. A piece of coarse sandpaper on the floor will do the job if you work the door back and forth until there is no further contact. A little sanding on the edges of the door may take off high spots that are rubbing.

Here's a door that can take it. Interior panel is of corrugated yellow plastic. It's weatherproof, almost unbreakable, will take a lot of banging and pressure, can be washed without streaking, lets in a lot of light, never needs repainting. The frame is redwood, left to weather naturally. Glass in an existing door could be replaced with plastic, but this one would be easy and inexpensive to build. Added bonus: A child's figure easily shows through the plastic, so he will be seen by another child approaching from the other side at a dead run. Don't forget an extra handle at child height.

HINGES LOOSE: Put a wedge under the door bottom to take the strain off the screws. If screws spin around and won't tighten, try using new and longer screws or get some sheet metal screws which have threads all along the shank. If neither of these methods works, the holes are probably stripped. Take out the old screws and fill the old holes with wood putty or wooden plugs coated with glue. Wait until putty or glue is thoroughly dry and then put in new screws. Sometimes it may be necessary to move the hinges to a point where screws will go into fresh wood. Gaps left where hinges were formerly positioned can be concealed by gluing in a sliver of wood, sanding and staining it.

DOOR SWOLLEN ON ALL SIDES: Now use a plane, but set it for as thin a cut as possible and use it on the hinge side. Take off only a little at a time, always working from edge to center of the door. Try door frequently. It may not take much to make it fit.

WARPING: Remove the door and put it across a couple of sawhorses. Weigh it down with about 50 pounds of weight on the curved surface area for a day or so.

After you've completed a door repair and replaced the door you may find that the latch no longer hits the strike plate. Remove strike plate, fill the old mortise, mark where the latch now hits, and then chisel a new plate mortise.

16

Sandwich Doors That Slide

Pine strips and plastic make these stylish problem-solvers

Sliding translucent doors are great problem-solvers because they do so many things so efficiently and attractively. Since you can easily make these doors yourself from stock 1″ x 4″ lumber and flat plastic panels, they are both inexpensive and decorative.

Use them to:

• Turn a dull garage into a bright one—especially important if you use it as a workshop.

• Enclose a carport for weather protection.

• Replace a swinging access door to a garage, in places where wind often bangs a hinged door.

• Form a movable partition in any large room—and do it without loss of daylight.

• Replace any interior door of your home to gain space and light.

• Do the work of a sliding patio door wherever glass creates a privacy problem.

What makes such doors as these fingertip-easy to operate is a combination of their light weight and the new availability of appropriate hardware. For operating sliding doors your choice is no longer limited to overheavy, clumsy barn-door stuff on the one hand or flimsy closet-door track-and-carriers on the other.

Now on the market is aluminum sliding-door hardware rated heavy-duty. It will handle doors weighing up to 100 pounds, allowing ample margin for its use even with full 7' x 8' garage sliders. Maker of the kind used here is Acme Appliance Mfg. Company.

Required for a pair of bypassing doors for a double garage is one 192" length of No. 1338 double track and hardware set No. 1400-BX.

For single doors the hardware requirement is even simpler: a packaged set of single track hangers and floor guide for your choice of 24", 30", 36", or 48" door.

If you frame your doors with nominal 1" x 4" lumber, most readily available in pine, you need only cut it to length and assemble.

What you are producing is a sandwich. The bread is the pine lumber and the meat is a sheet of flat FRP—fiberglass-reinforced plastic. The kind we used is called Filon.

You can get Filon in colors, both brilliant and subdued, as well as white. But for architectural use my favorite is the kind the maker calls Clear, which it is not. It is highly translucent, in a shell-like way resembling the effect of the Japanese papers used in those movable Oriental walls called shojis. The heavy type is best, at least for large doors or for exterior use. It is obtainable in a grade called Filoplated, which carries a fifteen-year warranty.

Bypassing doors for a double garage are fingertip-easy to operate. The translucent plastic panels make a brightly lighted garage, day or night, especially desirable when it doubles as a home workshop.

BUILDING THE DOOR. The drawings show how to cut parts for the overlapping frames. The idea is simply to make two frames that have the same overall dimensions but have joints at different places, for maximum strength without complicated joinery.

Lay out parts to make sure they are the same size. Then assemble *one* frame, with glue and ½″ corrugated fasteners. Use two fasteners on one side at each joint, one on the other side. For exterior doors, use waterproof glue.

Butt joints like these aren't very strong, but never mind that. The sandwich construction takes care of this problem.

Coat one side of the frame with adhesive. Filon adhesive, made by the manufacturer of the flat plastic sheeting, is ideal. But

Sandwich system of translucent Filon plastic sheets between 1″ x 4″ pine on 2′ centers makes both the fixed wall, at left, and sliding door of this home laundry. Advantages: generous daylight, warmth, doors that open a full 4′ yet are entirely out of the way when open.

In full-sandwich construction, upper and lower pine frames are same dimension as plastic sheet—4′ x 7′ in this case. Three layers are held together by corrugated nails and Filon adhesive.

if this is not available, white wood glue such as Evertite is equally strong for a door not exposed to heavy wetting.

Cut the plastic to size if necessary and lay it on the frame. Doors more than 4' wide will require two pieces of plastic, cut so that their joint falls on a wood strip.

Build the second wood side of the sandwich right on top of the plastic, first spreading glue on the underside of the wood. Use glue and corrugated fasteners (sometimes known, amusingly, as "wiggle nails") at the joints.

Nail the two frames together, nailing right through the three elements of the sandwich. Use galvanized nails, placing them about every 12".

Alternate method. There is an alternate way to construct these doors. We've used it, and it works well and is even stronger than the system just described.

The drawback is that it requires you to rabbet all the framing pieces for one side of the door. This means some extra effort and also demands that you have a suitable power tool, such as a jointer.

Its advantage is that it enables you to make a door that is several inches larger in both dimensions than your plastic. Thus, if you need a pair of 30"-wide doors, you can make them both from a single 48" sheet of plastic by cutting it in two.

So, assuming you have a tool for rabbeting, choose the method giving the most economical use of your Filon sheets.

To use this method, rabbet the inner edge of each framing piece, and both edges of any in-between piece. The rabbet should be at least ½" wide and as deep as the thickness of the Filon.

Rabbet only the parts of your first frame. Then glue the Filon into the rabbeted frame before gluing and nailing the second frame to the first.

You may wish to paint or stain the frames to match your house. Otherwise, a good choice of finish is black Stain Wax (Cabot makes it). The crisp contrast supplied by the black frames goes well with almost any architecture.

A good tip on finishing: Do at least the edges of all the pieces before assembling with the plastic. Then you won't have the tedious, almost impossible, task of cutting in the paint product right next to the plastic.

Instructions for the simple job of mounting the track and hanging the doors come with the hardware. The package also includes a wrench for adjusting carriers so that doors hang neatly even from framing that may not be perfectly level or plumb.

Stain Wax, Filon, and aluminum are all low-maintenance

materials even in difficult areas such as the seacoast, so your doors should need no care beyond an occasional dusting or hosing.

If Stain Wax finish gets chipped or marred, you can fix it by rubbing with a rag dipped in the wax. There is little weathering, so matching is no problem.

Same overlapping layout of pine strips is used for this 7' x 8' garage door. As an alternative to full sandwich construction, this picture shows the pine strips rabbeted so that the sheets may be set in before covering with other set of strips.

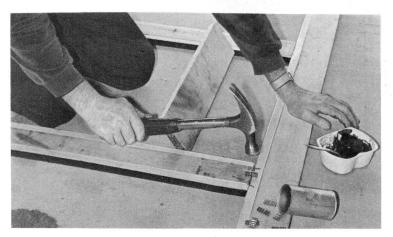

Closeup shows how joint is made with corrugated fasteners and waterproof glue. Although such a joint is initially weak, it becomes very strong when second layer of frame reinforces it.

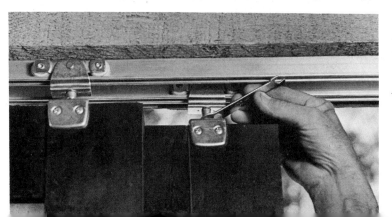

Heavy-duty aluminum track easily supports the weight of a big garage door made of pine 1" x 4" and Filon plastic. Four-wheel Acme hangers like these will take doors up to 100 pounds. They come with a wrench for height adjustment.

Plastic floor guides are available for sliding doors. But large doors need something stronger and better adapted to fastening to concrete. This one, made up of scraps, is fastened to floor with screws in masonry anchors.

Here is a sliding version of the Mondrian-inspired Dutch door shown in a previous chapter. It serves as a source of daylight for a large bathroom, also providing ventilation and access to a private little deck.

Here is how this Mondrian door and the Dutch-door version are built—still another alternative to the sandwich construction described in this chapter. Rabbeted frame takes Filon plastic sheets in varied colors, which are then held by strips nailed in.

The Mondrian pattern and the construction methods shown in this chapter are applied to a double door. One panel could be a fixed one, if you wish, to give the effect of a large door opening and bring in more light. Create your own painting in a door by going through books that feature such painters as Mondrian, Klee, Miro, Picasso. You'll get ideas and inspiration that lend themselves to creativity.

These door panels look like a wall when closed. Because they are extremely lightweight it is no effort to slide them, nor do they require heavy hardware. Using methods described in this chapter, you can quickly build them from wood strips and sheets of flat Filon fiberglass-reinforced plastic.

17

Molded Carvings Rescue
Old Doors

**How to use moldings and carvings of plastic to add
instant-wood distinction**

When you use the remarkably realistic moldings and carvings now
available to rescue battered old or plain new doors from drabness,
you're right in the trend of the times.

With a selection of rectangular plaques, circular medallions,
and straight and curved trim, you can convert a low-priced slab
door into the equivalent of a costly hand-carved one. The same
methods, by the way, can do great things for built-ins and furniture.

Add the easy art of antiquing to the use of these new
carvings and you get an impressive result. Any furniture or woodwork surface, however ancient and dented, takes on charm when
antiqued; and these molded carvings offer perfect texture for the
color and shading the antiquing process produces.

Most of these products, like the Designer Carvings that
you see used here, are carefully cast from plastic materials chosen
to give maximum fidelity to wood. They resemble the wood
originals closely in texture, feel, and appearance. And they respond
like wood to sawing, sanding, drilling, gluing, and nailing.

The carvings are so elaborate in themselves that restraint
is called for in their use. Only rarely will you want to use more
than two shapes in a single project, and often one is enough. The

most useful combination is narrow molding to form a border around a group of square or oblong plaques or round medallions.

The fact that the molding is made in a quarter-circle as well as straight pieces lets you design borders that look as if carved in place.

To cut strip moldings to length needed, or to divide a medallion or plaque when necessary, cut with an ordinary handsaw or power saw. A fine-toothed blade will reduce or eliminate sanding.

Fasten the molding to the surface with any good wood glue. Coat the back of the molding, place it accurately, then either clamp or weight it down heavily or secure it with a few small brads.

No special finishing techniques are called for. The carvings accept stains or paints much as wood does. In most situations you'll prefer to use some kind of wiping technique to emphasize the intricate lines of the carvings.

A good way to do this is with one of the antiquing products now widely available in paint departments. Each type comes with

This was a plain slab door—neat enough but like a million others. A combination of moldings and medallions made it one of a kind. Materials and methods used are shown in the other photos.

its own directions, but the basic procedure is pretty uniform. Apply base coat, whether brush-on or spray, to the entire surface of both the woodwork and the carvings. Let it dry, then apply the glaze coat. Wipe this lightly while it is still tacky. Just how you wipe decides the effect you get, and no one piece will ever be exactly like another.

Generally it is best to wipe flat areas rather lightly to highlight them, and bear down a little more vigorously on carved surfaces. A little experimenting will show you what you can do and the interesting type of results you can get. It's almost impossible to get a bad antiquing job.

Some antiquing is even more elaborate, calling for a three-coat job. The last coat is usually gold, used sparingly.

Antiquing materials may be obtained separately or in kits, which may include a clear finish coat. Some are oil-based and some are water-based. The water-based give a quicker drying and finishing time, often only a few hours from start to finish. The final clear finish coat is needed only on surfaces subject to considerable wear.

Available shapes include 2¼" and 1½" moldings, in 2' and 3' lengths; 12" and 7" round medallions; 7" x 7" and 7" x 15" plaques; 5⅞"-radius quarter-circle.

Above left

Begin door project by sanding surface if glue is to be used or a stain finish is planned. This old slab door will be turned into the beauty you see in the other photograph in spite of its dents, scratches, and cigarette burns which resulted from its previous use as a desk top.

Above right

Antiquing begins with base coat, applied to all surfaces and allowed to dry. Glaze (in this case gold over the white base) is brushed on, partially wiped off with rag. Knob or handle is carefully chosen bit of driftwood from the Carmel beach.

Below

Here is another slab door in the process of taking on a new look. It has been sanded to remove enough of the old varnish finish so that glue will take hold. You'll get more interesting results if the door has gouges and dents, so add a few with a piece of chain or a hammer, if your door is perfectly smooth.

18

Locks For a Safer Home

Combination, deadbolt, and auxiliary hardware types are keys to door security

The lock on your front door may be an open invitation to burglars. Builders feeling the cost-and-profit squeeze often put in cheap locks. So even if your house is quite new it may already be a candidate for better door hardware. As for older locks—they are often battered and corroded, may show signs of the day someone tried to jimmy his way in because of a mislaid key. Not uncommon is the old lock that offers little security yet balks the keyholding owner himself until he remembers to jiggle the key or hold the knob in just the magic position.

The truth is, the ordinary front-door lock bars only the most inept of intruders—and you, when you have forgotten your key. It's a cinch for a burglar to defeat it by slipping in a bit of cardboard or a plastic credit card, which he can carry about with him without the risk attached to being in possession of burglars' tools. (Years ago he'd have slipped off his celluloid collar and used that.)

One partial remedy that costs nothing is to drive a finishing nail through the door stop, the wood strip the door closes against. Place it right opposite the point where the door latches. This will often slow up a burglar, and burglars are in no position to waste time.

A new house, incidentally, has a special kind of vulnerability. Any workman or delivery boy who was given a key during construction may have retained it or had it duplicated, for sale to a professional or for a contemplated burglary career of his own.

At least one manufacturer has an ingenious answer to this common problem. He makes entrance locksets so designed that the first time you use your owner's key all the keys that workmen have had are permanently locked out. The system is called Kwikset Protectokey, "the lockset with a brain."

For an entrance door that already has a functioning lock, addition of an auxiliary combination-operated bolt creates both security and convenience. At least two manufacturers now offer these convenient, secure pushbutton locks.

One kind, called Preso-Matic, has ten pushbuttons, each numbered. You must press the correct four in the correct sequence to open the door. Since four digits can be combined in 10,000 different ways, the odds against beating such a combination are 10,000 to 1 for each attempt. If that's not good enough for you, you can have a similar lock with a seven-digit combination that raises the odds to 10,000,000 to 1.

No key is needed for this Preso-Matic door lock. Press the combination and it unlocks immediately. There's an instant one-button exit and nightlatch on the inside, and lock is guaranteed to be pickproof. Polymer buttons insure against wear from use or weather. The antique-bronze lock shown costs less than $20, can be installed in solid-wood, hollow-core, prefab, or metal.

Yet you, or anyone in the know, can open the door in a fraction of the time normally spent fumbling for a key.

On the inside there is an instant-exit "unlock" button. There is also a built-in nightlatch you can use when you are home to make entry impossible even to a person who knows the combination.

This Space Age lock, used at Apollo headquarters, is made in styles to fit various home designs. It is quickly installed, using instructions that come with it. The combination can be changed at any time by removing an inside cover plate, turning two spring clips clear of the slot in the lock housing, lifting out two combination slides, and slipping in new ones. These are obtainable from the maker at modest cost. They permit change of combination for security reasons and also allow the owner to have like combinations on two or more doors.

Another auxiliary combination lock, the Simplex, features an inconspicuous little circle of five numbered pushbuttons warranted to baffle any burglar. You make up and set your own combination, using as many or few of the buttons as you like. And if, for example, you choose to set the lock for "push 3 and 2 at the same time, then 4," pushing them all at once or one at a time won't open the lock. So the chance of accidental solution is negligible.

Since the Simplex is primarily a surface lock, installation calls for drilling only two holes, $\frac{3}{4}''$ and $1\frac{5}{8}''$.

A lock like this, the maker reminds you, is the only kind that can be opened in an emergency by telephone instruction. (Barring, that is, the phone call that tells someone where you have buried a key.)

Not much bigger than a walnut—but a lot tougher to crack—is this Simplex combination deadbolt lock. It gives the homeowner any pushbutton combination he wishes from 2,200 button-sequence possibilities. Available from hardware stores, locksmiths, or directly from the manufacturer.

These locks come in brushed chrome or satin brass, are said to have a thirty-year life. Models are made for other household uses—on a medicine chest, closet, desk, liquor cabinet, or tool chest. One type fits a metal door.

In addition to auxiliary locks, which have round bolts, one model offered by Presto-Matic has ordinary latch action. It is to be used primarily as a replacement, making the usual door-knob-and-latch unnecessary.

With the auxiliary types you will still need knob and latch. You can leave the present lockset on to do this job. If you do this, you should park a key somewhere outside for getting in when you have locked both locks—by accident or for extra security. If you don't feel the need of the second lock for occasional use, re-place it with a nonlocking set of the kind used for some interior doors.

You can stay with a key lock and still improve your security system. If yours is a tubular lock, like most made in recent years, you should be able to find a superior, deadlatch-equipped replace-ment for it that will fit the existing holes. For those wishing to improve ordinary locks of its manufacture, Kwikset offers an inexpensive deadlatch. You merely remove the spring latch and install the replacement.

If removing an old lock leaves an ugly hole the new lock

Safety-first replacement for an old lock comes with this set that includes a deadlatch and superior mechanism. It is designed to be installed in two bored holes in the door, comes with detailed draw-ings and instructions.

won't cover, a modernization kit may be the answer. This kit consists of latch plate, strike plate, front and back trim plates.

Security is by no means the only aspect to consider in updating door hardware. Locksets are now made in many period and modern styles, each in a variety of metals and finishes. For additional variation there are escutcheons to go with the locksets— these too in many patterns. You may choose from, for example, Spanish, Aztec, Roman, and Greek motifs.

Still another device for adding to door security is a chain guard. The ordinary thin ones are of limited value, since one kick will break them or tear them from their moorings, but stronger types are available. Especially good are the ones that have key locks, since these may be fastened even when you are away from home. An intruder who encounters the chain may be led to believe the house is occupied.

Photo left

You can install a modern lock in place of one of ancient design by using a modernization kit like this one. It consists of two rectangular trim plates, 3½" x 10½", plus oversize latch and strike plates. Its maker, Kwikset, calls it a sure cure for D.O.—doorlock obsolescence.

Photo right

Lockset being installed here illustrates three things: attractive design and finish available in today's locks; pleasing effect of 5" backset that puts knob further than usual from door's edge and protects knuckles from barking; and ordinary latch without deadlock. For greater security the latch shown here could be replaced by a dead-latch, at cost of about $2. Stout chain lock shown is key-operated so that it may be used even when no one is at home.

Still another auxiliary lock suited to an entrance door is a deadbolt that can be locked and unlocked from the outside with a key. One version slips vertically through several strong rings of metal. It is made by the New England Lock Company.

One nervous householder put three locks on his front door to be sure of safety, only to have his house rifled by a thief who easily entered by the back door with its single old-fashioned lock. Intruder-resistant hardware is at least as important for back doors as front, since professional burglars have a natural preference for entrances not visible to passersby.

The same goes for sliding glass doors. The locks that come with many of them are easily forced with a knife or other small tool. An easily installed patio door lock is a long metal bar that swings down to make forcing impossible. A length of heavy dowel or old broom handle will do the job as well, if less neatly, when it is laid in the channel where the door slides. This method is workable, naturally, only with patio doors that slide inside the fixed section of glass.

A determined thief can still get in by breaking a substantial section of glass, or cutting it out with a glass cutter. And even this method becomes almost prohibitively difficult if your patio door is tempered glass. It should be, anyway, as a precaution against accidents.

PART IV

WINDOWS AND SKYLIGHTS

19

Ideas For Better Windows

**Choose from windows of aluminum, steel, wood—windows
with glass that won't break, frames that are vinyl-wrapped,
colors that let in a little sun or a lot**

Windows that leak? Drafts? Decaying wood, termites, breakage
hazard? These are all ailments characteristic of houses both old
and new. Some windows refuse to open easily. Others throw a lot
of glare into a room.

Your house may have been built at a period a few years
ago when contractors were picture-window happy, and your picture windows not only destroy your privacy but give no really
worthwhile view. These are some of the window problems you
can solve yourself with the ideas in this section.

You can not only find replacement panes, sash, and hardware but whole new window units that slip right into the old frames.
Aluminum, steel, and wood window units are available with
factory paint jobs or plastic coatings that need no paint. Ordinary
wood now comes pre-treated to resist moisture, termites, and
fungus. Windows with too many panes are now easy to clean—if
you get the kind with snap-out bars. You can also get windows
with pivoting or removable panes as well as some which raise in
the conventional fashion but can also be tilted in for easy cleaning.

You can replace your old windows with wood units that
are wrapped in while vinyl, a material guaranteed for a quarter-
century of use. Vinyl weathers slowly, changes little in color, can
be painted if you wish. Although vinyl-clad windows and sliding

doors cost as much as 20 percent more than plain wood, they will be worth it in appearance, durability, and the no-maintenance surfaces. Vinyl also replaces old-fashioned putty in joints, too.

Storm doors and windows, vinyl wrapped, won't rot, peel, crack, or chip, and every crack is sealed against wind leakage and rattling.

SUN PROBLEMS. Too much sun? Too little? The right windows will take care of either situation. Glass comes in many colors, including a new type which goes from dark to bright depending upon the day. Gray or blue will reduce sun heat and shut out glare from desert or seashore. If you want to replace an entire solid wall with a two-story expanse of glass, part of it can be tinted and the rest can be clear, depending upon your climate and how the sun hits various areas of glass. Lower areas can be glazed with safety glass.

Many building codes now require that only tempered, laminated, or wired glass may be used where large areas of glass are a hazard. Whether or not the code requires it in your area, it would be a wise precaution to protect your family and guests by replacing danger spots with nonlethal glass.

Where light is wanted but view is not, there are better window materials than ordinary glass. Obscure glass is the traditional solution, but today's plastics are easier to handle and more modest in price and offer a variety of imaginative solutions. Flat fiberglass-plastic, such as the white Filon seen here, combines nicely with plywood grilles, widely available in many patterns.

You can make such a window this way. Hold grille in place by setting it into the frame of the window or door; or fasten it to the plastic with clear adhesive, which is rolled on.

Newer than glass, and absolutely safe against breakage, are plexiglas acrylic windows in unusual shapes—some like the port-holes on ships or in oval design. Acrylic plastic windows are problem-solvers in areas where glass breakage from vandalism, or even a stray golf ball, is a hazard.

WINDOW WALLS. Any homeowner can add a window wall. Sometimes you have to live in a house for a while before you feel the need of a window wall. Let's say you buy an old house and decide later that you can change the feeling of a whole dark room by knocking out a wall and bringing in the outdoors. Window walls seem to double the space of a room by giving the illusion that the outdoors has been brought into the house.

Lack of a dramatic view outdoors is no problem. A tiny screened or fenced garden, an aviary, or a small deck seen through a window wall give a feeling of openness.

If you own a period-style home, you may wish to retain that appearance in the front of the house; but even a restored Victorian can benefit by a window wall if you add it at the side or back of the house. Near a kitchen, dining, or recreation area, that window wall will give you modern planning and pleasure while you still retain the basic Victorian look.

As far as appearance goes, it's not so much what kind of windows you use in your home-improvement project as it is how you arrange them. Here you see perfectly good windows spoiling the appearance of a good house. Lacking is a unified and consistent relationship.

Same house, equivalent windows—but a far more unified and serene effect. And, assuming those small windows in the living room are made to open, better ventliation as well.

Windows do not have to be centered in a wall. They can be a whole wall, a two-story wall, or come short of the floor to leave room for a window seat, shelves, or planter. When glass does not come to the floor, the room feels more secure and, of course, has better possibilities for room arrangement and furniture placement.

Some people feel cold if the entire wall is made of glass, although the temperature of the room may be comfortable. A window which comes short of the floor by a foot or two makes the room more cozy.

VENTILATION. Not all of a large window area needs to be fixed glass. A window wall can have panels or sections that swing out. A few panes can slide or be screened. You can also add sections of glass or wood louvers at the top or bottom of the fixed window sections.

Awning-type windows swing up, out, and will not let in rain, when they are wide open. If you live where winter is severe, choose double or triple glass to give good insulation. Combination storm and screen window systems save the seasonal argument over when to take down the one and put up the other.

Unconventional window placement is often functionally best. Short, high windows like these supply daylight that covers the room well. At the same time they insure privacy and, in a one-story house where they are fairly close to the roof overhang, they let in much less of the sun's heat in summer. And they don't interfere with furniture arrangement.

One of the worst things windows do is produce glare. You'll get far less of this with a single large opening—which need not be a single piece of glass—than with several smaller ones. Glare comes mostly from contrast between windows and dark areas between them.

Choose window shapes primarily to get the kind of light distribution your room needs. A short, wide window like the horizontal one at left produces a broad, shallow distribution of light. A tall, narrow window (right) naturally gives a thin, deep distribution.

Windows brought nearly to the ceiling (top) will cost little more than ones cut off lower, may even save money by simplifying wall construction and finish. Value of the extra glass up high is in daylighting the distant parts of the room that need the illumination most.

KITCHEN

BEDROOM

Unless you're taller than 6'4" (which puts your eyes about 6' from the floor) or shorter than 5', these are the window-head and sill heights that will give you a good view of the outdoors. Between these heights, avoid horizontal divisions more than 4" thick. All these sketches are based on data from detailed studies made by the University of Illinois Small Homes Council.

DINING ROOM

LIVING ROOM

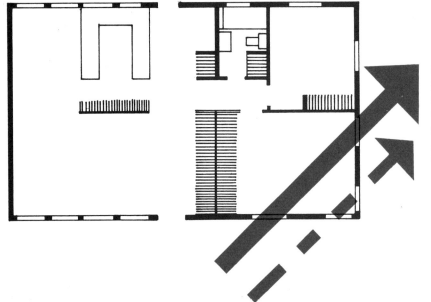

Corner windows and those near corners produce less effective lighting and far less ventilation than those well away from exterior corners. Arrows indicate the difference in the flow of air.

Whether you use frameless tension screen like these or prefer another type, screen only the part of the window that can be opened. In respect to its primary function of admitting daylight, a screened window is only half a window: University of Michigan Engineering Research Institute has found that full screens block out about half the daylight.

Roll-up inside screen is a useful answer to bug problem where window is large and not regularly opened. Since screen is usually rolled out of sight, it interferes less often with view and daylighting. Another important daylighting principle: avoid heavy, dark curtains that hang an appreciable distance over the glass at top or sides. The Michigan researchers found these cut three-fourths of available daylight.

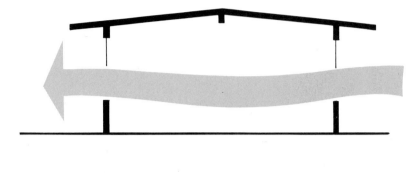

Thorough ventilation depends as much on strategic placement of window openings as it does on their area. Good comfort conditions are produced by pairs of openings low on opposite walls.

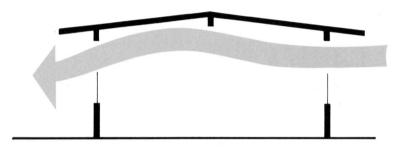

High openings are far from worthless: they carry off warm air stored at ceiling level. But they do less for human comfort than window openings of the same size placed lower.

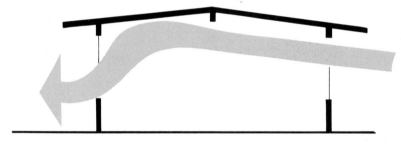

Effect of one high opening and one low one depends upon the direction of the breeze. Poor ventilation shown here will improve somewhat—but not to a maximum extent—if wind direction shifts.

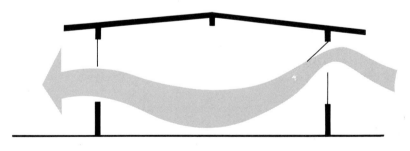

The unsatisfactory condition shown in the previous sketch can be remedied to a large extent by an arrangement that deflects the breeze to body level. Also helpful: trimming back bushes that block air currents.

20

Build a Window Wall

Create your own view—with plenty of warmth and sunshine— by putting in a new window arrangement of modern flexible units or stock glass fixed in wood framing

"Brighten up the corner where you are." So says the old song. One prime way to do it with a house is by building a window wall. There are few features that can do so much to make an old house newer, a new house more livable, or a porch useful full time.

It has all been made easier for the amateur builder by the introduction of a complete range of factory-made units. You need only frame them in, join them together, and nail on trim to produce a full-scale, custom-designed wall of glass.

Four kinds of units especially deserve your attention. By using any one or two of these types, you can design just about any kind of wall-of-glass you like.

1. Gliding windows come in a variety of sizes up to 6' tall. They come in pairs—two sash that slide in one frame. When closed, the sash are side by side; one moves inward to bypass the other for opening. Since the windows don't swing, a simple framed screen may be put on the outside.

You can buy gliding units complete—including glass, hardware, and screens—ready to set into any opening and nail into place.

A set of wood louvers consists of boards and spacer blocks. Here the first of the spacers is being nailed for a second set of louvers to match the unit already completed at right.

A great part of the heat loss of which windows are guilty comes from the cracks around unweatherstripped windows. Simplest answer in building a window wall is to use, for all moving windows, factory units that have built-in weatherstripping—which give extra dividends in keeping out dust and moisture.

Combining wood louvers with areas of fixed glass is an effective way to provide ample ventilation.

In older houses where fixed windows are still good but ventilation is inadequate, louvers can often be added at either top or bottom of existing window areas. In a bathroom, hallway, or laundry where light is adequate but more ventilation is desired, louvers fill the bill. Sometimes, for reason of safety or privacy, it is desirable and feasible to remove an existing glass window and replace it with a section of louvers, either permanent or movable. Louvers can be purchased ready-made, or you can make them yourself.

Construction can be simple if you have the patience to cut a lot of little blocks the same size and shape. These little blocks separate the louver boards.

Length of the individual louver boards depends in part on the way your building is framed and the appearance you want. Up to about 3' long, nominal 1" lumber works well. For lengths greater than 3', there is danger of warping or twisting later on; better use full inch, or nominal 2" lumber.

Eight-inch-wide boards, used as they come from the lumber yard, work out well for most buildings.

For simple cutting, good weather protection, and privacy, tilt the louvers 45 degrees. This takes advantage of one of the best features of louver ventilation: plenty of air circulation on hot evenings without giving prying eyes a look-see.

Windows consisting of glass louvers give effectively controlled ventilation in generous amount. Such units, easily installed, also allow full entrance of light without seriously blocking view.

2. Triple-purpose units offer a fine flexibility for working out your own designs. They consist of glazed sash fitted into weatherstripped frames, come with the needed hardware for opening, and with screens if you wish. Put them in one way and they're outward-opening awning windows. Turn them over and they open inward in hopper or bin fashion. Installed sideways they're outswinging casement windows.

3. View or picture windows are fixed-glass units for any place where ventilation is not needed. Most often they are combined with other types. You can combine two or more to make a window wall that looks uniform but provides whatever amount of ventilation you figure you'll need.

4. Basement units are modest little numbers that often fit into fancier surroundings than their name implies. They've been successfully combined with gliding windows for extra ventilation at ceiling level. At least one maker offers basement units hinged both top and bottom so they can be opened either way or removed without tools.

Design your window wall with six things in mind: view, daylight, sunshine, heat loss, ventilation, and privacy.

YOUR VIEW. This is no problem if you're blessed with a fine one. Some of us are not, and so we must create our own. A fenced yard or a few well-placed shrubs may be well worth looking out upon. Even five feet of space between a house and a property line can often be converted into a private, enclosed garden if a wall of glass opens onto it.

Scale your windows to the view. A long horizontal window is logical if you look out on a range of mountains. But a narrow garden may call for a glass wall that is tall and not so wide.

If the shape of your window wall is fixed by something beyond your control—for instance the proportions of an existing porch—you can help things by your choice of heights. The main thing here is to avoid heavy horizontal framing members at eye level.

Remember, though, that eye level can vary from room to room—even from person to person. If you're a six-and-a-half-footer and your wife's a foot shorter, try your ideas on her before you convert them into wood and glass. And especially consider her if the windows are for the kitchen.

Some arbitrary figures for window heights have been worked out by the Small Homes Council at the University of

Illinois. Use them for a starting point. Try to avoid heavy horizontal window divisions between 42″ and 80″ from the floor in the kitchen, and 48″ and 80″ in a bedroom. For dining room the figures are 30″ and 80″. And in a living room, the ideal is to have a clear view from 10″ above the floor to 80″.

Don't be afraid of too much daylight. Glare is the thing to avoid—glare and contrast. A single big bank of windows will produce much less glare than a few small openings with dark spaces between.

How big should your window wall be? Building codes often call for window area at least one tenth as great as the floor area of the room. At least twice that much is better and is becoming the rule in good new homes in most climates.

The higher in the wall you place the window, the better daylight will penetrate into the room.

Bay windows and corner windows accomplish less per square foot than ordinary ones do, so far as daylight is concerned.

Don't screen any more of your window wall than is necessary. Screens can cut daylight in half.

Design your window wall in such a way that curtains can hang beside the glass instead of partly covering it. Glass that is permanently covered by draperies is wasted.

SUNSHINE AND HEAT LOSS. Sunshine is controlled first of all by the wall you choose. A north window wall is ideal for dependable daylight but a heating problem in winter, because it lets in no sushine to balance the loss. East and west windows are sun problems part of the day, and there is no simple and effective way to control the excessive summer sun unless you have trees right where you need them. A wide overhang will cut down the problem, however, and so will awnings and shutters.

A south window is the thing, of course, when combined with a generous roof overhang. Such a window wall will, in most parts of the U.S., take in more heat in the form of sunshine than it will steal during nights and dark days. A heavy curtain, drawn at sunset, helps too.

Storm sash is the usual answer to excessive heat loss, but a handier one is now available for many window walls. The triple-purpose units (Flexivent) are now offered with insulating glass if you want it. This is double window glass (not expensive plate) with a sealed airspace. But don't use it if you live above 3,000 feet; your atmospheric pressure won't be great enough to balance that sealed within the window.

THE GOLDFISH BOWL. A window wall that faces the street is strictly for the goldfish—and there have been a million streetside picture windows built in recent years.

So face that glass wall toward a distant view or your own outdoor living area if you can.

Don't face it toward any nearby property you don't control. One family in Babylon, Long Island, did that. They aimed their enormous window wall into a lovely stand of timber untouched since the Indians cleared out. It was bought a few months later, by a man who admired the first people's window so much that he put one just like it in his house. He placed it facing right into its twin.

The moral to all this is: a window that has to be curtained all the time is just an expensive uninsulated wall.

STEPS IN BUILDING A WINDOW WALL

1. Begin by framing the opening, shimming if necessary to make all parts plumb and square. Use masonry nails or screws with lead anchors to fasten to concrete, stone or brick.

2. Check the opening you're about to put windows into for any variation from plumb, square, and level. Cut 2″ x 4″s or other lumber to frame the opening strongly.

3. Paint-prime the units before you install them. If they are the new all-vinyl clad windows you can leave them in their natural color, usually white, or paint them to match the house. If you're painting around units, be sure to keep paint off the weatherstripping and hinge slide channels. For waterproofing, follow the old rule of letting the paint lap slightly onto the glass.

4. Place the first unit in the corner of your rough opening. Wall it—but don't drive the nails all the way in. You may want to make some slight shifts later for perfect alignment.

5. Now toenail in the second unit. Corrugated fasteners provide the simplest method of joining the units together. Place the fasteners at about 8″ intervals, and use them inside as well as out. Trim will cover them.

6. Check for level as you go along, and again when you finish the bottom row. If—and this is not unusual—your sill turns out to be not quite level, you can fix things by shimming up one end of the bottom units.

7. You'll find that a second row of windows stacks easily on the first. Toenail windows to wall member. Fasten to each other with wiggle nails—corrugated fasteners.

Here is the semifinal step in building a window wall the easy way. Strips about 3″ wide cut from 1″ x 4″s have been nailed flush with the inner edge of the 2″ x 4″s that frame the wall. The rabbet thus formed has received a bead of glazing compound. Glass has been pushed firmly against it. Now it is only necessary to nail in the stops and clean off any excess compound.

Use these instructions as a general guide, to be supplemented by the detailed, illustrated instructions that will usually accompany window units you buy.

A most flexible and economical way to add a window wall for many situations is by building it all yourself. This need be no more difficult than installing stock units if no moving windows for ventilation are called for. You can get around even this problem easily enough if wood louvers of the kind described earlier will fit into the scheme.

The essential secrets of building a superior fixed-window wall easily are two: designing for glass in stock sizes; and setting it by an uncommon but simple method. You do no cutting, and you get a good job without needing a glazier's skills.

Most glass is set into a frame, held with glazier's points, then sealed with putty. It takes practice to do this rapidly or well; if it isn't done just right it may not last.

The best thing a window wall does for a room is bring the outdoors visually inside, increasing both the cheer and the apparent size of that room. It does this most effectively—oddly enough—when the outside it brings in is bounded by fences, hedges, patio walls.

Lighting in a room is improved when not all the glass is concentrated in just one wall. Another principle also shown here: keep horizontal divisions in a window wall below or above the view if possible.

181

You'll find it much easier to use this method of setting wood stops. Professionals use it for big windows or for deluxe installations. When they do it, it costs more than the ordinary method. But it is simple and foolproof (and much better looking) and so it is the perfect do-it-yourself system.

For a window wall at minimun cost, begin by building a frame of 2″ x 4″s. Make the opening ¼″ bigger each way than the glass size. Use dry lumber of good quality since some of it will be exposed to view.

Complete the frame and form rabbets for glass by nailing on lengths of 1″ x 4″ lumber after first ripping a ¾″ strip off each piece. Inside edges of the narrowed 1″ x 4″ can be set flush with the edge of the 2″ x 4″. Save the strips.

Seal the wood, including the strips you ripped off, with a prime coat of the paint or natural finish you prefer. Run a bead of glazing compound, using the tube type in a caulking gun. Just as good, but slower, is to backputty with glazing compound or very soft putty, using a putty knife.

Then put the glass into place, pressing gently all around until the glazing compound fills the space between glass and wood.

Nail in the stops (the strips you ripped off the 1″ x 4″s). If the window is likely to catch much rain, be sure that enough compound is pushed up to form a seal between glass and stop. If necessary, add some more before setting stop. Or fill any gap by pushing putty between stop and glass afterwards.

21

Glass For Your Windows

What to use, and how to buy it. Some tips on installing it

It is possible to get a lot or a little for your money when choosing and buying glass for windows, doors, partitions, and the like. It's mainly a matter of knowing which glass will do what, how to plan for its use, and how to buy it. Then you won't pay double or triple prices because you've ordered by the sheet instead of the case or put in plate where heavy sheet glass would do as well.

WINDOW GLASS. Often called sheet glass, this was the only kind used in most houses until the window wall and the picture window came in. It comes in two thicknesses—single strength and double strength—and two qualities, A and B.

The only difference between A and B is in the number of small defects and waves. Most sheets in a lot of B quality you'd have trouble telling from A. Many dealers, especially in the West, don't stock A quality because they don't think it is worth paying 25 percent more for. You can get along without it very well.

Choice between single and double strength is primarily a matter of window size. Single strength is the logical thing to use for small panes and is generally considered safe up to about 30″ square. There are many glaziers who don't like to use it that big, however. A good rule to follow is double strength for anything over about 2′ square.

Once you get into double strength, the big question is how large can you go. That's important because there is a sharp price jump when you go from double strength to crystal sheet or plate. It can be used as large as 40″ by 48″ inches without disaster, but you might prefer to play it safe and go by some figures worked out by a glass-company engineer. Unless you have to figure on a wind stronger than 70 miles per hour, you can safely use DS in such sizes as 38″ by 48″ and 34″ by 72″, he calculates.

You can use these figures to work out quite an attractive window wall at about one-fourth the cost of the big sheets of plate glass. Go right across the room with 30″ by 72″ double strength placed vertically. The perhaps 30″ of wall below the glass can be plain wall, built-in bookcases, or ventilating louvers.

Glass by the case can save you as much as fifty percent over the cost of purchasing it by the piece. At that discount you can afford to use glass liberally in anything you build or remodel or inclose.

A case of window glass is whatever number of sheets will come out the closest to 50 square feet, so buying by the case doesn't mean you're stockpiling for years to come. Cases of very large sheets are 100 square feet.

CRYSTAL SHEET is heavy window glass of good quality. It is the economical thing to use when the opening gets too big for double strength. If you need only a few sheets you'll find that it costs very little more than DSB bought the same way. But it runs about twice as high as double strength by the case.

Current Northern California prices on crystal sheet run from 90 cents to a dollar per square foot. Architects often choose between crystal and plate (which costs twice as much) on a basis of the kind of view to be seen from the window in question. If it is a short view, of your own backyard say, crystal sheet will do perfectly. You'll never notice slight waviness. But if you have a view of the ocean, or the next county, it calls for plate.

PLATE GLASS is polished to approximate optical perfection and there is absolutely nothing wrong with it except the price. It lists in the West at $1.50 a square foot—a bit more if the size gets above 50 square feet.

Another thing about cost: With plate and usually with crystal you are likely to be using sizes bigger than you can handle and more expensive than you can afford to take a chance on breaking. You'll likely be paying the installed price, which varies a good deal. Current price is about $2 a square foot—for glass and labor.

Standard plate glass in the glazing quality is best for a window. It may be either ⅛" or ¼" thick, the latter being what you'll want for a big view window.

The variety called thick plate may be anywhere from ⅜" to 1" or more in thickness. It is called for only where there is an enormous window or a bad wind problem or both. Most of it is used for tabletops and shelves and aquariums and things like that.

HEAT-ABSORBING PLATE GLASS is the same product as is used in many automobiles now to reduce heat and glare. It is most often used in west windows, particularly along the beach. The tint is so slight that you will not be aware of it in a room unless there is plain glass or an open window alongside.

A new type of glass, which you've already seen in sunglasses, changes its color automatically according to the amount of light intensity outdoors. On a sunny day this glass appears dark in a window. On a gray day the glass seems to be clear and untinted.

Heat-absorbing glass is a comfort to both eyes and body but it is no substitute for air-conditioning. Although it cuts out the infrared rays that constitute half the heat in sunshine it heats up in the process; and some of this soaked-up heat is then reradiated into the room. Under average conditions where plate glass keeps 13 percent of the sun's heat out of the house, heat-absorbing glass will exclude 29 percent.

You can figure the cost of this kind of glass at about two and one half times that of ordinary plate.

TINTED GLASS in other hues is used mostly for shelves and partitions and decorative effects. It is usually plate and costs about the same as heat-absorbing. One variety, a strong blue in color, is sometimes used where glare is terrific, particularly where a house faces the rising or setting sun across a body of water.

Glass with a copper tint on one side is another new type of double glass which does very well for a house with an ocean view.

HEATED GLASS is the newest thing for houses in extra-cold climates. Developed by PPG, this double-glazed window has an inner pane surface warmed by an electrically conductive coating. Glass temperature is controlled by a thermostat. No drops of moisture or frost can form, and chilly drafts are nonexistent.

SAFETY GLASS, now required in many areas for new construction, can be used to update the sliding doors in any home. If your doors are a standard size, the dealer may have sheets of tempered glass in stock to fit. Since tempered glass cannot be cut, it may be necessary to special-order for your job, usually the case with older doors of a non-standard size.

OBSCURE GLASS is fine for windows where you have a view you're better off without. Such glass, or its equivalent in translucent plastic, is used a good deal for partitions, too, where light is wanted but clear vision is not. A wall of it might be just the thing to let light through to a basement recreation room where part of the basement is used as a garage. For something like that or for any large partition you'd want the thick variety, perhaps 3/8", referred to as decorative or structural glass.

Thinner figured glass is used for entrance panels, sliding cupboards doors, shower enclosures.

There is quite a variety of unusual patterns and colors in various thicknesses. You can find wide and narrow corrugations, stipples, rough patterns, cross ribs, plain ribs, diamond designs, and combinations of these.

The common kind of wire glass is an obscure glass with a kind of chicken fence in it as protection against fire and breakage. It is not very attractive. But a new version of this idea is so good looking that it is being used for decorative partitions.

This type is polished plate glass—no pattern—with a grid of plain wire in it. It does the work of wire glass without the unpleasant appearance.

Still another form of glass that is neither fully transparent nor opaque is the transparent mirror. It is polished plate with chromium or silver on it but not painted over like an ordinary mirror.

Used in an entrance door it is a mirror for a person outside (where the light is stronger) but a window to the householder inside. Of course it works the other way around at night if light is stronger indoors than out.

One way this material has been used in a bathroom is as a cover over a recessed light. With the light off you have a mirror. When the light is turned on it shines right through. Transparent mirror glass is expensive, but any glass dealer who makes mirrors can make it for you at about half the price.

INSULATING GLASS is two, or occasionally three, panes sealed into a single unit with air spaces between. It is the vastly superior modern replacement for ordinary window plus storm sash. Like any insulation, it will usually pay for itself over the years in fuel saving as well as comfort.

Double glass, however, is not much protection against the direct rays of the sun. They go right through. The usual variety, consisting of two sheets of $\frac{1}{4}''$ plate with a $\frac{1}{2}''$ airspace, ranks about midway between an ordinary single window and one of heat-absorbing glass in reducing heat from sunshine.

However, if one of the glass layers is heat-absorbing glass (and this variation is widely available) 42 percent of sun heat is kept out. This is nearly twice as much as is excluded by plain double glazing, and it's about half again as much as a single thickness of heat-absorbing glass keeps out.

Where double-glazed units really function is as barriers against loss of heat from the house in cold weather. That's what they are for—that and preventing steaming up and also making it a good deal more comfortable to sit near a big window on a cold evening.

Originally all insulating units were plate glass but you can now buy this kind of glazing in window glass, too. Those made of $\frac{1}{4}''$ plate cost around $4.50 or so a square foot. You can save about one third by using the window-glass kind unless you need large panes.

ONE-WAY GLASS is a remarkable material that may solve some problems around your house. But the jokes about people who installed their one-way-vision glass wrong-way-out are based on a misunderstanding. It isn't the side of the glass that makes the difference, it's a matter of light. The person on the darker side sees the one on the lighter side.

This kind of glass is often called a transparent mirror. A factory-made type has an evaporated chromium alloy on one surface. It should be installed with the coated side toward the room into which the view is desired.

Most glass companies can produce an equivalent material. This is two sheets of window glass, silvered but not painted, and mounted back-to-back for protection of the silvering.

Although the stuff is fairly costly in any form, it is worth using because of the fascinating and useful things you can do with it. A newspaper crime reporter in Los Angeles uses it in his office door so he can see his "copy" before it sees him. Stores use it to detect customer theft. Scientists, photographers, and college psychology departments use it. A square of it mounted in a wall between office and showroom of a jewelry store foiled a robbery. It might be useful in a home, if it were installed between playroom or nursery and the kitchen. A mother could keep an eye on the children without being obvious about it.

This is what a caller will see if you set a piece of one-way glass into your entrance door: the reflected image of himself. From inside you'll see him, without being seen.

Here is one-way, or transparent-mirror, glass set into a bathroom wall. For ordinary use it is simply an exceptionally clear mirror with no distracting surface reflections. But mounted behind it are fluorescent lights. When turned on they shine right through the transparent mirror to illuminate the looker's face.

Most usual use is, of course, in the entrance door, where it gives the people inside first look at callers. To the outsider such a pane of glass is simply a mirror reflecting his own image. However, the person hidden inside the door can see him perfectly. It works this way in the daytime only. At night it would give the caller a good look into a brightly lighted house. This can be avoided by having the hall or entrance light reasonably dim and the light much brighter on the outside.

This, as well as another, and more novel, use is shown in the photographs.

22

Skylights:
Windows In Your Roof

These ultra-efficient sources of daylight are indispensable in some common remodeling situations you may encounter

Daylight from above will illuminate a dark closet, a gloomy hallway, a depressing kitchen, or a shaded porch. A skylight may be far more desirable than a window or a window wall where neighbors are close or the view is of a kind better left unseen.

Sometimes a skylight is the only way to bring in daylight, as for an added interior bathroom or half-bath. And a skylight can ventilate as well.

Ability to ventilate, in the case of skylights designed to open, gives them special utility in showers, laundries, and kitchens that may need air as much as light. A skylight is ideally located to rid a room of moisture rapidly. Besides the skylights that hinge open, there are types with built-in ventilating fans.

The shape of your roof need not interfere with your installing a skylight. Whether the roof is steeply or gently pitched or dead flat, there is a skylight that will do the job.

If you don't want light in the roof, there are other ways of sky-lighting your home. Windows high under the eaves, a clerestory window where the roof level changes, a row of glass along the ridge of the roof, or just a block of glass dropped in here and there in the roof, will bring light just where you need it.

Skylights don't necessarily have to be large. Sometimes a tiny one will give adequate light to a dark closet or interior nook and do away with the sharp light which an added window might give.

You can add a cluster of round or randomly placed rectangular skylights to give gentle diffusion and provide a soft pattern of light throughout a room. Glass blocks are useful for this type of skylighting.

Not only do skylights bring in light but they are useful for spotlighting paintings, planters, or sculpture. A whole room roofed over with skylighting material can provide an interior court-garden that will be useful year-round in most climates.

Speaking of climate, you will need to know quite a bit about the nature of yours before you start cutting holes in the roof and installing skylights at random.

In many seashore locations where temperatures do not vary much from one season to the next, the warmth of skylights may be welcome every day of the year. But in a climate where temperatures get extremely high in summer and below zero in winter, a skylight may bring in too much heat—or let too much out. Take a good look at that spot where you plan to put a skylight. Observe it at various times of the day. Will it be shaded all day, have sun all day, or some of each? A skylight in full sun in a hot climate will be a heat trap. There is also danger of fading and bleaching effects on wood, carpets and books.

In a cool climate a skylight may be quite an added blessing. Even on a cloudy or foggy day it will transmit enough warmth to make an appreciable difference in your heating bill.

For hot weather or full-sunshine areas there are solutions to control skylight heat. An indoor pull shade (mounted horizontally directly under the skylight) can be used during the hottest part of the day, or an adjustable shutter unit that fits under the dome of the skylight will filter out the sun's rays and still let in plenty of light. Plastic Engineering Company of Tulsa, Oklahoma, makes such a unit. An outside louvered cover will also filter out glare and send an interesting light design into the room.

Some control of heat and light can be achieved through your choice of skylight material. You don't have to have clear glass or plastic. Colored panels or translucent ones with patterns or imbedded materials such as flowers or ferns are not only beautiful but diffuse light and keep out some of the heat.

Unlike most building items, skylights and some of the things they can be made of have come down in price over the last few years. One you build yourself can cost you as little as a dollar a square foot.

Skylight in this roof not only brings pleasant, soft, glareless light to the dining area but makes possible the development of a small indoor garden. In an existing house a corner-garden could be added by building a box and putting crushed rocks in the bottom, then placing potted plants on the rocks.

Furthermore, a skylight may be an essential item. Without it you might not be permitted to add that extra bathroom or a new laundry. FHA approves a skylighted bathroom and will credit the skylight to the window area of the room.

The next three chapters show three kinds of skylights suitable for homes, and tell how to make or install them.

The first is the simplest to use: a factory-made skylight you can buy ready for installation in a rectangular opening cut in the roof. It is also the most expensive.

The other two call for the use of corrugated or flat fiberglass-reinforced plastic. Corrugated has the advantage of being readily available, often in single odd sheets at very low cost. Its shape is so strong that it will not usually need any support except at the edges.

Facing page

This attic was transformed into an extra dressing-room and bath by skylighting it and adding a shower and a wide Formica-topped counter. Front of counter and wall also are plastic laminate.

A skylight should be strong enough to support the weight of a man, in case someone needs to step on it. Building codes usually require that glass skylights be wire-reinforced. Plastic, especially in a curved or domed shape, is strong enough to support a person. Any variation in design may require advice from your local building inspector.

Flat plastic sheets need some internal support unless the skylight is to be quite small. Except for this requirement, however, they are easier to work with than the corrugated and are a surer bet for producing a leak-free skylight.

When is a skylight not a skylight? In this case it's a porch roof made of the same corrugated plastic often used for skylights. Where an ordinary, opaque porch roof would have darkened this living-room corner, translucent plastic actually makes it lighter than when there was no roof outside at all.

23

Install a Double Dome

A factory-made skylight is easy to put in, offers efficient light-gathering and ventilation—plus a view of the sky if you want one

Today's plastic bubble skylight is a marvel of efficiency. Double-domed for insulation, easily opened for ventilation, it seals itself tightly against leaks or drafts, is shaped to wash itself in rain.

Like any skylight, the new plastic-and-aluminum kind is by its nature a super-window. When open it exhausts used air straight up far more rapidly than any vertical window can. And it brings in many times the light of most windows because it faces directly toward the sky.

This bubble skylight, called Ventarama, has been designed for easy addition to your existing home. With its integral copper flashing, it need only be dropped into a hole in the roof, sealed, then framed inside for neat appearance.

A bubble skydome can bring light and air to a bedroom without the expense and awkwardness of an added dormer. It can turn a dark bathroom into a bright one without loss of privacy. It can make a garage corner into cheerfully efficient workshop or laundry space. It can inexpensively open up an attic for add-a-room remodeling.

And what if you must place your new skylight where it can't be easily reached with its aluminum-pole operator? Just use a motorized model, operated by a toggle switch placed wherever you want it.

These skylights are sized to fit standard framing. The 22″ x 30″ and 25½″ x 45½″ oblong models are hinged on either narrow or wide side, and there are 30″ and 45½″ square models as well. Inner domes of acrylic plastic may be either clear or white translucent. Screens are included.

Because it faces the sky, a new double-bubble skylight will give your home a super-efficient window. It will do it without loss of privacy, too. an important feature in this bathroom.

HOW TO INSTALL A DOUBLE-BUBBLE SKYLIGHT

1.

2.

1. It's own screen is a lightweight and handy thing to use in choosing location for your skylight. To mark corners for roof cut, drive long nails from below right through shingles or tar.

2. Cut through tar and gravel with chisel to expose an area of roof the size of your skylight. If yours is a shingled roof you'll have to clear a larger area. Save best shingles for reuse.

3. Saw through roof deck or boards to make an opening just the size of the skylight, with about ½″ to spare. Allow room for adding to rafters or headers for strength if needed.

4. If yours is a built-up roof, scrape off gravel in strips 4″ from roof opening. Apply heavy coating of roof cement. Skylights ordered for shingled roofs come with suitable flashing.

5. Drop skylight into place on fresh coating of roof cement. On shingled roof, place bottom shingles first, then flashing, and then the other shingles.

6. On a tar-and-gravel roof like this one, just fasten down the skylight with galvanized roofing nails driven through the flashing.

199

7. Complete the outside job by pressing the loose gravel into the fresh plastic cement. Result: inconspicuous low-profile skylight that looks as if it had always been there.

8. Complete your skylight installation indoors by adding trim. This may be wide boards from roof to ceiling when these elements are separated, or mere mitered frame as here, stained to match woodwork.

24

Build a Corrugated Skylight

Large or small, a single sheet of readily available plastic builds it

The skylight you see here was used to bring light and cheer into a dark kitchen, all without disturbing the interior arrangement or stealing wall space needed for storage.

With corrugated fiberglass-supported plastic, you have a wide choice of color. For a warm climate, one of the cool greens or blues might be most desirable, preferably in one of the heat-reducing grades offered by some of the companies, notably Filon. For the cool, foggy climate in which this skylight was constructed, yellow was chosen for its bright, sunny feel even when the sun is not shining.

The skylight shown uses a full 40" x 96" sheet of plastic. At a cost of about $20 it does a job that would run into three figures if done with a manufactured model. A small skylight can be built in this way for as little as $5.

Since a skylight is constantly exposed to weather, it is usually worth while to buy the best grade of fiberglass-plastic available. The material used here, Filoplated Filon, is a special grade that carries a fifteen-year guarantee.

HOW TO INSTALL A CORRUGATED SKYLIGHT

1.

2.

1. Begin by framing the opening. Material used here is 2″ x 6″ pine. Bring tarpaper flashing up the sides all around and top with metal counterflashing, as shown here.

2. Top the opening at each end with corrugated filler. This is available in either rubber or redwood. Topping material being nailed here along side is redwood set in mastic. Makers of corrugated plastic can supply these accessories.

3.

4.

3. Cover the end and side sealer strips with a waterproof mastic. The one seen here is actually a waterproof vinyl flooring cement. Excellent and readily available is waterproof panel adhesive, in tubes for use with caulking guns.

4. Having a helper makes it easier to drop the sheet of corrugated plastic into place without smearing the mastic. As with so many home jobs, you don't have to be a married man—but it helps.

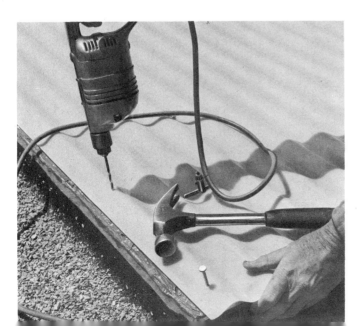

5. Nail every 6″ along the sides and in alternate corrugations on ends. Aluminum screw-shank nails, the kind that come with washers, are best. Pre-drill nail holes. Apply any necessary trim inside the house for appearance, and the job is done.

203

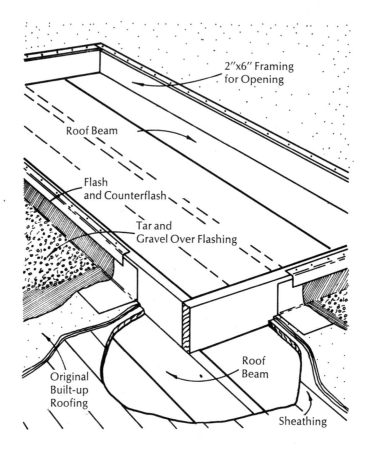

2"x6" Framing
for Opening

Roof Beam

Flash
and Counterflash

Tar and
Gravel Over Flashing

Roof
Beam

Original
Built-up
Roofing

Sheathing

Position the roof opening so you cut as few beams as possible.
Sketch shows how it can be done by removing only a section of
one beam, with ends being supported by metal hangers.

25

Plastic Skylight Is Easy To Build

No special corrugated sealer strips are needed when you make a skylight of flat fiberglass-plastic

A big diffusing skylight you can build for well under a dollar a square foot is quite a building bargain. This one has transformed the landing above a stairway from a dark trap into the brightest spot in the house. It lights the hall and stairs effectively on moonlit nights too. You could use a similar skylight to brighten a bathroom or kitchen, a garage or shop.

Its basis is a 4' x 6' sheet of flat fiberglass-reinforced plastic (Filon). For durability it's well to use the heaviest grade.

Like its corrugated cousin, the flat plastic comes in color as well as "clear," a highly translucent, milklike type for maximum light transmission. If you want a little less light, and no color, there's a good alternative—the snowier variety called white. If you wish to insulate, avoid condensation, add an architectural touch—cover the ceiling with another sheet of flat Filon; fasten every 6" along exposed beams and rafters.

1. Frame is six pieces of 2" x 8" pine, two straight sides and four pieces band-sawn to a gradual arc and put crosswise. Frame extends above roof surface.

2.

3.

2. Drill holes at 6″ intervals to fasten the panels as seen here. Extend panel 1″ beyond frame all around. Extend roofing paper up frame from built-up roof to serve as flashing. Use metal for other roof types.

3. Use aluminum roofing nails with a screw shank and neoprene washer to fasten panel after running heavy bead of waterproof panel adhesive around top edge of frame.

4. From above, your skylight will look like this. It is well to allow about 2″ of excess plastic all round to carry off water. Sketch in previous chapter gives some hints about flashing.

5. And here's the new skylight from below. Add molding or other trim for appearance, if needed. Scrape off any excess adhesive that may have oozed out.

4.

5.

Bathroom Modernizing

26

Update Your Bathroom

With new ideas and new equipment you can turn it from the most old-fashioned to the most modern room in the house

A house built only a few years ago is a half-century old in its bathroom design. Most bathrooms are small, dark cubbyholes, inadequate for the needs of one person much less those of a growing family. Old bathroom fixtures are often unsafe and inappropriately designed for the size and shape of the people who use them. But this is changing in the better new houses—and you can change it in yours.

Professor Alexander Kira, who headed a Cornell University five-year research program on bathroom development, concluded that: "In many respects the bathroom is in about the same stage of development as the kitchen was years ago when a stove, sink and ice box sat in splendid isolation against opposite walls of a room and storage was accounted for by some unreachable fixed shelves often in the next room."

Professor Kira's remarks have led bathroom manufacturers to do something about this state of affairs. So you can now find fixtures and accessories that didn't exist a few years ago.

An up-to-date bathroom does not end with the necessities; glamour, with all the glories of the ancient Roman spa, can be yours. Today's bathroom can have a steam shower, a sauna bath, built-in radiant heat and spot-heating devices, whirlpool in the tub, a toilet seat that also cleanses you, a built-in scale, twin tubs or a double-occupancy tub.

Like the automobile manufacturers, bathroom producers have become safety conscious. Moldy or stained strips and bathmats are passé. You can have a tub with a built-in nonskid surface that is four times as safe as the older type is even with a mat. There are built-in grab bars at different levels, soap dishes at several heights so you won't fall down scrambling for a bar on the floor. Your chances of scalding or freezing from a quick change of temperature are no longer inevitable. There's a pressure-balancing valve that automatically assures a constant water temperature no matter what happens in the rest of the plumbing. It's just a question of which gadgets and appliances are most in demand in your family, which ones you can afford, and whether present bathroom space will hold all the innovations that appeal to you.

You can have carpet on the floor, walls that look like rare wood or actually are rare wood with an impermeable melamine-plastic finish. You can have marble tiles on walls and floor, or synthetic marble which duplicates the real thing at lower cost. You can have any color you want in bathroom fixtures and ac-

Your remodeled bathroom can be as Space Age as you like—right now. All the equipment shown in this "idea" bathroom-universe is available. In fact, American Standard dreamed up the design just to show off its line of new fixtures.

An interior space or one where a window would create a privacy problem suggests use of a skylight. This is best combined with a ventilator, such as the one seen on the tiled wall here, which may be controlled by an automatic switch. This small bathroom is visually doubled in size by generous use of mirrors.

Compartmenting has converted this big, old bathroom so that each of three areas may be used at the same time. For elegance, a plastic-finished woodgrain (Marlite) paneling was used in the dressing-room section. Colored panels, also with an easy-care plastic finish, were used in the smaller compartments to give light and beauty. Note the concealed-lighting fixture above the dressing table. This could just as well be a skylight, circumstances permitting.

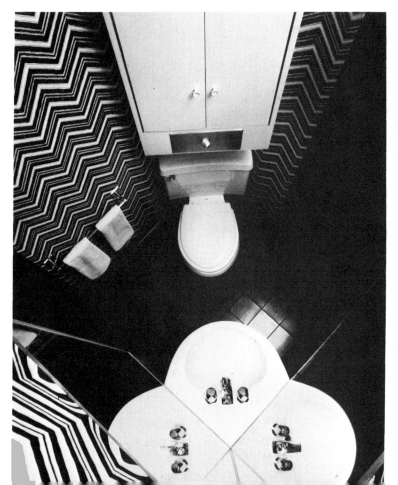

Here's what you can put into a space as little as 4' square —without crowding. What looks like four lavatories here is just one, set into a mirrored corner to produce an illusion of spaciousness. The dramatic wallcovering is washable. Heat, light, and ventilation can all be supplied in a room like this without using wall space by installing a combination ceiling device made by NuTone.

213

cessories. The tub can be sunken. The toilet can be wall-hung. You can have several shower heads at different heights. The medicine cabinets can be concealed, locked without keys, lighted. The ceiling can be luminous.

If your home is a very old one, you are luckier than the fellow with an outdated bathroom in a fairly recent house. Years ago space was not so expensive. Bathrooms were large, ceilings high, and it was not unusual to find such features as an easy chair, a chaise longue, and a wood-burning fireplace.

A large old bathroom can be remodeled into a partitioned bathroom, if you wish, with a separate small room for tub or toilet. If your bathroom is on an outside wall, it may be feasible to add a picture window and small, fenced outdoor garden to bring the outdoors into the bathroom without sacrificing privacy.

Today's bathroom is a special kind of living area, meant to be one of the most beautiful and comfortable rooms in the house. It should also be one of the easiest rooms to maintain.

REDECORATE A BATHROOM. Remodeling an entire bathroom can be a major task and huge expense; therefore, think first of how you can keep the present fixtures and make changes that do not require moving the plumbing. A solid but ugly floor can be carpeted with self-stick vinyl or carpet tiles. Now on the market are Ozite carpet tiles which have a self-stick backing that permits you to take a tile up at any time, scrub it, and put it back without destroying the self-stick surface. These tiles come in pastel colors and are easy to cut with a scissors.

Yours may be one of the houses with a too-dark bathroom. Solve this problem with a skylight and bring in the sun. If you can't do this, then a suspended luminous ceiling could be added to give the illusion of daylight.

Old walls can be renewed with scrubbable vinyl paper, melamine-surfaced panels, ceramic tile, mirror tile, washable velvet velour. Ozite self-stick tiles are now being used on walls as well as floors. They help to soundproof a bathroom.

One carpet maker suggests bringing the floor right up the outside of the tub and predicts that the day may come when tubs will also be carpeted inside. And we'll all wonder how we could even have put up so long with hard, cold, unlined tubs.

You can also panel around a tub with three watertight fiberglass panels and do away forever with grout and falling tiles.

It's not so much what you can do, but what do you want to do, and how much can you afford to spend. If the basic design of your present bathroom still pleases, it may suffice to put in a new floor and cover the old walls, both projects easy enough for

Early American bathroom was added to part of house where a slab floor prevented putting drains below. Special high-outlet tub and wall-hung toilet make it possible. Period touches come from red bandanna wallcovering and shower curtain, reproductions of old gas lamps, ladder-back chair, braided rug, and a random-width pegged-oak floor.

Cutaway shows how the tub, also shown in the Early American bathroom, works. It looks like any other bathtub, but the drain clears the floor by more than 2".

a wife to do these days. An old-fashioned bathtub with claw feet doesn't need to be discarded if the enameled surface is good. Put in new faucets with temperature control, add a telephone shower, box in the tub itself, and tile the outside.

INSTALL A BIDET. But of all devices the one that will most completely revolutionize bathroom hygiene is a bidet ("bee-day"). Americans most often meet it for the first time while traveling in Europe, and particularly France, where it has been regarded as a necessity for a long time. Its name means "little horse," and it is said to have been developed to cleanse the parts of the body that come into contact with a saddle.

We no longer spend much time in the saddle, but we are all concerned with improving bathroom hygiene. If your bathroom has space to spare, or if you are building a large new one, a bidet beside the toilet, as shown in the photograph, is a natural arrangement. Most plumbing manufacturers now include a bidet in their line. In the limited number of U.S. households where one is found, the bidet has almost invariably come to be regarded much more as a necessity than as a luxury.

Since a bidet is most often used in conjunction with a toilet, the logical idea of combining the two has occurred to someone. So now we have the American Bidet. It serves most of the same purposes as the regular bidet, and often does them better. Since it takes up no floor space and involves no major plumbing changes you can have one in any existing bathroom.

It replaces an ordinary toilet seat, and in appearance it closely resembles one—but it houses a warm-water valve and nozzle and a warm-air blower.

At a flick of a switch, a jet of clean warm water washes the perineal area of the user. Another flick of the switch in the opposite direction sends out a gentle stream of warm air for drying purposes. Bathroom tissue may be dispensed with.

All mechanism for operating the appliance, including heating the water and air, is hidden within the hollow polypropylene-plastic shell.

The American Bidet fits any of the basic types of toilet bowls, including one-piece, wall hung, and case types. Plumbing connection is to the cold-water line below the tank or ahead of the siphon-jet flushing mechanism. Electricity for heating the water and heating and blowing the air is obtained by plugging into any ordinary outlet. If you're remodeling the bathroom, install an outlet just behind the toilet bowel for this connection.

Lid and seat still raise independently just as on the ordinary toilet seat. All connections, wires, fan, motor, and heating elements are insulated. Water is released at about 94 degrees, nearly body temperature, so it feels neither too hot nor too cold.

Children, elderly people, and handicapped members of a family soon learn to use the bidet, a device which vastly reduces the danger of infection. Two included accessories are a feminine-hygiene tube and a low-enema tube which fit over the water nozzle.

ABOVE-THE-FLOOR DRAINS. One plumbing problem, often without a solution in the past, can now be solved. If you have a concrete slab, or a situation where there are rooms below and exposed plumbing would be unsightly, you needn't be stopped dead for lack of suitable fixtures. Now you can get both a toilet and tub (Kohler) in which all necessary drains exit above grade and go out through the house wall before going down into the ground.

With roughing-in above the existing floor level, the concrete slab need not be disturbed, nor is there a need to build a false ceiling below an existing wood floor in order to conceal exposed pipes. Fixtures using above-the-floor drains look very much like other tubs and toilets, but installation work is simplified.

Bathtub and toilet of this kind come in six colors as well as white. The tub is 16″ high outside and 13″ inside to permit the bottom to be raised above the floor. The toilet is a reverse-trap closet with quiet, efficient flushing action, is floor-mounted and close coupled, and has its outlet center 4″ above the floor.

Only the platform shape tells you that this toilet, like the tub, has been especially shaped to drain above floor level. Eljer makes these units, NuTone the heater-light-fan above.

Changing basic plumbing fixtures such as toilet or tub involves more work and planning. Usually you can switch over from one type of toilet to another. A noisy, inefficient model can be exchanged for a silent, self-cleaning, self-ventilating type. But to install a wall-hung toilet may require adding to wall framing.

In making major plumbing changes, consult the local building department and find out requirements and whether you will need a permit. Most building inspectors are helpful and sympathetic toward do-it-yourselfers who wish to make improvements. It is much better to find out what you're allowed to do *before* you tear out walls and plumbing. If some aspect of your plan is illegal, the inspector can often suggest an alternate method.

You may wish to work with a contractor or plumber on a basis where he does the rough-in work and you do the finishing. Most plumbing shops will at least throw in telephone consultation at no extra charge when they sell fixtures to the homeowner.

SOLVING THE SPACE PROBLEM. Before investing time and money adding gadgets to a bathroom, it is important to stop and take the long view. Consider the future needs of your family. As children grow into their teens there never seem to be enough bathrooms.

Solve this problem by refurbishing the old bathroom at minimum expense and add a half-bath. Or you might be able to compartment a large old bathroom and make it usable by more than one person at a time.

Does your present bathroom lack storage facilities? Usually there is space available between the studs for fitting in narrow shelves, medicine cabinet, extra towel rack, built-in folding scale, miniature heater. Build a cabinet above the toilet, below the sink, change over to sliding doors instead of swing-out types, add a counter around a sink basin, put in a heat lamp aimed at tub or shower-exit, update old cabinets with new hardware, use the backs of doors for towel racks or for mirrors.

If bathroom space is hopelessly small, consider the possibility of stealing a little space from another room. Half a wall, one foot in depth, taken off a bedroom may be just room enough to add storage space and a dressing table to a bathroom.

One way to bring beauty into a bathroom is to add a tiny garden. If you have an available space, even a foot or so wide, you can make it a part of your bathroom by putting in a glass wall or sliding door. A tall fence or hedge will take care of the privacy problem.

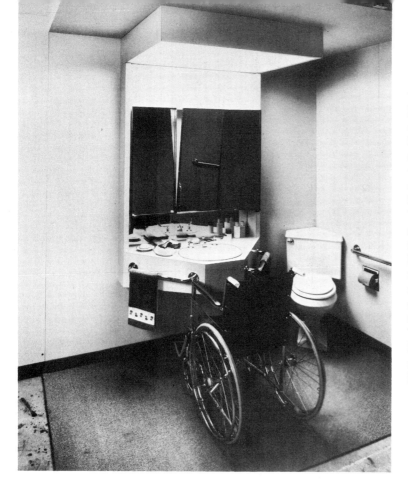

This is a highly specialized bathroom arrangement but one that could be vitally important in a household including an invalid. Triangle toilet fits neatly into a corner. The towel bar near it also serves as a grab bar. The small lavatory has easily accessible counter space and faucets with wrist-action handles, similar to those used in hospital scrub rooms. They are easily operated by people with arthritis or muscular problems. The cabinet above the sink has a special tilt-down mirror. Wheelchair can be brought close to lavatory.

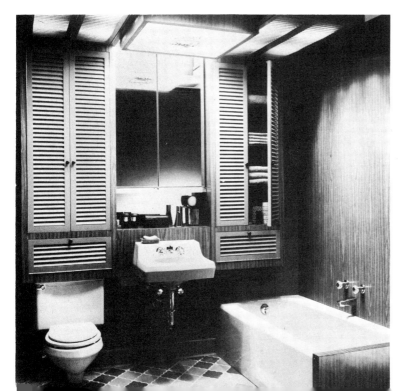

Widely available wood louver units are the key to this bathroom decorating scheme. A dropped-ceiling unit permits soft light to come through translucent fiberglass panels, while the added louvers diffuse the light and give an unusual pattern. Louvers could equally well be used with skylights that otherwise allow too much glare and heat during summer months. Matching wood louvers on cabinet doors provide ventilation as well as a decorative note. Louvers are painted to match the paneling of laminated plastic in Ceylon teak pattern.

Luxurious bathroom "sanitary area" places low-slung, quiet toilet alongside bidet, since these devices are often used successively. Control panel for bidet is mounted on storage cabinet.

Looking much like the ordinary toilet seat it replaces, the American Bidet does the cleansing duty of a bidet and provides warm-air drying as well. And it consumes no bathroom space.

Wall-hung toilet like this can solve several home-improvement problems at once. It ends the messiness around the base of the ordinary toilet, permits wall-to-wall carpeting or other floor-covering, eliminates trying to put plumbing into slab floor, has exceptionally quiet flushing action, and has short, rounded-front shape for tight spaces.

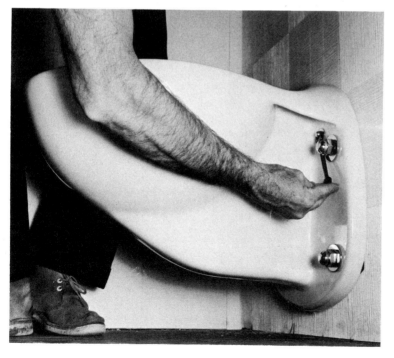

This unusual wall-hung toilet has its tank concealed within the wall above. Access to flushing mechanism is from above, by means of either a door or a removable shelf.

Heavy steel hanger is what makes a wall-hung toilet feasible. To install it you will usually have to provide additional studs.

The difficult job of fitting a sink rim has often discouraged the amateur plumber. This problem can be solved with a self-rimming type that is now available in white or colors (Kohler). All you need do is drop it into a cutout counter top. A waterproof adhesive or sealer is used to prevent leakage under the rim.

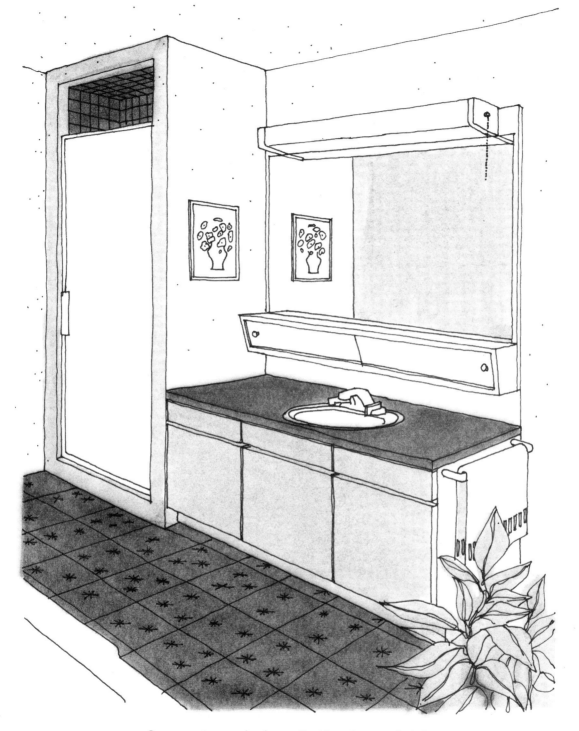

One way to supply the really big mirror so helpful in updating an outdated bathroom is by adding a unit like this. In addition to mirror, it includes a sliding door cabinet, a shelf, a fluorescent light, and a convenience outlet.

1. To install the new mirrored unit, provide firm framing support to take mounting screws at the four points marked X.

2. Hang mirror and add the vanity compartment at the bottom, a simple screwdriver job. Bring in electrical supply.

3. Mount the light at the top and make the electrical connection. Slip in sliding mirror doors—and that's it.

Upgrade the most-used thing in your bathroom by replacing the old lavatory. New circular lavatory with single-lever faucet sits in a plumbing-concealing vanity. It is made of ordinary fir plywood in the simplest possible design, ornamented by adding Filon carvings. To do such a job, use the carvings in the way described in Chapter 17.

With a little more outdoor space available you may be able to pave part of the area and add a sunning or lounging space to the bathroom.

Another way to make a small bathroom seem larger is to add mirrors. One wall of mirror will create spaciousness. Add a planter opposite the mirror and you will see your garden twice, even if the planter is only a few inches wide. Some plants thrive in the steamy, tropical temperatures of a bathroom.

One small bathroom improvement that is especially worth considering because it involves so little effort is addition of a built-in scale. In our weight-conscious era, a scale is regarded by many as a near-necessity; but, stumbled over, it may also be a first-class nuisance.

Building in a scale made for this arrangement involves no more than cutting a properly dimensioned hole in the wall and inserting the scale housing in this opening. The scale and its platform flip down instantly for use, disappear equally quickly when not wanted.

27

Tips On Working With Tile

Putting in new tile, replacing old tile, or adding a few tile to replace broken ones is a do-it-yourself job

If you add a bathroom to your home, you may wish to do some of its surfaces in ceramic tile. And if you repair or remodel an old one, chances are there will be tilework involved.

If only a few tile are broken, it is not hard to replace them —but matching an old color or pattern may be impossible. A good solution is to remove not only the broken tile but a few others as well and put in their place decorative tile or tile of a contrasting color, to create a spot of accent or interest.

In many situations you may find it easiest to work with tiny Japanese tile that come in sheets mounted on cloth mesh. They can be cut to fit difficult areas, but often don't need cutting at all. The array of colors and designs is large, so you won't have any trouble finding something that harmonizes with your bathroom.

The photographs cover problems you're most likely to meet in tiling a new area or repairing an old one.

For large jobs it's best to rent a tile cutter like this one from your dealer. Have him show you how to use it.

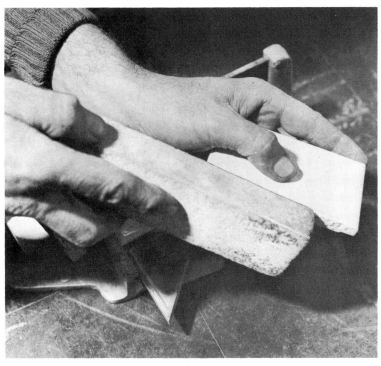

Cut edges of tile can be smoothed by rubbing with a carborundum stone or with emery paper wrapped around a block of wood.

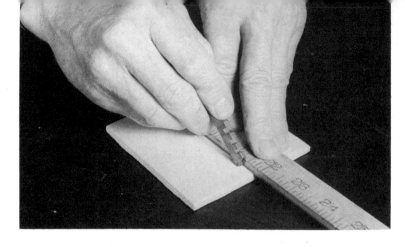

To cut tile without a tile cutter, first score the tile with a glass cutter . . .

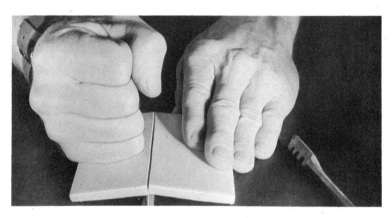

. . . then place it over a triangular file and break it off with a sharp blow.

To cut off a narrow strip, score with glass cutter, put tile in a vise, and snap it off with a quick motion.

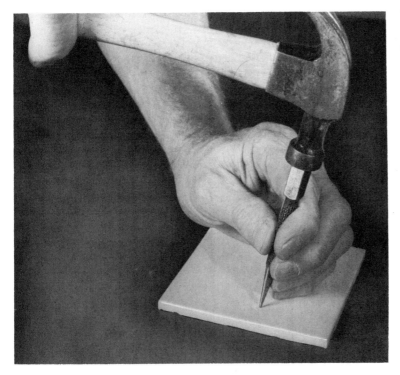

To make a small hole through a tile, first chip away glaze with nail set or sharp tool . . .

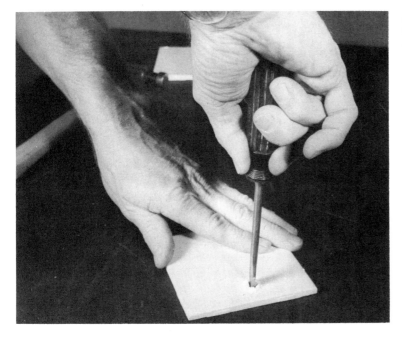

. . . and gradually enlarge the hole to the correct size with a screwdriver.

When laying a new area of tile in mortar, first nail down mesh such as chicken wire.

Mix mortar to peanut-butter consistency. Lay level bed of mortar, then place tile after soaking them in water.

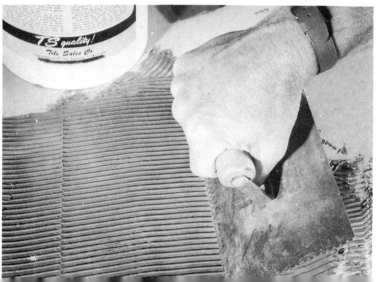

Tile adhesive is handier than mortar for most jobs on vertical surfaces. Seal surface first, then spread adhesive with notched trowel.

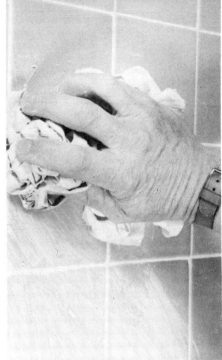

Photo left
Tap tiles level as you work by using a wood scrap placed over several tiles at a time. It's best to wait a day before grouting.

Photo right
Grout comes in dry form, must be mixed to creamy consistency with water. Work into gaps, then wipe off excess with a damp cloth.

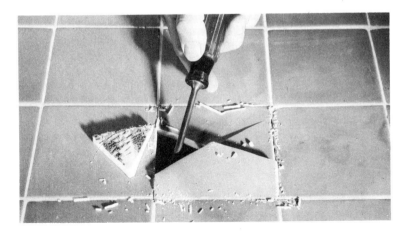

To remove damaged old tile, score in X pattern, break, then pry off in pieces with a screw driver. Clean and level the area before putting in new tile.

Cutaway model shows steps in salvaging an old tub: frame, cover with plywood, spread on adhesive, and cover with new tile, trim.

28

New Walls For Your Bathroom

Foam-backed plastic laminate is waterproof, goes up in big sheets, is durable and requires little maintenance

Foam-backed plastic-laminate wall panels are a new home-improvement product quite different from anything ever available before.

Water can't hurt them because the face material is Formica laminated plastic $\frac{1}{16}''$ thick. This is backed by $\frac{1}{8}''$ polystyrene foam which has enough give for smooth installation over tile and other slightly irregular walls. It is known as Panel System 202.

The panels are made in 4′ and 5′ widths, lengths to 10′, for installation between two-part moldings. The base part of each molding is nailed or cemented to the wall, the panel is then put up with contact cement, and the decorative second part of the molding is snapped in to cover the joint. This avoids the super-accurate fitting some wall materials require.

PREPARATION OF OLD WALL. A sound tile wall may need no work. But if any tiles are loose they should be cemented down, and any missing ones should be replaced with scraps of plywood. Protruding trim tiles at top of a wainscoting or at floor may have to be knocked off and the wall built up to level with gypsum board or plywood.

233

Panel System 202, in "Classic Cremo Marble" pattern, durably transforms this bathroom. Visible on two walls are the snap-in moldings that simplify getting a neat fit at corners and where sheets join.

Any plaster or plasterboard that has been damaged by moisture should be cut out and replaced with exterior-grade plywood. This should be done in any case above tub and shower pan, using strips of plywood 6" wide.

To insure a permanent bond with the new panels, any wallpaper or vinyl or fabric wallcoverings should be removed. Painted surfaces may need scraping or sanding to remove blisters or flaking. The wall should, of course, be made sound and solid by additional nailing if needed. And any grease or soap or other dirt should be cleaned off.

MOLDING. Cut and apply the base part of each length of molding. You'll need it at corners, at any exposed edges and where seams come, but not at floor or ceiling.

Attach base sections of molding with nails every 6" to 8" where there is solid backing. Where wall is unsupported, use contact cement.

PAPER TEMPLATES will simplify cutting the panels, especially for irregular walls or ones having plumbing or outlets for which openings must be made.

Make templates with heavy paper and 1½" masking tape. Begin by fastening paper at the ceiling with masking tape. Tape on additional pieces of paper until the wall is covered, punching any plumbing fittings through. Keep paper trimmed back about 1" from corners or finish line of panel, making up the space with tape.

234

Maximum moisture resistance makes this new bathroom panel system useful everywhere in the room, even in tub and shower enclosures. Blue Starflower is one of many abstract, marble, and woodgrain designs.

For the new look in bathroom improvement, two harmonizing patterns of Panel System 202 are used here. Regency Walnut and Blue Starflower have been combined to give variety.

HOW TO INSTALL BATHROOM PANELING

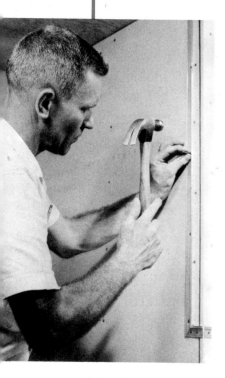

1. Begin installation of paneling by nailing or cementing base section of molding. Decorative part of each molding strip will snap into this base after panels are cemented up.

2. Large 202 panels with cutouts, like this one, are most safely cut after making a paper template. Then they should be tested for fit, as shown here, before contact cement is applied.

3. Formica's Contact Adhesive 140 should be applied to panel backs and to wall, using short nap roller. Brush is better for corners and tight spots. Porous surfaces may require two coats.

4. As soon as contact cement is dry, place panel carefully in proper location and press and roll for good adhesion. Use a rubber mallet or a hammer and short block of 2″ x 4″ in corners and around edges.

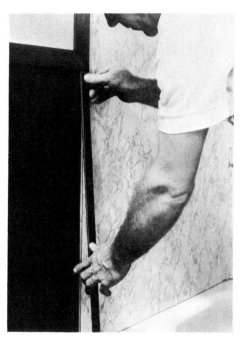

5. Finishing touch in the 202 System is Formica-clad decorative portion of molding that snaps into base part. Strip being snapped in here is Spanish Oak woodgrain pattern that separates panel of this finish at left from creamy marble pattern around tub

Now use dividers to mark a cutting line on all edges of the template. Allow $\frac{1}{16}$″ clearance at top and bottom, $\frac{1}{8}$″ at molding. Mark for all plumbing or fixture cutouts.

Remove the template and tape it to the panel for cutting with a fine-toothed saw, 24 to 32 teeth to the inch. Use brace with expansion bit, hole saw and saber saw to make any cutouts required. Square cutouts should be drilled first and made with slightly rounded corners to prevent panel from cracking.

Trim and smooth edges with block plane. Round any inside corners with a round file.

PLACE PANEL on wall without adhesive first to test the fit. Clearance of $\frac{1}{16}''$ along top of tub should be obtained by use of a shim, such as a scrap of Formica.

To be sure you can get the panel into precisely the position after adhesive is applied, put a piece of masking tape on tub edge and panel face and make a location mark.

Apply brush-grade contact cement after reading all safety precautions. Coat back of panel and all of wall, including molding flange. When cement is dry, place panel carefully since it will grab at once and be impossible to move. Press with roller, using hammer and block of wood in tight corners.

COMPLETE MOLDING by cutting each decorative part to length with hacksaw and pressing into base piece. Burrs should be filed off first and serrated tongue rubbed with paraffin for easy attachment.

Sealant for joints and edges is supplied by the manufacturer of this system. You should apply it at all panel edges around the tub or shower pan and at ceiling joints.

The job is done—with every prospect of durability and minimum maintenance. Since the surface of your new walls is the same as the Formica of countertops, it may be cleaned with a damp cloth or soap and water. For stubborn stains or marks use suitable solvents, such as lacquer thinner; but don't use harsh abrasive cleaners that can scratch or dull the surface.

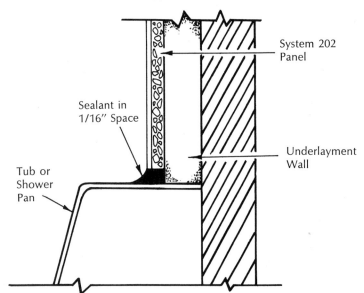

System 202 Panel

Sealant in 1/16" Space

Underlayment Wall

Tub or Shower Pan

Wherever System 202 panels are to sit on top of a tub or shower pan, tape shims in place to prevent actual contact. Use any $\frac{1}{16}''$ material, such as scraps of plastic laminate. After panels are in place, remove shims and fill the gap with sealant.

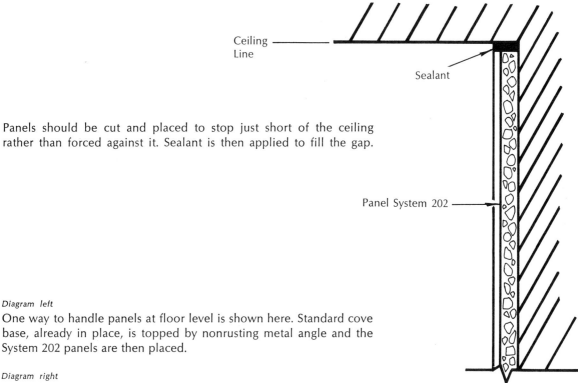

Ceiling
Line

Sealant

Panels should be cut and placed to stop just short of the ceiling rather than forced against it. Sealant is then applied to fill the gap.

Panel System 202

Diagram left

One way to handle panels at floor level is shown here. Standard cove base, already in place, is topped by nonrusting metal angle and the System 202 panels are then placed.

Diagram right

Where the previous wall has had no cove base, or it requires replacement, this detail will be the easiest method to follow. Bring panels approximately to floor level, then apply base.

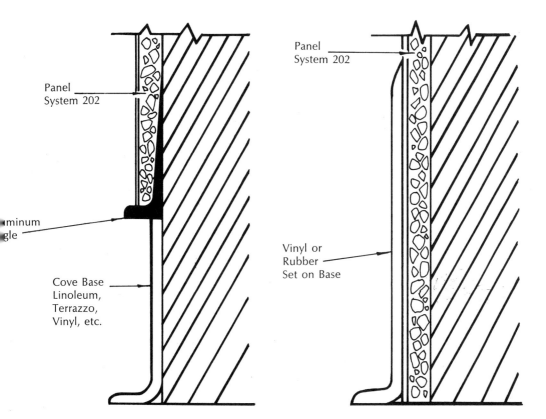

Panel
System 202

Panel
System 202

minum
gle

Vinyl or
Rubber
Set on Base

Cove Base
Linoleum,
Terrazzo,
Vinyl, etc.

If you are combining new bathroom walls with a suspended ceiling (as described in another chapter) continue panels to a couple of inches above desired ceiling height. Then apply bracket or supporting trim strip directly to surface.

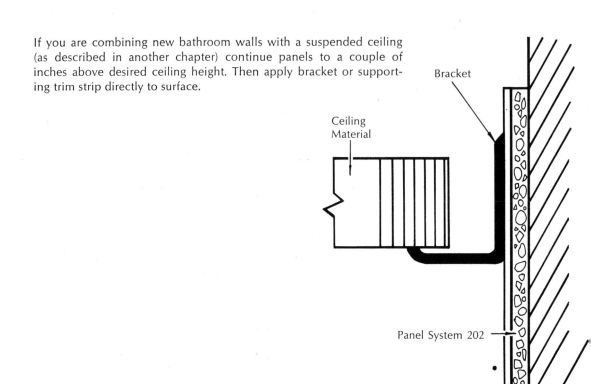

Bracket

Ceiling
Material

Panel System 202

Door
Jamb

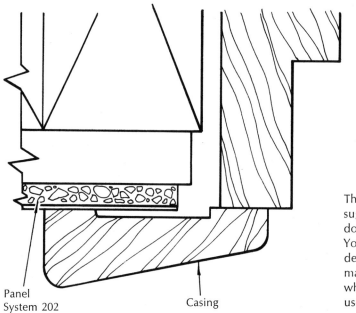

Panel
System 202

Casing

This is the manufacturer's suggestion for treatment of door and window jambs. You may prefer to alter it, depending on what trim material is available and whether it is feasible to re-use what you have removed.

29

When Is a Tub More Than a Tub?

When it's sunken, plastic-enclosed, fiberglass-backed, shower-equipped, and turned into a spa by a whirlpool bath

There are quite a few interesting things you can do to—or about—the tub in the bathroom you are improving or the new bath you are adding to your home.

For one thing, you can sink it below floor level, using either a factory-made tub designed for this treatment or one you build yourself.

You can use one of the super tub-shower combinations, or you can turn the tub you now have into a sort of compact health spa by installing a Whirlpool massage unit.

You can vastly improve both the appearance and the durability of the wall behind your tub by any of several methods. These include replacing or repairing the tile, as shown in a previous chapter; putting in new walls of foam-backed plastic laminate, also shown in a previous chapter; or using one of the fast-installation new fiberglass-plastic kits, as shown in this chapter.

And if yours is—or is to become—a tub-shower combination, you can avoid the various shortcomings of shower curtains by installing a modern tub enclosure with folding panels that open from both ends.

Let's begin with the sunken bathtub and its feeling of

Roman luxury. This need not be expensive if you install an enameled cast-iron tub especially designed to be placed as easily as an ordinary above-the-floor tub. A completely assembled, one-piece, corner sunken tub requires no tiling, comes in colors and several lengths.

The tub does, however, require approximately 25″ of space below the floor line. This means that you can't add a sunken tub just anywhere. The tub shown in the photograph was installed in a second-floor bathroom above a garage, so fixtures and piping underneath did not create a major problem. In some houses a sunken tub could be added in an area over a downstairs closet or above a room where the tub bottom could be concealed by a built-in cabinet.

Installing this tub on the ground floor is simpler unless there is a slab floor to contend with. Where there is a crawl space you cut a hole in the floor and drop the tub through. It would not need to be boxed in below the floor, but it should be wrapped or padded with insulating material to reduce heat loss.

Once the tub is in, you can add glamour by putting colorful tile on the walls, adding a planter, or installing unusual fixtures. The tub shown uses an Adjusto faucet. This sunken tub becomes a shower when the faucet is swiveled up to shoulder height. Because the tub bottom is below the floor level, shower splashing is minimal on surrounding surfaces, and it's possible to get by without a curtain. This arrangement also offers advantages for bathing small children or shampooing hair.

WHIRLPOOL UNIT. One of the most therapeutic things you can do to improve a bathroom without getting into a major remodeling job is put in a permanent Whirlpool unit.

Romans, Greeks, and Japanese started using water therapy for ills and for relaxation centuries ago. Now you can join them by adding a modern Whirlpool in the tub. It comes from Jacuzzi Research, Inc., and can be installed by a do-it-yourselfer with a little help from a plumber.

A Whirlpool unit, consisting of a visible chrome vertical pipe and a swiveling flow-control handle in the tub, plus a pump and motor concealed in a cabinet below or at the end of the tub, are all the parts supplied by the maker for this home spa.

You need approximately 2′ at the drain end of the tub to house the pump. Lacking this, you could put the pump beneath the flooring, directly under the tub. In some situations it is feasible and necessary to install the pump directly in front of the tub. Installation instructions deal with any of these situations.

Sunken tub like this is most easily built by casting a concrete slab for the base, erecting sides of concrete block, then tiling. This bathroom is made spacious and bright by use of glass, mirrors, and luminous ceiling.

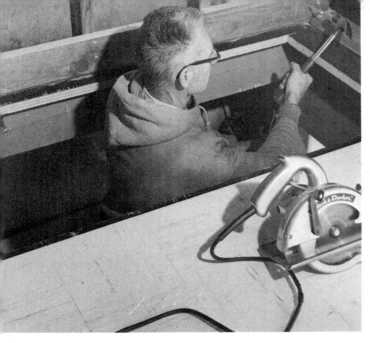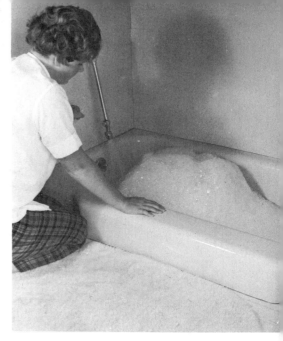

Photo left

Simple cuts form a rectangular hole ready to receive the sunken tub. All you need do is drop it in. Tub is heavy cast iron, so it remains in place without the need of adhesive or any fasteners.

Photo right

Tub is ready to use immediately. In a remodeling job faucets might have to be moved, but chances are that you'll want to replace worn faucets with more glamorous fixtures anyway. Wall surface around this tub is Formica in an aqua shade. Tub is pale yellow. Faucet shown here swivels up for shower position.

No special tub is required. The tub drains by gravity, and overflow fittings are included with the whirlpool kit. There is also a time switch which you mount on the wall. It can be set to operate the required number of minutes and then shut itself off. The plate that covers the timer is stainless steel with permanently printed operating instructions for the unit. Any householder who has had the experience of having an appliance misused because someone couldn't find the instructions will appreciate this feature.

If you are doing an all-out bath-remodeling job or adding one of the new large luxury bathrooms, you might want to add Jacuzzi's version of the Japanese bath which permits the whole family to have a hot plunge. This tub is 92″ long by 52″ wide and 38½″ deep. The tub shell is made of fiberglass-plastic and looks like a small swimming pool. For the package-unit installed you might have to put out nearly $3,000, but this cost can be cut by a handy remodeler.

Should you want something really unusual, a company architect will work with you to design a family spa in any shape or size desired. A project of this size is, of course, quite a different thing from installing a simple unit in a bathtub—more work, more cost, but bigger results. The spa-pool, without the agitation device

Another idea, using the sunken tub for beauty, incorporates tub area with a tiny terrace separated from tub by sliding glass door. This tub is surrounded by tile which converts the whole room into a shower stall. There are shower heads of different heights for "him" and "her". Lighting comes from a luminous ceiling. Lights above the tub could be heat lamps.

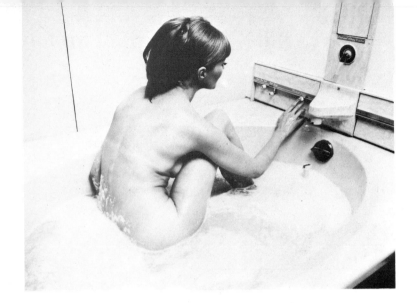

This oval-shaped tub is big enough for the name bathing pool. It has a control console that presets the temperature and depth of the water. There's a built-in hand shower for hair-washing and a Whirlpool turbulator, plus a fountain-like water spout that trajects a splashless flow of water in a controlled arc. This tub is 30 percent wider than a standard tub and is contoured for lumbar support. Tub edge is beveled to provide a comfortable headrest, and bottom of tub has a permanent slip-resistant surface.

Jacuzzi Whirlpool unit replaces conventional drain and overflow in this tub. Inset diagram shows position of pump and motor when installed at the end of the tub. In this case, pump mechanism was concealed in closet area behind the tiled wall. Regular use of a water softener keeps the Whirlpool operating mechanism from being clogged by water scum.

Whirlpool in action is inconspicuous. The small air hole at the top can be rotated to control the volume of water flowing in. Beneath the water is a star-shaped handle which the bather uses to control direction of water flow by pushing it with a toe.

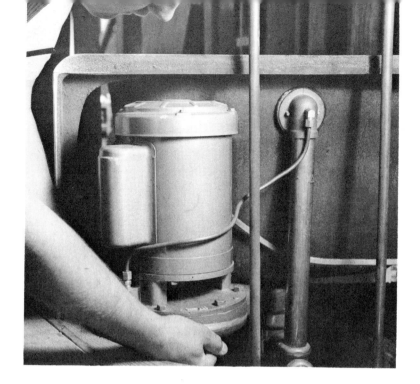

This Jacuzzi Whirlpool unit was installed in an under-the-sink counter area adjacent to the tub. When the remodeling job is complete, doors will hide the pump but make it easily available for servicing.

Display model shows how three pieces form a total above-tub wall liner for new or remodeled bathroom.

HOW TO INSTALL A WALL LINER

1. Cut hole in wall for soap dish, squeeze adhesive onto wall, then put main section into place.

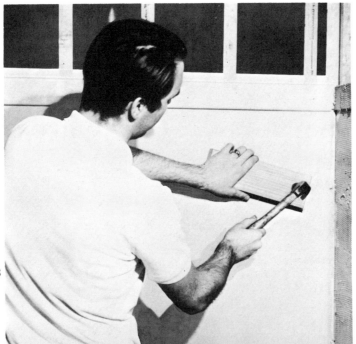

2. Pull liner away from wall, allow adhesive to set for five minutes, then replace and hammer as shown.

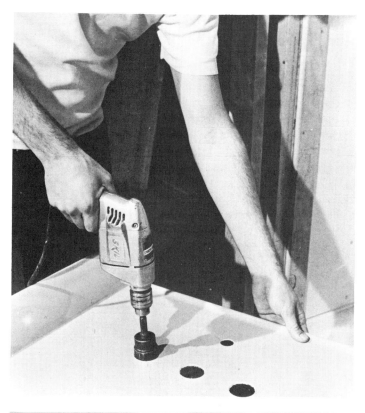

3. Install end wall liner in the same way after cutting plumbing holes with hole saw or drill and saber saw.

4. After other end-wall liner is permanently in place, calk joints with synthetic rubber included with kit.

249

in operation, makes a small swimming pool—ideal for teaching a child how to swim in a controlled, safe situation, or a place for an adult to take exercise in water.

KEEP WATER OFF THE FLOOR. When your tub also serves as a shower, flying water can be pretty hard on the floor and walls around it. In redoing your old bathroom or adding a new one, consider a modern molded-fiberglass-plastic three-piece wall.

The one shown in the how-to-install-it picture series is called Tubwal. It comes in several colors as well as white, has a molded-in soap dish, and installs with mastic that comes with it.

Another desirable addition to the tub that acts also as a shower is a sliding enclosure to replace shower curtains that blow, stick to you, let drafts in, and let water leak onto the floor.

This folding tub enclosure comes in a compact package, has detailed instructions for assembly.

HOW TO INSTALL A TUB ENCLOSURE

1. After measuring space and cutting off top and bottom rails of enclosure as needed, assemble on floor.

2. Self-stick foam tape is included as part of this unit. Apply it to both sides and bottom of the enclosure.

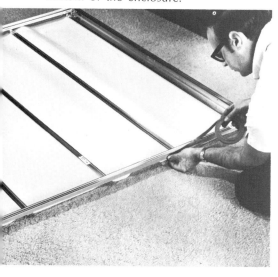

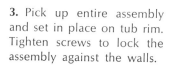

3. Pick up entire assembly and set in place on tub rim. Tighten screws to lock the assembly against the walls.

The one shown in the photographs is called Showerfold. It opens from either end of the tub. This eliminates the old problem of a door that opens only half way and gives you a bad time every time you have to reach in to clean the tub. It also eliminates the nuisance of trying to bathe a child in a half-open tub.

Showerfold panels are flexible, crackproof, and shatter-proof. They move easily on spring-loaded rollers. Because of their material, the doors won't mildew or mold. The track is designed to be easier to clean than most of its predecessors.

There are also models with center openings and models to fit showers.

An enclosure like this need not be a permanent installation. One type now offered goes up with foam tape used to keep it tightly pressed into place in a way that does not mar the wall. You can take your tub enclosure with you when you move and still have no complaints from a landlord about holes in the wall.

30

Update Your Showerbaths

Add a shower attachment to a bathtub, build a new shower, or update a battered old one

You have some quite interesting options in improving a shower or adding a new one.

You can do something as simple as adding a telephone shower attachment to the plumbing of your present tub, thus turning it into a shower without cutting into a wall. You can transform a primitive metal stall shower into a quiet, lighted built-in one. You can go all the way and build a new shower, using tile-setting techniques shown in a previous chapter—or use the most modern seamless system, described later in this chapter.

For quicker results, still at moderate cost, you can install one of the modern circular units of reinforced plastic, following the steps shown.

The telephone shower first came to the attention of Americans when they met it while traveling in Europe—and found it a most welcome convenience. Apparently a Danish invention, it is now available in many versions all over the world, with American companies offering a number of types of these personal hand showers.

You can use a telephone shower either while you are sitting in the bathtub or in the ordinary way while standing up. The hand-fitted shower head can be directed at any angle you wish. It is especially good for shampooing or for bathing small children or, as one manufacturer suggests, bathing a pet. Since this device is easily controlled by the bather there is less than the usual need for a shower curtain.

A telephone shower can also be used as an addition to an existing shower arrangement. This add-on telephone shower means that short women and children can take a shower without getting their hair wet.

One company has a chrome-plated, rubber-lined hose with a shower head attached to a 24″ bar. The shower head slides up or down to any height needed. The angle of the spray can be adjusted with a finger, and the vertical bar doubles as a grab bar. One model has an adjustable spray which goes from needle hard to soft as you turn the collar of the head.

Adjusto faucets, which are tub-fillers as well as shower heads, provide a shower when in an upright position, can be partially lowered to provide a more comfortable shower for a child or invalid, and can be swung all the way down to fill the tub.

One of the nicest things you can do for your family in the shower department is provide water at a controlled temperature— guaranteed to produce neither instant gooseflesh nor scald. The mechanism called for is a special valve, sold under the name Temptrol. There are models for showers and others for use with tub-shower combinations.

Wherever the expense of automatic temperature control would not be justified, a problem-solver worth considering is a faucet that enables you to see the temperature of the water before you feel it. The Colortemp faucet has a push-pull acrylic dial. Turn it to the left until the aperture on the faucet shows full red and only the hottest water flows out. Turn it to a full blue color on the right and extremely cold water flows. Setting for moderate temperature, of course, is in the middle with both colors visible. All this simplifies pre-setting the temperature before turning on the faucet. This color system also works as a safety feature for children, who can understand the temperature settings easier with color than they can with letters.

You can not only incorporate some of the above fixtures in your shower-remodeling job, but you can work out a custom shower-head panel with an assortment of sprays at different heights. Some manufacturers sell shower accessories or complete shower-panels that can be fitted into a remodeling plan.

UPDATING AN OLD STALL SHOWER. An old stall shower is often dark, dank, drafty, not very pretty to look at—and inclined

Photo left

"Shower tower" with two heads is a home-improvement feature guaranteed to diminish domestic strife. Use the upper head for shampooing, lower for child or for woman with hair to protect from water, both for extra vigor.

Photo right

Telephone shower can be part of tower, as here, or installed as addition to any new or existing tub or shower. In addition to its showering virtues it is handy for rinsing the tub or the shower wall.

You can make your own combination of shower heads and shower and tub controls on a panel when remodeling a bathroom. Or use a factory-made combination like this one. Ceiling unit is light, heater, and fan all in one.

Photo left

Non-scald valve is equally an assurance against chill when water-line temperature changes suddenly because someone in the house has turned on a tap or flushed a toilet. Temptrol '76 is for shower; other models are for tub-showers.

Photo right

Color-coded fixture gives visual clue to temperature setting. And, unlike some modern bathroom devices, this one can be operated by a stranger without fumbling. Similar models are available for tub, shower, lavatory.

to go *boing-g-g* every time you bump it with an elbow.

Fortunately there are four improvements you can make in the old one you already have in your home or on the new one you're about to install. Each change will help. Combined they'll turn it into a shower cabinet that is solid, light, and warm.

The steps, shown in the accompanying photographs:

1. Pad the walls for solidity and quiet.

2. Add dome light to provide warmth and light which not only make the shower easier to use but get rid of dankness and darkness that encourage mold and fungus growths.

3. Frame and wall around the cabinet to give it a built-in appearance.

4. Install a glass door so you can throw away that annoying shower curtain which lets in drafts and encourages mildew.

To make the walls of a stall shower solid and quiet, pad them wherever you can. Scraps of batt-type fiberglass insulation are good and so are bits of insulation board

Install a ceiling light kit made for the purpose, or make your own from a heavy grade of flat Filon plastic. By using a hard-glass infrared bulb you can have heat as well as light.

Build in the stall shower by framing the opening with 2" x 4" lumber and covering with wall material to match the rest of the bathroom. Finish the opening to fit stock shower door.

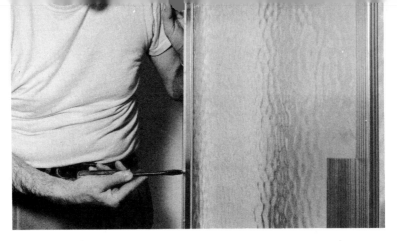

Hang shower door. This one is glass but others are made of rigid or flexible plastic. You can make your own door by using a sheet of flat or corrugated plastic.

NEW TYPES OF SHOWERS. The best of the modern stall showers are a vast improvement over the familiar metal ones. Many are made of fiberglass-reinforced plastic for a minimum of seams and an end to difficult maintenance problems. One of the round ones shown in the pictures solves the problem of how to put a new shower in limited space, or it can be used as a replacement for an old metal one too far gone to salvage.

Or consider building anything from a shower or tub to a whole room and then plastic coating it. This is made possible for the do-it-yourselfer by the same seamless flooring products discussed in the section on floors. They work on walls, counters and cabinets as well as they do underfoot.

The process for doing an entire room is essentially the same as for floors, but some of the techniques will vary because when you plastic-coat a shower—or a whole bathroom—you will have many vertical surfaces to deal with.

A seamless bathroom, or area within a bathroom, poured or rolled on in coats of plastic, will have no cracks or crevices or joints to harbor bacteria, soap scum, dirt, or mold. It will consist of a continuous surface you can clean with a cloth and still retain that new look after thousands of showers.

If you're doing over an old room, seamless plastic can be applied to whichever surfaces need refinishing. You can build a new shower of waterproof plywood with poured-concrete receptor and cover every inch of it, including the ceiling, with a continuous plastic coating.

Not all seamless pour-on materials are alike. Some are usable as they come from the can. Others must be mixed in just the right proportions, because they differ chemically. For an acrylic type, such as Flecto, you will find instructions in the chapter on seamless floors in an earlier section. If you choose a urethane-epoxy type such as Dur-A-Flex, you should proceed as follows. You will notice that some of the general hints given here apply equally to all types of seamless jobs.

HOW TO INSTALL A CIRCULAR SHOWER

Swan fiberglass-reinforced plastic circular shower is a deluxe built-in version of the free-standing shower shown in the how-to-do-it picture. The plastic door slides.

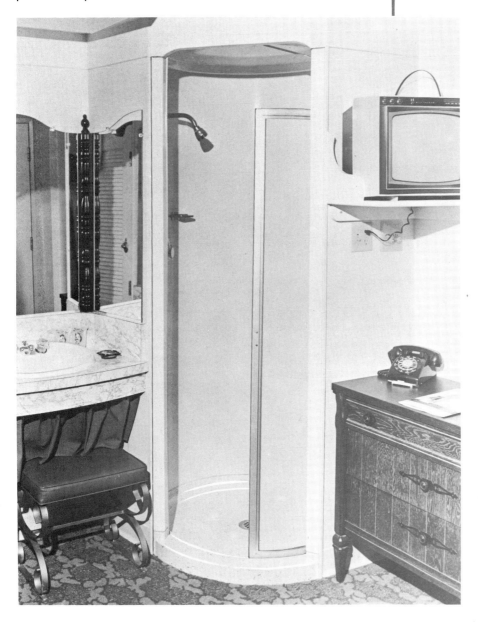

1.

2.

1. Free-standing 36" molded circular shower arrives in two cartons, weighs under 50 pounds including curtain.

2. Locate drain, using receptor as template. If a hole cannot be cut in the floor, place shower on wooden platform.

3. Assemble wall to receptor. Aluminum jambs fit on molded knobs and shower wall fits on a ledge on receptor.

4. Curved aluminum extrusion fits over the top edge of the wall and is held with a screw and nut at the rear.

3.

4.

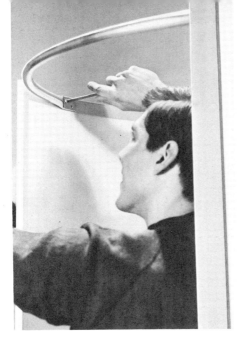

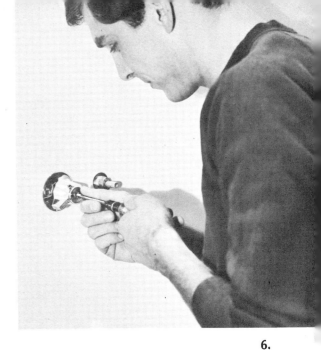

5.

6.

5. Four screws attach curtain rod to extrusion. Six others attach wall and jambs to receptor at bottom.

6. Holes for plumbing can be made with drill, saber saw, or even pocketknife. Ragged edges will be covered.

7. Install piping and screw showerhead into place. Place soap dish (included in kit) and fasten to wall.

7.

261

8. Once plumbing has been supplied, assembly of shower kit may take as little as fifteen minutes. Colors: yellow, blue.

1. Clean and prepare any old surface by scraping or sanding. If it's an old shower, soap scum, mildew, and water deposits will have to be removed by scrubbing with a commercial soap-removal product or kerosene. Cracks and corners may need to be cleaned with a sharp tool such as a screwdriver. If there is wax on the surface, use a commercial dewaxing product. A good finished job will depend on the throughness of preparation.

2. Mix the two-component epoxy that will form the base into which colored chips are broadcast. Work with adequate

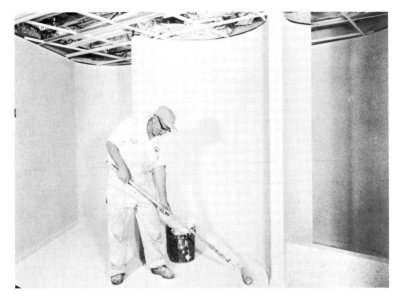

With availability of roll-on seamless plastic products, it's now feasible to make your bathroom walls and shower—and even tub if you like—of wood coated to form a continuous, impervious surface.

ventilation. This material is nonflammable and of low toxicity, but in an enclosed space such as a shower or small bathroom, the fumes may be irritating to eyes and lungs. Open all windows and doors or work with a face mask, especially if you know you are sensitive to plastic materials.

3. Base coat is white but you can tint it with Universal coloring in amounts up to six fluid ounces per gallon of epoxy. The flakes you will imbed in the surface come in many colors and you can use one or a combination of several. Spread a uniformly thin coat with a medium-nap roller. In doing a high wall or a ceiling an extension handle helps.

4. Within three to five minutes after applying the epoxy, spray on a fine mist of clean cool water. You can use a garden-type sprayer for a large area, or a small sprayer where the area is not large.

5. Immediately start broadcasting chips into the moistened epoxy coating. On a shower wall, throw them with an underhand pitching motion. Complete coverage is important. Once you've covered about 100 square feet, again spray on a fine water mist to be sure the chips are wet down and adhering to the surface. Avoid puddling on any horizontal surface. The entire area you are working with should be coated, misted, sown with chips and wet down. Try to work quickly. Complete the whole step within five minutes.

6. Let dry overnight, at 70 degrees or more if possible. If some of the chips are sticking out or forming bumps, smooth with sandpaper the next day.

7. Put on two or more protective coats of the clear urethane, number depending upon how much use the surface will get. Sand, and dust, between coats. One good thing about this product is that you can always add another coat or touch up a small area. Patching won't show. If a surface gets more use than you'd figured on, add another coat of plastic weeks or months later. For a shower, occasional wiping with a cloth dipped in water-ammonia solution restores the shining surface.

31

It's a Tub *and* a Shower

It does more than either—or both. It costs less. You can build it yourself

Which will you add to your home—tub or shower?

Why not both at the same time? Here is a combination you can build yourself. It can be adapted to the space you have, even to an area too small for a conventional tub.

Basically it is a tiled shower with its front built up about 14 inches to hold a bathful of water. It works as a tub, as a conventional shower, or as a sit-down or kneel shower.

Some of its versatility comes from its hinged-elbow fixture. Point the faucet down and it fills the tub. Swing it high and it gives a normal shower. Set it between and it becomes a sit-down shower, shampoo bowl, shower bath scaled to a small child, even doubles for a laundry tub.

The diagram shows, in cross-section, what to build. The photographs show how to perform the principal steps.

For sure watertightness, the tile that forms the tub is best set in cement mortar. The rest may be put on the easier way, with waterproof ceramic-tile cement.

Dimensions of the shower-tub can vary a good deal. The one shown in the photographs has proved to be of convenient size: about 30″ x 48″. The drain pipe can come through the floor at the center. For stopper, when used as a tub, obtain a dime-store flat rubber sink stopper.

Here's how the combination tub-shower fits into the end of an updated bathroom where space was too small for an ordinary tub. High side makes it a tub—but also prevents shower splash. Another good idea: give your bathroom a luminous plastic ceiling like this and add a red heat lamp for after-shower comfort.

Bring hot- and cold-water lines in on a side wall on 6" centers. End each with a ½" threaded nipple long enough to extend just beyond the surface of the tile. Height should be about 30" above the top of the low wall forming the front of the tub. Absolute minimum is 28¾" to prevent shower head from ever reaching water line, which would be contrary to plumbing codes.

Before spreading the mortar, put tile to soak in a pan of water. Soak just the tile that will be installed in mortar. Tile for mastic installation should be dry. Mortar, especially that for the walls, should be mixed quite stiff.

To prevent splash, you'll probably want to put a stub of a wall at the front, at least on the side opposite the head. The simplest thing is to make this one tile wide.

A variety of trim is offered for most kinds of ceramic tile. But you can avoid the problem of using it, just as was done with the tub-shower shown here.

Carry the sidewall tile to the ceiling and it will need no

266

As a shower this build-it-yourself combination has the triple advantage of roominess, high front to stop splash, adjustable-height shower head.

When you want a tub, swing down the faucet. You have a shampoo setup, too. The tub ledge is wide enough to sit on when the tub is used for a footbath.

trim. Finish the three edges that form the door opening with the tiny multicolored tiles that come mounted on cloth mesh. Cut them into suitable strips with a scissors.

On the larger tile you can make straight cuts by scribing with a glass cutter, then breaking the tile across a big finish nail. But a tile cutter is quicker; the dealer you buy your tile from will probably lend—or at least, rent—you one.

He should be able to supply a nipper too. You'll use that to nibble bits off the pieces of tile where they must fit around the drain and the water pipes. It's not difficult if you remember to take many small nips. You'll find additional tips on tile work in a previous chapter on just that subject.

If you want to spend more time than money, shop around for your tile. Consider using seconds, but look them over carefully. Some are nearly perfect, others pretty bad. For the shower in the pictures, seconds costing only 39 cents a square foot were used.

Although a door is neater, a curtain may be more convenient as well as cheaper for a shower-tub having as many uses as this one. The curtain and rings you see are standard store-bought items. The rod they hang on is a piece of ¾" Do-It-Yourself aluminum tubing.

HOW TO INSTALL TUB-SHOWER

1. Frame and box solidly with lumber or exterior plywood to a height of about 15". Continue up to ceiling with 2" x 4" studs not more than 16" apart to take sheetrock or other wall material.

2. Threaded end of drain-pipe stops an inch or so below floor level. Screw on lower part of shower drain. Do not bolt on upper section until the waterproof pan has been placed.

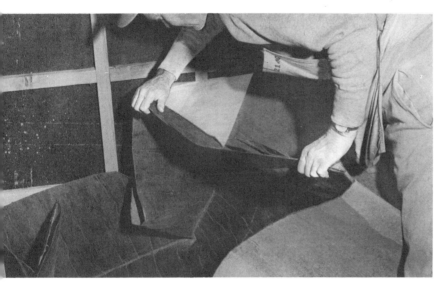

3. Waterproof pan may be plastic or—as here—reinforced laminated paper. Use type available and accepted locally. It should be big enough to come about 15″ up each wall.

4. Nail the pan in place around the top. Notch the framing slightly if necessary so that sheetrock will lap over it a little and fit without bulging. Bolt on the top of the drain.

269

5. Cover the area of the pan with fine mesh. This supplies reinforcing and, more important, gives the mortar something to stick to. Staple or nail it around the top.

6. Line the shower with ½" plasterboard. Waterproof by giving it a skim coat of ceramic-tile adhesive, "painting" it on with the unnotched edge of your tile-adhesive trowel. Seal cracks, joints, and point where plasterboard meets shower pan with this same adhesive.

7. Spread mortar on bottom of pan, sloping it slightly upward from drain to sides. Screed sticks lightly tacked in place will help. Pull them out after leveling the mortar. Premixed mortar, sold in sacks, is easiest to use.

8. Lay floor tile, then spread mortar on walls as high as the bottom of the plasterboard and place wall tile. Firm tile into place with hammer and block. All tile to go into mortar should be soaked thirty minutes first.

9. Then spread tile adhesive on walls and continue up. Complete the job with whatever type of trim you wish to use. Grout all the tilework and wipe clean as shown here.

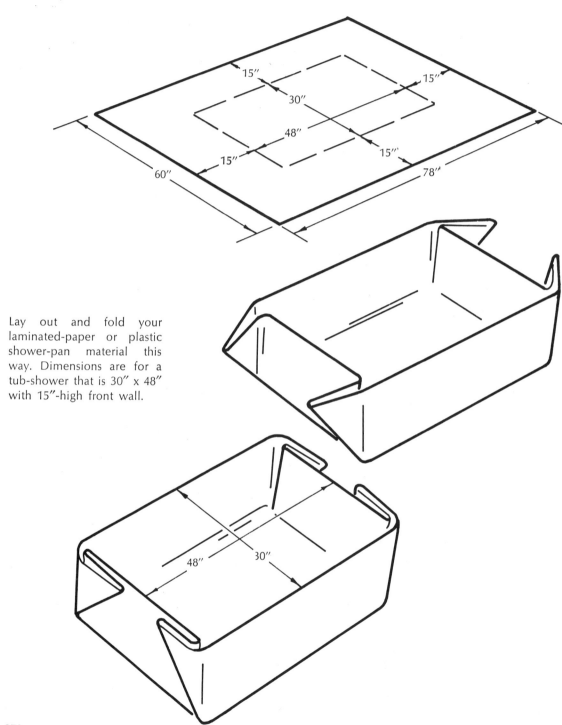

Lay out and fold your laminated-paper or plastic shower-pan material this way. Dimensions are for a tub-shower that is 30″ x 48″ with 15″-high front wall.

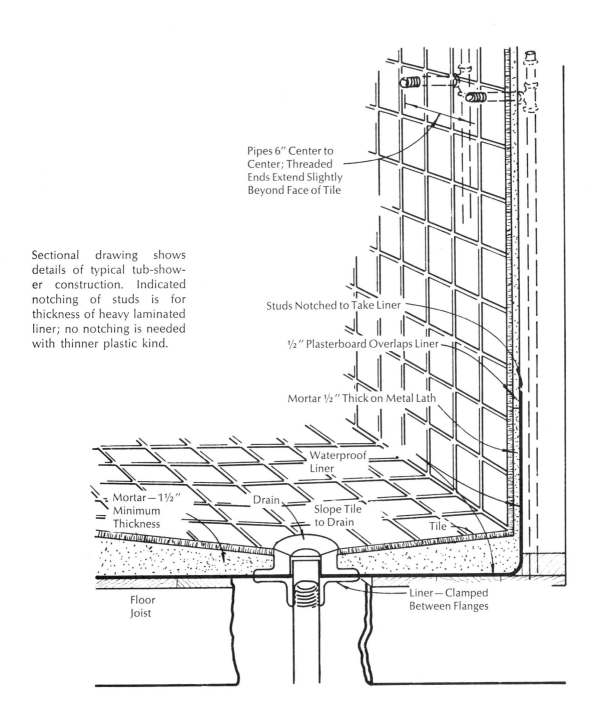

Pipes 6″ Center to Center; Threaded Ends Extend Slightly Beyond Face of Tile

Sectional drawing shows details of typical tub-shower construction. Indicated notching of studs is for thickness of heavy laminated liner; no notching is needed with thinner plastic kind.

Studs Notched to Take Liner

½″ Plasterboard Overlaps Liner

Mortar ½″ Thick on Metal Lath

Waterproof Liner

Mortar — 1½″ Minimum Thickness

Drain

Slope Tile to Drain

Tile

Floor Joist

Liner — Clamped Between Flanges

32

Bathroom Heat, Light, and Ventilation

Brighter lighting, instant heat, more effective ventilation are three comforts that demand priority in bathroom updating

With the electrical devices now offered, you can add light, heat, and ventilation piecemeal or at a single swoop.

To solve the heat problem you can install a fan-assisted ceiling heater, an infrared radiant unit, or an inconspicuous but powerful small heater that tucks into the wall between the studs and starts delivering warm air the moment you turn it on.

Where space is at a premium a little heater like the one shown fills the requirements by taking up only a 4″ x 14″ wall opening. The finished grille size is 5″ wide by 15¼″ long. The only part that protrudes into the room is the grille. An additional feature of this heater is its versatility: add little plugs that come with it and it changes from 1,000-watt operation to 1,500 or 2,000.

You can have a wall thermostat if you wish, or the usual on-off switch. If, for any reason, someone blocks the flow of heat with furniture or clothing, your house won't burn. The heater has a safety cut-off thermostat.

The rough-in box comes in two pieces. The top section can be slipped through a 4″ x 14″ opening between studs. After the bottom section is put into place, the top section easily slides down to make up the completed rough-in box. The heating unit can then be snapped into place in the box.

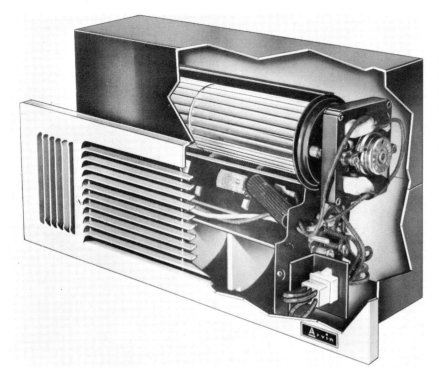

Only the white grill shows when this heater is tucked into your bathroom wall. Mechanism includes blower, safety cut-off, and removable plug at lower right for changing capacity.

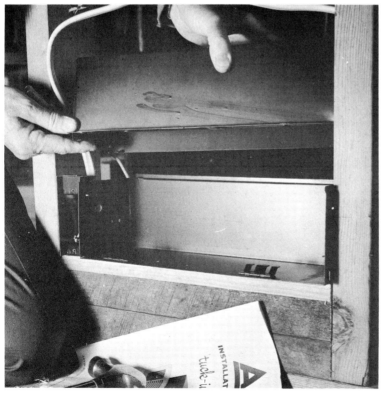

In existing construction the top section of the rough-in box is slipped through the 4″ x 4″ opening between studs. After bottom section is in place, top section slides down to form completed rough-in box. Heating unit then goes into box.

This heater operates silently enough so it won't wake up sleepers if it is used in the middle of the night or early in the morning. Another feature—edges of the heater stay cool, keeping the adjacent wall from becoming dangerously hot.

SPOT HEATING WITH LAMPS. If spot heating, rather than area heating, is what your bathroom needs for maximum comfort, the easiest way to supply this may be with an infrared heat lamp or a bank of them, aimed at a spot where a wet bather stands while using a towel. A heat lamp is also a quick hair-dryer.

You can add a heat lamp by putting an extra fixture in your present ceiling or by putting in a "false" translucent ceiling. The photographs show how this can be done.

Another method of installing an extra heat lamp is to buy a swivel-type fixture for the bulb and place it high enough on a wall so it will aim down or can be aimed at the tub or shower area. Use a hard-glass lamp that won't shatter if splashed with cold water.

If your bathroom needs better ventilation and a fan is the answer, you can add quick heat and extra light at the same time with units like those offered by Nutone. One is a ventilating fan

Photo left

For new construction, the two-piece box may be installed in one piece at rough-in time. Junction box is already attached, so there is no separate wiring required. Plaster or dry wall frame is an integral part of the rough-in box.

Photo right

Single heat lamp in homemade fixture is an economical way to add spot heat to a chilly bathroom. You might also install one over the spot where a baby is bathed or, in the kitchen or dining area, where food must be kept hot.

paired with a couple of infrared bulbs. The fan in the other is accompanied by a larger heating element and a diffusing light fixture.

Installation consists primarily of providing a hole in the ceiling to fit the box and grill, and connecting the vent opening to the outdoors by means of standard 4″ round metal duct. Wiring must be run to a suitable switch and to a source of power, of course.

Typical of the switches offered for devices of this kind is one for the heater-light-ventilator. It fits into a double-gang switch box and provides an ordinary toggle switch for turning the light on and off independently. A second switch has four positions to handle all possible combinations of ventilator and heater: ventilator alone, heater alone, both on, and both off.

To encourage use of a pre-set combination of these things or to discourage leaving the device on long after the room is out of use, an additional time switch can be added. This fits an ordinary switch box and controls power entering the selector box. It is set for any number of minutes up to sixty by the person entering the bathroom. It automatically turns off if the user forgets to do so when departing.

Photo left

Electrical part of heat-lamp installation consists of ordinary octagon box and porcelain socket, fed by wall-switch-controlled cable. Mounting bracket cut from plywood scrap places socket at proper height for dropped ceiling.

Photo right

Plastic ceiling section is a piece of white Filon. Two edges are framed for stiffness, the other two edges resting on ledges nailed to wall. Hacksaw blade in saber saw is used to cut out circular opening for hard-glass ruby heat lamp.

Heater-ventilator contains a pair of 250-watt infrared lamps, usable alone or together. The fan exhausts 70 cubic feet of air per minute. In triple unit, also made by NuTone, light, fan-driven heater, and fan ventilator are separately controlled.

33

Build Your Own Mini-Sauna

With a Solo Sauna Door and a 3′ x 3′ closet or corner you can have a sauna

Cost of a typical sauna bath can run up into the thousands of dollars—even more if you must add a whole new room to house it.

But a mini-sauna that you can build into your home for $500 or $600 can give you all the benefits of a big, expensive one. The difference is that only one person, or possibly two, can use it at a time.

A sauna is quite different from a steam bath. (You can have one of those in your home, too, if you wish. An electrically operated attachment is available to build into a shower.) A sauna produces oven-dry heat that millions of devoted users, mostly Finns, believe religiously is of incalculable benefit to health and to spiritual as well as physical well-being. Finns have been using saunas for centuries, so bathing by heat is no innovation. You sit in your sauna and bake, and sweat, for periods of a few minutes to the better part of an hour at temperatures ranging from 180 degrees to somewhat above the boiling point of water—believe it or not.

You can create this personal sauna of yours anywhere in your home that there's a 3′ square of space to spare.

All you have to do is build a mini-room or line an existing closet. And install a door.

The door's the secret of it all. It's called a Solo Sauna door, and it's made by Viking Sauna Company. It's a 2' x 6'8" solid-core Philippine mahogany slab door with heating unit, control, timer, window, and light fixture built into it. It comes complete with hinges and catches, ready to connect to an ordinary 20-ampere electric outlet that you must have or provide beside the door about a foot from the floor.

Whether you build a new closet or line an old one for your sauna, it should be 31½" to 48" wide and 34½" to 36" front to back. Make ceiling height 74" to 84". These are all inside dimensions. Make your sauna the minimum size and it will heat up in twenty-five minutes. The maximum size will take an hour of pre-heating.

Viking Sauna Company will sell its door as part of complete freestanding package prefabbed for home assembly. Or you can purchase the door alone, to build into your home as shown in the how-to picture sequence.

Insulate walls and ceilings with full-thick mineral wool. To fit the door the floor should be ¾″ plywood over 2″ x 4″ sleepers. Carpet with sisal or Ozite indoor-outdoor.

To conform to traditional sauna seating, build a bench about 15¾″ wide and 32″ high across the back of the tiny room. Provide a step 8″ high. Make these of 2″ x 2″ and 2″ x 4″ redwood.

For maximum benefit from your minimum sauna, don't overdo its use. Even Finns don't sauna-cook themselves every day or for long periods. Try twice a week, with each session consisting of two ten-minute periods followed by cool showers or tub or pool plunges. Top off the session with a rest period before dressing.

You may even find out how the Finns got so tough.

HOW TO INSTALL A SAUNA

1. Unless you are using an existing closet, frame your sauna space with 2″ x 4″ studs. Add either 1″ x 3″ horizontal furring or 2″ x 4″ blocking as shown here. Space 2″ x 4″'s either 16″ or 24″ to take standard insulation.

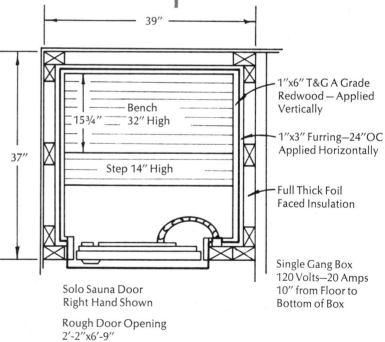

39″

37″

Bench
15¾″   32″ High

Step 14″ High

1″x6″ T&G A Grade
Redwood—Applied
Vertically

1″x3″ Furring—24″OC
Applied Horizontally

Full Thick Foil
Faced Insulation

Single Gang Box
120 Volts—20 Amps
10″ from Floor to
Bottom of Box

Solo Sauna Door
Right Hand Shown

Rough Door Opening
2′-2″x6′-9″

2.

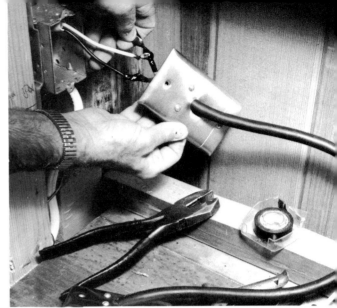

3.

2. For quick heating and economy of operation, insulate the sauna space thoroughly. Use full-thick, foil-lined fiberglass, tacked or stapled into place. Frame the ceiling in the same way, putting in a double layer of insulation if space permits.

3. The cable and two metal cover plates come with Solo Sauna door. You connect the cable to an ordinary 115-volt outlet (fused at 20 amps) beside the door and to the box in the door itself. Electrical requirement is 1,700 watts.

4. Line the sauna—walls and ceiling—with smooth, unfinished lumber. Kiln-dried redwood is the usual choice. This is Georgia-Pacific's saw-textured 1″ x 6″ paneling, with smooth face exposed inside the sauna, textured face outside.

5. Door comes with hinges and bullet catches already installed, for quick hanging. Fasten on the door handles and install a step and bench of redwood 2″ x 4″s, carpet with Ozite indoor-outdoor— and your sauna is ready to use.

4.

5.

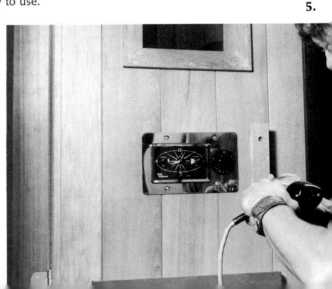

Unless you have an icy Finnish lake or a swimming pool handy, a sauna is most properly used in conjunction with a shower. So a location near a bathroom is preferable. Best of all is right in the bathroom, as mirrored here.

PART VI

Modernize Your Kitchen

34

Your Kitchen Tomorrow

Free-wheel as you attack kitchen improvement. Today anything goes—if it works for your family

There is little doubt that your kitchen could stand improving. Consider these two factors:

1. As the work center of your home, the kitchen is too important to neglect.

2. As the mechanical center of your house, it holds most of the things that wear out or that become obsolete as better devices are developed.

By the same token, there is a great deal to be said for keeping your kitchen up to new-home standards year by year through a series of home improvements. This will interfere less with its use than all-out remodeling at long intervals will. It probably will be less of a chore and far more economical; and at worst it will soften the economic blow by spreading the cost over a longer period.

The essential rule for this piecemeal remodeling through a series of lesser improvements is: begin with a knowledge of what the newest things are for kitchens of today and tomorrow, an understanding of how they can be used effectively, an appreciation of which ones are worthwhile for your particular kitchen. Visualize, and preferably commit to paper, the campaign of which each improvement is to be a part.

You can be far less doctrinaire about your kitchen plan than architects and home economists used to say you should be. Don't concern yourself about whether yours is properly called a U plan or an L or a corridor or a one-wall and whether it uses up every available cubic inch of space.

A kitchen is a very personal thing. As long as it pleases, and works for, the people who are going to use it—anything goes.

The modest kitchen planned and built by the author for his own home, for instance, is notable for the things it doesn't have. There is no linoleum or vinyl or other resilient flooring. There are no hinged cabinet doors, in fact no above-counter cabinets at all. There are no light fixtures and there are no windows you can open or see through. Also lacking is any wall surface that is painted and would, consequently, require repainting someday.

These usual things were not omitted to be arbitrary. It was just that it seemed better to do what each of them does in other ways that would be more appropriate to this particular house and its people.

The floor is slate, to make it continuous with the dining-area floor and the living-room hearth. The below-counter doors slide, so that they will be out of the way even when open, and so that they could conveniently be made of flat Filon plastic with its washable, built-in color that never needs painting. A light and airy kitchen was made possible by having no cupboards above the counters, and the lost storage space is not missed because there's a walk-in pantry instead.

With the kitchen side of the house very close to a neighbor, a common condition in the charming but crowded village of Carmel, California, it seemed best to get daylight through windows of translucent plastic instead of glass. For its view, the kitchen looks the other way—through an opening to the two-story window wall of the living room, which faces south.

Artificial light is from invisible fixtures. A section of the kitchen ceiling 2′ wide and 12′ long is made of white plastic with six ordinary porcelain sockets mounted above to take 60- or 100-watt bulbs.

Ventilation is provided through an above-the-range fan and a large sliding glass door in the adjacent dining area.

Walls that did not, and will not, need painting were achieved by continuing the rough-redwood paneling of the entry-way and the dining room into the kitchen. Other wall surfaces in the room are Peg Board of the kind having a permanent and colorful melamine-plastic surface. Such walls take hooks and shelf supports and other fixtures and so are highly functional.

Whether or not any of these ideas will work for your own kitchen, they are worth noting because of what they say about the kitchen of the 1970s. It should be designed purely for its job and the tastes of its owners. It can ignore all preconceptions of what a kitchen is supposed to look like.

One of the best reasons for being free-wheeling in your approach to kitchen improvement is that only then will you be able to take full and effective advantage of today's enormous choice of new materials and new pieces of kitchen equipment.

You'll be tempted by such things as these: a microwave oven, priced below $500, that will cook a meal right on a serving plate of plastic or paper or fine china in a few minutes; a device that mashes and presses a week's trash into a compact rectangular bundle encased in a plastic bag; a range-top, with no visible burners, that looks like a slab of white marble; even a computer system that will take over calorie counting and meal planning if you can afford to spend $10,000 and send your wife to a special two-week course in programming (included in the price).

Maybe you'll want to remodel around the appliances you now have, while waiting for such things-to-come as the ultrasonic dishwasher that has no moving parts to break down.

If you are reacting from the severity of the kitchens of the recent past, you may want to go for the homey look. Patterned carpet shows spills less, gives comfortable feel along with actual comfort underfoot, though you probably will prefer less pattern than this if your kitchen is small. This carpet, foam-backed for softness, is Ozite Country Fare. An easily achieved alternate to these carved cabinet doors is plain old or new plywood ones with Filon Decorator Carvings glued on and antiqued.

To give easy access to a sink for two people at once, put a jog in a counter. Scenic panel above sink is washable plastic - finished Marlite, placed to give the pleasant illusion of a view window where one was not possible before.

Yours may be one of the families with a romantic attachment to the past. You can have a little of both worlds. There's a huge, friendly cookstove just like Grandma's, but now it uses electricity or gas. One model has a wood-burning compartment. You can update with fixtures that use electricity in old-fashioned-looking kerosene lamps. Even the braided rug of the past is available with a vinyl coating that gives it today's practicality with yesterday's charm.

Whatever you plan for the kitchen in your present home, it is unlikely you'll settle for the hospital-white kitchen of a few years ago or the dirt-gathering inefficient room which your female ancestors took for granted.

Washable, durable wall, floor, and counter surfaces are now do-it-yourself materials. Old appliances and cabinets can be updated with new surfaces and hardware. A kitchen that is still basically satisfactory can be made more useful with one or two major changes and a number of small renovation projects you'll find throughout this book.

You may want to start by considering a few of the appliances that are a part of the kitchen revolution.

A large kitchen can become both multi-purpose and a modern stepsaver through division into two or three separate areas. Here a fireplace-divider creates a small sitting room, at left; working kitchen, at right; and dining area, behind the divider. In a major home-improvement project, gaining dining space in a kitchen often permits adding old dining-room space to living room where it is badly needed.

Do you have the problem of trying to turn a small, dark space into an attractive kitchen? Use the highly adaptable ideas shown here. Luminous ceiling, with dimmer control on wall, makes the kitchen light. Yellow cabinets make it bright. Kitchen carpeting makes it warm and comfortable. Use of Marlite wormy chestnut paneling makes walls washable. For unity, which keeps the kitchen from seeming as small as it is, wall, ceiling, and floor materials all continue into adjoining room.

Unused corner of a kitchen —or it could be another room—can be turned into a planning center, useful also for bill-paying, letter-writing. Self-edged desk top of plastic laminate, applied as described in next chapter, contrasts with wood-grain walls of Georgia-Pacific's Handy Panel, hardboard pre-drilled for hanging things.

OVENS. A poll of housewives showed that the most hated job in the kitchen was cleaning the oven, so it is fair to say that a self-cleaning oven is a must for any kitchen that would call itself modern. This cleaning job can now be done by the oven itself, more efficiently than any woman could do it.

You'll have a choice of types. An electric or gas oven that uses the pyrolytic, or high-heat, cleaning method costs about a hundred dollars more than the ordinary oven. During a three-hour cleaning cycle, which you set by a special clock, the oven burns off stains, grease, and spills from all interior surfaces including the racks, window and light. Cost of each cleaning session averages about a dime, and during the cleaning process the oven is locked. Efficient insulation within the oven walls keeps the kitchen cool even though cleaning is accomplished at very high temperatures.

Newer on the market are ovens, both electric and gas, which do not use this high-heat method. They "clean as they bake" by a process called a continuous cleaning or catalytic system. A range using this type of oven-cleaning process will cost up to $50 more than the usual range. This system is not as effective as the high-heat method. Furthermore, the catalytic finish on the oven interior may be harmed if you use strong cleaners or detergents

292

Three-in-one range top has special appeal for anyone doing a major kitchen-improvement project. Electric charbroiling grill is made feasible by ventilating device in center, converts to griddle in seconds. Burners, left, are of the new ceramic type. Jenn-Air Corporation makes it.

If your kitchen-improvement plans include a built-in range and there's no space for both range top and separate oven, a drop-in combination may be the answer. Many manufacturers offer ranges of this kind.

This wall-suspended electric grill can be a quick addition to a kitchen in need of added facilities. Fasten it to an exterior wall, vent it right through to carry off smoke and odors, and connect it to a source of electric power. Accessories convert it to a French fryer, rotisserie, or nonstick griddle.

on it. It doesn't cost an extra dime for each cleaning session in this type of oven, nor does the oven have to be out of use for several hours while the cleaning process is going on, as it does in the pyrolytic method.

Your choice will depend upon how much you want to spend and upon the type of guarantee offered. Ovens using self-cleaning methods not only cost more but may not last as long as the twenty-year-old range you're thinking of replacing.

REFRIGERATORS, too, are changing. One type features an ice maker that controls the size of ice cubes. Many have automatic ice cube and ice water dispensers. Most have a choice of colors and unusual decorator surfaces. You can have a "mod" refrigerator in wild colors or patterns, one with a front of exotic wood, or one that matches the wallpaper and kitchen curtains. Some refrigerators have panels that slide in and out so you can change the color and surface of the door front, whenever you tire of its looks.

Refrigerators come in many sizes. New types of insulation make it possible to get more inside space for food storage and less outside bulk. There are huge walk-in combination freezer-refrigerators, slim models that are only a foot or so wide, and tiny models which don't look like refrigerators at all. They slip under a counter or fasten on a wall, have exterior surfaces that resemble fine wood, and sometimes have wheels so they can be moved from one room to another.

Do you like to prepare refrigerator meals or freezer-foods in advance? Then you may wish to add an accessory in the freezer department. It's called "Seal-A-Meal." This appliance heat-seals meals in plastic pouches so that air is removed and food can be stored safely in a freezer until needed.

CABINETS are an expensive and vital part of any kitchen, with possible exception of one in which a pantry takes their place. There never seem to be enough of them. You can avoid the expense of replacing them by remodeling the old door surfaces or by dressing up the old cabinets with new fronts.

Cabinet fronts which are dented, gouged, varnished, or painted are good candidates for antiquing. The more damage the better, as explained in the section on do-it-yourself antiquing. This process is easy for an amateur to use and is an economical way to rescue old surfaces that seem hopeless.

Another method of saving the well-built old cabinets is to dress them up with new surfaces of plastic-laminate, or wall-covering material. They could also be renewed with a few coats of the same seamless plastic material used on floors. New hardware is a help in updating old kitchen doors and drawers.

It's quicker and far less costly to fix up old cabinets that still work than to tear everything out and start over. In many older homes the cabinet work is better than any you could buy to replace it. With any leftover energy you can add a few cabinets in a vacant area such as a dead spot above the stove or refrigerator. Another job worth doing is to add shelves, partitions, and sections to large cupboards in order to store trays, pot lids, food, and gadgets efficiently without stacking them or wasting a lot of space.

FLOORS nearly always need renovating, even in kitchens only a few years old. Today the big choice is between carpet and a resilient flooring material such as vinyl or vinyl-asbestos.

There's no getting around the fact that the kitchen floor is a target for grease and stubborn stains that are not going to come out with the swish of a damp cloth. You can, however, now get carpet highly suited to kitchen use. Nylon, olefin, and acrylic fiber

Woodgrain surfaces seen here, as well as the self-edged counter tops, are done in Formica. How to work with plastic laminates for kitchen improvement is detailed in the next chapter.

materials not only resist most stains but they take to hard scrubbing without losing color or design. If you choose a tapestry, paisley, or mod pattern, the kitchen carpet will conceal any really stubborn stains and clean well with detergent and water.

One good solution to the kitchen carpeting problem is to use self-stick olefin squares that come with their own built-in adhesive, go down quickly, can be rearranged at any time to hide damage or wear. A square or two can easily be replaced or doused in the kitchen sink for a thorough scrubbing.

There are self-stick squares available in vinyl and vinyl-asbestos, too. Or you can now tackle a floor renovation in which you use wide sheet material, following the instructions in the chapter on how to lay vinyl flooring.

PLAN before you start. Remember, the most expensive thing a kitchen remodeler can do is to change the plumbing and wiring. Save money and energy, if possible, by fitting new appliances into the same locations as their predecessors.

Go over your present kitchen. Maybe a few small changes will make a big improvement. Adding a sheet of Peg Board can turn a bare wall into a storage area. A dead corner can become a small kitchen-office.

Consider adding an appliance that provides extra counter space at the same time. A dishwasher could have a cutting-board top or a ceramic-tile surface to take hot dishes. If you need more hot water in the kitchen, think about adding a counter-top water heater and surfacing it with a material to match the rest of the kitchen counters. One homeowner added a counter-height refrigerator and used a slab of marble for the top surface to give his wife the pastry-rolling surface she'd always wanted.

One trend in kitchen planning is to go out of the old kitchen and look for other areas in the house where a mini-kitchen could be added. Recreation room, porch, and study are all candidates for a counter, an extra plug-in or two for electric appliances, and a miniature refrigerator.

Imagination and plenty of planning are the clues to getting good results in the kitchen renovation. Changes made on paper won't cost you a thing. Concentrate on the small jobs you can do yourself, and don't forget that sawdust, plaster, and paint are a bigger nuisance in kitchen updating than they are in any other part of the house.

You might start by adding a mini-kitchen somewhere else in the house. Then you can use *it* while you make bigger changes in the main kitchen.

35

New Tops For Old Counters

Change your kitchen environment by resurfacing with plastic laminates, now immensely varied and easier to work with

The basic material for covering kitchen counter tops is plastic laminate, such as Formica. In improving your kitchen, it is very likely that you will be working with laminates, as described in this chapter, or with one or more of the alternate toppers covered in the next chapter.

In addition to the familiar plain colors and patterns, today's laminates come in such surprises as rustic weathered pine, white or green leather, oak woodgrains in muted color tones of green, blue, and red. Use them for both countertops and such vertical surfaces as cabinet doors where surfaces get hard wear and need frequent cleaning.

As well as in standard sheet form, plastic laminates can be purchased in complete countertop shape, called post-formed. For about $5 a lineal foot you get a complete countertop, seamless, including the coved backsplash, ready to be dropped onto existing base cabinets.

Usually, though, you will be working with the sheet material, covering horizontal and vertical surfaces separately. You can obtain laminates in sizes up to 5' x 12', so that almost any installation you are likely to make can be seamless.

Just how you will do the job will depend upon whether the front edge is to be covered with a molding strip of some sort. You may prefer a self-edging method instead. If you do edge with laminate, do this before applying the laminate to the main surface. The photographs show how to do it.

Edges and top of this table are covered with plastic laminate, applied as described in this chapter. Note provision of electric outlet and storage place for coffee-pot and other appliances. Floor is cork.

Close-up view of same dining table shows self-edging —and a surprise feature. In open position, table reveals two-burner electric range top for at-table cooking of anything from pancakes to sukiyaki. Necessary safety provision for such an installation is switch control for range that automatically cuts current when top closes.

Matching Formica sink counter and cabinet doors give this kitchen clean lines and harmony. Doors lift out so they can be damp-washed on a flat surface. By using two different colors of laminate, one on each side, the cabinet doors can be reversed to change the color scheme of the kitchen. Simple inexpensive finger indents are all the hardware needed.

Plastic laminate, with extensive use of self-edging, played a large part in this economical but attractive kitchen - improvement project. Matte-finish Formica was used. Old cabinets, with new doors of Douglas fir plywood, were given a decorative touch with molding and old - fashioned door-knobs for handles. Hinges on cabinets are spring-loaded to prevent open-door hazards. Cake box is antique. Milk-glass light fixtures, vinyl-asbestos floor tiles, and window shades are new.

Counter for kitchen, or elsewhere, gains versatility when alternate surfaces are provided. This counter, edged and surfaced with white Formica where a smooth surface was wanted, has small sections of glass tile, called tesserae, in shades of green. To apply such tiles, which come in foot-square sheets, peel off backing paper, glue in place, and grout. To accent the green, in this counter, a few individual tiles were chosen at random, pulled out before adhesive set, and replaced by a red or yellow tile.

HOW TO APPLY PLASTIC LAMINATE

1. PREPARE THE SURFACE. Remove the old surface material, scrape off old adhesive as far as possible, and sandpaper the surface to make it smooth and clean. An old counter top that is rotted or delaminated or otherwise unsound should be replaced or covered with plywood or particle board.

Even a new surface or a sound old one should be inspected for dents or voids. Any irregularities will telegraph through and affect the smoothness of the result. For this reason, rough, unsanded plywood is not suitable.

2. CUT THE LAMINATE. Keep cutting to a minimum by designing any new counter top or table to fit available sheet sizes. There are many ways to cut plastic laminate. Choose one or more of the following, depending upon the shop equipment you happen to own.

A utility knife equipped with a tempered high-carbon-steel blade is the handiest tool for many cuts. As the photographs show, this is a score-and-break method, so it will work easily only for comparatively short cuts.

Circular power saws with fine-toothed blades cut laminates easily. Any blade not intended for cutting hard plastics or metal will dull quickly, however. To avoid chipping, make the cut so that the teeth are cutting into the decorative side of the plastic. With a portable circular saw, this means with decorative side down.

An electric saber saw with a hard-steel blade is ideal for making cutouts, as for sinks, and can also be used for straight cuts of laminate sheets. Cut with the good side down. (This is difficult to do in the instance of sink cutouts made after cementing plastic to counter top, so don't bother. Any chipping will be covered by the sink rim.)

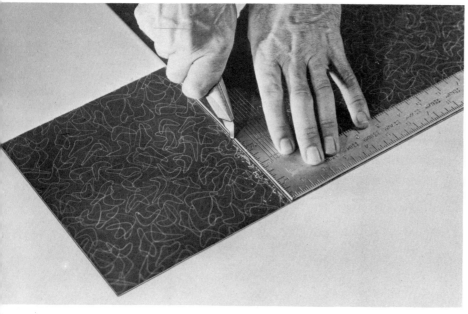

Use a tempered high-carbon-steel blade in a utility knife to get clean, true edges on plastic laminate. Score surface lightly with point of blade, then more firmly and deeply. Break sharply upward. This score-and-break method is especially useful where a curve or intricate shape must be cut.

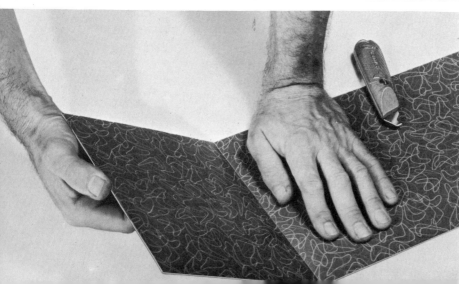

Cutting with a fine-toothed handsaw should be done with the good side of the plastic up and with the saw held at a low angle to minimize chipping. A small metal-cutting handsaw with replaceable blades is useful for straight cuts and excellent for making cut-outs, if you lack power equipment.

Plastic not yet glued down can be cut with a tin shears, but cut oversize to allow for chipping that may occur. Cut with decorative side up.

With all cuts, support the laminate firmly as close to the line of cut as possible. Allow about ⅛″ of extra material as a margin of safety. You will trim this off later.

3. APPLY THE ADHESIVE. Stop first, though, and read the safety warnings on the can. Many a home-improver, amateur or experienced pro, has destroyed a kitchen or a house by ignoring these precautions.

Like other lacquer-solvent products, contact cement will burn and its fumes can explode if they meet a flame or even a tiny spark. Of course, this means no smoking, no fires, no pilot lights burning. It also means you should unplug any electrical appliance, such as a refrigerator, that can produce a spark when its motor starts.

Equally important is ventilation, for the good of your lungs and eyes as well as for fire safety.

For vertical surfaces, such as cupboard doors that cannot easily be taken down and areas being self-edged, apply contact cement with an animal-bristle brush.

Use a natural-bristle brush to apply contact cement to an edge. Since brush coat will be thin and edges are often porous, two or even three coats may be needed. You can use this method to apply wood trim.

For small areas, or for lack of a notched metal trowel, homemade wooden paddle may be used for spreading contact cement. Notches control quantity of cement used, desirable even for a small repair job.

A brush or a makeshift wooden paddle may be used for horizontal surfaces, but the usual applicator is a small metal trowel or spreader with notched edge. Get one when you buy your contact cement. The notches control the amount of adhesive you apply, so you automatically get the right quantity.

It was the development of contact cement, by the way, that turned the Formica kind of product into something for any of us to use. Formerly, ordinary wood glues were used, water-resistant ones around sinks of course, and they work fine. But they must be clamped or sandbagged elaborately while the glue is setting.

Spread a coat of contact cement on the back of the laminated-plastic sheet. Immediately apply a similar coat on the wood surface to which it is to be glued. Be sure that you get complete coverage on both surfaces. Allow the cement to dry. About thirty to forty minutes is usually long enough and anything up to about two hours should be safe.

The surface is tacky, but not wet. Test it by lightly pressing a bit of kraft or wrapping paper against it. The paper should come away without lifting any of the cement. If you are delayed and don't get around to bonding the surfaces within two hours, you can reactivate the cement by applying an additional thin coat to each surface. Let this dry, too.

304

A bare wood surface may be so porous that much of the cement will sink in. You will see dull spots as the cement dries. Such a condition calls for an extra coat. A really first-class job requires that both surfaces have a heavy, glossy coat. Flakeboard, hardwood, and the plastic laminate are comparatively nonporous.

4. APPLY THE LAMINATE. When the two cemented surfaces touch, the cement bonds immediately. *No adjustment of position is possible.* It is extremely important to position the sheet precisely before the two glue surfaces touch.

The best method of positioning the laminate is to cut a heavy sheet of brown wrapping paper into several pieces. Put these on the wood surface so they overlap each other and completely cover the glued area. Place the laminate on top of the sheet of paper and adjust it for perfect fit. Move the first piece of paper out a few inches at a time, gently pressing the laminate to the wood surface as you go. Then remove the other pieces of paper one at a time.

When laminating a very large sheet to a long counter, try to impress a helper into service. He can hold one end of the sheet of laminate above the surface while you position it from the other end.

Accidents do happen. If you inadvertently let the laminate sheet grab hold before it is in the right position, there is still hope. Dump or brush lacquer thinner under the laminate and force the two surfaces apart a little at a time.

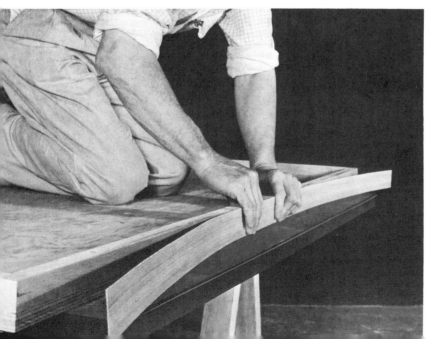

Press self-edging laminate strip into place and then beat with a rubber mallet or a hammer and padded block of wood. This operation should be completed and the edging trimmed flush with the top surface before contact cement is applied.

Wrapping - paper technique is a lifesaver when placing plastic laminate. Gently cover dry adhesive-coated surface with two or more overlapping sheets of paper. Drop laminate into precise position wanted, then pull out paper one at a time.

5. PUT ON PRESSURE. Once the sheet is in place apply heavy pressure to the surface. Start in the center and roll toward the edges. Be sure to roll every square inch of the surface. A 3″ hand roller provides the heaviest concentration of pressure. A rolling pin is a help, too.

For critical work, such as edging, use a rubber mallet or a hammer and padded block of wood to get the best bond. If you fail to get a good bond in some area, you can reactivate the cement with heat. Use a heat lamp or an ordinary light bulb, not flame. Warm the area, then press the two materials together, maintaining pressure until they have reactivated only within about the first three days.

If you have a joint that hasn't adhered perfectly, proceed much as with the disaster mentioned earlier. Apply a solvent such as lacquer thinner or one recommended by the maker of the contact cement. Force it under the joint with a small brush or squirt it

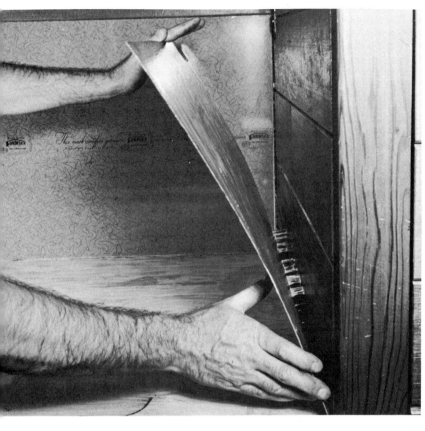

If small areas are being done or if surface to be laminated is vertical, wrapping paper may not be needed. Fit sheet carefully at one corner, then at rest of edge before letting more of it touch the surface.

in with an oil can. Peel back the material slightly as you go. Then you can reapply cement and go through the gluing process again in the same area. Roll the joint firmly and thoroughly.

6. FINISH THE EDGES. Satisfactory self-edging or edge-bonding may require first building up the thickness of the edge to ½″ by nailing strips 1½″ or 2″ wide or ¾″ particle board, plywood, or lumber to the underside of the exposed edge. Sandpaper until the strip and original edge form a flat, smooth surface.

Cut a strip of laminate slightly wider than the edge to be covered.

Apply two coats of contact cement to the wood edge and one to the back of the laminate.

After adhesive has dried, put the strip into place so that it is at least as high as all the points at the top surface of the counter. Roll and beat.

Then trim flush with the surface, using a block plane and hand file unless you have a router with a flush-trimming bit suitable for use with plastic laminate. A pair of bits—one for flush trimming, one for beveling edges—can often be rented, along with a router if needed.

Trimming the edge of the surface sheet of laminate is done in much the same manner. But file this final edge to a bevel, and then finish with fine sandpaper, preferably mounted on a sanding block. This will give a velvety-soft rounded edge.

An alternative to self-edging is metal molding. It is made in various widths for this purpose, commonly comes with suitable screws. Although many people will agree that metal trim is less attractive than self-edging, its use is easier and quicker. There is the further drawback that some types will make black marks on clothing of anyone who rubs against it while working. Coating the edging with clear plastic or even paste wax may help.

Plastic laminates are difficult to harm except by cutting or by applying heat in excess of 275 degrees. Thus boiling water won't hurt your new counter surface—but an electric iron or a pan right out of the oven or off the stove can do so.

Surest protection for your laminate-plastic counter top is provision of alternative surfaces nearby or within it. Ceramic tile and marble can stand more intense heat. Wood makes a cutting surface in which knife nicks will be less objectionable.

For an old laminate counter top in which a section or two has suffered damage, there is a simpler solution than total removal. Just replace the damaged area with one of wood, for cutting, or tile, to take hot dishes. It will look and be appropriate, and it may prevent damage in the future.

36

Counter Tops You Pour

For better work surfaces, adapt the materials and methods originally meant for floors and craftwork

All new in recent years are pourable plastic products excellent for topping kitchen counters and indoor and outdoor tables, desks, and other built-ins. They offer interesting alternatives to plastic laminates, described in the preceding chapter. Since you pour them in place, they are easier for the inexperienced householder to work with. And, for the same reason, they are a simple and economical solution to covering areas that are irregular in shape and hence wasteful to cover with a sheet material. In addition to the more obvious places, you may want to cover such nuisance areas as window sills on which ordinary finishes deteriorate so rapidly.

Of these pouring plastic materials, the one most readily available and offered in the widest variety of color effects is the seamless-floor product sold under such names as Flecto and Dur-A-Flex. You'll find detailed information on working with these in the earlier chapters on pouring floors and updating showers.

A counter on a tabletop is usually so much smaller than a floor that you can apply additional clear-sealer coats without running to excessive cost. In addition to providing the greater durability you may need for counter-topping, these added layers of plastic will produce an attractive appearance of greater depth in the finish.

Some manufacturers offer finishing kits that are essentially the same thing as those for pouring seamless floors, but are intended specifically for counters and tables. The difference is in the pigments supplied. These are unusual colors, often wild metallic ones, and foil flakes. A shimmering gold floor would be a bit much, except possibly in a night club, but a small table or a dining counter can afford to glitter.

To produce a new and brilliant surface on any table or other work surface, first prepare the surface by filling any cracks and gluing down any loose veneer.

1. Then sandpaper the surface until it is fairly smooth. Although these heavy plastic coatings have the great virtue of filling and concealing many irregularities, the liquids will tend to sink into deep cracks and holes so that they will still show.

2. Mix equal quantities of the two epoxy ingredients in a clean plastic pail. The temperature of the room should be at least 70 degrees so the plastic will harden properly. Stir the mixture for two minutes to assure proper blending.

3. Pour part of the material onto the surface and spread it with a medium-nap roller. Spread uniformly as thin a coat as possible, but make sure that the old surface does not show through. Avoid leaving roller marks. *Spread rather than roll.*

Within three to five minutes after this material has been applied, spray on a fine mist of water. Use a hand sprayer, or for small areas, a bottle of the kind used to apply window-cleaning spray.

Immediately broadcast chips into the coating. Cover completely. After you've done a few square feet, again spray on a fine water mist, completely wetting the chips. Avoid puddling. Continue this process until the entire area is coated, misted, chipped and wet down.

4. Allow to dry overnight. Temperature during the drying period should be at least 70 degrees to insure complete evaporation of moisture.

5. The next day, scrape off protruding chips or bumps with a straightedge trowel.

6. Now give the surface two or more coats of the clear finishing material. The table top shown in the photograph was given three coats. You can add extra coats, or even patch a thin area, at any time later.

You have created a surface that is nonporous and so does not absorb dirt and bacteria. It needs no waxing. Its luster can be restored with ammonia in water. Most liquids, including ink and oil, will not stain it.

Photo left

To edge a counter or tabletop with wood, cut thin strips to the proper width, preferably mitered at the corners. Fasten them on with wood glue and finishing nails or with contact cement, used as described in the chapter on plastic laminates that precedes this one. With some topping materials, self-edging is feasible—as shown in the photographs on "seamless" finishes and marble-like plastic.

Photo right

When working with topping materials using water-soluble epoxy for the base coat, light moistening is required at several stages. Glass of water and window-spraying device are handy for dampening. This old table got base coat and a heavy sprinkling of gold flakes.

The seal coat being rolled on here is an extra—not necessary but highly desirable when the original surface is something like old linoleum that might bleed through. With a chip coat like the gold-flake one used here, it also flattens the chips for smoother result.

With all the "seamless" methods of counter-topping, whether sold for floor use or modified for furniture-finishing, final two or three coats are clear plastic. Urethane is used here. It can be brushed, rolled, or troweled on, but often spreading with a straightedged piece of wood or molding gives a smooth result.

Pour-in-place flooring products of the acrylic-plastic type are also excellent for topping counters. A base coat, usually white, is allowed to dry, then followed by clear acrylic into which colored flakes are tossed. Same acrylic is rolled or spread on to provide one or more protective glaze coats.

Same acrylic seamless-floor product is used here for floor, counter top, drawer fronts, and cabinet edges. A battered old chest of drawers, formerly used in a workshop, was rescued to form the basis of this kitchen.

Here a tiny, wasted corner is turned into a kitchen office by addition of a desk top. In another room, it could equally well be a dressing table. Top is built up on a wood frame with ¼"-plywood surfaces, to fit over matching strips first nailed to the wall. Top is finished before hanging, using seamless-floor acrylic.

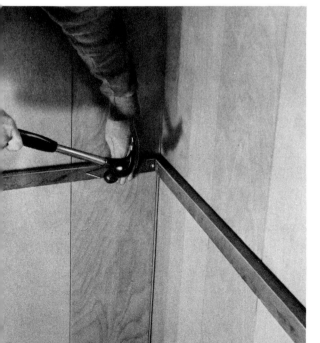

Another flooring material that is beautifully adapted to pouring counter tops lets you do the whole job in a single giant step. Since the most successful way to use it is by blending two or more colors into a marble-like pattern, it is found under such trade names as Desert Marble. It consists of a single molasses-thick liquid plastic to which a small amount of catalyst is added just before use. A sequence of photographs accompanying this chapter shows how to mix and pour and blend Desert Marble.

The topping materials described so far, like the plastic laminates to which the preceding chapter was devoted, cover a counter or table with an opaque layer. The appearance of the result is determined by the color or the topper you choose.

But what if you like the appearance of a natural wood top? Or have a material, such as a fabric or wallpaper or other wall-covering that you would like to use? You might want your counter top finished to match a wallcovering or a curtain material you are using in the same room.

For any of these situations the product of choice is a clear casting plastic. The photographs show the use of a kind called Castoglas.

To use it, you just mix it, pour it on, spread it evenly, let it dry, then sand the surface. Then you pour and spread a second coat, roll on a sheet of heavyweight laminating film (obtained from the same source as the casting plastic), push out bubbles, and allow to set up. This process gives a brilliantly smooth, shiny surface. The steps are shown in the photographs.

Infinite variation in result is possible. The most important is the choice of the surface over which to pour the plastic. Most often, perhaps, this will be natural wood. This is the best looking surface for almost any table, counter, or shelf—but it is hopelessly delicate for most situations until given protection with casting plastic.

But you may have reason to prefer some other effect, whether for getting color or strong pattern into a dull room, matching an existing material, or covering an unattractive old surface. Then proceed as described above and shown in the pictures.

For still another variation, experiment with embedding thin objects in the layer of casting plastic. These might be leaves or ferns or grasses.

A matte surface will often be more attractive or appropriate than a shiny one. You can dull a shiny plastic surface by rubbing with 0000 steel wool and then polishing with rubbing compound and furniture wax.

1. Desert Marble topping job for table or kitchen counter begins with addition of catalyst to white and colored plastics. Three or more colors may be used.

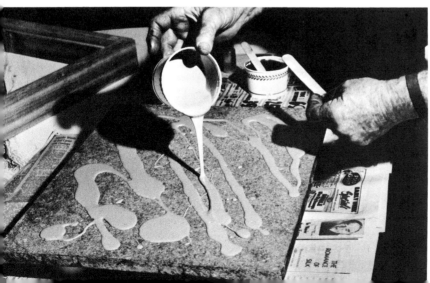

2. After mixing, pour base color—most often white or slightly tinted—onto counter or tabletop in a random pattern. Tongue depressers are handy for spreading.

315

3. Also in random fashion, pour on smaller quantities of the second color—and other colors, if any more are being used.

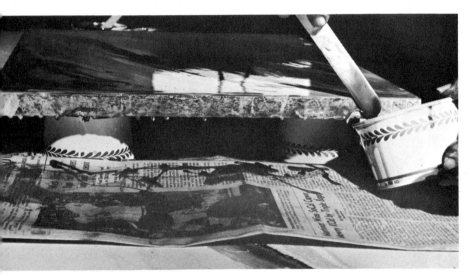

4. To convert this mess into something bearing a remarkable resemblance to marble, blend the colors with a stick and a paint brush, using brush to bring the plastic to a uniform level. Edges may be covered too.

5. Your finished counter top will look more like this—or quite different, depending upon the extent to which you carry the blending process. This type of topping material gives you an exceptional degree of control.

HOW TO APPLY CASTING PLASTIC

1. To surface a counter top with clear casting plastic, mix and pour the material, then spread evenly with cardboard. If there are seams or joints, as with this top of flakeboard surrounded by wood tiles, seal and fill them first.

2. Let the first plastic coat harden, then sand it with medium-grit sandpaper. Apply a second coat of plastic on dry, dust-free surface.

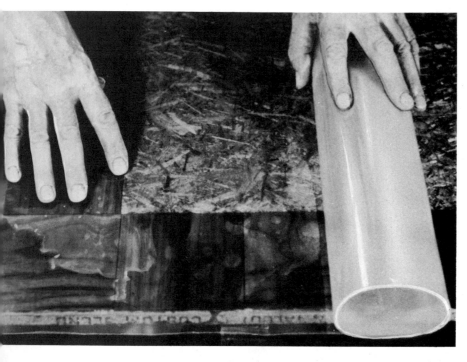

3. Roll a sheet of heavy-gauge laminating plastic film over the wet casting plastic. Without this step, the topping material will not harden smooth and level.

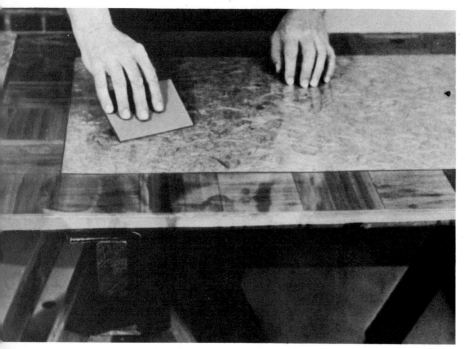

4. Working from the center toward the edges, spread the casting plastic evenly under the film. Watch to see that you are removing all air bubbles.

5. Peel off the film after the casting plastic has hardened. This film produces a plate-glass finish. Rub with fine steel wool and rubbing compound if you want a duller finish.

Sometimes wirebrushing is best way to rescue an old top (left). Process scrubs out the softer part of the wood, leaving the hard grain exposed for a better wearing surface. Brushing can be done with power, using a scratch wheel in a flexible shaft, as here, or chucked in an electric drill; or it can be done by hand, using a wire-brush of scrub-brush shape. More interesting results are sometimes—not always—obtained by first charring the surface with a butane torch (right). Apply clear plastic after wirebrushing.

37

Ventilating Your Kitchen

Install a fan, with or without hood, to rid your kitchen of damaging grease, moisture, heat and odor

Tests made at Purdue University reveal that twelve pounds of water vapor a day are produced in the ordinary kitchen. You generate almost a pound of vapor when you prepare a breakfast for four people. This moisture can make its way inside walls and condense there, forming puddles and damaging the paint inside and out. Wooden framework may even rot.

Getting rid of this moisture, along with grease, smoke, and odor is the job of the kitchen fan.

The Home Ventilating Institute recommends that kitchen air be changed—or cleaned—about fifteen times an hour. A ducted fan changes the air by pumping it outdoors through a vent in either the sidewall or the roof. The duct should be as short as possible, with minimum number of turns. It should remain full size all the way.

Ductless fans are less effective, but often are easier to install in an existing house. They do not discharge air to the outdoors. They do, however, filter dirty air to remove contaminants and then send the cleaned air back into the room. They cannot remove heat and moisture.

Both ducted and ductless ventilating fans may be found built into range hoods. Often you have your choice of the two types in range hoods that are otherwise identical.

The working capacity of a ventilating fan is commonly figured in cubic feet of air moved per minute. You can use a simple calculation to determine the size of fan to install.

Multiply the length of the room by the width and then by the height, all in feet. This gives you the cubic footage. If you divide this by four, you will have the fan capacity needed to move the air of the room every four minutes, or fifteen times an hour.

You may prefer to choose a fan of greater capacity, possibly one that will change the air every two minutes instead of every four. The heavier fan is a real advantage when food is scorched or some kitchen operation produces a large amount of vapor.

If you do choose a fan of generous capacity, you will find that it also produces quite a bit of noise. A multiple-speed switch gives you some control of this, since you can run the fan at low speed most of the time, stepping up the capacity, and the sound, only when you really need to move a lot of air.

As far as appearance goes, a fan is usually just a fan— that is, an opening partly covered by a grille of some sort. One new through-the-wall fan, however, is designed to take decoration into account. Its visible part consists mostly of a rectangular brushed-steel plate with air-intake occurring around its edges. The metal plate is attractive enough, at least by comparison to the appearance of an ordinary fan, and it can be covered with some decorative material or with a bit of the wall material of the room.

When you install a range hood containing the fan, you have an opportunity to improve the appearance of the kitchen substantially. You can use such a hood to add color accent to a kitchen or to update the whole feeling of the room. Just install a hood of copper or stainless steel, or one enameled to match other things in the kitchen.

An example of the unusual hoods offered today is a roll-out model of silver-anodyzed aluminum, mounted on nylon casters so that the unit can be left out of the way when not needed. Placed over the range, it can be pulled out to ventilate most effectively either the oven or the range burners. The fan goes on automatically when the hood is pulled out, shuts itself off when the hood is retracted.

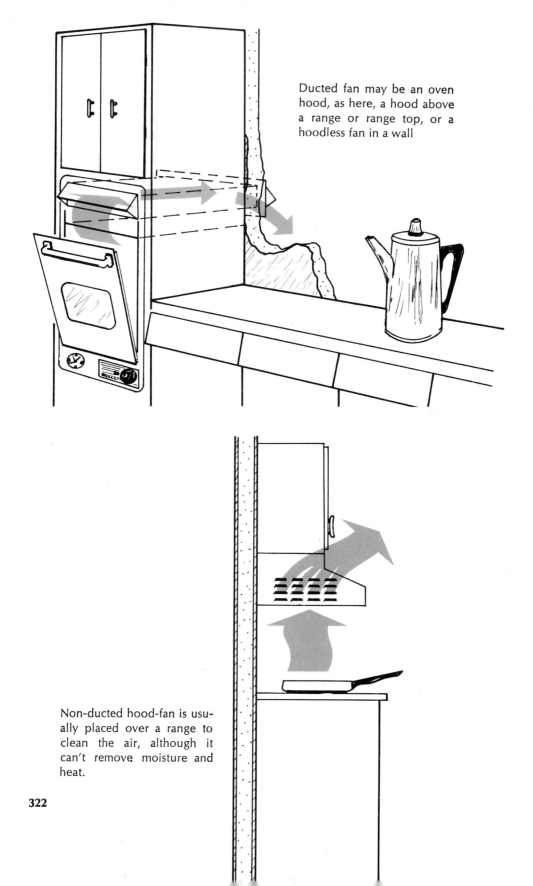

Ducted fan may be an oven hood, as here, a hood above a range or range top, or a hoodless fan in a wall

Non-ducted hood-fan is usually placed over a range to clean the air, although it can't remove moisture and heat.

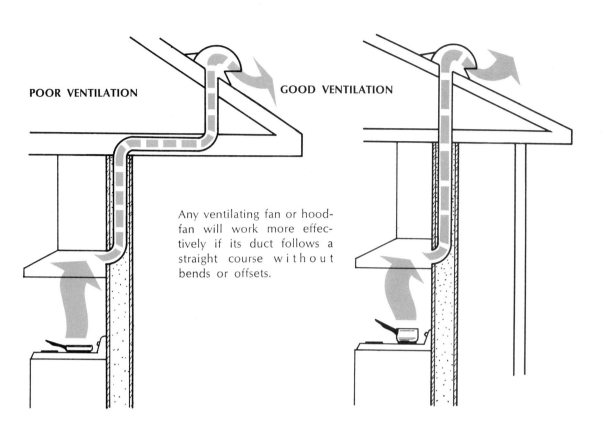

POOR VENTILATION

GOOD VENTILATION

Any ventilating fan or hood-fan will work more effectively if its duct follows a straight course w i t h o u t bends or offsets.

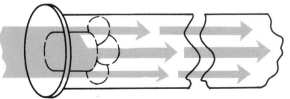

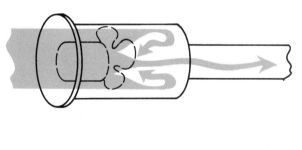

Constricting the ductwork in your ventilating installation produces an efficency loss. Keep all the duct full size.

323

Propeller fan is usually a stamped disc with three or more blades set at an angle to deliver a maximum amount of air against relatively low resistance. It uses little power but also it fails to overcome resistance.

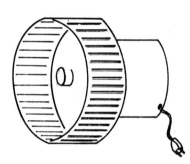

Centrifugal blower is commonly called a "squirrel cage" fan. Air is sucked into the center of a revolving wheel and discharged at right angles into an expanding scroll. This type has maximum ability to overcome resistance but it requires more motor power.

Mixed-flow impeller combines the best features of propeller and blower. Blades are set at a pitch at the intake and are like a blower at the discharge end, so less motor power is required than for centrifugal blower.

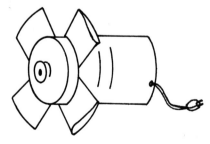

Axial-flow type is an improved version of the propeller blade. It is built on aircraft principles and overcomes resistance by driving air at high speed through a close-fitting tube.

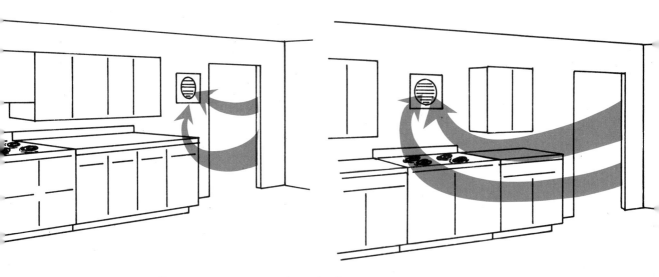

Even more important than the kind and size of ventilating equipment you use in your kitchen is where you put it. Prime location is directly above range top, the source of most heat, odor, moisture, and smoke in most kitchens.

This hood features old-fashioned charm but efficiently solves the problem of a cooking center in an island or pass-through counter, a situation unsuited to an ordinary hood-fan. It comes in four different widths and several colors, has twin blowers and two aluminum-mesh filters.

  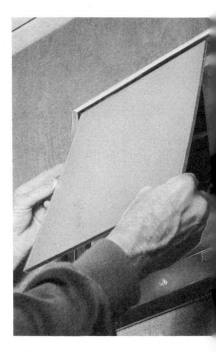

Top left

Installing a through-the-wall fan is often the easiest, and sometimes the only way to add ventilation to an existing kitchen. Begin installation by cutting through both wall surfaces, then fastening main unit into place with screws.

Top center

Aluminum frame snaps on and surrounds fan box, creating concealed intake ports. This NuTone fan can be installed in walls from 5″ to 10″ thick. It delivers 200 cubic feet of air per minute, usually sufficient for a room with 100 square feet of floor area.

Top right

Brushed-aluminum snap-on center panel is attractive as it stands, can also be painted or otherwise covered to match features of the room. In this case, the piece of rough-sawn redwood plywood just cut out of the wall was trimmed and cemented on.

Opposite page

Hammered-copper hood gives a romantic look to this kitchen, demonstrates that ventilating equipment can contribute to appearance as well as comfort. Kitchen walls, including the range backsplash, are plastic-surfaced hardboard paneling for quick cleaning.

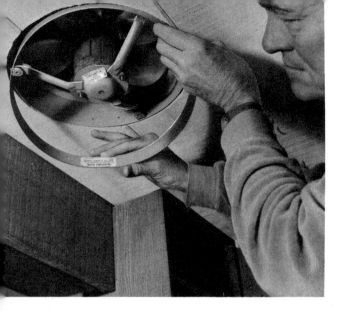

Above left

For a kitchen where a range hood would not fit in, next best thing is a high-quality, high capacity fan. This one is being placed in a ceiling opening, where it connects to a duct that discharges through the nearest outside wall.

Above right

This kitchen fan uses a permanent filter of aluminum mesh. It can be removed in a few seconds for cleaning, keeps grease from coating inside of duct. Most ventilating fans should be oiled once a year, cleaned often enough to prevent dangerous accumulation of grease. Clean motor by wiping with paper towel. Do not submerge.

This solid-state control permits continuous variation of speed, is the same type used with the through-the-wall fan. It fits an ordinary electric-switch box.

38

Your Kitchen Power Center

Build a mixer-blender-juicer-grinder into your kitchen counter —or make a special portable cabinet for it

A multiple-purpose food center can concentrate into a single compact space many of the kitchen chores most efficiently done by motor power. Such a device is basically a mixer that operates from an electric turntable installed flush with the top of a kitchen counter. But accessories permit it to do many other jobs. It becomes in turn a food blender, an ice chopper, a meat grinder, a knife sharpener, a juice squeezer, a shredder-slicer.

While the kitchen is its usual habitat, the power food center has so many noncooking uses that you may prefer to build it into something portable. Then it can move from kitchen to family room or porch or patio when the ice crusher or the blender— which makes excellent milkshakes and malteds—is wanted for a party. It could also be moved from one house to another.

The installation photographs with this chapter show how to build a power center into either a fixed kitchen counter or a movable counter that you can make of plywood.

329

Photo left

Kitchen power center turns into outdoor dairy bar here. Cabinet was built to match kitchen counters for height, given retractable casters for shifting to other locations. Top, holding power unit, was glued up from strips of maple, could have been chopping-block stock from lumberyard.

Photo right

Grooved plywood, called Texture 1-11, was used for cabinet sides. One fixed shelf provides bracing and location for magnetic door catch. There is generous storage space for food-center accessories and food items. Grooves permit adding removable shelves.

If it's not possible to match existing cabinet doors, or if you want something richly distinctive, cover your door with tooling copper. Then tool it with a ball-peen hammer, as the author's daughter is doing here to the matching backsplash. Consult Chapter 15 for details on how to do this.

Power-driven turntable that is the heart of the food center looks like this. In a fixed installation, power cable is brought through knockout and connected to wires shown here. For a movable cabinet, a regular cord is used and plugged into convenience outlets.

Addition of parts seen in these pictures converts food power center into mixer, blender, ice crusher. Other accessories provide for grinding meat, squeezing juice, sharpening knives, and shredding and slicing.

HOW TO INSTALL FOOD POWER CENTER

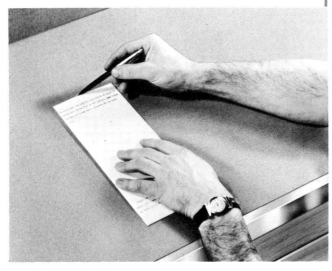

1. Place the template (included with the unit) on the counter top or cabinet in the desired spot. Make sure that the front of the template is at least 1″ behind inside face of cabinet.

2. After marking around the template, cut opening in the counter top. Remove the knock-out on the side of the junction box that is most convenient for wiring. (For dead corner or 6″ cabinet filler installation use the bottom knock-out instead.)

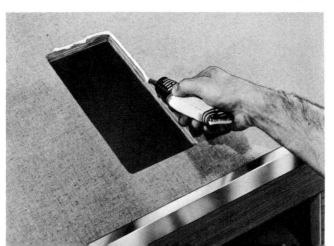

3. Put a bead of sealing compound around the edge of the opening in the counter top. Place the power unit into the cutout with the nameplate facing the front of the cabinet.

4. Turn screw clockwise until clamp bracket is tight against underside of counter top, locking the unit securely in place. Correct pressure can be determined by resistance being built up. Then put a dab of sealing compound over screw.

5. Run wires through 90-degree - angle clamp and connect to the appliance circuit of the kitchen, following your local electrical code. Unit draws 3 amps.

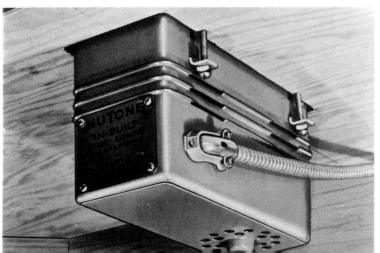

6. Connect power to the two leads in the junction box and fasten on the nameplate with the screws furnished. Clamp the flexible tubing with the clip mounted on the housing. Unit must be grounded.

7. When installing the food center in a space used by a drawer, pull the drawer part way (under proposed location of power unit) and measure from counter top to drawer bottom. Make sure there is clearance for the unit when installed. Dimension to top of counter should be at least 6¾".

8. To allow the drawer to pull all the way out, it is necessary to cut out part of its back wall. To do this, pull drawer out part way, drop square down into counter opening (on each side) and mark back of drawer. Draw parallel lines ¾" further out, to allow opening of 1½" wider than cutout of top.

9. Cut out the back of the drawer along the lines you have drawn to a point at least 6¾" below the top of the counter. This allows the cabinet drawer to move freely after the unit is in.

39

Built-Ins For a Better Kitchen

Add convenience and efficiency to the work center of your home with permanently installed devices

Like the multi-purpose food center described in the preceding chapter, many of the appliances a modern kitchen needs can be built in instead of plugged in.

One big advantage of a built-in is that it often uses up no useful storage space. So building in the appliances shown here can free space equivalent to an added cupboard or cabinet. Since a built-in ordinarily is ready for instant use at any time, it gets used —instead of remaining stowed away.

A built-in toaster of the kind shown is always accessible at a fixed spot in the kitchen, yet not out in the open getting dusty or taking up counter space. It can be taken from its niche for use in another room if wanted there.

Possibly the biggest advantage a built-in dishwasher offers over a portable one is sound control. Either a dishwasher designed for building in, or a portable that you install as shown in the photographs, can be muffled and shielded.

A dispenser for paper towels, plastic wrap, waxed paper, and aluminum foil can be set into an ordinary wall. It concentrates several items where they are easily found, and it reduces kitchen clutter substantially.

A faucet that provides super-hot water is one of the newest helpers for kitchens. You can install one on your sink by connecting its 2-quart tank to the household water line and to a source of electric power. Since it instantly provides water at temperatures far above those at which an ordinary water heater would be set, it is the built-in—and far handier—equivalent of an electric tea kettle. It won't fill the room with steam nor boil dry. It is most useful in making beverages such as instant coffee and in speeding up cooking operations that call for very hot water.

When you build an electric can opener into a wall, instead of hanging one of the ordinary kind on the surface, you save space and reduce the feeling of clutter.

To solve the problem of keeping food warm, you have a choice of many devices. You can set into a counter top a section of radiant glass similar to the hot trays sold for portable use. Or you can, at tiny cost, mount one or more infrared heat lamps above a counter, using the hard-glass kind that won't shatter when struck by water. Or, more elaborately, you can use space under a counter to build in an oven-size (and oven-priced) hot food server. Its drawers will keep all the food for a family dinner or a party hot and in good condition for several hours.

A water-treatment device will improve a kitchen in a most fundamental matter—and one that becomes more of a problem in many communities each year. Some water supplies are best treated with specialized conditioning equipment, such as water softeners, iron-removers, and so on.

But your supply may be such that an ordinary filter will provide the needed improvement. There is now a family of devices, the Fram Water Filters, that you can install in limited space. One size is intended for basement installation where it will filter all the household water. A more compact type fits under most sinks to handle just kitchen water. Either one may be had with filter elements which remove dirt and sediment or taste and odor.

When you build in a dual-use toaster, it is almost flush with the surrounding surface. It tilts out just far enough to let you slip in one to four slices of bread. To move it to the dining room, recreation room, or patio, lift it out of its box and un-plug the cord. It becomes a table toaster with brushed-chrome finish and simple automatic pop-up "light-dark" control. There's a safety switch to prevent operation when the toaster is closed into the wall. Slots in the toaster are large enough to take the new toasted-cooked foods such as instant waffles or tarts.

This unit stores paper toweling, wax paper, aluminum foil, plastic wrap, or any other roll-packaged material in space ordinarily wasted within a standard stud wall. The cabinet is 11" high and 16" wide, has a satin brushed-chrome finish and a special hinge design that permits the door to be removed and dunked in the sink for easy washing. The can part—everything except the door and its handle—is identical with the unit used for the built-in toaster.

If your kitchen was built before dishwashers became the usual thing, perhaps the most useful single updating you can accomplish is addition of one. It need not be one designed for building in. Economical solution shown here is adaptation of an ordinary portable one to built-in use by providing a niche with door above. Hot-water line to provide faucet was extended to the back corner. No cold-water line is required. Drain could be to sewer, but in this case it is a length of threaded pipe extended through the wall to outdoors. Walls of cabinet are heavy exterior-grade plywood to muffle sound; and front panel is plywood covered by wood paneling to match the room. Since this panel remains fixed except if repair or cleaning is needed, it is held by two screws.

Access door above built-in portable dishwasher is hinged at the back and lined with plastic laminate for protection from moisture. Since this installation, made by the authors, is near the dining table, most dishes never reach the kitchen at all. Open shelves at right and others behind sliding doors at left are used for dish storage, as is cupboard above dishwasher. With access door closed, it and adjoining tiled counter provide space for buffet serving.

Though intended mostly for kitchenettes, this compact dishwasher-sink provides fast updating for any kitchen. Simply move out existing worn-out cabinet sink and replace it with this unit, made by Hobart. It is 4′ wide and its dishwasher is an intrinsic part of the sink, for quick hookup to existing plumbing. You have your choice of porcelain, stainless-steel, or plastic top.

Instant foods, frozen foods, dehydrated foods have changed our ways of kitchen living and cooking. We need hotter-than-tap water for preparing quick meals, making cereal or instant coffee, thawing packaged frozen foods. Solution to this kitchen need, a device called Instant-Hot, gives you 150 to 190 degrees tap water from a special faucet.

This automatic electric can opener fits into the wall, is almost invisible when closed—especially if you camouflage it with a door insert that matches your present kitchen cabinets. If you're painting or paneling the old kitchen this can opener will blend right in and add no cluttered look. It requires a rough-in area 7½" high, 3⅝" wide, the cutout area shown in the photograph. Clearance required: 10" from bottom of unit (for can height) 5⅛" from left side (for door). Step-by-step instructions on its use, cleaning, adjustment, and replacement blades are permanently printed on the inside of the door along with the name and address of the manufacturer.

Most elaborate form of kitchen food warmer is this type, with drawers and thermostatic control to provide temperatures to 190 degrees. Since its wattage is only 900 and it is available in 115-volt as well as 230-volt model, it is easily connected to power.

PART VII

IMPROVE YOUR HOME SYSTEMS

40

Update Your Electrical System

It doesn't take an electrician to replace outdated switches and outlets with functionally and esthetically better new ones

You can do a lot to modernize your electrical system from a wall box. These small metal boxes contain the switches and outlets that put your system to work. Replace these old units with modern ones, and you have—within the limits of existing wiring—a new system.

The boxes are easy to get at. After turning off the electricity, you remove the cover plate with a screwdriver. You touch only the wires that are already exposed inside the receptacle box. You unhook these wires from the old switch or outlet, rehook them to the new one, and put the cover plate back on. That's all there is to it. (Learn how to make decorative copper-enameled cover plates in Chapter 42.)

It's a job anyone can do. Modern switches and outlets fit the same wall boxes in the same way as the old ones. By putting in new units, you can have switches that turn off or on noiselessly, light up or glow in the dark, respond to the touch of an elbow when your hands are full, or turn off the lights after you've had time to get into bed. You can have outlets that turn on at a switch, lock plugs in their sockets, or keep children from poking in dangerous bits of metal.

New combination units also make your wall boxes do double duty. If you need extra outlets—and most homes usually do—you may be able to get them by converting single-purpose wall switches to new switch-plus-outlet combinations. You still have the switch, but then you have an outlet, too.

With the same type of combination, you can convert an ordinary outlet to a switch-controlled one, so that you can operate kitchen appliances without plugging and unplugging them all the time.

This is no way to treat an electric cord—but it dramatizes one of the improvements you can make in your home's power system. Replace an ordinary receptacle with one of the locking type, and the plug won't fall out

Newly styled switches and outlets, shown here mounted together in an ordinary double-gang box, look quite different from old ones. You can get these devices and their cover plates in a wide variety of colors.

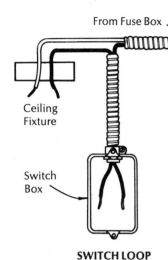

From Fuse Box

Ceiling
Fixture

Switch
Box

SWITCH LOOP

Use this drawing and the next one to help you tell whether you can add an outlet to an electric box that now contains only a switch. If only two wires enter the box, this is a switch loop from the ceiling fixture and cannot be used to power a receptacle. Of course you can still substitute a silent switch for an old noisy one or install a dimmer.

If four wires come into the box, then one pair will be from the fuse box, and you can substitute an outlet for the switch. Or you can replace the switch with a switch-outlet combination. The switch part of the combination can continue to handle the job of the switch you've taken out, and the outlet will be available for plugging in portable devices.

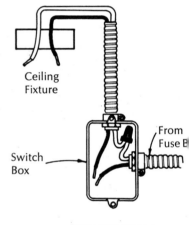

Ceiling
Fixture

Switch
Box

From
Fuse B

PARALLEL LEADS

THAT EXTRA OUTLET. If you have a wall switch that has power available, if both sides of the circuit pass through the receptacle box, you can incorporate a valuable bonus—a convenience outlet. Switch-high outlets are more convenient for many uses than baseboard outlets.

To find out whether you can add an outlet to a switch, turn off the electricity (by pulling the main switch or branch fuse), then remove the cover plate and the two screws that hold the switch in its box. Lift the switch out a little and see if two or four wires enter the box.

If there are only two, you are looking at the insides of a switch loop. Actually the two wires are a single lead from the power line, cut so that the switch can be inserted in series. You can replace this switch with any other switch, but you *cannot* add an outlet because you have only one side of the circuit, the hot side, passing through the switch box.

346

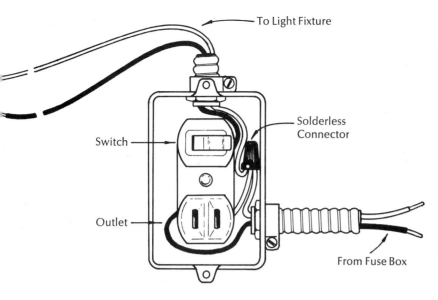

To Light Fixture

Solderless Connector

Switch

Outlet

From Fuse Box

To connect the combination device, attach the black wires as shown. At the point where the two white wires are connected together, attach a short white wire and connect it to the second (white metal) terminal on the new outlet. Insulate the white-wire splice by using a solderless connector; or solder the splice and tape it. *All this with the current shut off, of course.*

Don't ever try to use the metallic cable covering (or the ground wire in nonmetallic cable) as the other side of the circuit. This is not designed to carry prolonged current loads and has a high electrical resistance. If wired into a circuit it may become hot and start a fire *without even blowing the fuse.*

However, if you find four wires entering the box (usually two two-wire cables), you can replace the old switch with a switch-outlet combination. You can install the combination so that the new switch controls the same fixture as the old switch did and the new outlet is permanently "on."

If you want to get fancy you can get a combination that has two switches and an outlet (it fits the standard receptacle box). Then you can use one switch for the overhead lights and the other to control a lamp or appliance plugged into the outlet.

Remember, though, that adding outlets does not increase the current-handling capacity of your circuit, which remains the same as it was.

Look for a second terminal screw connected to the first one by a metal strip, and fasten your second wire to this. If no second terminal exists, twist the two wires together, plus a third short wire called a "pigtail." This should be of the same gauge as the others (usually No. 12). If in doubt, snip a short end off an old wire and take it to the hardware store.

Carefully solder the three wires together and tape them, or use a solderless screw-on connector. Then fasten the pigtail to the terminal screw.

A combination switch-outlet can also be used in any box that now has only an outlet, for instance to control kitchen appliances. This will work even if you find only two wires at an outlet box, as at the end of a circuit.

MAKING "PIGTAILS." In some cases, you may find it necessary to connect two wires to the same terminal, as in hooking up some types of switch-outlet combinations. Direct connection of more than one wire to the same terminal screw is not permitted by electrical code.

Incidentally, when you replace outlets that may be used for heavy appliances or power tools, put in the three-hole grounded sockets that take the new three-prong appliance plugs. These are made so that the third contact is automatically grounded to the receptacle box when you screw in the outlet. You can still use your old two-prong plugs in the new outlets.

SILENT SWITCHES THAT SHINE. New switches don't make the noise that the older types do. There is a new rotary switch with a silent twist knob instead of a toggle lever, as well as a quiet mechanical toggle and the noiseless mercury type.

The rotary-switch knob glows in the dark. Some toggle switches—mechanical and mercury—have neon lamps in the toggles. The latter serve as reverse pilot lights. If the light is off, it tells you at a glance that a switch has been left on. If you prefer a more positive indication, then you'll go for the opposite type of pilot-light switch—one that glows when the juice is on.

SWITCHES THAT LOCK. If you want to make sure that no one can tamper with a switch, replace it with one of the locking type. Essentially this is a toggle switch except that the toggle is made in the form of a removable key.

With another type, you can be like the fellow in the old joke who was so fast he could flip a switch and hop into bed before the light went out. This delayed-action switch turns on exactly like an ordinary switch, but it takes its time when you press it to "off."

SHOCKLESS OUTLETS. Children can't poke scissors into special shockproof receptacles. These are designed so that nothing but a proper plug can make electrical contact. Another safety device is a replacement cover plate that bars the way to hairpins, scissors, and toys.

Another nuisance is that old receptacle that won't grasp a plug and hold it. The remedy is a twist-lock outlet. When you push

Only tool you need is a screwdriver to replace your old switch with a full-range dimmer. Make *SURE* that electricity is turned off at the fuse- or breaker-box, remove cover plate, disconnect switch, and connect new dimmer in the same way, then put on cover plate.

a plug into this, it holds with conventional tightness. But if you twist the plug, the prongs lock so you can't pull the plug free—convenient for appliances such as a vacuum cleaner which may be subject to accidental tugs.

LIGHT DIMMER. These things used to be cigar-box size and they cost up toward $50. Modern solid-state physics has dwarfed both their price and their size, and now they fit an ordinary box. So you can put one in where a plain switch now dwells without any more fuss than when changing switches.

The simplest dimmer looks like a switch and has high, low, and off positions.

Where a dimmer will have much use it may be worth your while to use a full-range kind, which has a dial to set for whatever intensity you wish. Pressing in on the dial turns the light on and off. A light controlled by a dimmer turned low makes an excellent night light as well as a deterrent to intruders when you are away during the evening.

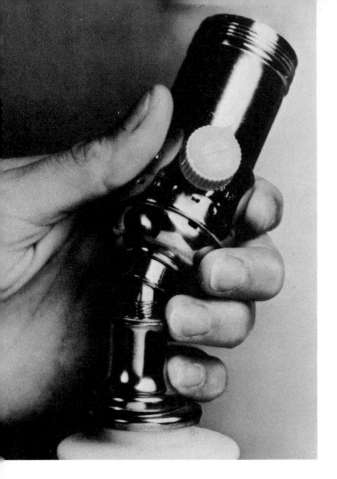

Any lamp can have its own full-range dimmer. Just replace the old socket with the dimmer socket you see here (left). Another handy device is the feed-through switch (right) you can install on a lamp cord wherever it will be most convenient.

DEVICES THAT AUTOMATE. Photoelectric cells and clock timers have been around for many years, although mostly limited to commercial use. Now you can obtain devices of both types made to fit into your existing switch and receptacle boxes. Unobtrusive though they are, they can bring remarkable convenience into everyday life. These are covered, along with other automating ideas, in the next chapter.

41

Bring Automation to Your Home

**Timers, photocells, radio-controlled motors—put them to work
and they'll make your home more up to date than most new ones**

Pushbutton living? Why bother?

Today you can shove your home right past that primitive stage into true automation. In the process you'll make your house a more comfortable and safer place. You can do the same for your yard and porch or patio, your garage, your workshop, and your vacation house if you happen to have one.

What you do is program your electrical devices to go on and off under the control of time clocks, delayed action switches, photocells, and combinations of these genii. Then they'll function on schedule without your having to remember or move a finger or even be there.

And for the minority of devices where you want flexibility of control more than programming, new devices put pushbuttons where you want them—or make them portable through sound or radio waves.

With your automation program you can create such household conveniences as these:

Lights that stay on just long enough to get you safely from garage to house—or from one room to another or from door to bed.

- Air conditioners that start to cool your house an hour before you get there.
- Illumination that leaps from room to room to convince any lurking burglar that you're there when you're not.
- Coffee pots that warm up while you steal that last dream.
- Sun lamps that refuse to crisp you even if you fall asleep under them.
- Battery warmers or engine-pan in your garage that go to work before you're up to get your car ready for easier cold-morning starting.
- Furnaces that heat your bedroom and bathroom while you begin to wake up.
- Radios that sing you to sleep and then stay silent until it's time for you to get up.
- Shop heat lamps that stay on just long enough to speed paint drying or glue setting after you've knocked off for the day.
- Refrigerator or water heater in your vacation house that rests for five days, then goes into action on Friday night in anticipation of your Saturday arrival.
- Swimming-pool filters and safety alarms that operate without a thought on your part.
- Sprinkler systems that water your lawn or garden with exact consistency even when you're off on vacation.
- Fireplaces you can start blazing on a chilly morning without stirring from your bed.
- Lights or radios or other electrical devices that you can turn on from your bedside or other distant parts of the house without installing special wiring for the purpose.
- Bedroom curtains that keep you in the dark till you wake, then slide quietly back when you touch a bedside button. Or even, at a pre-chosen hour, open of their own accord to tell you it's time to get up.
- Garage doors, whether sliding or overhead, that open as you approach, turn on a light for as long as you need it, then close and lock themselves.

AUTOMATED DOORS, either pushbutton or radio-controlled, are feasible for almost any garage now. Even a garage that is short of headroom or is equipped with sliding rather than overhead doors is no problem to many of the newer operators.

An operator that uses a heavy screw drive, such as the Moore-O-Matic shown in the illustrations, is adaptable to both overhead and sliding doors. With a little ingenuity and an operator of this kind you can construct a dumbwaiter, a moving partition between rooms or within a large room, or a roof that opens and closes over a patio.

To operate an overhead door, the motor part of the operator is suspended from the garage ceiling or a ceiling beam. The other end is fastened directly above the center of the single or double door. A moving bracket will then open and close the door as it travels along the drive screw.

A much less common trick is adapting this device to open a sliding door, but the results are equally good. The motor end of the operator is mounted just higher than the door and just beyond the edge of the door when it is closed. The far end of the screw is secured above the other end of the door. When the screw turns, the door slides.

In the case of a pair of bypassing doors, the choice of which door to attach to the operator is made for you: it must be the door that is closer to the inside of the building—else you'd have to mount the whole operator outdoors.

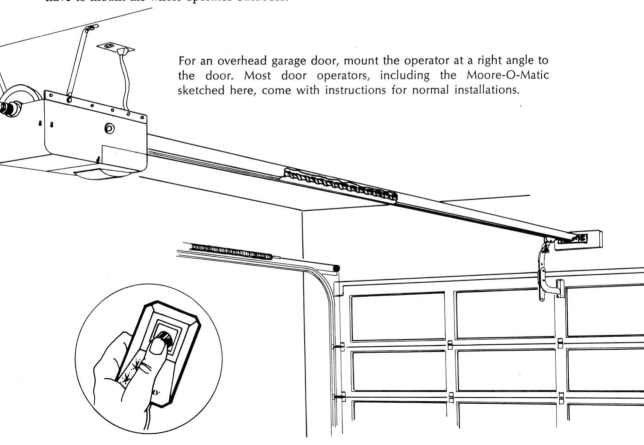

For an overhead garage door, mount the operator at a right angle to the door. Most door operators, including the Moore-O-Matic sketched here, come with instructions for normal installations.

To open and close sliding doors, the operator must be mounted in an unusual fashion. It goes directly above the door and parallel to it. For pushbutton operation (instead of radio control, or to supplement it) switches may be attached at the point the boy is touching.

One rather surprising fact is that a single operator, controlled by a radio transmitter in each car, is enough to do all the necessary tasks for a pair of bypassing sliding doors on a two-car garage. That is, you really need an operator on only one of a pair of doors to eliminate the nuisance of ever having to get out of your car to open or close a door. It works like this:

If the car you wish to drive is in the stall guarded by the inner door, open that door by motor. If you wish to take out the other car instead, open its garage door manually. Either way, close the garage by pushing the radio button as you drive off.

If someone takes out the other car, he must open the door on his side manually, then close the garage by radio as he drives off.

When either person returns, he has only to press the radio control to open a door guarding an empty stall. If he finds that the other car is still away, he closes the outer garage door manually. This leaves the garage ready to open by radio upon the arrival of the second car.

It sounds pretty complicated, but it works, and it doesn't take long for the family to catch on to the handy system. The garage doors are never left open to expose the garage contents nor invite an easy theft from a passerby.

AUTOMATIC CURTAINS are possible in several forms—a matter of what type of control you want—but the essence of the scheme is an electromagnetic traverse rod called Electrac. It is made by Kirsch Company, a manufacturer of many types of curtain hardware.

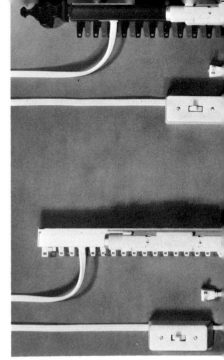

This is a traverse rod that you install much like any other —except that it requires an electrical connection. A "power capsule" travels along the traverse rod when electricity is turned on, pulling the curtain open or closed behind it.

There are three ways you can cause this to happen:

1. You can push a switch up (or down). This switch can be anywhere in your house that you can reach with the electric cable from the outlet box installed near one end of the track. It can, for example, be at the head of your bed to open bedroom curtains when you wake up.

2. You can touch a button on a portable transmitter of precisely the kind used for radio-controlled garage doors. The receiver part of this control is installed within a few feet of the end of the curtain track.

This radio method is desirable if you want to be able to draw the draperies from different parts of the room, or of the house, at different times. Its greatest advantage, however, is that it permits flexible installation in an existing home where it might be difficult to run cable for a switch control.

The electric track comes in two styles. At top is the decorative kind, with finial, rod, and rings that show at all times. Below is the conventional type, suited to most modern houses. Power capsule (most easily seen at top) moves along track when power is on, pulling drapery.

Electric curtain track looks much like any other traverse hardware. But the curtain moves at the touch of a button (beside the curtain or far across the room), by radio control from anywhere you wish, or automatically night and morning at a preset time. The special timer that does this job thus serves as a gentle alarm clock as well.

355

3. Or you can fully automate your curtain control with a time clock that will close your curtains each evening and open them each morning—at times you have chosen in advance. Standard timers, as described later in this chapter, won't do for this special job. The curtain control must be held at "on" or "off" for several seconds, since the curtain will stop moving as soon as the power is cut off. So this chore calls for a special kind of timer that holds a pulse for ten to twelve seconds instead of merely changing from on to off. This timer is available from the Kirsch people, who make the track.

Any burglar, thinking your house is unoccupied, is never going to be sure, when the draperies are open and closed each day. So if you add an automatic curtain system to an automatic on-off light system, you'll be adding protection to your home whether you're there or not.

FIREPLACE AUTOMATION can be added to your home in any of three forms.

If you have an electric fireplace you can make it automatic in precisely the same way that any other electrical appliance

This realistic "driftwood" chunk heats up and radiates warmth in the gas flame of this fireplace, converted from woodburning for the convenience of automation. Pilot light, tiny generator, and pushbutton (or thermostat) make fireplace automation possible in any home.

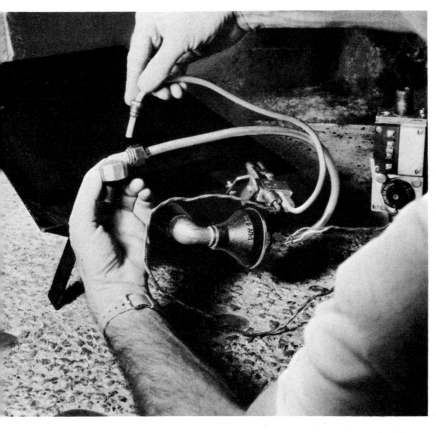

Converting your fireplace to automation is done by adding burner pan with pilot light and tiny generator mounted on it, all controlled by a device (extreme right) of the kind found on gas furnaces. The bell-shaped object just below the generator is an air-intake to produce a sootless blue flame.

can be made automatic: by plugging it into an electric timer clock of suitable capacity or wiring it through a time switch. Details on these devices are given later in this chapter.

If you are adding a gas fireplace to your home, you can obtain one as automatic as your modern furnace. That is, it can be turned on or off by means of a pushbutton—far away from the fireplace if you like—or by a thermostat.

But you can also convert any ordinary fireplace to automatic burning of gas. To do this, run a gas line into the fireplace by way of a shut-off valve. Best thing to use is a valve made for a gas-fiber log kindler, the kind of valve that uses a large, removable key. Then you can convert the fireplace back to wood-burning whenever you wish. You'll find details on installing a kindler in the last chapter of the section on fireplaces.

If you have installed such a kindler, or if your fireplace was already equipped with one, it's no great chore to add the automation.

Pilot is lighted by turning the control button to pilot setting and pressing in with one hand while the other holds a match as shown here. Wire to a thermostat or switch in any convenient part of the room permits instant remote control. There is no connection to the electrical system of the house.

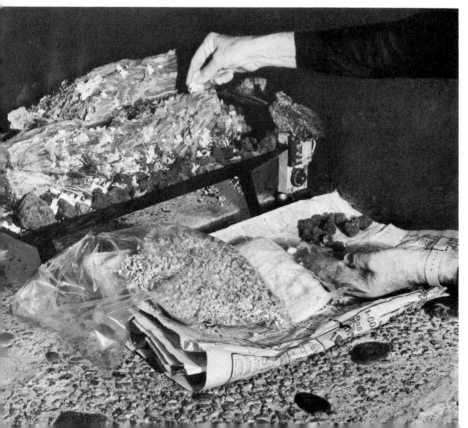

Maker of the burner pan and controls (see Appendix) also offers realistic "logs" and the accessory kit seen in the foreground. It includes vermiculite to fill the pan and filter gas through and materials to glow and sparkle in the flame.

What you do is connect the gas line to a pan-style burner, available from manufacturers such as Rasmussen Iron Works (see Appendix for address) and handled by hardware stores and fireplace-accessory shops. The burner has an air-mixer, or you can get one for it, so the gas will burn with a blue flame that is free from soot. To all this you connect a control and safety device with a pilot light, much like the arrangement on a gas furnace, and available from the same source as the burner pan.

A tiny heat-operated generator is situated close to the pilot flame, and the electricity it makes can be carried through an electric cable to any place within 50 feet. You bring this cable to an ordinary switch box, which can contain a thermostat or a switch, as you prefer. At a touch of this switch the gas goes on in the fireplace and is ignited by the pilot. Touch the switch again and the gas goes off.

So if you place the switch beside your bed you can turn on your fireplace—bedroom or living room—before you get up in the morning.

To complete your arrangement for an attractive gas fire and get a realistic look, you will fill the burner pan with vermiculite granules. These come with the pan. Place ceramic gas logs on top for effect, or group chunks of volcanic rock.

MULTIPURPOSE REMOTE CONTROL is possible with a device called Teleswitch. You can use it to turn any electrical device off or on from a distant part of the house. In its simplest form it consists of a fist-sized box that you plug into an outlet and connect to your lamp, television set, or other electrical items—and a portable "wand." Like a remote control for a garage door, this wand has a pushbutton. Press it and the distant switch is flipped on or off by ultra-sound. It will not operate through a wall.

A more sophisticated version of Teleswitch can be operated from one room to another throughout the house. Plug the switch unit into your appliance and the wand into any outlet, and distance is no problem. A third version is made with two channels, to control two different appliances with the same wand. Prices of the different types range between about $20 and $40.

Another version of the same idea has the virtue that the sending instrument is a tiny whistle, smaller than your little finger. Blow it from across even the largest room and it will turn on or off a switch that you have plugged into a standard electrical outlet. The switch can control any electrical device of capacity up to 350 watts.

The manufacture of the Whistle Switch offers a larger and more elaborate device called Sonuswitch, which will handle appliances up to 700 watts—which might include a coffeemaker or small heater.

This one works with the same whistle, but responds only when the sound is two little blasts close together. You can also make it work even when you aren't carrying the whistle, since it will respond to other quickly repeated sounds that fall within its 14–18 kilocycle range of sensitivity. These include hand claps, a rap on the door with your key ring, and even a "psst, psst," sounded up close.

A specialized safety device from the same maker is Pool Sitter. Place and connect it in a swimming pool and it picks up all sounds so that you can monitor use by children from a distance; and when the pool is out of use it can be set to turn on an alarm when anyone enters the pool. You can set the sensitivity control to detect an object as small as a penny. And of course it can be moved to pick up the sound of an intruder anywhere else in your house or grounds.

PORTABLE TIMERS are the simplest and most flexible controls for lamps and other light-duty appliances.

To use one, plug it into any outlet and plug your lamp or appliance into it.

The basic, or general purpose, model has a twenty-four-hour dial that must first be set to the right time. There is a lever to place for the desired turn-on time and one for turn-off. With these set, the timer will do its work day after day without further attention. There is a manual on-off switch to use at any time you may wish to assert your own will.

The single most important use for timers is to operate lights in your absence in hope of persuading a potential burglar that you are there. But burglars know about timers, and an attentive one may discover that your light is going on and off with suspiciously precise timing night after night. To defeat him, you can now obtain a timer that goes on automatically as darkness falls—and then randomly staggers its turn-off time to fool a watcher.

Portable timer is a plug-in device especially useful with lamps and other movable electrical appliances. It can start a coffee percolator beside, your bed at wake-up time, turn lamps off and on to fool burglars or provide night safety.

Photo Left

Metal-box time control is best for permanent installation, must be wired in rather than just plugged in. Of the many versions made, this is among the more elaborate. Called Astro Dial, it compensates for seasonal change in onset of darkness.

Photo Right

Where most timers repeat on a twenty-four hour cycle, this elaborate one permits a different pair of settings for each day of the week. Use it to program appliances for a different schedule on different days.

In choosing a timer, one important thing to note is its current rating. A low-priced model may be limited to 875 watts (7 amps), while a more expensive type will have a rating of 1875 watts and easily handle any portable appliance, even an electric heater.

Although a timer of this kind is best for all-round use, some of its specialized cousins are handier for single jobs.

Clock-timers are kitchen and shop helpers. Use them for roasters and other cooking appliances and for heat lamps in the gluing or painting end of your workshop. They're easy to set, offer the advantage of a quickly read electric clock as a bonus. They're not for timing intervals of more than a few hours nor will they repeat day after day without resetting.

A radio-timer hitched to your set will let you go to sleep to music, awaken you the same way—if you choose the right station. One of these is easier to set than a general-purpose timer for varying bedtime hours, offers the extra features of a bedside clock and a buzzer alarm that sounds ten minutes after the music starts.

Other portable timers are even more specialized. One is for fans, another is for window air conditioners and a third converts an ordinary electric refrigerator into an automatic defrost model.

TIME SWITCHES in rugged metal boxes with hinged lids are usually designed to be more-or-less permanently wired in. Since they do the work of portable timers but handle far heavier loads they are best suited to controlling heavy appliances, furnaces, and permanently connected lighting.

They offer extra features too. Even the ordinary models may be obtained with extra screw-on trippers to permit two—or many more—on-off cycles each day.

A time switch selling for around $10 is likely to be rated

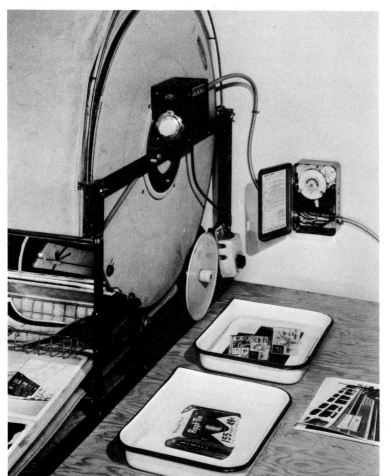

Simple time switch can control a furnace or a home music system — or a print dryer in a darkroom.

at about 4,000 watts. It can easily handle a multiple job, such as controlling simultaneously a post light, porch light, garage light, and living-room outlet. In its 250-volt version it can handle a fair-sized electric room-heater of the permanently installed type.

For controlling your furnace you can find a time switch tailored to almost any situation. You have only to specify whether your system uses a single thermostat, a day-night twin, or separate day and night thermostats; and whether the thermostat uses line or low voltage. The time switch will let you go to bed in a house that is beginning to cool off for the night and get up on one already warmed for dressing. And no money will be going into heating when you don't want it.

All these types of switches also come in what one maker, Intermatic, calls Skipper models. With these you can cut out Saturday and Sunday or any day of the week if you like.

Seven-day time switches—more costly, of course—let you choose on and off times individually for each day of the week. Intended primarily for commercial lighting and heating uses, they also appeal to the family whose arising time changes abruptly when the weekend rolls around.

A recent development is a time switch that adjusts itself to the length of the day. It will come on at sunrise and go off at sunset, or at times related to these, changing its clock time as the season rolls on. It must be factory calibrated to the latitude in which it is to be used.

Homeowners will find new miniature models of time switches useful. One is a standard timer—handy for outdoor lighting installations—so small that it fits on a standard electric handy box. Since it is attractively finished in gray with a gold-and-white dial and is only 3¼″ thick, it will mount unobtrusively on a porch or patio, or even a living-room wall, where a bulky time switch would appear out of place.

For rooms where appearance is especially important, there is a timer housed in a flush-mount box primed to paint to match your living-room walls. Closed, it's a neatly designed on-off switch, for manual control of lights or outlets into which you may plug appliances; but inside is a time switch to handle them automatically whether you're there or not. Its junction box requires a 5″ x 5″ hole in the wall only 2¹³⁄₁₆″ deep.

One specialized time switch is made to control lawn sprinklers. Wired to your pump or master valve, it will turn water on or off at any hour. It comes in two versions—for seven-day or twelve-day programming—and can provide different schedules for each of three areas in your yard.

This timer mounts on an ordinary electrical outlet box, controls any lamp or other appliance you plug into it. You can use one to replace an existing receptacle without having to add any new wiring to your home.

DELAYED-ACTION SWITCHES offer the easiest and cheapest route to electrical automation. The most usual type looks much like an ordinary toggle light switch. Push it to "on" and the light (or appliance up to 10 amps) that it controls goes on. Push it to "off"—and nothing happens for half a minute or so. And then it clicks slightly and turns off the light.

Meanwhile you've had time to get from garage to house, porch to street, up or down a flight of stairs, or down a long hall or across a room.

Since in all but its internal workings a delay switch is similar to an ordinary one you now have in your house, the changeover can be made easily. Just turn off electricity by flipping main switch or breaker or taking out fuse. Then remove the cover plate, take out your old switch and install the delay kind in exactly the same way.

Cost—usually under $3—will often be made up by power savings, the convenience features costing you nothing.

A delayed-action switch is really a low-cost interval timer that is pre-set for only a brief delay. For some lighting, heating or ventilating needs you may prefer an actual interval timer.

One now offered is so compact it will fit on an ordinary single-gang switch or receptacle box or handy box. As you turn it on you also set it for any number of minutes up to sixty—or, in another model, up to twenty hours. It costs under ten dollars and will handle 13.8 amps of light or heating or motors to ¾ horsepower.

PHOTO-ELECTRIC CONTROLS are especially useful for yard and porch lights. They turn lights on at dark and off at dawn without ever needing resetting or other attention.

You have a choice of shapes. These magic eyes come in housings to fit electric boxes, conduit connectors, or post lights. They also come already built into yard-light reflectors and lamp holders.

An old problem with photo controls has now been solved in two different ways. To avoid shutting off from casual light sources, such as headlights of passing cars, some of the controls are equipped with a built-in delay. This keeps them from responding to any light that strikes them for less than twenty seconds. Another manufacturer merely uses tiny louvers to shield his cells from light coming from anywhere but the sky. Of course

Any existing electric outlet becomes a photocell control when you plug this little box into it. It will automatically turn on a lamp at dusk, shut it off at dawn.

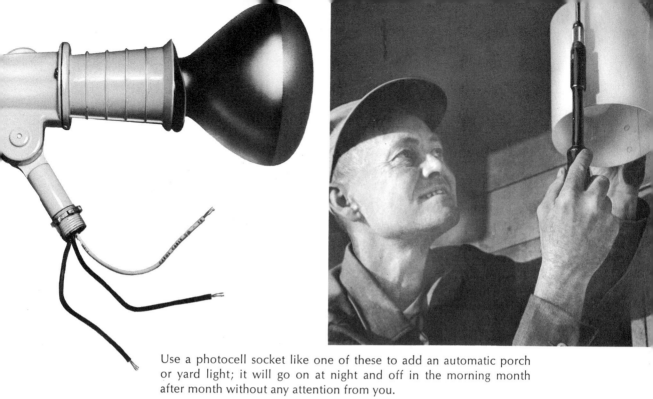

Use a photocell socket like one of these to add an automatic porch or yard light; it will go on at night and off in the morning month after month without any attention from you.

not everybody who wants his yard lights to go on at dusk cares to have them burn all night.

The best solution is to wire the photo-controlled light circuit through an ordinary on-off switch. The light comes on automatically each evening and you turn if off manually at bed-time—if you remember. You must also remember to push the switch back to on some time the next day or nothing will happen when darkness falls again.

One answer to the problem—urged by the Intermatic people as the most flexible—is to combine a time clock with a photo control. Let the latter do the turn-on job while the clock handles the turn-off, at midnight or whenever you prefer. Combination devices combining both types of control in a single unit are also on the market.

Another maker has worked out an economical answer that fits ordinary home needs. It is a portable plug-in photo-electric control with a built-in switch and automatic reset.

Left to its own devices, it will turn your lights on at dusk and off at dawn. But you have the option of using its switch to kill the juice when you go to bed. And it will *still* turn them on again the following evening without your having to remember to restore its operation.

The gadgets to automate your home get smarter every day.

42

Make Enameled-Copper
Switch and Outlet Plates

**Metal-enameling becomes a home-improvement art when you
use it to make unique replacements for those dull plastic covers**

Enameled-copper plates of your own design will add a new color
note to every room of your house.

The process is the same as the one used to produce
jewelry and decorative dishes. Essentially it consists of arranging
dust-fine grains of glass on clean copper and then fusing the
glass permanently to the metal at a temperature of about 1500
degrees.

The heat you need is most easily supplied by a small
electric kiln, sold in hobby shops or by mail from craft houses
for $10 to $20, depending upon its size.

However, if you want to experiment before investing and
already own a propane torch, you can use it as the heat source.
Using the hottest flame available, pass the torch back and forth
under the copper plate until the glass melts into a smooth coating
and fuses solidly to the metal.

For best results with a torch make a simple reflector kiln
by cutting a section out of an empty tin can with a tin snips, as
shown in the photograph. Any can at least 4½″ high will do.
Punch two holes near the open end and run a bit of wire across.
This will make the thing more rigid and will give support to the
plate you're enameling. The can retains and concentrates the heat
of the torch under the plate you're enameling.

Heavy copper blanks, already cut and shaped to form single and double switch plates and outlet plates, are available from hobby shops, or by mail from craft suppliers. From the same sources you can obtain a few simple materials. The switch plates cost about 75 cents each. Tiny jars of colored enameling-glass cost less than 50 cents each. The dust-fine glass is available in hundreds of shades. You also can get glass in thread or lump form to use in creating unusual effects over the basic coat of enameled-glass.

Esther Julian, of Santa Barbara, California, created this Siamese switchplate. Method: Place stencil after firing base coat, dust on second coat of enamel, remove stencil, clean up rough edges around design with a small brush, fire again in the kiln.

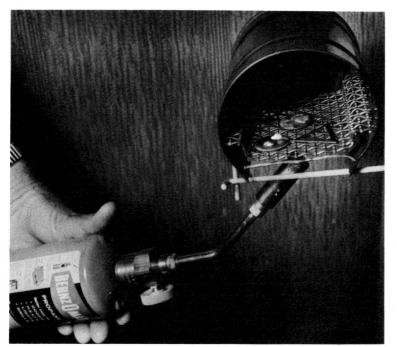

You can make an inexpensive heat-reflecting kiln by cutting away about a third of an ordinary can. Run a piece of wire through two holes to give additional support. Support the tin-can reflector on some kind of wire frame similar to the one shown here. Be sure you keep it well clear of any flammable material. A shelf bent from wire mesh will support the work.

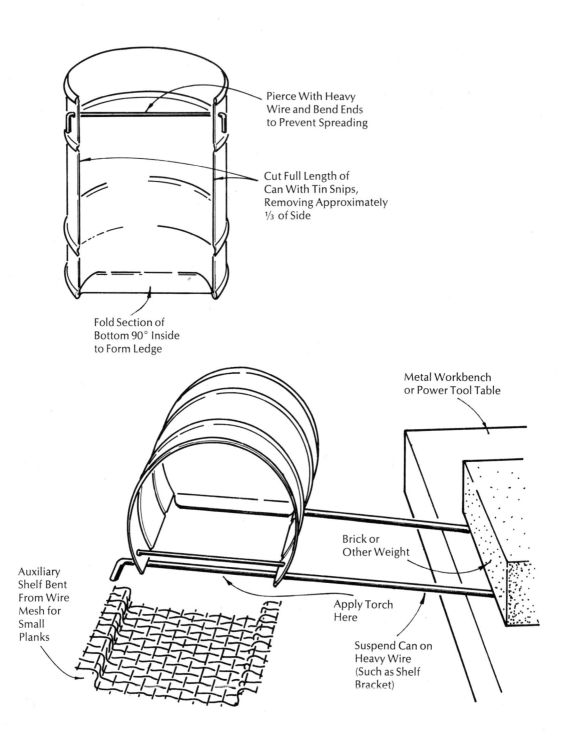

Pierce With Heavy
Wire and Bend Ends
to Prevent Spreading

Cut Full Length of
Can With Tin Snips,
Removing Approximately
1/3 of Side

Fold Section of
Bottom 90° Inside
to Form Ledge

Metal Workbench
or Power Tool Table

Brick or
Other Weight

Auxiliary
Shelf Bent
From Wire
Mesh for
Small
Planks

Apply Torch
Here

Suspend Can on
Heavy Wire
(Such as Shelf
Bracket)

You can carry the craft further by experimenting with brush-on wet enamels and crackle enamels that form patterns. You may want to add effects with metal wire or brush-on paints that are then fired like powdered enamels. Gold and platinum lustres, gold and silver foils, and confetti-colored bits of glass can be used for an infinite variety of effects or designs.

If you don't trust your artistic talent, you can buy tiny motifs, costing less than a dime, to fire right into a coat of clear enamel (called flux) over a basic first coat. Such forms as miniature golf sticks, cowboy boots, antique autos, animal or floral designs come ready to use.

To start out you'll need at least the copper plate, one or two jars of colored enameling-glass, an ounce of lavender or binder oil (often a thin coat of gum tragacanth is used) to hold the enamel in place until it is melted. You'll also need a spatula and an asbestos pad to handle the hot plate when it is taken out of the kiln. A heavy weight, or an old iron, is also useful to place on the hot enameled object as soon as it comes from the kiln. This will prevent buckling and warping of a plate which must fit flat against the wall.

The step-by-step photographs show the basic process. You can improvise as you observe the results you get. Names of copper supply shops are given at the end of the book. Most of these companies also send out catalogs which include detailed information on various enameling techniques.

One great thing about enameling switchplates on copper is that you can change the results as you go along. Just dust another coat of enameling powder right over the first design, put the plate back in the kiln for re-firing, and you'll get a new color and a new effect. You can keep right on doing this until you're satisfied. Enameling artists often put on as many as fifteen coats of enamel to get special depth effects.

Put the plate on the wall as soon as the metal is cold. Its beauty and colors are permanent. Or put it there until the next time you redecorate, then add more enamel, refire, and you have a new plate at almost no cost.

Once you've mastered the enameling technique, you'll find other ways to use it. Enameled-copper cutouts add decoration to drawer handles and cabinet knobs. Enameled rectangular shapes can be combined to make a wall mural. Enameling artist Esther Julian, who made the cat plate shown, designed a mural consisting of seventy-two pieces fired individually in a small kiln and then assembled to create the mural.

1.

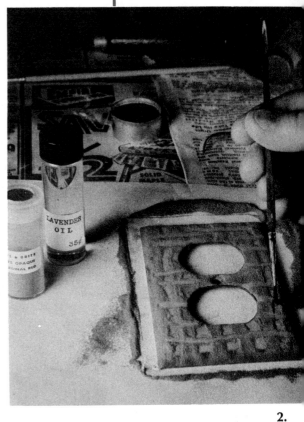

2.

1. Clean the copper. Use ordinary kitchen cleanser or special copper cleaning material available from a hobby shop. Rub, rinse thoroughly, wipe dry. (Do not clean with steel wool or bits of the metal may remain to mar the finished enamel coat.) Keep fingers off the surface after you've cleaned the plate; oil may keep enameling glass from adhering to the metal.

2. Brush the surface with lavender oil, or use a thin coat of gum tragacanth. Then sprinkle on the enamel, covering metal surface evenly until it looks like velvet and no copper shows through. Enamels often come with a sifter-top bottle. Use this, or get an 80-mesh sifter to shake enamel onto plate. Catch excess and dump back into can. You can create a personalized design as this enameler is doing with a brush.

3.

4.

3. Sgraffito is the word for patterns drawn in enamel with a pointed stick. This plate was fired with clear enamel, called flux, before dusting with blue enamel. Final result will be a pattern of European road signs in gold on blue for home of an international traveler.

4. Lumps of special glass can be used on plates to melt into unusual jeweled effects. When the plates have been fired, you'll get the results you see here. Completed plate is cooling on an asbestos pad.

5. Lift switchplate in or out of the kiln quickly with a spatula. Heat escapes rapidly, so do not keep the kiln cover open more than a few seconds. The whole process from dry enamel to red-hot flowing glass should not take more than three or four minutes. An orange-rind wrinkled surface on the plate is indication that your kiln was not hot enough or you did not leave the plate in long enough to melt the enamel completely.

6. When lumps of glass melt on a switchplate you can create strange designs or shapes by using long metal hooks in a technique called swirling, as shown here. Tip: After removing plate from kiln, immediately weight it down with a heavy object such as an old iron, or your plate may not fit smoothly against the wall.

5. **6.**

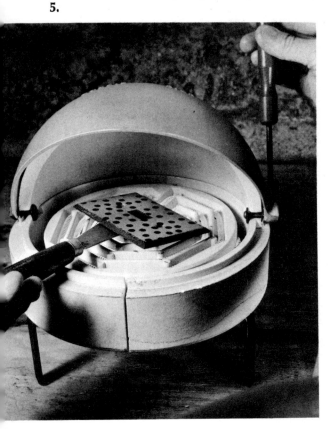 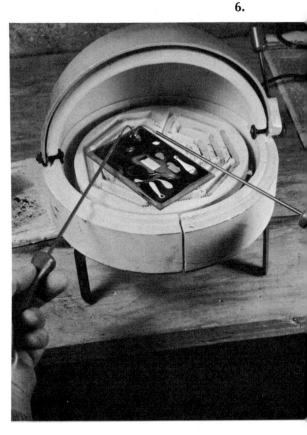

Build a Luminous Ceiling

Unobtrusive, glare-free, broad-source lighting can help restyle your house

Where would you want a luminous ceiling?

Kitchen: By all means. There's no room in which even, glareless, all-pervading light will be more welcome.

Dining room: Not the whole ceiling, but perhaps in the form of a table-sized panel directly over the dining table.

Living room: Generally not. The spotty light that comes from individual lamps is less efficient than overall lighting, but it seems far cozier.

Bedrooms: No. But in a large bedroom a sewing center will be improved by a luminous ceiling covering a limited area.

Bathroom: Here is an ideal spot for a luminous ceiling covering most—or preferably all—of the room.

Workshop: Splendid, though perhaps something of a luxury. But a section of luminous ceiling, placed over workbench or tools most used will be well worth its cost in safety alone if you do much of your work under artificial light.

Family room: Most likely in the form of two or more sections.

The essential elements of the simplest luminous ceiling are a framework holding rectangles of translucent material and a series of ordinary light bulbs evenly spaced around the ceiling.

For each bulb you will need an octagon electric box and a porcelain socket, plus enough electric cable to connect them to each other and to the source of electricity.

If there is already a ceiling light in the room, you will be able to connect to its box. Otherwise you will have to run cable from a source of electricity and perhaps install a switch.

In all cases, naturally, *be sure that power is off before touching wiring.*

Use a type of wiring cable allowed by your electrical code, normally whatever the house was wired with originally. Romex is easiest to handle, generally accepted.

If your luminous ceiling is to cover the entire room, or as much of it as you wish to illuminate fully, allow one light for each 10 or 15 square feet of ceiling. If the ceiling must illuminate an area much larger than itself, you may want one socket for each 4 to 5 square feet of luminous ceiling.

These figures will give quite even and attractive lighting. Exact intensity, which will depend upon wall and ceiling color as well as how the room is to be used, is something you can modify later by choice of light-bulb size.

The diffusing material that forms the actual luminous ceiling is usually fiberglass-plastic. This material, most commonly seen in corrugated form and used for such things as patio roofs, is also made in flat sheets and in rolls of flat material under a number of trade names including Filon. The roll material, being thinner and less expensive and easier to cut, is usually the best choice.

For a handsome effect like this, frame your luminous ceiling with an eggcrate of lumber that matches the trim of the room. Diffusing panels here are white Filon fiberglass-reinforced plastic.

When your room is as small as this kitchen, it is well to make the entire ceiling, or most of it, the light source. Wall-to-wall lighting, like wall-to-wall carpeting, adds to size of room.

For the greater stiffness needed for longer spans, use flat sheets. For even greater stiffness, use the corrugated type; the 1½″ corrugations make a more attractive ceiling than the larger corrugations that are ordinarily seen in outdoor installations.

Although tints are available in some types of fiberglass-plastic, it is usually wiser to use white or the almost-white the makers of Filon call "clear." Tinted bulbs can be used to gain color, and they are must more easily changed for white if you wish. You might also want to try this suggestion: lamps in different pastel colors will give striking effect.

To estimate the cost of the ceiling, figure 40 to 80 cents a square foot for the diffusing material. Add on about $1.50 for each light (cost of box, porcelain, cable and bulb). Cost of wood needed for framing will vary a good deal, but usually won't amount to much.

A typical luminous ceiling installed by the author wall-to-wall in a bathroom 4′ by about 8′ used three lights (with 100-watt bulbs) and cost just under $23, including switch and switch box.

For the most unobtrusive framing, use T-sections of aluminum (sold for this use) or wood. Make each wood T-section by gluing two strips of wood together. Stem might be a 1" x 4", crossbar a 1" x 2".

A silent mercury switch, by the way, is well worth the extra half dollar it costs. The silent switch adds an appropriate touch to the luxurious feeling that the ceiling gives.

To frame for a ceiling in a large room, fur down in any way that will provide a series of ledges on which the diffusing plastic can rest. The method will depend upon the ceiling structure of the room. If your new ceiling is part of a major home improvement, you will probably be able to frame it with the same kind of material used elsewhere in the room. Just run a trim strip all the way around the room at the chosen distance below the existing ceiling. Then, for a narrow room, merely run crossbars. For a wider room, run supports both directions. You can do this in eggcrate fashion.

An alternative to wood construction is the use of aluminum angle and T-section material that is sold for just this purpose. You fasten angle pieces all around the wall, then join them with one or more T-section pieces. These, in turn, are joined by other such pieces. Building material dealers often can supply these parts. They can be ordered from either Sears or Ward's, who also stock

When one room serves two purposes—such as cooking and eating—a limited area of luminous ceiling can help make the visual division. Where spans are long enough to produce sag, counteract it with wire ties from the new framing to the old ceiling or beams above.

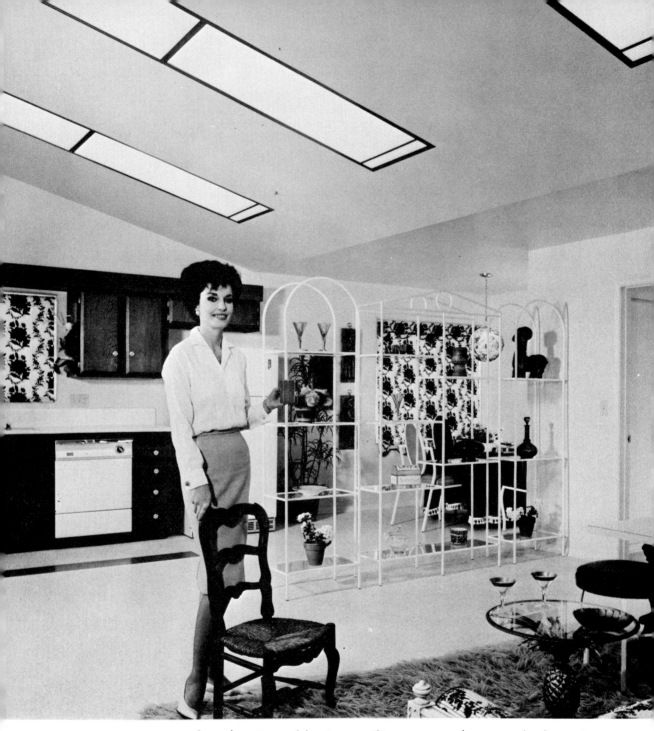

Spaced sections of luminous ceiling are a good compromise in a room too large for wall-to-wall treatment. Also especially desirable in a large room is a dimmer instead of an ordinary switch. With one of these a luminous ceiling can even serve as a night light.

Mini versions of the luminous-ceiling idea make attractive area lighting. You might adapt this idea to any place where work or reading makes good illumination important: bed, sewing table, game table, hobby corner. For such an installation over a dining table, try pink bulbs to flatter complexions.

A special version of the ceiling-that-illuminates is the light soffit, easily built of the same lumber used for construction of the room. By its location under a high window, this soffit serves a daytime lighting function as well as a nighttime one: its diffusing plastic gathers daylight and showers it onto the part of the room directly below.

Man's end of this luxurious bathroom uses a ceiling lighting fixture built like one section of the overall luminous ceiling above it. The walls and cabinetry are rosewood and black, the oversize El-jer lavatory is blue, and the carpet and towels are gold.

This long vanity counter is an idea adaptable to any bathroom with space for it. The makeup compartment is lighted from below, while the lady who uses it is lighted by an overhead fixture that gains effectiveness be proximity to mirror.

380

Photo Left
Much of the effect of a luminous ceiling can be produced by painting a ceiling white and illuminating it strongly. The steel ceiling in this experimental house effectively reflects light from a number of fluorescent fixtures especially made of steel mesh.

Photo Right
An enormous fixture like this, with its 24 square feet of diffusing surface, gives broad-source lighting much like that from a true luminous ceiling. The authors made it for their two-story living room by assembling three pieces of framed luminous-ceiling Filon. It uses a 300-watt bulb.

a variety of translucent panels in 2′ x 2′ and 2′ x 4′ dimensions. If you like one of the patterns available and the dimensions in which they are offered suit your plan, substitute this kind of diffuser for the fiberglass-plastic. The cost will be about the same.

It is best to plan the grid so that the plastic diffusers are not more than 4 feet square. Large pieces are difficult to handle for cleaning. If you use fiberglass-plastic in the economical roll form, one dimension will be limited to the 30″ width in which this material is sold.

Heavy plastic can be cut with a handsaw or—more easily—a reinforced flexible cut-off wheel on a circular saw. But a tin snips will do well with the flat type. The thinner Filon that comes in rolls cuts nicely with a household shears.

Five photographs show the steps in installing a light fixture especially made for a tile ceiling. Sprinkling a number of such fixtures about the ceiling will give broad illumination, much as a luminous ceiling does.

44

Your Music-Intercom System

It can play your records and tapes, pipe music or your voice through your house, wake you in the morning, answer the door, take messages, watch over a baby

The best of modern intercoms are so versatile that building one into your home may be well worth your while even if you don't need an intercom.

It is this remarkable versatility, too, that has brought systems of the kind shown in the pictures to such popularity in new-home building. Because they are so usual in upper-bracket new housing, adding one to an existing house is an effective updating operation.

Since intercoms can do so many things, the first problem is selecting the one that does best the things your house needs most. Here are the things that can be done by one or more of the models offered by just one company, NuTone, Division of Scovill, in Cincinnati. Use this list to establish the priorities for your own installation.

1. Intercommunication among various rooms or outdoor areas of a house, or between them and outbuildings. Thus your intercom is a sort of house telephone. Because a modern system, with its solid-state parts, uses no more electricity than a clock does you can leave it on all the time.

2. Doorbell amplifying. This is accomplished by wiring electronic door chimes into the system. Then they will sound in all the speakers throughout the house.

3. Door answering. If you wish to communicate with a caller from wherever you happen to be—and in safety—you can include a speaker at the door or gate. The caller hears your voice in this speaker and also replies through it by holding down a "talk" button.

4. Door opening. For even greater convenience combined with security, you can have an electrically controlled latch on your gate or front door. This is not actually part of the intercom system, but the parts come from the same dealer and a door-opener is often installed along with the intercom—since an intercom is what makes it so useful. Essentially it is a latch in which the plate pulls away from the door lock when a solenoid, or electromagnet, is activated by a touch of a button.

5. Fire and burglary protection. Like some of the other new features, this is not available with all intercoms. But it can be made part of NuTone systems by addition of a control alarm unit and one or more smoke-heat detectors. It can include an outside horn and flashing beacon that alerts the neighborhood at the same time that internal alarms are relayed and sounded through the intercom speakers.

6. Radio reception. All but the simplest or most highly specialized intercom systems include a radio receiver. It may be limited to an AM, but often includes an FM as well. The master unit, which houses the radio tuner and amplifier and intercom controls, will also have a speaker. Radio music is piped to the other speakers in the system, and your intercom messages will be heard over it.

7. Record playing. This is accomplished by plugging in a turntable or changer, music from which will then be heard in all the speakers. Speakers made especially for use with some of the systems shown are now available.

8. Tape playing and recording. As with record players, any tape device may be connected to your music-intercom system. You may use a casette player-recorder, cartridge tape player, or a reel player-recorder. Any of these can be used to play music throughout the system, of course. And the recorders can also tape music directly from the radio tuner or the record player—as well as directly if connected to a microphone.

9. Stereo music. The most elaborate music-intercoms are equipped for FM stereo reception and for handling stereo music from record players and tape players. Naturally these require two speakers, well separated, for each room in which stereo reception is wanted. Less important rooms may be equipped with single

Chairside location was the most convenient placing possible when this music-intercom system was added in the authors' home. Since this is a stereo system, speakers are external for necessary separation. Seen at right are closed cupboards housing record and tape players and an open one for storing records.

speakers, for music without the stereo effect and for intercom purposes.

10. Message taping. A brand-new development is incorporation into the master unit of a casette tape recorder-player. This location, and the inclusion of an "alert light," make it so convenient to use that it serves as a family message center. It can also record and play back radio programs.

11. Listening in. When you wire a room for a full intercom system, you are "bugging" it as well. But in a perfectly acceptable way, since the microphone is both evident and easily defeated by turning the volume setting to off. This means that you can hear any sound made by a baby or a bedridden invalid in a distant part of the house. With the volume control on the room speaker turned up, set that channel at the master unit to "listen." Any sound in the room will now be audible over any other speaker in the system that is turned on.

12. Morning awakening. Any intercom-music system, like any radio, can become a musical alarm clock. Just wire it through a timer, as described in the chapter on automation in the home. With an intercom, however, this method has the drawback of putting out of action the other features—communication, door chime, alarms—that you might wish to have on all night. One of

This view of the authors' installation of a 2071 series NuTone intercom shows phono and tape-recorder cabinets open. Identical cabinets may also be obtained for record storage. Connected to this master unit are hi-fi speaker pairs in living room and bedrooms, singles in porch, shop and at door.

NuTone's new models, the same one that offers the casette massage center, has a timer built in; and another of its systems can give complete flexibility by use of a special remote speaker that incorporates a clock timer. Install one of these in your master bedroom. Set the alarm at bedtime and the music goes off till the chosen morning hour, while other functions remain on and ready. If you want music to go to sleep by, a separate timer will supply this for as long as you set it for, up to sixty minutes.

With all these possibilities—and who knows what new features may be added, even while this is on the press?—an intercom-music system does a lot of modernizing for any home. While choosing your system calls for these many decisions, installation involves only two major operations.

One of these is building in the components—the master unit, any accessories you choose, and the speakers. Since all these parts are designed to fit between studs in standard frame construction, this is usually no great problem. Just cut a hole in the wall and mount the metal box, which comes with each component, with the screws provided.

Location of your intercom master is a highly personal choice. A busy kitchen is a logical place, since it keeps the person working there in easy control of the music and at the same time provides instant communication with the rest of the house and the front door.

Another popular location is within arm reach of an easy chair that is frequently occupied.

Music accessories—tape and record players—should be within a few feet of the master unit, ordinarily as close as possible. A commonly recommended height for master and accessories is at least 32″ from the floor. A location nearer the floor, as seen in some of the photographs, is convenient only when operation is to be by someone sitting down.

In choosing a place for the master unit, keep in mind that it must have an electrical supply. And it must be placed so that it is possible to run wiring from it to each speaker location. Con-

Installation of this typical intercom master unit is in three steps. Steel box is mounted in wall and connected to power. Four screws fasten chassis to box after speaker connections have been made. Then the walnut-trimmed front goes on, also held by four screws, and the control knobs are slipped on their shafts.

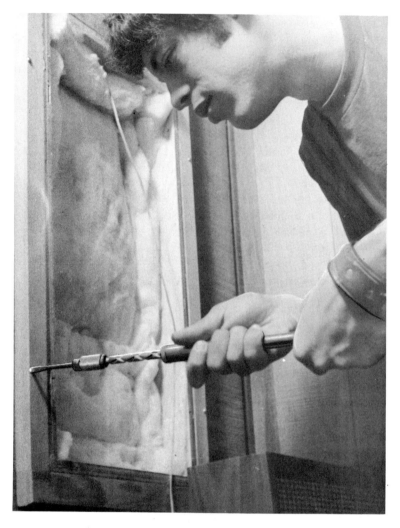

Living-room speakers for the intercom-music system seen in the previous photographs contain a pair of 3½″ tweeters and a 12″ woofer, yet fit into ordinary frame walls. External part seen at bottom of picture is walnut, fits over fiberglass - padded housing being installed within a wall

sider all the attic, basement, and outdoor possibilities for the wire when conditions in an existing house make it impractical to work within walls.

Each principal room of the house deserves a speaker, as does any patio or porch or workshop that is in frequent use. In deciding whether an only partly detached room (such as a kitchen in an open-plan house) needs its own speaker, consider intercom and door-answering uses as well as music listening. One of the most important functions of an intercom system is saving steps— and throats.

Where intercommunication aspect is not needed, or wiring to speakers is not feasible, this music center can be mounted for a built-in look. Whether shelf- or wall-mounted or incorporated into a room divider, it becomes part of a home-improvement project as no freestanding music system can. Tambour doors conceal stereo record and tape players and radio for AM, FM, and FM stereo. With a pair of extension speakers, this system serves second room.

Photo below left

This unit is monaural so can include its own speaker. It is the master for what is called a centralized system and contains all the controls. Only 3-wire cable is needed to connect it to its remote speakers.

Photo below right

In contrast to the unit installed in the room with the turned-on wallpaper, this one controls a decentralized system. Although it requires 8-wire cable, it can be wired from speaker to speaker. You may find this an important advantage in putting a system into an existing home. With this system, each speaker is its own control center for music, door answering, and intercom.

Photo left

Another virtue of a decentralized music-intercom system is that it permits use of a timer-speaker like this in your bedroom. When you set the alarm at bedtime, music is silenced but the intercom feature remains on. Music starts again at the chosen morning hour to awaken you. There's a sixty-minute timer for music to go to sleep by.

Photo right

If you are especially interested in clock and communication features, you may prefer to combine an elaborate master unit like this one with simple speakers in other rooms. Radio music at master and elsewhere is provided. Cassette tape recorder makes the unit a family message center, can also record from the radio. Clock timer permits up to an hour of music after it is set to go off during the night and on again in the morning to do the work of an alarm clock.

PART VIII

BUILT-INS
AND STORAGE

45

Put Your Walls to Work

Every home needs more cupboards and cabinets for concealed storage. Here are ways to build them, often without stealing any space at all from the room

Full-sized closets are fine, but even one that's a mere two feet deep robs a room of a significant amount of useful space.

The ideas this chapter offers for your adoption are different: many of them take no space away from the room, and the others take so little that it usually wouldn't be missed.

Varied applications of three principles make this possible:

1. Storage units built into walls occupy, partly or entirely, space otherwise wasted. The mathematics of this are surprising. Studs and stud spaces in a wall 12 feet long use up something like 32 square feet of floor area. You reclaim the greater part of this when you turn it into storage. At today's building and remodeling costs, 32 square feet represents at least several hundred dollars.

2. When a storage unit hangs on a wall instead of sitting on the floor, it may take away nothing from the effective space of the room. It also follows that a unit reaching from floor to ceiling holds far more for the floor space it takes up than one that is only table high.

3. Organized space is often worth two or three times as much as the same space without well-placed partitions and shelves. When the arrangement can be modified as needs change, the space becomes even more efficient.

Facing page

Combination of window seat and vertical and horizontal bookcases, all continuous, gives this room's storage a unified appearance. Paneling is random-width tongue and-groove redwood finished with Stain Wax. Idea worth adopting: Vertical center strips support long self spans without partitioning shelves.

392

Shelves and cupboards set flush with the surface of one wall take up only half the space of surface ones. A unit like this (built of Western pine boards) can go into a wasted recess of a bedroom wall or combine back-to-back with another to fill out a wall that is partly closet.

No space is wasted here. Sliding doors that give access to closed storage space below shelves and window seat look like marble but actually are Marlite, a hardboard with an extremely durable surface. Even the short wall that holds the plumbing has several cubic feet available for organized storage of toilet items

MEDICINE CABINET ON PANELED WALL

1. These three photographs show steps in building a medicine cabinet in a newly paneled bathroom. Frame is ¼" prefinished plywood with short lengths of the same material laminated into place to support the shelves—each of which is two thicknesses of the paneling laminated back to back.

2. Trim added to the front of the cabinet is a standard outside-corner molding supplied by Weyerhaeuser for use with its paneling. It has been modified and installed here to provide a slot in which a door of flat fiberglass-reinforced plastic can slide. Shelf at author's right thumb is halfway between top and bottom of cabinet.

3. Plastic door (made of heaviest available grade of Filon in "clear" grade) is flexible enough to bow while being snapped into grooves. When resting at cabinet bottom it conceals four shelf spaces, leaves top two open. Friction in top-trim slot holds it open while lower shelves are in use. Decorative pull is slice of manzanita burl.

1. **2.** **3.**

1.

2.

1. One good way to make semiconcealed between-studs cabinets for any paneled wall begins with cutting these four pieces of lumber. Two vertical pieces, seen in foreground, have slots to take shelves, will usually be about 3½" wide to correspond to wall thickness. The horizontal have no slots but are ½" wider and have ¼" grooves plowed ¼" from one edge.

2. The four pieces go together like this and are then nailed within the stud space. The door, a rectangle of the material used to panel the wall, slides between the grooves.

3.

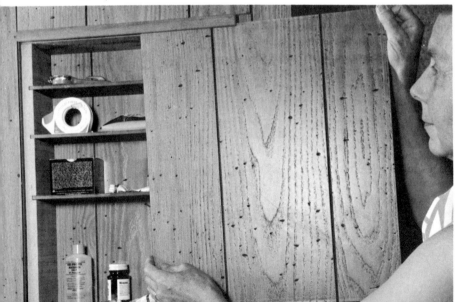

3. The between-studs medicine cabinet looks like this when completed. Although not invisible, it is so inconspicuous as to add little to any feeling of clutter in a bathroom. A pull or handle could be added—a decorative fragment of burl or driftwood, for instance—but none is actually needed.

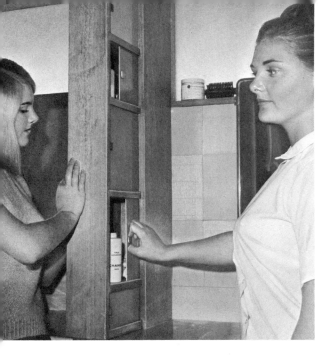

Photo left

Making virtue out of necessity, this stud wall covers a plumbing vent pipe—while separating twin lavatories, housing a light fixture, and storing cosmetics. Doors made of flat Filon translucent plastic slide in grooves cut in the shelves. Pulls are squares of glass tile.

Photo right

Neater storage for small objects is provided when some of the shelves in a bookcase wall are converted into closed cupboards. Two circular-saw kerfs in each half are spaced at $1/4''$ intervals, those in the upper shelf being deeper than those in the lower for easy insertion of doors.

Concealing garage and carport clutter is a particularly effective home improvement because these areas are so often visible to so many people. You can make doors like these by gluing wide redwood boards to long 1" x 4" strips, putting battens at joints to conceal them.

397

Photo left

Here a wall system of Masonite hardboard paneling and slotted metal strips is used to create an auxiliary kitchen, also used as a photographic darkroom. Paneling for such systems is inexpensive and is available in a variety of woodgrain patterns.

Photo right

Special storage-wall systems simplify construction and permit easy changes. This one, offered by Masonite, combines prefinished wall paneling with slotted strips into which metal hooks fit. The hooks hold such special fixtures as bookshelves and magazine racks, can support cabinets you make yourself or wide brackets to hold up an ordinary slab door to turn it into a desk, as here.

The same kind of system seen with hardboard paneling can be created with grooved plywood such as Texture 1-11. Slotted steel strips are a standard hardware-store item and come with shelf supports of varying width. A wall like this could hold cupboards and a desk.

399

A wall with a smallish window punched out of its middle is neither attractive nor an efficient use of space. Here's an answer if there's one in your house. Drawers and stock louvered doors combine with shelves of Ponderosa pine. Note how scale is preserved and a solid feeling produced by using thicker ⁵⁄₄" pine for the wide shelf.

This total-flexibility storage unit is quickly constructed if you use pregrooved plywood (Texture 1-11 is the name of the pattern) for the shelf supports. Prepasted lining papers, fabrics, and foils offer an easy way to add smooth, brilliant color to sections of the plywood or hardboard back.

Make the addition of ample wall-storage space part of a paneling job. Concealed storage is a prime way to reduce clutter while adding to efficiency. Plastic-finished walnut-grained hardboard is framed with 1" x 2" pine strips to give the doors needed stiffness. Back wall, continuing behind dresser, is same walnut pattern predrilled for hanging shelf brackets, pictures, various storage devices.

46

Build a Room Divider

When's a wall not a wall? When it makes one room into two yet lets each continue to share the space of the other

A room divider is a kind of partial wall that gives each of two areas its own identity without fully cutting it off from the other. Unlike a wall, it adds either decoration or storage and display space. Usually it provides both.

Very often a room divider is light enough, or is caster-mounted, so that it can be shifted or removed as the function of the room changes.

Among the furnishings you add by building them into dividers are: cabinets of all sizes and shapes to fit special accessories, counter space, a fold-out desk, radio and tape- and record-playing equipment, an extra heating unit, a fan, a room cooler, a degree of concealment for an ugly existing radiator, book shelves, storage space for snacks and bottled goods, a box-frame to display a painting, a planter, a bulletin board, a display for a collection of specimens or photographs.

Does your house lack a private entryway? Many older homes have a front door that opens right into the living room and lets in drafts while destroying privacy. In this section you will find photographs and information on how to build a divider that not only adds a private entryway but also provides a coat-closet.

If you entertain often but don't want your living room to look like a cocktail bar, you can conceal a snack-and-drink counter in a room divider and have it open only when you want it.

You may not need to consult a psychologist to solve the problem of youngsters' quarrels. Often it's a lack of privacy, or of a place for personal possessions, that leads to family friction. A room divider can give each child his own special place with cabinet space and study desk. If you want to, you can provide a see-through area above the desks that can be closed or open depending upon the wishes of the users.

The photographs in this chapter show a variety of dividers. One of them may work out perfectly for your home. More likely, though, since each house and the people who live in it form a unique combination, you will prefer to treat these designs as suggestions and adapt some of the ideas they offer.

Below left

Open shelves hung on poles make a divider with minimum visual interference. Effort and skill required are minimum too, since all parts can be purchased ready for assembly. Pressure against ceiling holds poles rigidly upright, so there are no screws or others fastening devices to leave traces behind if divider is removed.

Below right

Peg Board takes many kinds of metal and plastic fixtures, is the basis for this easily constructed divider. The plastic surface of this special Peg Board wipes clean with a damp cloth. It is obtainable in various woodgrains, as shown here, and in plain colors.

Some design methods shown for a working wall in the preceding chapter are put to work to make a highly flexible room divider. Texture 1-11 pregrooved plywood provides the slots that permit changing position of each shelf and cupboard. Since the plywood backs can be placed on either side, the unit can present one blank face (permitting its placement along a wall if desired) or access can be divided between the faces. If this divider is used to house a record player, the vertically partitioned spaces used here for magazines can be turned to record storage.

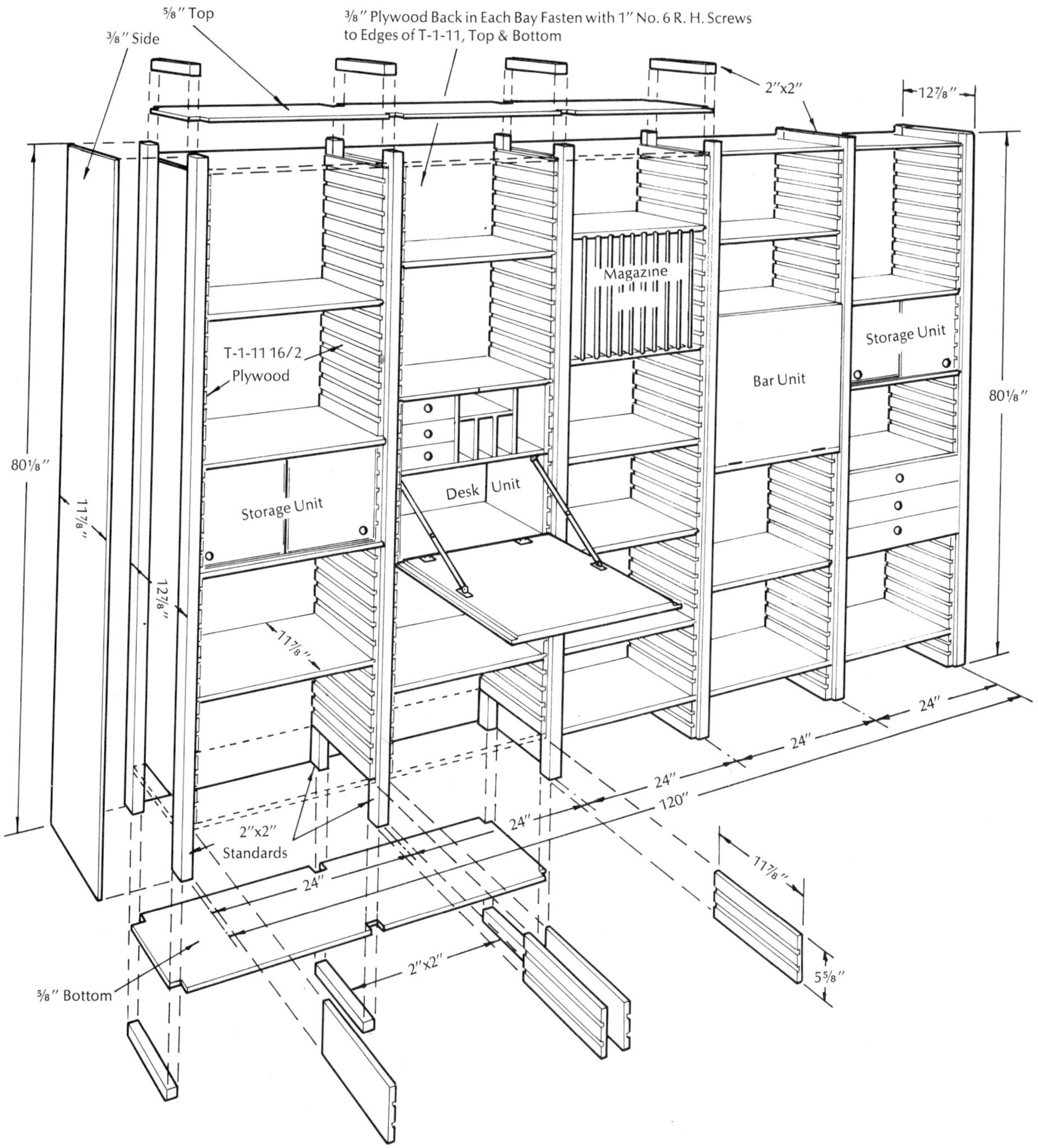

5/8″ Top
3/8″ Side
3/8″ Plywood Back in Each Bay Fasten with 1″ No. 6 R. H. Screws
to Edges of T-1-11, Top & Bottom
2″x2″
12⅞″
Magazine
Storage Unit
T-1-11 16/2
Plywood
Bar Unit
80⅛″
80⅛″
11⅞″
Desk Unit
Storage Unit
12⅞″
11⅞″
24″
24″
24″
24″
120″
2″x2″
Standards
24″
11⅞″
5⅝″
2″x2″
5/8″ Bottom

Redwood divider separates a bedroom from its private sitting room, offering storage for games and papers (at lower right) as well as books. Glowing coils and copper reflector of the radiant electric heater in the center of the wall provide cheer as well as warmth. Use of redwood lumber 2″ thick makes for a comfortably massive effect, is also a way to make long shelves that will carry the heavy load of books without sagging.

Peg Board holes simplify storage uses without tempting anyone to drive nails. Units like these are light enough to remove and convert to other uses when no longer needed to divide a room used by two boys into bed cubicles plus a dayroom.

Here are the two aspects of a room divider made to function effectively from both sides. Designed by Gideon Kramer for plywood construction, it serves a living room and its dining area well. It would adapt easily for use in a family room or near a front door. As shown here, the divider is 18" thick, 6' high, and about 8' long. The large doors slide on regular closet-door hardware. The small ones have curved edges for a nice design touch that makes finger pulls unnecessary.

407

Above left

When two areas of the house require only a visual hint to separate them and there's no space (or possibly need) for additional storage, a lacy screen may be the best type of divider.

Above right

Screen made of fiberglass-reinforced plastic is unaffected by dampness and blocks view almost completely without cutting off light. Another virtue is its built-in color that never needs renewing.

A freestanding screen seems more casual than a partition, has the advantage of easy removal if its use is only seasonal. Lightness of this one, made by weaving strips of flat Filon plastic around wood framing, contrasts with solidity of permanent dividers seen at right.

This is a big, solid storage-divider, but thanks to the ten casters it secretly sits on and the moldings that fit it snugly to floor and ceiling, it can move to another room—or from a position in the middle of the room to one against a wall—at any time. The desk, with its top of wood strips laminated together, folds up. The various cupboard and cabinet units can be interchanged or moved to different heights because the compartments in which they sit are lined in an unusual way: with Western red cedar bevel siding applied upside down to create a series of ledges. If you're interested in building one like it, or in having details from which to work in designing a unit of your own, you'll find information in the Appendix about how to order a plan sheet. In honor of its caster arrangement, this movable storage wall has been named the Caravan by the Western Wood Products Association for which it was designed.

This comfortable king-size bench is actually a capacious storage unit and divider, suitable for a large area such as a family room, or a porch or patio. The framework is covered by boards and battens to harmonize with the construction of the authors' home, walls of which are to be seen behind it. Finish, also in harmony with the house, is Cabot's heavy-bodied stain in sagebrush gray. In adapting this idea to your own space and needs, you may wish to alter the sheathing material to go better with your house. Foam cushions are covered with fur fabric; for use in an unprotected outdoor spot a good covering material would be plastic that sheds water.

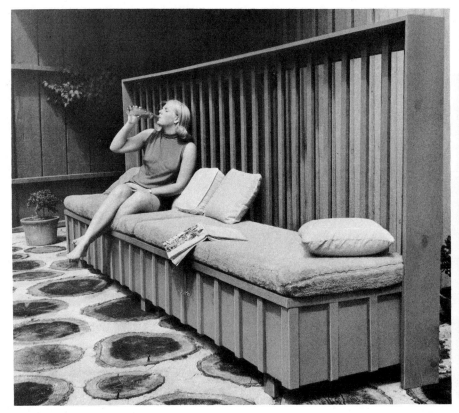

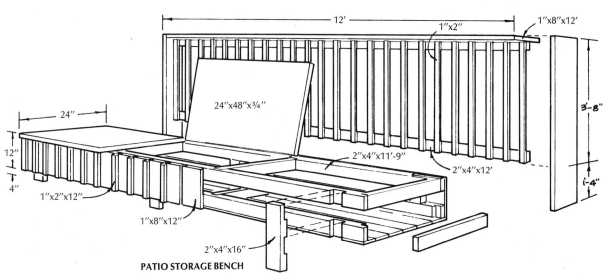

PATIO STORAGE BENCH

410

HOW TO BUILD THE STORAGE BENCH

1. Assemble the 2" x 4" framing pieces as shown in the diagram into a pair of skeletons like this. Then give one of them a bottom by covering it with hemlock flooring or plywood—exterior grade if the unit goes outdoors.

2. Saw notches into the edges of the flooring to match the leg notches in the frames. Put on the six notched legs, holding them temporarily in place with clamps or nails.

411

3. Now secure legs strongly by placing a ⅛″ x 1¾″ flat-head stove bolt at each of the twelve joints between leg and frame.

4. Put on sheathing of plywood, shiplap, or other siding, or boards and battens as here. Use three pairs of heavy galvanized 4″ T hinges to mount lids of ⁵⁄₄″ ponderosa pine or ¾″ plywood (exterior grade for outdoor use).

5. Make screen by assembling a frame as shown in the diagram. Cover with staggered 4' lengths of 1" x 2" or use wider boards for a different effect. Stain or paint to match your house.

47

Hang a Desk

Like any furniture not resting on the floor, a suspended desk is neater and more efficient in its use of space. One of these desks has an ingenious typewriter drawer you can build

An unused corner turns into a streamlined study space or dressing table when you hang a desk on the wall. By keeping it off the floor you'll not only provide plenty of leg room, but you'll also simplify cleaning under it.

The first of the desks shown in this chapter forms a study corner in the master bedroom of a home built by the author. The top surface is tapered to offer minimum interference with a doorway. Topped and edged with walnut-grained Formica, the working surface wipes clean and will not be stained by writing materials or cosmetics.

Desk side and fronts of drawers are Philippine mahogany to match the paneled walls of the room. Cork squares at one side form a pinup board. Cupboard with sliding doors of translucent fiberglass-plastic is built into the studs to get additional depth without using up desk space.

An unusual feature of this desk is a typewriter shelf that disappears when not in use and really works when it's out.

It meets all these necessary specifications:

1. It slides silently in or out at a touch.
2. It has a sound-muffling, nonslip surface.
3. It's heavy enough to give no bounce under anyone's typing touch.
4. It provides extra space to hold papers when copying.
5. It has an instantly folding front that matches the other drawers.

You can include a working shelf like this in almost any kind of desk you may want to build. Or you can add it to an existing desk to replace a drawer.

For the sliding mechanism, use a standard rolling drawer slide, sold by lumber yards and hardware stores.

Shelf can be a piece of $1\frac{1}{8}''$ plywood used here, or laminated of thinner plywood to thickness of $1''$ to $1\frac{1}{4}''$. Working surface can be cork floor tile, glued on, or the Ozite carpet tile described in the chapter on goes-anywhere carpeting.

Shelf size depends on desk design and typewriter to be used. This one is $12'' \times 25''$.

Fasten the sliding hardware to the shelf and to the inside of the desk. Screws and instructions come with the unit.

Make a drawer front to match the desk. In remodeling an old desk you may be able to adapt the front of the drawer you're replacing.

Use a length of continuous ("piano") hinge to fasten front to shelf. Screw one leaf on the hinge to the front so that the pin is $1''$ or more from the bottom. Fasten the other leaf to the underside of the shelf.

To control the action of the hinge, mount an ordinary cupboard catch (about 50 cents in any hardware store).

When you pull out the shelf for use, touching this catch lets the front drop down out of the way of the typewriter carriage. It then forms a useful shelf.

When you hinge up the front afterwards to slide the shelf in, the catch grabs of its own accord.

To complete the job, put on a drawer pull to match those on the other drawers.

Both more elegant and more easily built than a freestanding equivalent, this desk-dressing table occupies a corner between two doorways. Wood is Philippine mahogany to match the walls and the chair, which also was designed and built by the authors. Details on constructing this sturdy typewriter-height pullout shelf are given in the text.

Out of use, an in-the-wall desk takes up no room space at all. You can install a readymade one or build your own. This unit, by Swanson, is made in fruitwood finish, fits between the studs of any 4"-thick wall. Rough dimensions are 30¼" wide and 12¼" high. Be sure there are no concealed wires or pipes in the section of wall you're going to cut out.

This compact combination of shelves and a table with a suspended drawer becomes a desk or a dressing table, depending on where you use it. The elements are available as parts of a wall system of brackets, shelves, shelf supports and desk tops with drawers (Dorfile). Made in a choice of walnut or white, these elements can be reorganized, changed in height, or transferred to another wall or another part of the house when redecorating is in order.

Peg Board, that old flexible-storage favorite for shops, garages, and kitchens, is quite acceptable in other rooms in its new prefinished forms. Accessories for this Masonite Royalcote in walnut grain include brackets to take heavy shelves and desk tops as well as the usual hanging devices.

417

Add a Formica-covered sheet of plywood and a shelf to a wall of
Peg Board and a kitchen corner becomes a hobby center or a home
office. Paneled walls as well as Peg Board have a plastic surface
that wipes clean with a damp cloth.

48

Put a Safe Into a Wall

Even a lightweight, inexpensive safe can protect your valuables from fire and theft—if you conceal it inside a wall and choose its location craftily

There are three good reasons why installing a safe should be part of your home-updating program.

Security. Household robberies are on the increase, but a sneak thief or even a burglar usually is not a professional safe-cracker. He wants to get in and out of a house in a hurry, taking whatever valuables he can gather quickly. He isn't prepared to blow a safe, nor does he expect to find one in the average home. He probably won't even search for a safe that's built-in and concealed. If he does find the safe, he can't easily open it, especially if it's a recessed type with a lock that can't be hit from above with a heavy object.

One home safe features a patented relocking device that's one step ahead of the burglar. It holds the door in a locked position should the thief be clever enough to knock or pry off the lock.

Safes come with either tumbler or key locks. If you use a safe with a combination lock, you can change the combination if the house is occupied temporarily by someone else.

Security from fire is the best reason for putting family papers and valuables in a safe. Safes of the kind covered in this chapter are all fire-resistive and will store papers safely for more than a hour of very high temperatures. A home fire is normally put out within a short time. Papers in a safe are also protected from smoke and water.

Economy. You don't have to pay rent each month on your home safe. The unit lasts as long as your house and its initial cost is low. The price of the safe may easily be saved by not having to pay a lawyer to replace a misplaced legal paper.

Convenience. Although you may prefer to have a box for your valuables at a bank, there are times when papers, bonds, or jewelry must be brought home for use. A home safe doesn't keep banking hours.

A safe at home will also protect you against yourself— the times when you tuck away birth certificates, insurance policies, coin collection, or property papers in a drawer, book, or even under the mattress and then forget where you put them. At times of illness or death lost papers can inflict undue hardship on members of the family who cannot locate them. With this special locked vault of your own there'll be a definite place for every member of the family to put things where they will be at hand.

Soon to be concealed, this Mosler combination safe is permanently recessed into the back of a stone fireplace wall in a home built by the author. The safe is impossible to remove and is doubly protected by its own tumbler lock and its deep recess into a solid masonry wall. There is no way to knock the tumbler off with a heavy instrument and no way to pry it out of its bed of cement mortar.

A gray mirror door, hinged, has been added to conceal the safe. The mirror, made inconspicuous by its color, is convenient for a quick checkup on hair or makeup for members of the household before answering the door and by guests arriving or departing.

A major remodeling or the addition of a fireplace will give you a chance to build a safe into a masonry wall without any extra work. This Hercules safe has been set level and wedged into place before stones and concrete fasten it permanently into a bedroom fireplace wall. Drilled flanges are used when installing in existing wall.

421

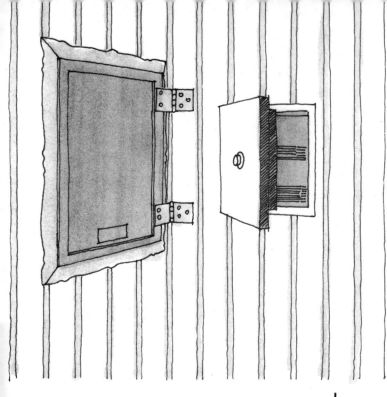

This safe mounts flush with the wall where it can easily be covered by a painting.

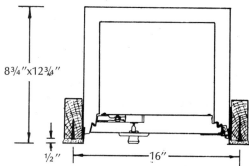

8¾″x12¾″

½″

16″

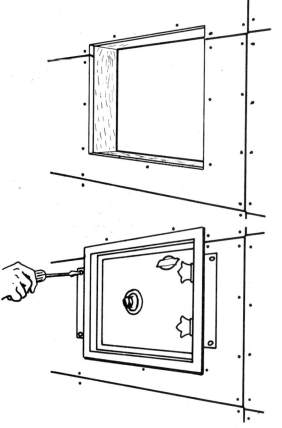

Wall vaults like those shown can be obtained in sizes to fit between conventionally placed studs. The safe goes into the opening as in the sketches, is fastened to studs with screws, and paneling or other finished wall then covers the flanges. In walls of ordinary depth the safe will protrude into the room behind it, so a location opposite a back corner of a closet is desirable.

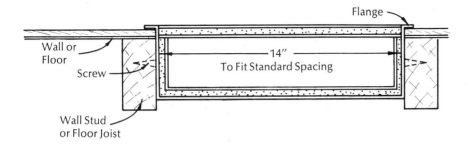

Wall or
Floor

Screw

Wall Stud
or Floor Joist

Flange

14"
To Fit Standard Spacing

A thin vault can be installed in any wall since it goes entirely between the studs. This type is designed to be added to an existing wall after a simple, rectangular cutout has been made. Door works to either right or left, depending upon which side of safe is placed up.

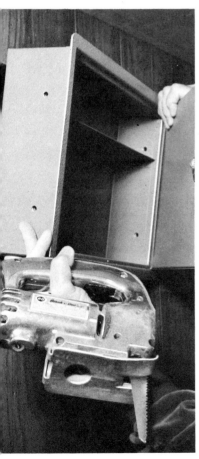

LOCATION. Where do you put a safe? The obvious place is on a wall behind a picture or mirror. But you don't need to be quite that obvious. You can build it in behind a heavy piece of furniture or make it look like a part of the wall itself, especially when you recess it far enough so any decorative object covering it is flush with the wall.

One of the safes is less than 4″ thick and can be fitted into the floor under a concealing carpet or piece of furniture where it would take a lot of looking and physical effort for a stranger to find it. It could also be concealed in the wall of a dark closet behind clothing or a false wall panel. If you happen to be doing a paneling job, this would be an ideal time to put in a safe with a cover to match the wall material. Don't overlook one thing. Be sure to tell those who should know its location where it is.

Safes come in many sizes. One about 12″ square and 12″ deep is more than ample for most homes. An even smaller one (Nor-Gee) is designed to fit between wall studs. It's 10″ x 14″ x 3¾″ deep and is installed by fitting it between normal 14″-spaced studs. Screws go into studs from inside the safe, so once it's locked there's no easy way to remove the asbestos-lined unit. The narrow visible flange does not allow sufficient bite for a thief to pry the safe out of the wall.

49

Build a Better Closet

Compartment your closets, add shelves, line them with cedar, and the storage space you now have will look better, work better, smell great

You can't organize people, especially members of your own family. But you *can* bring a good bit of order into their lives, by providing them with storage facilities that have order built into them.

This means putting closets where now there are none. Or improving existing closets by adding partitions or shelves or drawers or boxes or bins or slots. And making closets and cupboards and chests more protective and much more pleasant by giving them tight new linings of cedar.

With the present choice of cedar materials it's much easier and more economical than it used to be to turn an ordinary closet into a luxurious storage space with a fresh natural aroma. Thin cedar boards do the same work as ordinary thick ones at less cost and you have the even more economical option of using an aromatic new flakeboard of cedar.

You can have cedar storage space, even if you don't want to line a closet, by using either form of cedar to line a cupboard or storage box. You may want to build the modern version of the cedar chest—a bedroom lounge seat with a cedar-lined interior, as described later in this chapter.

Each kind of cedar lining has its own special advantages:

Individual cedar boards offer light weight, supersmooth surfaces, beautiful color, wonderful odor. They cost more than the flakeboard panels and take longer to put up, but they are truly luxurious and will retain their beauty for the life of the house, needing only a light sanding occasionally to renew the strength of the cedar aroma.

Cedar panels of compressed red cedar flakes also have a fine odor. They are not as handsome as cedar boards but come in either 4' x 8' or 16" x 48" panels which are easy to fit into any shape and go up fast, require less skillful workmanship than matching tongue- and groove. This paneling is easy to use when lining a cabinet, windowseat, or odd-shaped storage area. Like the boards, this material should not be painted or finished in any way, since this would destroy the cedar odor.

USING CEDAR BOARDS

1. Start a closet lining job by removing all existing shelves, hooks, rods. If there is molding around the floor, take it up. Base board should also be removed for a more finished job.

2. If closet is unfinished, you may wish to start by fitting insulation of either fiberglass batts or roll material in between the studs to cut down heat or cold penetration. Next, tack or staple an odorless heavy building paper to the studding on the inside. If the closet already has wall material, you can skip this step.

3. Cedar boards intended for lining closets and cupboards come with a tongue cut into one edge and a groove into the other. The ends of each piece are of like construction. The idea is to make your closet as near airtight as possible, by putting the tongue of one piece into the groove of the one adjacent and pushing it up closely. The same process should be used in joining end pieces.

4. Put the floor and ceiling on first. To put down the floor, start against the wall opposite the door and work toward door opening. Fit pieces together as tightly as possible.

5. Just before you put down the last course next to the door, close the closet door and make a pencil mark on the floor along the bottom edge of the door.

6. Rip a piece of the lining to exact width to fill in the space between the piece just laid and this line, allowing just enough space to permit the door to close without binding. In laying the floor and ceiling follow the same instructions for matching up the pieces as given in steps 7 through 10.

7. After floor and ceiling have been lined, start on the widest wall. Select a piece of cedar two or three feet long, and with grooved edge down, you start your first course at the top of the base board. If there is no base board, on the floor, letting the

grooved end come up against the wall to your left. Pieces should run parallel to floor and ceiling.

8. Nail this first piece against the wall using a two-penny finish or casing nail. (If nailing to plaster, better use a three-penny nail.)

9. Next, pick out another piece of cedar of sufficient length to fill out the remaining space between the end of the first piece and the right hand wall; if the exact length is not available, then cut off a piece just long enough to fill in that space. In doing this measure from the grooved end. Now fit the groove of the second piece to the tongue of the first piece, and nail in place, first making sure the tongue side points upward. Do not throw out the end you have just cut off, but use it to start the second course, placing the freshly sawn end against the left hand wall. Second course should be laid in the same ways as the first. Continue almost to the ceiling, and then on the last course, you may find you need again to rip a piece in order to fill out the remaining space. For a stronger and neater effect, stagger the joints.

10. On the remaining walls, use a square to cut the ends of the strips, so there will not be gaps in the corners.

11. There are two methods of lining the inside of the door. First—start at bottom of door allowing enough room to clear the cedar lining already on the floor, and nail all pieces just as you have on the wall. Bevel off the ends at each side of the door to permit easy closing. Second—you could, instead, select two strips of cedar which are the full length of your door, allowing for the lining already on the floor and dress off the tongue with a hand plane, placing dressed side out. Outside edges should be beveled. Now fill in between these two side pieces, running the strips horizontal to the floor the same as on the wall.

For a perfect seal, complete the job by using ordinary weatherstrip around the door. Now you can replace the shelves and accessories, or build new ones to make your cedar closet really efficient.

USING CEDAR-FLAKE PANELS
1. To line a closet with cedar-flake panels instead of boards, start by measuring walls and any other surfaces that are to be covered.

2. You'll save time and material if you outline how the panels are to be shaped and used. The 16" x 48" panels are easier to work with than the 4' x 8' size if you have to carry the

material back and forth from a shop. Edges of pieces should be centered over wall studs where joints are necessary.

3. Use 1¼″ finishing nails to fasten panels over existing wall material. This material doesn't split. If you miss a stud, forget it and drive another nail. The one that got away won't show against the flake background.

4. For a neat finished effect apply trim. This may be the old molding salvaged or it may be new molding of cedar or a contrasting wood.

5. Try for as airtight a closet as possible. Weatherstripping around the door will help to seal in the aromatic result. No finish should be used on the panels, of course, or you'll seal in the very odor you want to circulate.

What does it take to turn your old-fashioned, wasteful walk-in closet into this? Stock pine shelving, louvered doors, and some careful planning. Note the slanted shoe shelves, the sliding rack for handbags, the large amount of ceiling-high dead-storage space that gets rid of so much clutter.

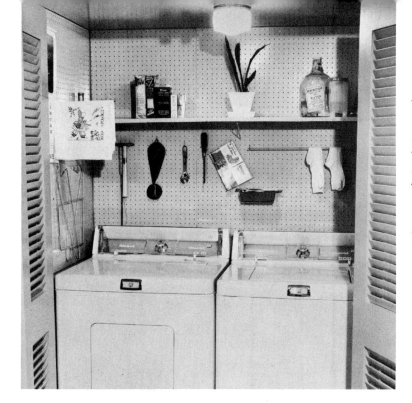

A tiny closet can become a laundry. Making the walls of Peg Board simplifies hanging tools, shelves, a drying rod. The louvered doors give necessary ventilation. Even if you have no closet you can duplicate this one by boxing in laundry units now sitting against a wall or on view in a kitchen or garage.

Photo left

Lightweight panels of compressed cedar flakes are easy to cut and fit into any closet, boxed-corner, or attic space to give attractive aromatic protection to clothes and blankets. Like plywood or hardboard paneling, they are most quickly applied by use of panel adhesive.

Photo right

Panels go up quickly with adhesive, 1¼" finishing nails, or a combination of both. Edges of panels should be centered over a wall stud. You won't need to worry about nails splitting the material or about setting them. They almost vanish.

Things are easier to find, and they go back where they came from, when you compartment a closet. To build a rack of shelves like this into a closet walled with Cedarline panels, use cedar boards. Good trick for building stout wide shelves: laminate two thicknesses of the cedar flakeboard together with wood glue.

Photo left

Odd-shaped corner in the master bedroom of the authors' home became a cedar chest, couch, emergency bed, and decorative piece of furniture. A small magazine bin fills in the angle at one end. Aromatic red-cedar tongue-and-groove boards are snugly fitted together to line a hinged plywood box, which is faced with Philippine mahogany boards to match the walls.

Photo right

The chest-couch seen in the other photograph looks like this when closed. The top is ¾" plywood hinged at the back and edged with a strip of Philippine mahogany that holds the blue and green foam-filled cushions in place. Natural look of paneling and couch was retained by rubbing bare wood with a mixture of white and clear Stain Wax. Interior cedar lining, of course, was left unfinished.

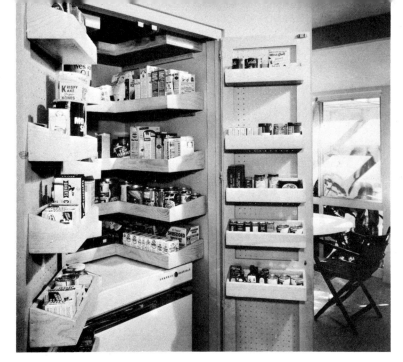

Wide space above an appliance is often wasted or used inefficiently for narrow shelves that don't hold much or wide ones that conceal what they hold. Use ingenious plywood troughs like these on walls and doors to store the most and keep it all visible. Peg Board doors provide ventilation needed for many appliances.

Photo left

Like most, this closet consists only of a single shelf above a clothes rod. Here is a closet that is not paying its way. The next three photographs show ways to multiply the usefulness of such closets.

Photo right

Where the vagrant closet is near the kitchen, compartment it for multi-shelf storage above the existing single shelf. And, if only a few garments must be stored in it, give it a bottom unit with compartments for grocery cart, table leaves, vacuum, plus bin with hinged front for cleaning rags. Shallower upper unit includes wine rack of hardwood strips notched into uprights and drilled for 1" dowels.

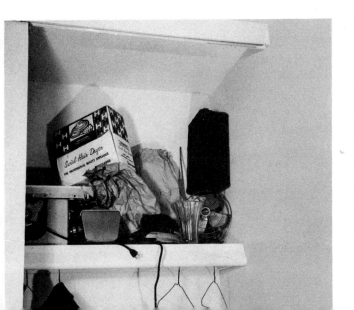

This division of closet space was designed for photographic equipment but could serve you equally well for other hobby materials. The eggcrate unit is best made of ½" to ¾" plywood with ¼" removable dividers.

Here again the storage unit is made of thick plywood with thinner removable dividers. To store bulky items, such as camping equipment, a full-width shelf is provided at top and supported by curving one of the dividers.

432

Whether you are reorganizing an existing closet or creating a new one by cutting a strip 2' wide off one end of a bedroom, flexible dividers are the safest answer. With its toy storage and low-level clothes pole, this closet fits its young owner but can be shifted instantly to other needs as she grows older or occupancy of the room changes.

Predecessor of the organized closet seen in the other photograph was the usual narrow rectangular space with a closet pole and shelf above. The plan for improving it called for spacing partitions to take existing chests of drawers. Homeowner not having these already on hand might prefer to space sections to take drawers directly in grooves as shown in the next chapter.

Framing for partitions is 2" x 2" lumber, to be covered on one side with panels of Texture 1-11 plywood. The grooves precut in this material, which ordinarily is used for house siding, form shelf supports when turned horizontally. Note use of clamps to hold framing.

Main purpose of this big kitchen closet, a compromise between ordinary cupboard and a walk-in pantry, is storage of home-canned
fruits and vegetables. There is also space for cleaning equipment and
extra dishes. You could add a similar storage unit to any kitchen that
can spare even half a foot along one wall. Gain extra depth if possible by using the space between the wall studs.

The inexpensive folding wood-slat door used to close off this hardworking closet opens at both ends, as can be seen by comparing this with the other photograph. Shelves are ⅜" plywood, which fits the waiting grooves, painted bright red. They slide out easily to permit new arrangements. Drawers to fit these grooves can be easily made of plywood with bottoms extended as shown in the next chapter

Mirrors make closet doors useful and solve the problem of matching doors to existing paneling in a home-improvement project. This low location of the clothes pole is good for a small child's room or for stowing garments such as shirts and blouses that are short.

50

Build a Bar

Recreation room, living room, dining room, kitchen—any of these may offer just the spot into which to build a refreshment-dispensing counter

When entertaining times comes you'll be glad to have a bar, whether for soft drinks, milkshakes, stouter fluids, or all three.

You are offered a choice of four designs here—to build or to adapt to your own requirements.

The first of them makes good use of the special characteristics of plywood. The strength of this material and the stiffness it possesses even in large sheets permits its use for free-standing construction without lumber framing. This design is presented in the form of detailed drawings as well as photographs so that you can reproduce it exactly if you choose.

Open the plywood bar and it offers an efficient serving counter jutting well out into the room. Close it and it fades inconspicuously into its corner, occupying only a few square feet of space. Hinged section with casters does it.

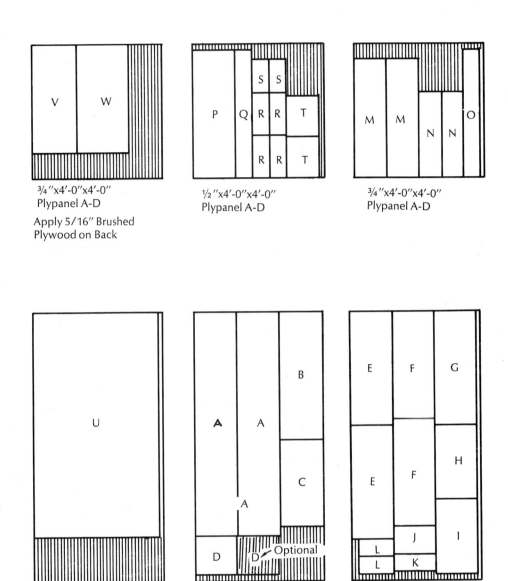

Cut parts to size. Rabbet sides A ⅜″ deep for back panel and fit matching pieces together. To sides, join bottom shelf B, facing strip O, divider Q, bottom P of light trough and partition C, being careful to keep entire structure exactly square. Glue and nail all joints.

PARTS SCHEDULE

Code	No. Req'd	Size	Part Identification
A	2	16"x80"	Side—Back Bar
B	1	$15^5/_8$"x$45^3/_4$"	Lower Shelf—Back Bar
C	1	$15^5/_8$"x$30^1/_2$"	Standard—Back Bar
D	1	$14^1/_8$"x$15^5/_8$"	Shelf—Back Bar
E	2	$15^1/_2$"x$40^3/_4$"	Side—Front Bar
F	2	$15^1/_2$"x$38^1/_2$"	Standard—Front Bar
G	1	$15^1/_2$"x$40^3/_4$"	Bottom Shelf—Front Bar
H	1	$15^1/_2$"x$26^3/_4$"	Shelf—Front Bar
I	1	$15^1/_2$"x$26^3/_4$"	Drawer Shelf—Front Bar
J	1	$9^1/_2$"x$15^1/_2$"	Shelf—Front Bar
K	1	6"x$15^1/_2$"	Divider Between Drawers
L	2	6"x13"	Drawer Front
M	2	12"x$42^1/_4$"	Bar Top
N	2	8"x$30^7/_8$"	Shelf—Back Bar
O	1	6"x$45^3/_4$"	Face of Light Trough
P	1	$15^5/_8$"x$45^3/_4$"	Bottom of Plant Box
Q	1	6"x$45^3/_4$"	Divider between Plant Box and Light Trough
R	4	$5^7/_8$"x$14^3/_8$"	Drawer Side*
S	2	$5^7/_8$"x12"	Drawer Back*
T	2	12"x$13^7/_8$"	Drawer Bottom*
U	1	$46^1/_2$"x80"	Back of Back Bar
V	1	16"x$38^3/_4$"	Door and Door Backing
W	1	$31^1/_4$"x$38^3/_4$"	Door and Door Backing
	3 Pcs.	16"x$79^1/_2$"	2" T 1-11 Doors and Bar Front**
	$3^1/_2$ Lin. Ft.	$^1/_4$"x1"	Filler
	$3^1/_2$ Lin. Ft.	1"x4"	Bracing
	1 Pc.	$5^1/_2$"x$45^3/_8$"	Obscure Glass
	1 Only	40-Watt-36" Long	Fluorescent Tube
	2 Pcs.	12"x$42^1/_4$"	Plastic Laminate Top
	$11^1/_2$ Lin. Ft.	For $^3/_4$" Edge	Metal Edging
	3 Ea.	"Soss"	Bar Top Hinges
	6 Ea.	For $^3/_4$" Plywood	Hinges
	2 Ea.	—	Pin Hinges
	3 Ea.	As Required	Rubber-Tired Casters
	1 Ea.	—	Door Stop for Bar

Miscellaneous—4d and 6d finish nails and glue

* Parts not identified on drawings by letters

** Cut from 3—1'-4"x8'-0" panels of Texture 1-11.

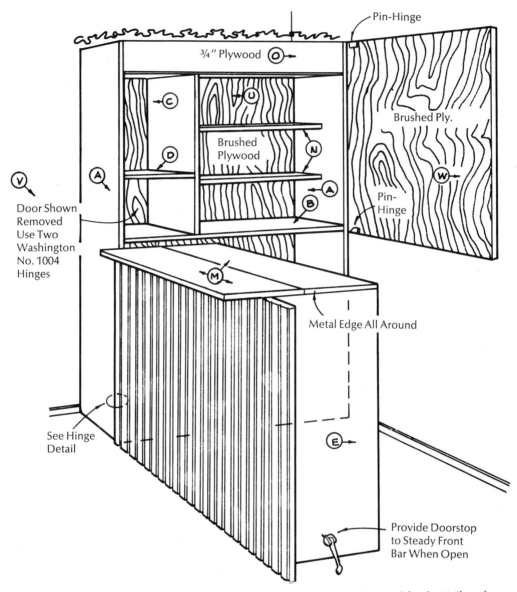

Pin-Hinge

¾" Plywood Ⓞ

Ⓒ

Ⓥ

Ⓤ

Brushed Plywood

Ⓝ

Ⓓ

Brushed Ply.

Ⓐ

Ⓑ

Ⓐ

Ⓦ

Pin-Hinge

Ⓥ

Door Shown
Removed
Use Two
Washington
No. 1004
Hinges

Ⓜ

Metal Edge All Around

See Hinge
Detail

Ⓔ

Provide Doorstop
to Steady Front
Bar When Open

Next, fit and nail into place the brushed plywood back. Nail and glue brushed plywood to back of door material and cut to size. Intermediate shelves may be nailed in position or installed with adjustable shelf supports after finishing.

Before assembling the hinged front bar, notch partitions F and K for the 1" x 4" nailing strip across the top. Because working space is limited, assemble these partitions with fixed top M, shelves H, I, J, bottom G, and hinged side E before exposed side E is installed. Apply Texture 1-11 front, hinged top, and casters last.

Move cabinet into place against wall and attach doors and hinged front bar after finishing.

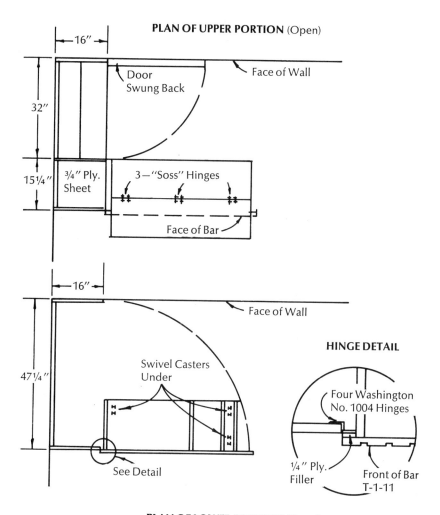

PLAN OF UPPER PORTION (Open)

16″

32″

15¼″

¾″ Ply. Sheet

Door Swung Back

Face of Wall

3—"Soss" Hinges

Face of Bar

16″

47¼″

Face of Wall

Swivel Casters Under

See Detail

PLAN OF LOWER PORTION (Open)

HINGE DETAIL

Four Washington No. 1004 Hinges

¼″ Ply. Filler

Front of Bar T-1-11

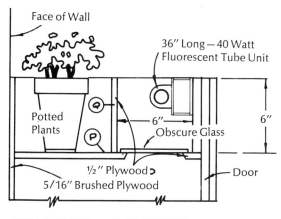

Face of Wall

36″ Long—40 Watt Fluorescent Tube Unit

Potted Plants

6″

Obscure Glass

6″

½″ Plywood

Door

5/16″ Brushed Plywood

DETAIL OF TOP CABINET SECTION

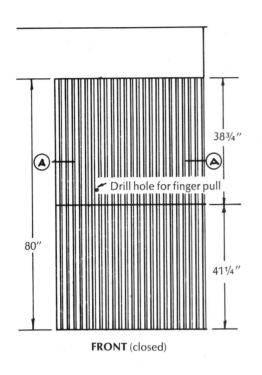

38¾″

A — — A

Drill hole for finger pull

80″

41¼″

FRONT (closed)

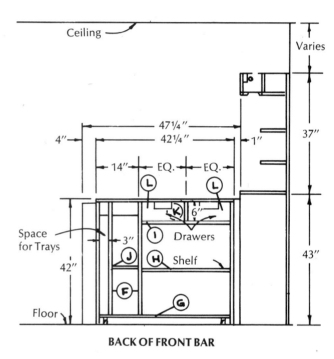

Ceiling

Varies

47¼″

4″ — 42¼″ — 1″

37″

14″ — EQ. — EQ.

L — L

K 6″

Space for Trays — 3″

Drawers

I

42″ — J — H — Shelf

43″

F

G

Floor

BACK OF FRONT BAR

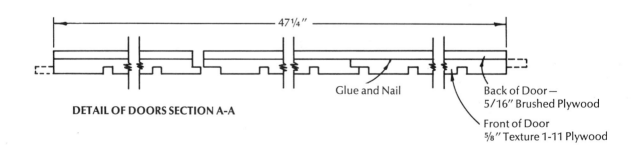

47¼″

Glue and Nail

Back of Door —
5/16″ Brushed Plywood

DETAIL OF DOORS SECTION A-A

Front of Door
⅝″ Texture 1-11 Plywood

442

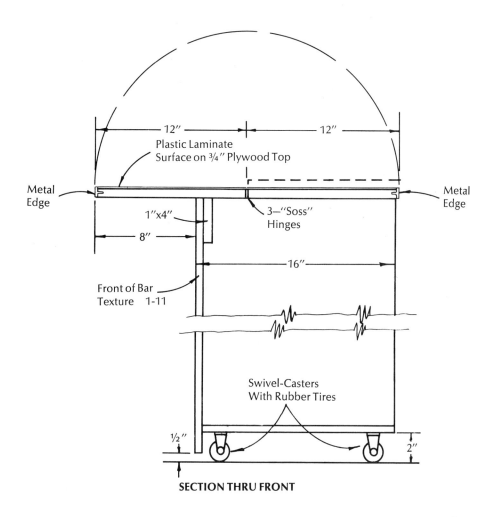

12″   12″

Plastic Laminate
Surface on ¾″ Plywood Top

Metal
Edge

Metal
Edge

1″x4″

3—"Soss"
Hinges

8″

16″

Front of Bar
Texture   1-11

Swivel-Casters
With Rubber Tires

½″

2″

SECTION THRU FRONT

Bib bar for lavish entertaining could easily be scaled down for a smaller recreation room. Walnut-grained hardboard of curved front is repeated in wall paneling except that the latter is pre-drilled for standard fixtures. Many more shelf brackets can be added as needed.

Corner of a basement family room becomes a refreshment bar when you add a counter and storage space. Hardware for adjustable shelves fastens directly to wall. Any narrow boards, plastic, or glass material can be used for the shelves. Walls, ceiling, counters, and front of the bar are all plastic-finished Marlite which wipes clean and will take a lot of punishment.

This versatile home project adds a new wall surface of textured wormy chestnut panels (Marlite) plus a home entertainment center closet-style. These tongue-and-groove panels go over any wall surface with a special adhesive and hidden clips. Instead of the two-light ceiling shown here, you could light the whole area evenly by using a translucent plastic panel, as shown in Chapter 43. Bar goes into hiding when louvered doors are closed. For even more unobtrusive doors, make them of the same paneling material.

51

Make and Install Drawers

There's no storage like drawer storage. You can improve your home by providing it generously, using prefabricated drawers or plywood ones that are easy to make

The trouble with drawers is that when you need them you usually want groups of half a dozen or so, making for a tedious construction process. One answer to this is simplifying construction to the ultimate. The drawings in this chapter will show you ways to build good drawers easily.

For even less labor, use existing drawers when you can. Molded plastic ones can be purchased. Wooden ones can be salvaged from old chests which you may own or can buy at low cost at garage sales. Even quite battered ones can be made much better than new by covering their fronts with plastic laminate using contact cement. Details on working with laminates, such as Formica, are given in an earlier chapter.

Along with the old drawer, you may wish to salvage the method of supporting it. Sometimes the whole case can be used if it is built into a storage wall so that its exterior is no longer to be seen.

For many purposes you can provide the equivalent of drawers by using bins. These may be molded plastic trays of various kinds, or they may be colorful plastic dishpans sold for less than a dollar in variety and discount stores. You don't suspend these like drawers but merely place them on shelves. Even shallow woven baskets in rectangular shape can be adapted to use as trays to take the place of kitchen drawers for knives and silverware.

As an instance of how bins can take the place of drawers at a great saving in effort, consider the problem of organizing the space under a new sink counter. Rather than load it with drawers, a considerable enterprise, you can partition part of it into cubicles to fit plastic dishpans, the rest to take trays, shelves, and other storage items that exactly fit your needs. Then equip the front with a pair of large sliding doors, perhaps of plastic-finished Peg Board. You'll have ventilation, good appearance, easy accessibility, and drawers that can be taken out and washed in soap and warm water.

Another problem that may seem to defy solution is that of a room that needs a chest of drawers but has no space whatever to spare. Sometimes you can find the answer by stealing space from an adjoining room that can spare it. Do this by putting drawers right through a wall. Let them slide into the room that needs them but occupy space in the room that can afford it. Box them in, of course, so that their shape becomes a table in that adjoining room.

A removable unit like this makes good use of space under a counter. Steadied in place by a screen-door hook, it can be taken out, drawers and all, for access to dead-storage space behind it. V-notches in alternate drawers make pulls that do not stick out.

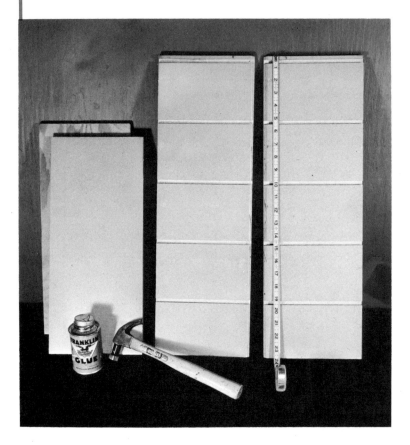

1. Working part of drawer case consists of four boards, or pieces of plywood, two of them grooved to suspend the drawers. Cut the grooves to fit the drawers, or use Texture 1-11 plywood (see previous chapter) and make drawers to fit the grooves.

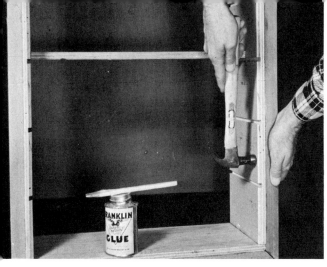

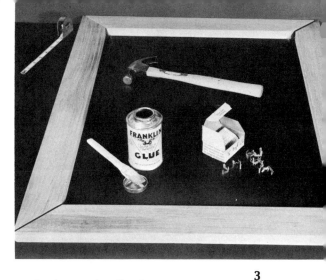

2.

3

2. Assemble four working parts with glue and nails. Fasten on a collar flush with the front edge of the case. If you are making a built-in, none of these parts will show, so any material can be used. And the case need not be the full depth of the drawers.

3. Make decorative frame like this, mitered for good appearance. Since it is the only part of the whole job that will show, except the drawer fronts, make it of wood chosen for good appearance with the other materials of the cabinet into which you are building the unit.

4. By nailing from behind, you can fasten trim frame into place without any nail holes showing. The center brace you see here is needed to keep the frame rigid. Place it so it will not interfere with operation of the drawers, or notch a drawer to go around it.

5. Whole case slips into an opening cut to fit in the front of the counter. A screen-door hook should be added to keep the case steadily in place while permitting quick removal for access to things stored behind it. You'll reach the hook by taking out one drawer.

4.

5.

This drawer, shown upside down, is easily made with saw and hammer. Butt joints are glued and nailed. The bottom should be ⅜″ or ½″ plywood for rigidity. The drawer front extends down to cover front bottom edge.

Additional strip of wood, glued and nailed to front panel, reinforces the bottom of this second type of drawer, made with hand tools. Reinforcing permits use of economical ¼″ plywood, hardboard, or particleboard for drawer bottoms.

Power tools make sturdy drawers easy to build. The picture shows one side (dadoed on outer face for drawer guide) being put into place. Rabbet drawer front (at right) to take sides; dado sides to fit drawer back. All four parts are grooved to take ¼″ plywood bottom.

Two types of guides, both calling for use of power tools, are shown here. As shown at left, the drawer side has been plowed before assembly to fit over a strip glued to the side of the cabinet. Procedure is reversed for the version at right. Here the cabinet side has been dadoed before assembly. A matching strip is glued to the side of the drawer. Even heavy drawers slide easily on guides like these if waxed or lubricated with paraffin after finishing.

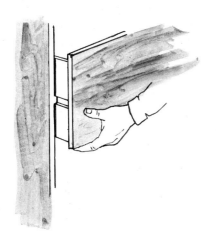 

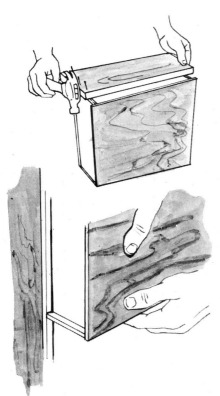

Extended bottom of this drawer fits into slots formed by gluing pieces of ⅜″ plywood to the inner surface of each side of the cabinet. Gap just wide enough to take the lip is left between the pieces.

52

How to Add Shelves Everywhere

While you're about it, don't forget what Cicero said a long, long time ago: "A room without books is a room without a soul." Include plenty of bookshelves

Is your home what the architect Le Corbusier called a "machine for living"? Shelves you can build will go a long way toward making it more efficiently so.

Innumerable spots in most houses call out for them. Waste space above and below clothing in closets . . . kitchen corners . . . blank living-room walls . . . bathroom areas below lavatories or over toilets . . . garage and carport walls . . . even those wasted spaces between studs in shop or garage.

Basic material is softwood shelving, most often surfaced Ponderosa pine in 1″ x 12″ and narrower dimensions. In 1″ x 4″ pine, Douglas fir or other construction lumber is just the thing for narrower shelves that tuck between studs.

For wider shelves, for which solid lumber is neither sufficiently stable nor easily obtained, plywood is a good bet. Unless it is to be painted, it usually calls for edge trim.

Don't overlook the possibilities of precut particle-board shelves, now beginning to show up in lumberyards. For cutting into small shelves a bargain material is sink cutouts. For a square-foot price often little more than that of plywood alone you get plywood surfaced with plastic laminate.

Where appearance is critical you may prefer to use hardwood. The variety most frequently offered in boards sanded and ready for shelving jobs is Philippine mahogany. It is commonly the least expensive of hardwoods, often costing no more than a good grade of softwood. Shop for the pre-packaged kind now sold in nominal 1″ thickness and in assorted widths up to 12″. The pinmark grade with its tiny worm holes is a good buy. You may prefer its appearance, and you will surely like its lower price.

Where shelves are to span long distances or carry heavy loads, don't overlook the advantages of using thicker lumber. Doing so may cost you little more than supplying intermediate supports, and it takes less work. It will give you a bonus both in appearance and in long, unbroken areas for storage of bulky things.

The gimmick is that suitable stock for heavy shelves is not easy to find at moderate price; and if you want wide shelves the problem is even more severe. An excellent answer is tongue-and-groove Ponderosa pine, which is sold kiln-dried in such dimensions as 2″ x 6″ and 2″ x 8″. Such stock can be joined to form shelves of any desired width. For some reason—possibly because it is mass-produced and widely sold for roof-deck and other construction—this material is commonly priced far lower than an equal amount of lumber in other forms. Put the groove at the shelf back where it won't show, and finish the front by planing off the final tongue.

Hollow-core slab doors of Philippine mahogany, handsome and inexpensive, make wide, thick shelves of surprising lightness and strength. They're limited, of course, to situations where you can use the standard dimensions—widths usually from 18″ up, length 80″.

Finish for shelves is usually dictated by the surroundings. Where there is free choice, an easy alternative to the traditional stain and varnish is one coat of Stain Wax. This comes in a variety of gray, neutral and wood tones and pastel shades. It can be applied with brush or rag, left alone for a few minutes, then rubbed off and polished with a cloth. The shelves are ready to use almost immediately, will resist almost any kind of marring, including water stains.

If the shelves are not a decorative item nor are their surfaces to show, then it is best to forget paint. It will be covered by the stored items, will be easily damaged, and will require laborious refinishing at intervals.

Prefinished shelves often come with a durable baked-enamel finish or with a vinyl-clad covering that lasts indefinitely. Formica-clad shelves are colorful, extremely durable, and handsome but somewhat more expensive, unless the shelving material is made from the inexpensive sink cutouts previously mentioned. Formica shelving is especially good in bathroom or kitchen where staining by moisture and cosmetics is a problem.

Hardware stores and lumberyards have a wide choice of brackets and fasteners for attaching shelves to walls, and your choice will be dictated by whether your walls are of wood, plaster, or masonry. The manufacturer or dealer can suggest the proper type to go with the shelves you plan. Masonry walls present a special problem, so you may need to rent an electric hand drill with carbide tip if you do not own one. With it you can drill a hole directly into solid concrete or stone.

You can buy anchoring devices which can then be hammered into the drilled holes. These anchors expand as a nail or screw for a shelf is inserted into them. Outside diameter of the anchor plug should be the same size as the bit in the drill.

TIPS ON SHELVES. In addition to methods and designs shown in the drawings and photographs, here are a few principles and hints drawn from experience. They are worth keeping in mind as you plan and build the shelves that will do so much to make your home a more workable living machine.

- Put shelves on backs of doors, especially inside cupboards and closets.
- Eggcrate shelving will store maps, drawings, prints. An eggcrate shelving arrangement will make a honeycomb for wine bottle storage.
- Revolving shelves make use of waste corners.
- Narrow shelves are more efficient than wide ones for small items such as spices and medicine bottles.
- Shelves for storing linens and placemats and trays should be very shallow to eliminate stacking of items.
- Rimmed shelves with wire-mesh bottoms make ventilated storage for fruits or vegetables.
- Step-up shelves of different widths give all stored items greater at-a-glance visibility.
- Good magazine-storage shelf space can be found in wasted space under a stairway.
- Plates, platters, trays fit well in vertical storage space. A large cabinet will provide a dozen such efficient "shelves."

Shelves slanted backward at about a 45-degree angle in a drawer will provide accessible storage for bottles or cosmetics without the jumble of ordinary drawer storage.

• Keep a shelf unit off the floor and floor space will still be available for other furniture.

• Space in hallway or along a staircase wall is suitable for narrow shelves without subtracting much width from the passageway. Or recess shelves between the studs along a stairway and provide book shelves that take no space at all away from passageway.

• Books seldom used can be shelved in wasted space above windows.

• A double-shelf unit facing two directions can become a room divider.

• Measure books and records before building shelves. Allow an additional 1½″ above books for finger room.

HOW LONG SHOULD A SHELF BE?

The distance a shelf can span without sagging noticeably depends mostly on its material and thickness—and the weight of the load.

Research done at the University of Illinois has produced some useful rules-of-thumb for spans:

• With ³⁄₈″ plywood, limit spans to 26″ for normal loads, 16″ for heavy loads; with ³⁄₄″ plywood, 46″ and 29″.

• Solid wood ³⁄₄″ thick can safely hold normal loads on a 48″ span, heavy loads on 30″. With lumber 1¹⁄₈″ thick, spans may increase to 66″ and 42″.

Books and records are typical "heavy" loads, while clothing, toys, and most dishes will be "normal."

The table below provides more detailed information for planning shelves to be made of nominal 1″ or 2″ lumber, or plywood in any of the usual thicknesses. It applies to lumber having no knots wider than half the width of the board, and to plywood used so the face grain runs in the direction of the span—the usual practice.

The figures given are the weights, in pounds per square foot, that each combination of span and material will support without sagging more than 1/240 of the span (1/20″ for each foot of length). Thus ³⁄₄″ pine lumber used for a 36″ span is acceptable for any load up to 38 pounds per square foot.

If greater spans are required, central support is necessary—whether of the type shown in the sketch, or a wall bracket.

TYPE OF SHELVING—ACTUAL THICKNESS

Distance Between Supports	Pine and Cedar Lumber		Douglas Fir and Larch Lumber		Douglas Fir Plywood			
	3/4″	1 1/2″	3/4″	1 1/2″	3/8″	1/2″	5/8″	3/4″
12″	670 lb.	2,685 lb.	1,134 lb.	4,537 lb.	163 lb.	330 lb.	593 lb.	817 lb.
16″	377 lb.	1,510 lb.	638 lb.	2,552 lb.	68 lb.	138 lb.	249 lb.	374 lb.
20″	222 lb.	967 lb.	356 lb.	1,633 lb.	35 lb.	71 lb.	127 lb.	191 lb.
24″	129 lb.	667 lb.	206 lb.	1,126 lb.	20 lb.	41 lb.	75 lb.	111 lb.
32″	54 lb.	378 lb.	87 lb.	638 lb.	9 lb.	17 lb.	30 lb.	46 lb.
36″	38 lb.	306 lb.	61 lb.	489 lb.	6 lb.	12 lb.	22 lb.	33 lb.
40″	28 lb.	223 lb.	44 lb.	356 lb.	4 lb.	9 lb.	16 lb.	24 lb.
48″	16 lb.	130 lb.	26 lb.	206 lb.	2 lb.	5 lb.	10 lb.	14 lb.
60″	8 lb.	66 lb.	13 lb.	106 lb.	—	—	—	7 lb.
72″	5 lb.	38 lb.	8 lb.	61 lb.	—	—	—	—

"Built-on" shelves can work like built-ins and still offer some flexibility. This system uses standard metal strips fastened with screws and taking metal shelf brackets that fit into slots.

Unlike dark strips and shelves that blend with the wall, these are brilliant white to contrast and add pattern. Big advantage of these shelving systems, sold in hardware stores and lumberyards, is the speed with which they can be installed, altered, or moved.

Hung high on a wall, a backless shelf system like this doesn't detract from the space of a room or its feeling of spaciousness. Magazine-rack accessories, offered for many shelf systems, are logical addition to shelves.

If you are doing over the walls of a room, you can allow for unlimited shelf installation by using paneling that comes with bracket-support strips as a feature. Virtually invisible, the strips are always ready when you want to add shelving.

Graceful shelving system seen here is self-supporting without attachment to ceiling or walls, can be installed for temporary use without marring room finish.

No screws are needed for these supports, either. They are spring-loaded to press against the ceiling. As shown here, the poles are reversed from their normal position against the wall for a different appearance.

Swing-out semicircular shelf unit solves the common kitchen problem of the wasted corner. It is built of Western pine and mounted on standard hardware. Equally ingenious is the corner mounting of the wall oven.

460

A welcome feature of any kitchen is plenty of storage room. This closet of Western pine region wood makes large utensils, lids, and pans easily accessible and the rough-sawn texture of the lumber has sound absorbent qualities, so the clatter of pots and pans, the closing of cupboard doors is reduced to a minimum.

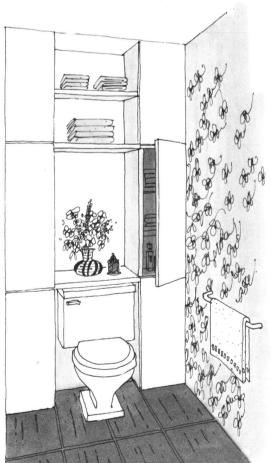

A storage wall of shelves—and cabinets as needed—takes up no useful space at all when it is planned this way. For permanent stability, set shelves into grooves cut into the upright framing, using glue as well as nails.

Doors that conceal shelves in a counter within a kitchen or between it and family or dining room can do double duty. Make them to hinge upward at convenient height with safe supports and they serve for informal dining and buffet serving as well.

Space just under a kitchen cabinet and near the wall is seldom used. Use it for a small, suspended spice shelf.

Steel brackets, sold by building-material dealers and hardware stores, can be the basis of folding shelves in laundry or garage. Out of use they drop out of way.

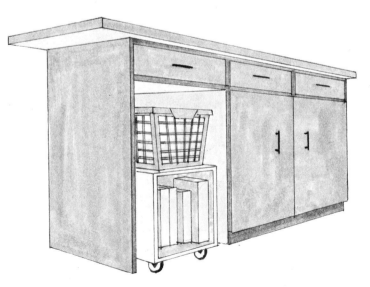

Build a shelf unit like this and equip it with casters. It can be part of a counter in laundry or kitchen.

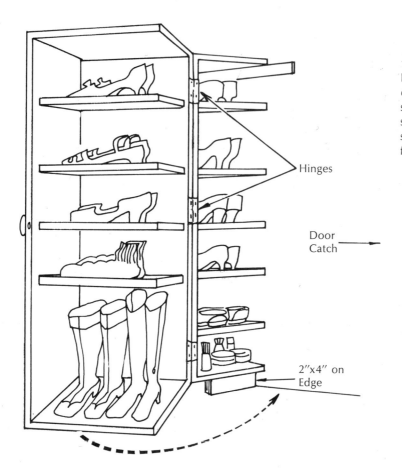

Half the clutter in many a closet is shoes. A hinged shelf unit like this stores shoes, or any other accessories, out of sight and away from dust.

Hinges

Door Catch

2"x4" on Edge

Hang a bookshelf with a fluorescent light built in. This one, built for a sofa too long for lamps at ends to be adequate, would also fit nicely over the head of a bed.

In a household that takes—and saves—many magazines, this sturdy case would be a welcome home improvement. Make it deep enough for all magazines, and build the top shelf narrower than the other slanted one below it.

Tongue-and-groove ponderosa pine decking makes long, wide, husky shelves for heavy-duty storage in basement, shop, or rear wall of garage. Nominal 2" lumber permits long spans. Vertical 1" boards set between shelves give support along back edges, while at front short lengths of water pipe are slipped between shelves to fit in shallow holes drilled before assembly. Since there are no solid center supports, the full length of each shelf can store long items—such as lumber or pipe.

Peg Board, either the ordinary hardboard kind or the plastic-surfaced that comes in colors and woodgrains, holds shelf brackets. An important feature here is the single wood strip, fastened with screws, that steadies all the shelves.

A movable miniature shelf unit, to hang on bathroom or bedroom wall, is made by framing a rectangle of Peg Board. Picture framing or molding to match house trim might be used. Shelves and hooks are white plastic.

467

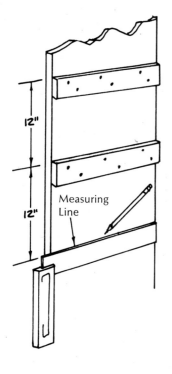

12"

Measuring
Line

12"

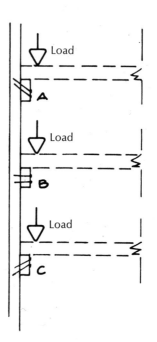

Load

A

Load

B

Load

C

If you are working without a power saw (table or radial) your basic method of supporting shelves will be with cleats. Use a square to establish cleat lines. Stagger nails to avoid splitting. Best nailing angle is shown at C, since the other two angles may let cleats pull away.

One way to make cleats less conspicuous is to set them back a little from the front of the shelf. Another is to bevel the ends. Or make cleats the full shelf-to-shelf distance as sketched here, and they won't show as cleats at all.

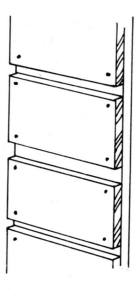

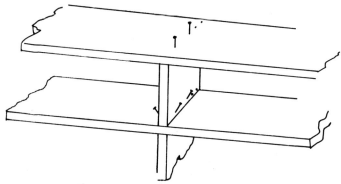

Above

Where shelves are too long for the weight they must carry, prevent sag by putting in intermediate supports. One end of each will have to be toenailed, as shown. Avoid visible nailheads by turning the unit upside down if possible while nailing.

Below left

An economical method of supporting shelves so heights may be varied anytime is with a row of holes drilled near each corner. Standard metal angles with studs fit the holes, or you can substitute short lengths of wood dowel.

Below right

For your more important groups of shelves you may prefer to use this system. Four strips are fastened to uprights and shelf supports clip into them. This method is especially tidy if the strips are set into grooves in the wood.

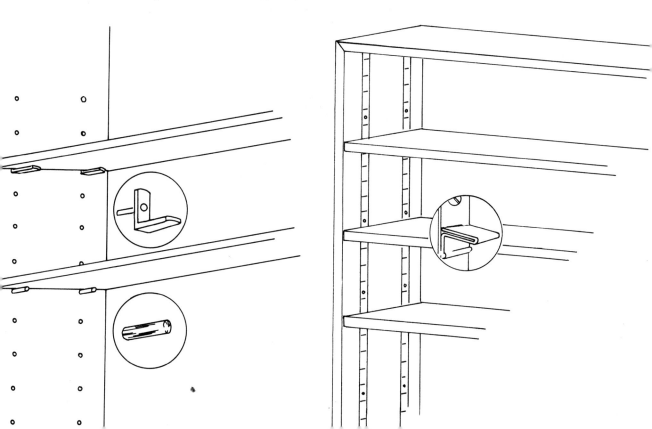

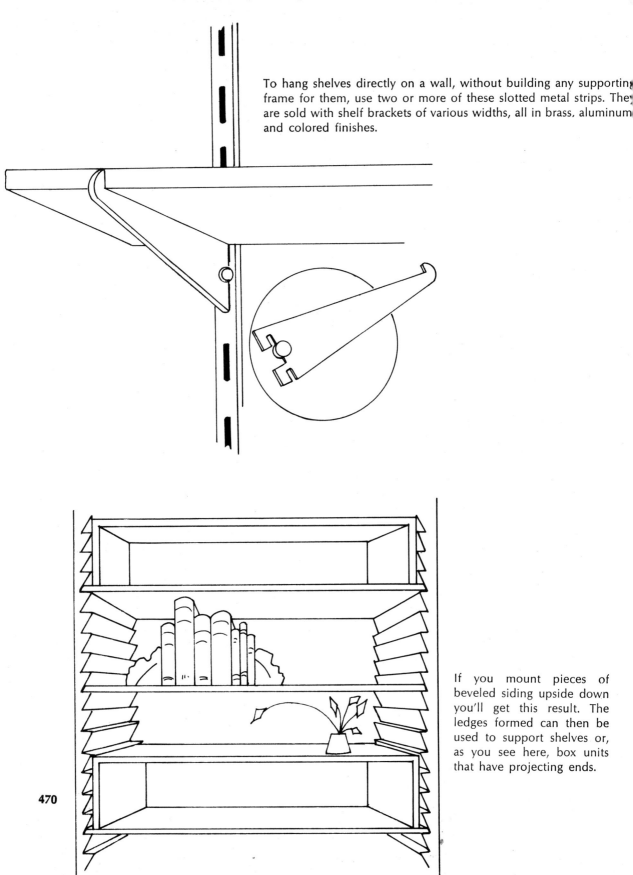

To hang shelves directly on a wall, without building any supporting frame for them, use two or more of these slotted metal strips. They are sold with shelf brackets of various widths, all in brass, aluminum and colored finishes.

If you mount pieces of beveled siding upside down you'll get this result. The ledges formed can then be used to support shelves or, as you see here, box units that have projecting ends.

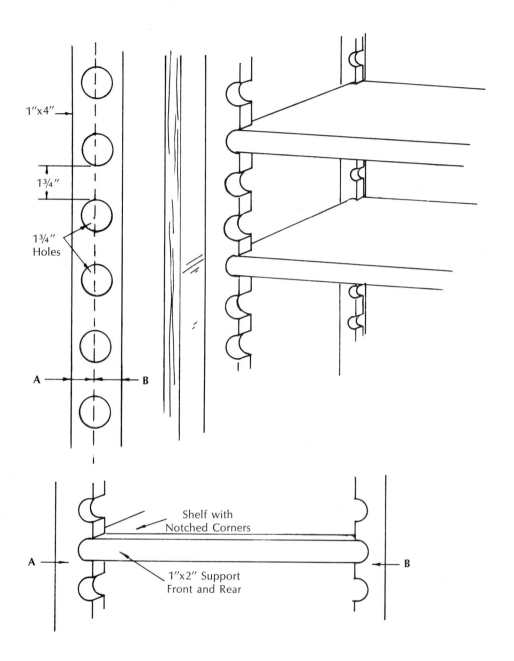

1"x4"

1¾"

1¾"
Holes

A — B

Shelf with
Notched Corners

A — B

1"x2" Support
Front and Rear

Bore a series of large-diameter holes along the center line of 1" x 4"
lumber, then rip the piece into two notched strips. Use a pair of
these at each end to support shelves with ends rounded to fit. Or
fit supports into these rounded notches to hold thin shelves.

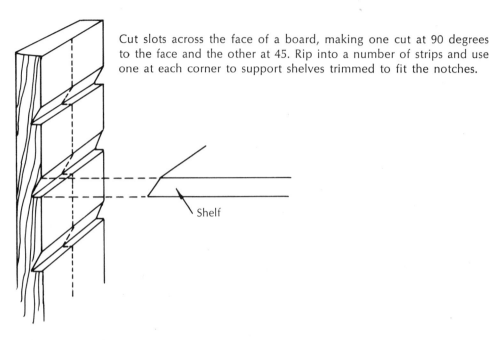

Cut slots across the face of a board, making one cut at 90 degrees to the face and the other at 45. Rip into a number of strips and use one at each corner to support shelves trimmed to fit the notches.

Shelf

Thick hardwood lumber (this is Philippine mahogany 1½" thick) is used both stylishly and economically to support these shelves. This method, like the variations shown in the last two sketches, can be used either for heavy skeleton framing, as here, or for support strips fastened to uprights. Random spacing of notches can be used without difficulties arising if you begin with a wide plank and dado the notches before ripping into narrower pieces.

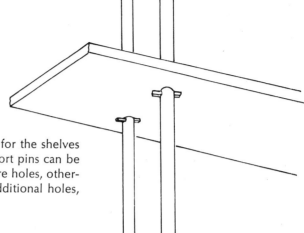

To build a big freestanding unit, use 2″ x 12″ lumber for the shelves and 1¾″ closet poles to hold them up, like this. Support pins can be square if you have mortising equipment to make square holes, otherwise ordinary ⅜″ or so round dowels. If you make additional holes, shelf heights will be adjustable.

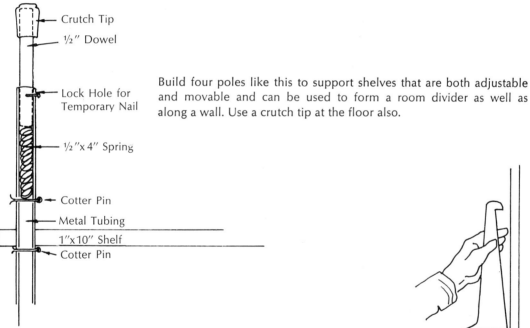

— Crutch Tip

— ½″ Dowel

— Lock Hole for Temporary Nail

— ½″ x 4″ Spring

— Cotter Pin

— Metal Tubing

1″ x 10″ Shelf

— Cotter Pin

Build four poles like this to support shelves that are both adjustable and movable and can be used to form a room divider as well as along a wall. Use a crutch tip at the floor also.

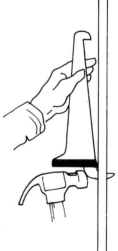

Clever shelf brackets that need no standards are called Tap-N-Hold. Drive the pointed hook through the face of a hollow wall and it seats against the back of the wall as you pivot the bracket to horizontal. Brackets come in several sizes, will support 20 pounds in drywall, 30 in ¼″ to ⅝″ plywood.

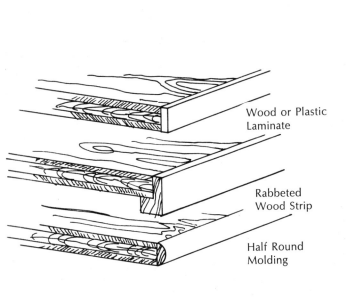

Wood or Plastic
Laminate

Rabbeted
Wood Strip

Half Round
Molding

Above left

Use plywood where wide shelving is needed or fine hardwood is wanted at moderate cost. Shelves to be painted will require filling of edge voids, and sanding, first. With natural finishes, use one of these edging methods, applying the edging with contact cement.

Above right

Edging with plastic laminate works best on wide edges. Thin shelves can be strengthened and given more imposing appearance by gluing a strip along the edge before applying trim. Another useful edging material is wood veneer, often sold in rolls of several standard widths.

Hanging shelf units or cabinets on hollow masonry walls is most easily done with fasteners that expand in the hidden core. Drill a hole with a hammer and star drill or with a carbide-tipped bit, then insert Molly fastener. With solid masonry, use a shield-type bolt that expands in a drilled hole, or fasten to surface with mastic.

In designing shelf storage, don't overlook the possibility of a unit at least partly covered by sliding doors. One like this can serve as a room divider, can provide a protected entryway, can become a freestanding closet, and still hold some wide shelves or narrower ones back to back.

Here's an easily constructed entry closet that supplies variable-height shelves as well as coat space and entryway protection. Its special feature is the bench that makes it handier to use as well as better looking.

Doors of the freestanding entry closet are textured plywood having an unsanded face with grooves cut at 2" intervals. Use of the same material for the bench top gives unity of appearance and a slat effect with minimum cost and effort.

Photo left

Give a shelf a sliding door and it becomes a cupboard, reducing appearance of clutter and protecting contents from dust. Sliding door of ¼" Philippine mahogany plywood slips between scraps from groove side of board, nailed to the edges of existing shelves.

Photo right

Rectangles of flat fiberglass-reinforced plastic (Filon) slide in double saw kerfs to turn these shelves into cabinets. Pulls are glass tiles (tesserae) cemented on; they have the advantages of being brightly colored, thin, and inexpensive—at most, a few cents each.

This crude cutaway model shows the basic method of providing sliding doors without buying special strips. Grooves at bottom are half as deep as those at top so that doors come free for removal when lifted. The sliding plastic doors work the same way but need only circular-saw kerfs instead of these wider grooves.

To provide for sliding doors without the use of power tools, glue and nail on narrow strips, preferably one square strip between two quarter-rounds. At top, fasten the outer two strips after putting the doors in place. When the method shown here is used, it is not feasible to make doors removable.

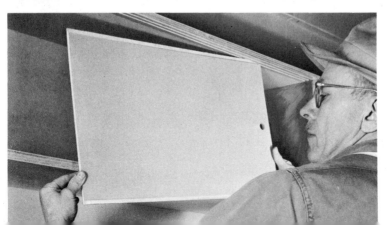

Sliding doors of a thicker material than fiberglass-plastic can be held in narrow grooves if they are made thinner along top and bottom by use of a jointer. The space saved this way can be important, especially if shelves are narrow. Plywood used here is the medium-density overlay type.

If a shelf unit has a stout back, you can hang it directly on a frame wall with woodscrews. Be sure they go through the wall material into the studs, normally found at 16" spacing. Overlay plywood like this is ideal for the spray-painting in brilliant contrasting colors that this case and its sliding doors are to receive.

In a position over a sink, if a shelf unit is to have doors they should be the sliding kind on which no one will crack his head. This cupboard and its shelves are made of the same redwood tongue-and-groove siding with which the room is paneled, mostly from salvaged short lengths. How a drawer unit was built in below this counter, at lower right, is shown in the preceding chapter.

The backs of shelf units and cabinets, usually of ¼" hardboard or plywood, are most often made full case size and set flush with edges—as at left here. But if instead you set the material as far back as possible from the edge—say ½" when the frame is ¾" stock—it will fade from view when the piece is placed against the wall.

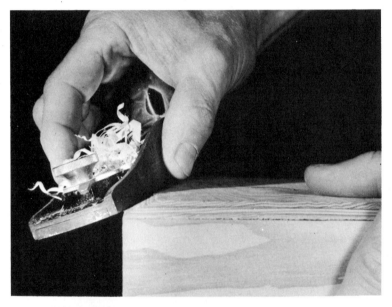

If the cabinet back is set flush with the case it can be made less conspicuous by beveling it with a plane.

For a particularly neat effect, if you are using power tools, rabbet the pieces making up the case. Then the back can be set in against the ledge provided by the rabbet.

When you are using only hand tools you can provide the equivalent of a rabbetted frame by nailing in wood strips to rest the back against. Quarter-round is the neatest.

Best of all: make the rabbet deeper than the thickness of the back material, as at right. The lip you produce in this way can be trimmed if necessary to get a good fit between the unit and the wall of the house.

A heavy-duty stapler like this will greatly speed up the work if you are making a number of cabinets. Tool-rental establishments often have them, or you may be able to borrow one where you buy your lumber. Even ordinary one-hand staplers will do with thin backing material, especially if you are using glue as well.

PART IX

ADD A FIREPLACE

53

Choosing a Fireplace

Preliminary tips on selecting a fireplace to improve almost any room in your house

"Start splittin' wood, Pop! Here comes our fireplace."

It's true. Almost anything, including one-day, do-it-your-self installation, is possible when you decide to update your home with one of the remarkable fireplace units they're making these days.

Other appealing aspects: guaranteed smokefree per-formance; brilliant permanent colors and new modern shapes, if you wish; or the traditional built-in look, with or without masonry.

You can now have a fireplace anywhere in your house including the kitchen and bathroom, upstairs or down. Best of all, you can have it without weeks of a torn-up house and a builder's bill that rips through a thousand-dollar bank account.

And every one of the fireplaces you see in this chapter and those that follow offers you one of the great comforts of life: the age-old pleasure of sitting before an open fire.

Are you prepared to work with masonry? Does your chosen location permit pouring a concrete base? Then you can build a traditional fireplace, using a steel circulator core to simplify your job. You'll build base, masonry shell and chimney—but the work-ing parts of the fireplace will come to you ready-made.

The next chapter tells about building a masonry fireplace.

Adding a masonry fireplace to your home is a big job—but use of a steel circulator core reduces the labor and makes far less skill necessary. For a better-looking job take a tip from this picture and substitute masonry slots for usual metal grill used for warm-air exhaust.

Stone-and-concrete fireplace wall can be as elaborate as this one built by the authors in their home. Metal grills are used for air intake below the cantilevered hearth, but air exhaust is through openings between stone mortared in. Barbecue at left and woodbox in center are part of same poured-concrete job done by a method similar to that shown in Chapter 54.

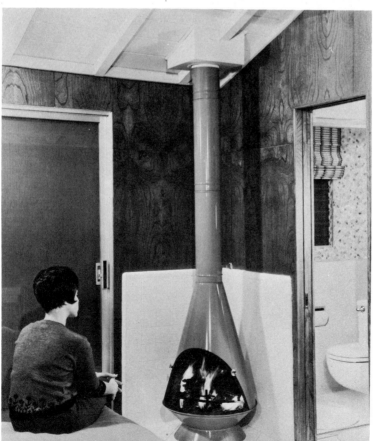

Ceramic tile matching that in adjoining bathroom was used for the hearth and the wall heat-shield of this slim enameled-metal fireplace.

Since the chimney must continue through to the roof, its location may be your first consideration when adding a fireplace to a basement room. Consider adding a similar fireplace in the room above, running both metal flues side by side to the roof where they can be covered by a double chimney. A photograph in the last chapter of this section shows how this is done.

The major preliminary to installation of a factory-made fireplace, as shown in later chapters, is laying a hearth. Since this must be fireproof, sheets of marble are excellent. Other possibilities: stone, slate, ceramic tile, glass tile, concrete, brick, paving tile.

Brick surround provides fire protection and lends a more traditional look to your metal-fireplace installation. This unit is designed to fit a corner, but similar models are available to fit other locations. Adding a fireplace is simplified by making use of an existing flue.

If you are putting in a fireplace where sparks may be a hazard, you may prefer one for which tempered-glass doors are available. To avoid fussing with mortar, you can lay bricks for a hearth like this by using epoxy or any thick construction adhesive or mastic.

Photo left
A prefabricated, quick-installation fireplace need not be metal. This is made of silicon-carbide crystals mixed with clay and hand-molded.

Photo right
If the situation permits, give your new fireplace importance by placing it on a raised hearth. Trim can be wood, as here, but surface should be incombustible—marble, stone, brick.

If your room or its furnishings seem to demand a traditional fireplace, there is still a nonmasonry solution. This black iron Franklin stove gives a fine view of the fire, is an efficient fireplace with doors open or closed.

As solid-looking as a masonry fireplace is this tile-trimmed one. But it's a factory-made metal unit, called zero-clearance because it can be installed on a wooden floor and right against framing. Pictures and detailed information on how to add such a fireplace to your house are in Chapter 57.

It shows a steel unit similar to a circulator but without the circulating feature. This noncirculator core has the advantage of coming with a prebuilt chimney.

You'll pour a base and build up a masonry shell to a height of about 3'. But from there up only carpentry will be needed.

If your house already has a flue, you can install your choice of wall-hung or freestanding metal fireplaces in a matter of hours. And even if your house has no flue, a modern metal fireplace—in brilliant enamel if you like—can be yours, again without masonry. These prefabricated fireplaces come in many sizes and shapes, all with prebuilt chimneys ready to run through the roof.

But what if you want a conventional in-the-wall fireplace that looks at home in, say, a Cape Cod cottage? You can have this, too, without ever touching an ounce of masonry. Use one of the new zero-clearance fireplace cores. The next to the last chapter in this section tells how.

For those who will give up the pleasure of a wood fire for the convenience of no-splitting and no-ashes, one of the metal types available is gas-fired. And there's even a convincing electric model you can move from room to room if you wish.

Also described in the succeeding chapters are prefabricated fireplaces of ceramic materials. These too come with their own prebuilt chimneys, making one-day installation by methods shown in the photographs quite feasible.

54

Build a Masonry Fireplace

Whether your material is brick, block, stone, or concrete, this steel-core method makes it easier

If you want to add to your home the permanence and solidity of a real masonry fireplace, a steel core is the homeowner's answer. It eliminates much of the labor and most of the skill ordinarily required for building a smokefree, woodburning fireplace.

There are many easier ways of adding a fireplace to your home than by building a masonry one. They are shown in the chapters that follow.

But where it is feasible to put a masonry fireplace there is nothing else that is quite so satisfying. Since such a fireplace involves first pouring a concrete footing, it is most likely to be a possible installation when it is part of a major home-improvement project. The job you see in the photographs was done by the author while adding a new master bedroom to his home.

You have your choice of two types of steel cores—circulating and noncirculating. The circulator has a double wall through which air flows by convection when it is heated by a fire. So it is far more effective in heating the room than an ordinary fireplace, or one built around a noncirculator core.

Unless your climate is very mild or the room is quite small or already well heated, the extra cost of the circulator is well worth while.

HOW TO BUILD A MASONRY FIREPLACE

Here are the basic details of building a masonry fireplace around a steel core. Depart from this as necessary when you use a different type of core, facing, chimney, and so on.

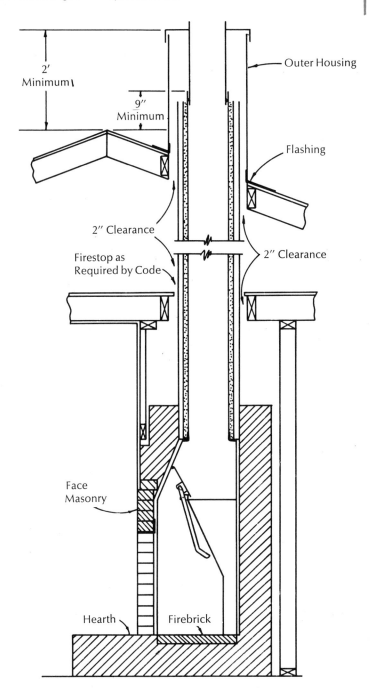

2'
Minimum

9"
Minimum

Outer Housing

Flashing

2" Clearance

Firestop as
Required by Code

2" Clearance

Face
Masonry

Hearth   Firebrick

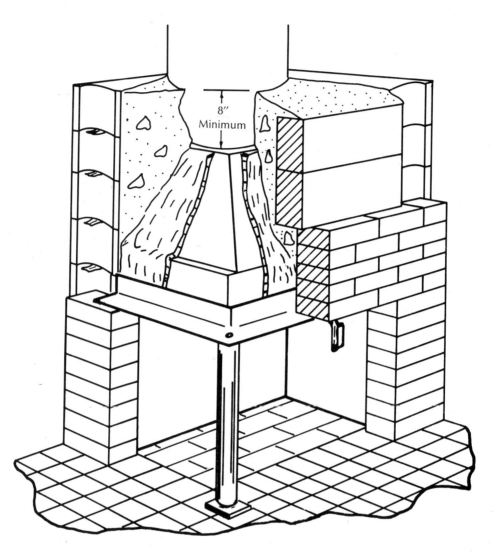

8"
Minimum

A corner unit calls for masonry construction like this. Concrete block is used for the back and side, which are hidden, and brick for the rest. This block-and-brick construction is an alternative to the stones-in-poured-concrete method you see in the photographs.

1.

2.

1. Begin your job by casting a concrete footing. Like a house foundation, it should go down to solid bearing below frost line. This footing is a foot higher than normal, to produce a raised fireplace, has sloping lip to discourage logs from rolling out and to make for easier control of ashes.

2. Post required for support of corner fireplace comes with unit, fits over socket cast in base—as seen in previous photograph. Box in corner is form to make an opening through the concrete for insertion of a second chimney for a similar fireplace on the lower floor.

3.

3. Here is the steel unit, complete with smoke shelf and damper. Angle steel seen in foreground will be held up by the corner post and will support the cantilevered masonry, as shown in the diagrams. Opening at lower right was cast into the concrete base to make a cupboard for storing wood.

495

4.

5.

4. With the steel core in place and protected by buffer of mineral wool (included with unit), concrete is poured against wooden forms. Flat-faced stones are set against the forms by hand as the pouring of concrete proceeds. With brick or block, forms are not needed.

5. Stone-in-concrete effect, so often used by Frank Lloyd Wright, can be enhanced by pulling off forms after a few hours and hosing down the face violently. This not only insures better exposure of the rocks but washes away cement so smaller stones give rugged texture.

Circulator cores ordinarily come without chimneys. In the past it was necessary and tedious to build your own chimney by using terra-cotta flue liners surrounded by masonry. Now, however, there is a metal chimney, called Metalbestos, on the market that eliminates all this labor. It is available nationally. You'll find more information about it in the last chapter of this section.

With the steel core you see in the pictures, the chimney problem is solved for you. A metal chimney and housing come as part of the package you buy.

You will have a couple of other buying decisions to make. Cores come in several sizes, most often in opening widths of 2' to 5'. Keep in mind that a larger fireplace than needed not only involves more money and more effort but also requires a larger fire for efficient operation.

496

Your other decision—whether to build a corner fireplace or one within a wall—will often be dictated by the shape of the room. Note that an ordinary unit may be placed in a corner so that it faces diagonally into the room. But a corner unit is used when you want full view of the fire from two directions. Units come in both left- and right-hand versions, so you must specify which you want.

Circulator units are offered for building see-through fireplaces as well. These are less effective heat producers since they lack a reflecting back wall. They also create a greater smoke problem since opening a door will often cause a current of air to go right through. Location of such a fireplace should be chosen with care.

Circulator units offered by different manufacturers vary in another respect that affects ease of construction. Some have smoke dome and downdraft shelf included in their steel construction. Majestic and Vega (see Appendix for addresses) are among the makers whose products follow this scheme. Some other units do not include this part because their makers believe you are better off

6. Here is a view of the form work required as construction approached the top of the steel unit. Prefabricated flue has been set in place. Rocks and concrete must continue on up until they reach a point at least 8″ above the begining of the flue. Construction may then be wood.

7. All form work seen here, including that at back and sides, will be removed as soon as the job is done. Topping base on which unit sits with firebrick, as shown in the diagrams, is recommended by most authorities. The authors have had no trouble from omitting it in several installations.

6.

7.

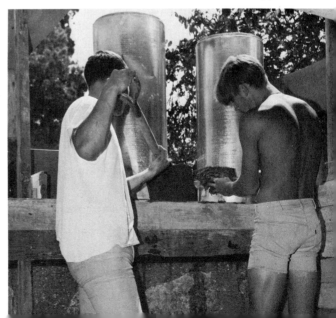

8. With flue extended through the roof, the chimney housing is cut to slope of roof and placed over flashing. Large double housing is required here because of second flue from the additional fireplace. More information and pictures on chimney installation will be found in the succeeding chapters.

forming a concrete smoke shelf as you build. This can be one of the more difficult parts of the job, however.

In planning your fireplace construction, allow for the one accessory which no woodburner should be without: a gas-fired log kindler. By making instant fires possible at any time without need of kindling, it may double or triple the usefulness of your fireplace. Its cost is only a few dollars—for a valve and some pipe—and its installation is simple if it is done while building a new fireplace. Details on this and some other possibilities with gas are also to be found in the last chapter of the section.

The drawings and photographs show the essential steps in building your own masonry fireplace around a steel core. For detailed treatment of building many types of masonry circulators, look up the author's book, *How to Work with Concrete and Masonry*.

55

Put a Fireplace Anywhere You Want It

Combination of lightweight, prefabricated unit and durable, firesafe metal chimney simplifies a major home improvement.

This is a fireplace installation that goes *anywhere you want it,* no matter how difficult the conditions. What makes this possible is a combination of prefabricated fireplace and prefabricated chimney and fittings.

The Acorn fireplace shown is made of welded steel finished in red porcelain enamel that makes polishing or refinishing forever unnecessary. Heat won't crack the surface, and soil cleans off with a damp cloth.

The chimney is Metalbestos, nationally available in an assortment of diameters and lengths. The sections twist-lock together and permit any total length wanted.

Because so many difficult conditions were met in making the installation shown here, it demonstrates several things:

1. With this combination you can put a fireplace in a room where there is no existing flue to connect to.

2. You can install it safely in a room made entirely of combustible materials—wooden floor, walls, ceiling.

3. You can put it in a second-floor bedroom or sitting room, as this one is.

4. You can do this even in a part of the house that cantilevers out over space, making a chimney foundation impossible.

499

Since there's little weight involved, you can now add a fireplace just about anywhere in your house that you want to. This one sits in a bedroom corner that is actually cantilevered out beyond the story beneath. The enameled-steel Acorn unit is red, hearth is gray-green slate, mosaic-tile chimney face is many shades of green.

5. And you can do it even if the room is at the front of your house where any chimney added to the outside might be objectionable.

The steps to follow in installing such a fireplace in your home are shown in the photographs.

Completing the job after that will be mostly a matter of personal taste in decorating.

After covering the framing around the chimney with gypsum board you can paint it to match the room or cover it in some other material for contrast. The room shown here was paneled in Philippine mahogany tongue-and-groove boards lightly wiped with white Stain Wax. The same paneling was used to cover the sides of the chimney, making it appear always to have been part of the room.

Since a noncombustible material was needed for the area right around the smokepipe, it was decided to use Mexican glass mosaic tile for the whole face. The tiles used are several shades of green, with occasional accents of brown, yellow, white, and red. They were glued directly to the gypsum board with ceramic-tile cement.

Since the metal face of the thimble into which the smokepipe fits lies flat against the gypsum board, the tile covers it as well.

500

Where the floor is combustible, some kind of hearth should be provided. This can be something as inexpensive as a sheet of metal or asbestos-cement board or a large flagstone. It should project at least 18″ beyond the fireplace at the front, 6″ at the sides. If you are not always going to use a fire screen (one is included to fit the Acorn) even more hearth area is advisable.

Masonry such as brick, flagstone, marble, or painted decorative tile makes the most attractive hearth. It may be built up to cover the feet of the fireplace legs if desired.

In this installation the hearth is made of thin slabs of gray-green slate laid in tile mastic on the plywood subfloor. Joints are filled with ordinary cement mortar to which black-oxide cement coloring gives a color close to that of the slate.

The test of any fireplace—and especially of its chimney—is what happens when the wind blows. This one is placed where the chimney takes full brunt of gales off the Pacific a few hundred yards away. It has been in regular use during shingle-lifting storms that shook the house and winds recorded at fifty miles an hour and worse. It has yet to give off any smoke in the room.

HOW TO INSTALL A PREFAB FIREPLACE

1. Essentials of the framing needed: four posts connecting 2″ x 4″s at floor and ceiling. An opening is cut in the roof for the chimney, and a platform is provided for the chimney support.

2.

3.

2. Chimney sections fit together and lock when twisted. After they've been fitted to the T-member that connects to the fireplace, they are continued up through the roof. Then the housing may be finished.

3. Chimney sections end at the top of the housing, which has been cut off to fit the slope of the roof and installed with its flashing to make a leakfree connection.

4. Housing top-assembly fits into top piece of flue and over chimney. An advantage of this type of top is that it provides excellent downdraft protection—downdrafts make some fireplaces smoke.

4.

5.

5. Whole assembly is made rigid and permanent by fastening with sheet-metal screws. The housing is very heavy galvanized steel, ready for priming and painting. Embossing adds strength besides giving masonry effect. Pacific ocean in the background here often sends in extremely high winds which have not disturbed or damaged this chimney in its ten years of existence.

6. Chimney housing arrives unpainted. Most others, as shown in one of the later chapters, have brick patterns painted on them. Since these are not particularly convincing imitations, it is just as well to give them a coat of neutral-colored paint.

7. Installation is completed inside by applying tile to face of chimney housing and then slipping in the fireplace flue connection. Fireplace units like this are available with legs, as shown, or with brackets for hanging clear of the floor.

6.

7.

56

How to Install a Fireplace in One Day

From hearth to chimney housing, adding a freestanding modern woodburner anywhere you want it can be a matter of hours

It used to be that quick and easy fireplace installation was possible only where an abandoned flue already existed. But now there are freestanding units that come with their own chimneys all ready to assemble and use within a single day.

Some of these interesting and unusually shaped fireplaces are shown in the first chapter of this section. Photographs in this chapter show one of the most attractive types, made of a Space Age ceramic, and demonstrate how you can use one to improve a living room, bedroom, study, or family room in your own home.

The method of installing this graceful Aztec (made by Condon-King) is in most respects the same as for other fireboxes from the same manufacturer. Many of the other fireplaces shown in the earlier chapter can also be installed in a quite similar way.

The Aztec comes complete except for hearth: spun-steel base, ceramic pot, screen and grate, black flue sections, collar, chimney housing, liner, and cap.

Two people, neither of them experienced with such fireplaces, made the installation you see here, doing it all on a single Saturday afternoon even with frequent delays for the photography you see.

This fireplace can be installed in even less time where a

HOW TO INSTALL A CERAMIC FIREPLACE

Space-age ceramic of the Aztec fireplace radiates heat effectively throughout the room, comes in a variety of colors. All materials, parts, including firescreen (at right) are included. It goes up so quickly you can light your first fire in a day.

masonry flue already exists. It is sold with chimney for the complete-from-scratch kind of installation shown in the photographs.

Begin the job by installing a noncombustible hearth, of material that should be at least ⅜" thick. A sheet of asbestos board is the simplest thing for a quick result. An area paved in stone or brick will take longer but give a more artistic appearance.

Slate was used here. It was put down with ordinary ceramic-tile adhesive. The joints were grouted with common portland cement.

With the hearth completed, you can proceed to install your fireplace as shown in these photographs.

1. Begin your installation by placing the spun-metal base where you want it, then bolting on the ceramic unit with its spacer and firepan. Metal baffle clips into pins inside the firepan.

2. Cut a circular hole in the ceiling and roof, centering it directly over the center of the fireplace. The diameter for proper clearance depends upon the size fireplace you use.

3.

4.

3. Remove shingles or other roofing to allow placing of the flashing included with the fireplace. Slip in the stainless-steel upper flue section and then slide on the outer housing as shown.

4. With the storm collar fitted firmly over the top of the outer housing, slip on the cap assembly and fasten it with sheet-metal screws. Cap should be 2′ higher than any part of the roof within 10′.

5. Make liberal use of roofer's plastic cement to restore the waterproof quality of the roof around the chimney flashing. With everything nailed down again, the chimney installation is completed.

6. Flue sections for this fireplace are 7″ in diameter and 24″ long. Place the first one, with its damper at the top, then add as many additional sections as your roof height requires.

5.

6.

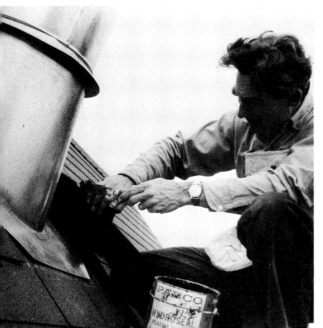

7.

8.

7. Insulating flue section goes through the ceiling for fire protection. You can obtain flue parts in needed lengths by supplying your dealer with a rough diagram of the construction of the room.

8. An ingenious adjustable collar covers the space between the flue and the ceiling. With this permanently fastened in place, you're ready to split some wood and strike a match to light your first fire.

57

Zero-Clearance:
Your Fireplace Miracle

Meet the build-it-yourself fireplace that's a part of your house without the work of masonry

It used to be that if you wanted to add a fireplace to an existing house you were forced to accept a compromise. Because of the need for a heavy masonry foundation, you had to put your new fireplace *where* you didn't want to—or use a freestanding prefab that didn't look solid and permanent the way you wanted it.

1. It must be a real woodburner—and big enough to take 2′ logs.

2. It must have the solid masonry look of an old-fashioned fireplace—not a Franklin stove or steel prefab.

3. It is to be built in an upstairs room smack over the center of a garage—or in some other location where a foundation would be impossible to provide.

4. It must sit on a wood floor and right against wood framing, yet be perfectly safe—and guaranteed smokefree.

5. Starting from absolute scratch, it must be possible to complete the job in less than two days—framing, finished wall, and all.

6. The whole job, from hearth to chimney, must cost less than $300.

A prefabricated fireplace device that is sometimes referred to as a "zero-clearance" unit fills every one of these requirements

This zero-clearance fireplace installation is similar to the one shown
in the how-to-do-it photographs, differs only in use of marble facing.
A fireplace in a free-standing column serves also to divide rooms.

to provide a terrific home-improvement bargain. This means that, unlike most devices that give heat, this one has been designed to be safe without several inches of clearance from wood framing or walls. Its maker, Vega Industries, calls it the Heatilator Mark 123. ("Easy as 1-2-3.")

Its secret is walls consisting of four layers of metal separated by insulation and by hollow spaces through which air flows to wipe away the heat. Sidewalls of the firebox are porcelain-enameled steel. The floor and back are heavy refractory bricks. The parts that don't show are galvanized steel.

Since the unit is light in weight and fire-safe right on a wood floor, you can install one anywhere you wish. The standard unit can go against a wall, become part of a room divider, or snuggle into a corner. Its rear is chamfered for corner use with minimum consumption of room space.

This slightly raised version of the goes-anywhere fireplace shows how well it can be made to harmonize with an unconventional room. Hearth is concrete, and the fireplace is faced with ceramic tile within a rough wood surround.

Period detailing is easily achieved with the zero-clearance fireplace unit. Within the carved trim on the wood-paneled wall, the necessary fireproof facing is large ceramic-tile squares, used also for the hearth.

Excellent for a corner location is this unit with its two open sides. Tile band at top of opening meets fire-safety requirements. Note how ingeniously the effect of a large masonry fireplace has been produced by comparatively few bricks.

For situations where you want the fire to be visible from two directions, there are corner models, both left- and right-hand. The Mark 123 comes as a complete package—unit, chimney, firestop spacer, chimney housing, roof flashing, and firescreen.

Whether you'll need extra parts depends upon where you install your fireplace. If you put it where the chimney can't go straight up through the ceiling and roof without interference from framing, you'll need a pair of offset chimney fittings. They're easy enough to use, but they add somewhat to the cost.

If your chimney-height requirement exceeds 11′ 8″ you'll need extra chimney sections, available in 2′ and 3′ lengths at around $10 a foot. For good draft and to meet building codes, your chimney top should be at least 2′ higher than any portion of the roof within 10′ of it. If the distance from this point to the floor onto which your unit is to go is more than 11′ you'll need extra chimney.

Another way around this, of course, is to put your fireplace onto an elevated hearth. A raised ("Swedish") fireplace of height up to about 18″ is very attractive in many rooms. Since your zero-clearance unit can safely sit on any kind of material, you can build a raised hearth of wood members, extending it beyond the front of the fireplace opening for safety.

These safety requirements are the same for a raised hearth as for one at floor level, and can be learned from your building inspector wherever codes are in force. A common requirement is that of FHA: "Outer hearth shall extend at least 16″ in front of opening and at least 8″ each side of fireplace opening."

The hearth can be marble, brick, stone, or 6″ or 12″ tile. The common 6″ tile seen in a couple of the photographs are convenient for both hearth and fireplace facing. Three rows of ten tiles each will give you a hearth exceeding the usual requirement, since the opening in the Mark 123 is 36″.

Facing at top and sides of fireplace opening must also be noncombustible. This may be marble or black glass (available from Vega) or other fairly thin material, such as slate or ceramic tile. Minimum permissible widths are 5″ at sides, 6″ at top. Here again you can meet the requirement by using 6″ ceramic tile squares, installed with tile adhesive.

This hearth and trim work can be done as soon as the unit has been placed within its framing, or it can wait till the chimney work has been completed, as shown in the how-to-do-it photographs. Doing it early has one advantage: the tile cement can harden while you finish the chimney work. You can then set off that first conflagration in your new fireplace without delay.

HOW TO INSTALL A ZERO-CLEARANCE FIREPLACE

1. Total fireplace package for normal installations weighs 413 pounds, a fraction of the usual fireplace weight. An ordinary rope hoist lifts the main unit to the second floor of the authors' home.

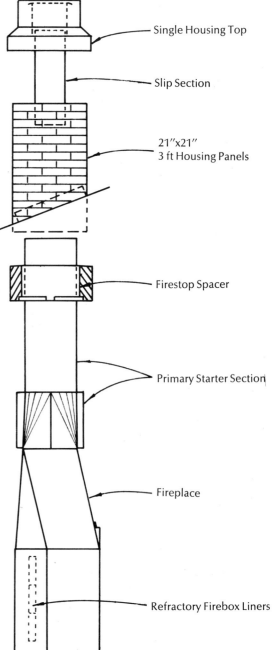

- Single Housing Top
- Slip Section
- 21"x21" 3 ft Housing Panels
- Firestop Spacer
- Primary Starter Section
- Fireplace
- Refractory Firebox Liners

514

2. All parts needed for a complete fireplace are shown here. Installation begins with placing the main unit in the desired location, then cutting 19″ square holes through any ceiling or roof above it to take firestop spacers.

3. Here you see the starter section of the chimney in position, fastened with sheet-metal screws. The framing of 2″ x 4″ lumber is to take rough redwood plywood paneling to match other walls of the room.

4. To cover the back wall with the refractory firebox liners, you must first remove a metal Z-section from the top of the unit. The durable fireproof liners then slide into place on metal flanges.

5. Glass and marble facings and hearth extensions come with installation instructions. Strip of wood clamped at the top of the fireplace opening supports the 6″ tile used while the ceramic-tile adhesive sets.

6. Panels of the chimney housing snap together, stay firmly locked after a tap with a rubber mallet. This single housing has 45-degree braces inside; double housings, for twin fireplaces, have X-braces.

7. Use a level to mark the two side panels of the chimney housing to correspond with the roof pitch. Then bend as shown. Housing is upside down. Metal parts in foreground are roof flashing supplied.

8. With housing and roof flashing in place, but not yet nailed, the slip section of the chimney and the housing top slide into position from above. Reshingling or other roofing job may then be completed.

58

Trouble With Fireplaces?

Here are ways to improve functionally the fireplace you have or the one you plan to add to your home

Some people have fireplaces and don't use them. Other people don't have fireplaces and don't want them. Either way, it's too bad. Because an effectively functioning fireplace adds immeasurably to the pleasure of a home.

It's not the fault of the people, however. The fault lies in the kind of fireplaces most of us have or remember living with.

The trouble with fireplaces—most of them—is that they . . .

. . . make too many ashes

. . . are messy to clean

. . . often produce smoke

. . . interfere with room planning and furniture arrangement

. . . waste their own heat and the heat from your furnace as well

. . . are difficult and expensive to construct

. . . are hard to build a lasting fire in

. . . and require wood-splitting, which is work.

The big news in fireplaces is that it is no longer necessary to put up with these faults. Whatever it is about fireplaces that bugs you most, there's a remedy at hand. Some of the remedies apply to existing fireplaces, others to ones you might want to add to your home.

ASHES? The most radical answer to the ash problem is a brand-new type of fireplace that eats most of its own ashes. Made by Malm Fireplaces, Inc., and called the Carousel, it's a circular metal fireplace that can be installed in the center of a room as readily as near a wall or in a corner. Although it has moving parts, baffles in the hood and an adjustable air intake in the door work together to create a spinning column of flame, an unusual sight to watch.

This whirlwind of flickering fire burns so intensely and efficiently that the fuel is completely consumed and about 90 percent of the ashes are sucked up and out the chimney. Since the intense flame has completely burned out the ashes, they are expelled in particles so small that they leave no residue on roof or lawn.

The fire in the Carousel is completely glassed in, so there's no danger of smoke, sparks, or ashes in the room. The glass yields fascinating reflections of the flame, also enables you to use it for foil-wrapped cooking for home picnics. It's all steel but light enough to require no special flooring or foundation. You have your choice of two sizes, 32″ and 42″ diameters, and ten colors.

MESS? If you want your wood fire in the open, rather than behind glass, you'll have to put up with heavy ash production. But you don't have to clean up the ashes the hard way.

What the built-in ash dump has always done for many masonry fireplaces, the Silent Butler now does for the prefabricated metal kind. It's a drawer beneath the firebox of Majestic's Contemporary. Just slide it out to empty, eliminating the dusty job of sweeping and shoveling out ashes.

SMOKE? One great advantage of all the modern fireplaces pictured here and described in this and the preceding chapters is that they have been designed to burn without smoking up the place.

There is no smoke problem, of course, with the iron-stove types that have doors, the Carousel with its glass enclosure, or the ones that burn only electricity or gas.

But the prefabricated metal ones are almost equally reliable, and many of the conventionally shaped steel units around which you can build a masonry fireplace now come with written guarantees of freedom from smoking.

NO SPACE? If you've hesitated to add a fireplace because there's no suitable wall, a fire-in-the-round may be your answer.

A fireplace of this kind consists of a great metal hood,

Without moving parts, Royal Carousel swirls its flame brilliantly and consumes most of the ashes it makes. Choose among ten colors in this home-improver's answer to the problem of ashes.

Barely visible drawer beneath this freestanding prefab catches ashes, makes their removal a cleaner and easier task. Masonry wall shield, which could be molded plastic in brick pattern, lends visual importance.

Something of a modern miracle is this zero-clearance unit that installs anywhere with the ease of a metal prefab. Made in both corner and wall models, it can be installed to look like a traditional masonry fireplace, as shown in the preceding chapter.

shaped like an inverted funnel, that is propped or hung over a base that holds the fire a foot or two above floor level. Or there may be no metal base but a sunken masonry pit for a firebox.

The new middle-of-the-room fireplace called Western is intended for both vacation and year-round homes. Its unusual features include a broad hearth all the way around that serves as a table as well, full 360-degree screen in brass or black that is mounted on rollers for easy sliding.

INEFFICIENT? The modern metal freestanding fireplaces all offer relatively high efficiency. Their whole hoods and chimneys effectively radiate heat into the room instead of taking most of it up the chimney.

For the masonry fireplace that looks best in most traditional houses, the modern answer to the heat-waste problem is the steel circulator core featured in Chapter 54.

In its newest form, such a core can be installed in an existing fireplace, converting your brick or stone woodburner into a modern circulator in minutes. And this without substantially altering its appearance.

The steel fireplace liner is called Heat-Master and can be ordered to fit any fireplace. Like the circulator cores that are used in building new fireplaces, the liner is a hollow steelbox that draws in cold air from the room. It heats the air, then expels it to warm a larger area than radiation alone can handle.

HEAT WASTER? In cold climates especially, the major charge brought against ordinary fireplaces is that they waste furnace heat as well as their own. They upset the workings of a well-balanced heating system when they are in use—and even when they are not, unless someone remembers to close their dampers. By convection they draw furnace-warmed air into themselves and puff it out their chimneys.

All too true. But modern versions of the Franklin stove effectively answer this criticism—because they have doors. Close the doors, whether you have a fire going or not, and you put an end to theft of furnace heat.

Some of these cast-iron beauties are brand new on the market, yet in form and function go back to the days of the statesman-philosopher-inventor they are named for. They are cast in sand molds by a process almost unchanged in three centuries. And five of the newest Franklin stove models offered by a leading manufacturer have just been reintroduced after a forty-year retirement.

Your present fireplace can take on the heating efficiency of a circulator model if you slip in a Heat-Master steel liner. It's made to measure. Cold air flows in at the bottom, warms, comes out at the top.

Reasons for the jump in sales of these iron fireplaces are practical as well as sentimental. They use their fuel efficiently since they have large radiating surfaces and full damper and draft control. They avoid the loss of room heat, something that is particularly a problem with an ordinary fireplace during the night after a day's use. A dying fire gives little heat, yet you can't close the damper on it. With a Franklin or other iron stove, you just close the doors.

HARD TO BUILD? The chore of constructing a fireplace is greatly reduced by the new models. With an existing chimney to hook up to, installing a freestanding metal fireplace takes a matter of hours.

The news is that the new metal chimney systems make it equally easy to put in a metal fireplace from scratch in a single day. And the leading flue manufacturer, Metalbestos, now has an all-stainless-steel, all-fuel chimney in sizes as large as four times that of the old ones. Inside diameters range all the way from 6″ to 14″—the largest being big enough for a man-size fireplace, masonry or otherwise.

These chimney sections come in 18″ and 30″ lengths, with various support fittings and insulated tees and elbows, as well as metal rooftop housings finished to resemble brick. The pipe sections have threaded internal couplers that lock with a

For fire without fireplace, try a cast-iron revival. The Franklin stove may be vented by stovepipe to a metal chimney at the ceiling or directly to a flue built inside, or as the exterior side of a masonry wall. Doors may be closed to prevent loss of room heat.

Your fireplace, new or old, ceases to be a sometime thing when you equip it with a gas flame for igniting logs without kindling. In the form seen here it is ½″ gas pipe ending in an ordinary cap into which a slot has been hacksawed. It is controlled by a shutoff valve, with removable key handle, placed so you can turn it on with one hand while lighting the gas with the other.

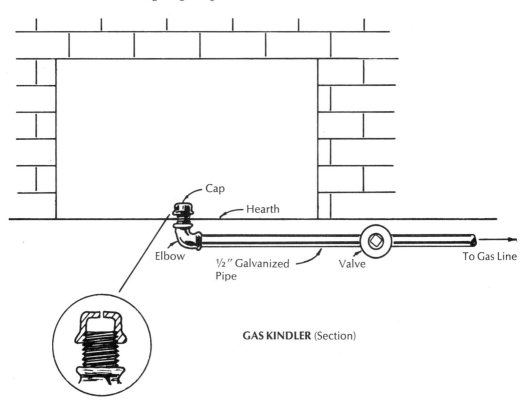

Cap

Hearth

Elbow

½″ Galvanized Pipe

Valve

To Gas Line

GAS KINDLER (Section)

simple twist. This makes installation a simple one-man job with no special tools required.

These modern chimneys are made possible by new insulating materials. Having seventeen times the insulating value of brick, they need be only 1″ thick. Even a 14″ flue is no fatter than a 7-incher used to be.

Efficient insulation and compact chimney sections are also the secret of the zero-clearance fireplace unit. This is the device that makes it possible for you—without previous experience— to install a fireplace of conventional appearance by yourself, and to do it in a day or two.

Zero-clearance refers to the fact that the galvanized-steel unit can be placed directly on a wooden floor and right smack against wood framing with complete fire safety. So your fireplace can go anywhere you want it, without a foundation—even in an upstairs room.

Basic installation of one of these instant fireplaces is as easy as for a freestanding metal prefab: locate unit where wanted; cut hole in ceiling and roof; add flue sections; terminate with roof-top housing; supply a hearth of incombustible material. Details and pictures are in a previous chapter.

The zero-clearance unit calls for one more step beyond the basics, however. Since it is designed to be built into a wall, you will still have the chore of framing it in and paneling over it. This adds nothing to the labor or cost, however, if you are building your fireplace as part of a remodeling or wall-paneling job.

KINDLING NUISANCE? If you've never owned a gas-fired kindler, you have no idea what a joy a fireplace can be. An auxiliary gas flame makes wood kindling entirely unnecessary and lets you get a fire going with big damp logs that otherwise would need laborious splitting and still might not burn well at all. After starting your fire it will sustain it without fussing, even during a party when you are busy with guests. And it makes your fireplace an effective trash incinerator.

On top of all this, a gas kindler is one of the cheapest little appliances you can install in your home. It consists of a pipe connected to your gas supply by way of a shut-off valve, a key-operated valve at the fireplace, and some kind of burner. For the simplest burner, just terminate the gas pipe with an ordinary pipe cap in which you have hacksawed a slot.

Keep this slotted cap low enough in the fireplace so that ashes can cover it. Then the gas flame will filter through the ashes and seem to be part of the wood fire.

Closeup view shows how realistic a manzanita "log" for use with a gas flame can be. Sand-filled pan contains burner for connecting to gas line and valve.

When gas flame is on, oak "logs" give realistic effect in their bed of blue and yellow flame. Automation can be added, with pilot light and either pushbutton or thermostatic control.

An alternative to gas logs is a gas-fire filtered through a bed of sand
on which volcanic rocks have been strewn. Rocks radiate heat.

Freestanding Firehood is a gas-fired version of the woodburning metal
fireplace. It comes with a high-temperature ceramic log, usually installs in half a day.

Electric fireplace comes in this semitraditional design as well as strikingly modern shapes and bright colors. It won't take the place of a real woodburner, but with its realistic red flicker it brings cheer as well as heat to a cold dismal room.

Now on the market are several types of manufactured burners—essentially a length of pipe with an air intake and a row of holes for the flame. The blue flame you get as a consequence is more efficient than the yellow one from a homemade pipe-cap burner, but may not be as powerful or as easy to light.

With any kindler you have an added advantage: you can convert from woodburning fireplace to gas-fired quickly. All you do is clean out the ashes and surround the flame with lava rocks from a patio-supplies house or fireplace shop. They will glow in the gas flame and radiate smokeless heat.

This form of instant fire may be a great convenience at some seasons. And the fireplace converts back to woodburning whenever you remove the rocks and store them away.

For a more elaborate conversion, use gas logs. The modern version, shown in the photographs, is not a gas burner in the shape of an improbable-looking imitation log. It is a burner con-

To install a Majestic Electric Fireplace, fasten the steel bracket to a wall with two screws, choosing a location in which the screws go into wall studs. Then lift the fireplace and slip over bracket.

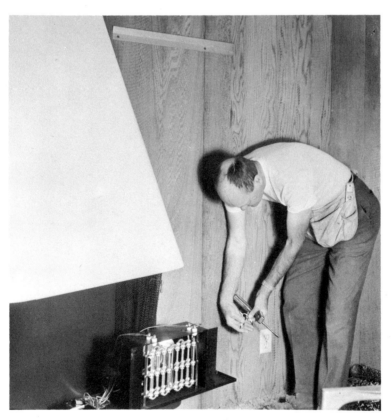

Electrical hookup completes the installation. With the 115-volt model, this means merely plugging into an outlet. The 230-volt heavy-duty type, however, will require special wiring for the load.

cealed under sand or vermiculite in a metal pan and topped by either a collection of rocks or several perfectly imitated logs. For even greater effectiveness, you can dust the logs with an assortment of fibers that will glow like everlasting sparks and embers when the fire is on.

A special advantage of this modern gas-all-the-way fireplace is that its automatic pilot can be turned off and on by remote electric pushbutton. You can start your fire any time without even going near the fireplace. Pushbutton control at your bedside can be a pleasant thing for a bedroom fireplace on a crisp morning. Such a switch can be controlled by a clock timer, if you'd like your fire to start even before you wake up. Thermostatic control is also available.

The same kind of ultramodern gas-log set is now available by itself. With it you can, temporarily or permanently, convert your present fireplace, whether masonry or metal prefab, to gas—electric pushbutton, clock timer, thermostat and all. Information on how to do this is in the chapter on automation in the home.

Your fireplace problem may be even more demanding. Suppose you have no flue and no desire—or perhaps space—to put in one. Or yours is a rented home, apartment, or cabin. The modern answer: an electric fireplace. All you need is an electrical connection and a wall to hang the fireplace on. Any wall will do.

Your electrical connection can be merely plugging in to an existing outlet, if you are satisfied with an output of 5,640 BTU per hour. That's what a 120-volt 1,650-watt model produces.

If you have, or can put in, a 240-volt three-wire circuit you can have more heat. Flip of a switch will give you a glowing log only or that plus either 2,000 or 4,000 watts of heat, thermostatically controlled.

In today's fireplaces you can have just about anything you want.

PART X

HOW TO ADD LIVING SPACE

59

Five Ways to
More Living Space

How and where to gain new living space from areas that now are not fully used.

Your house not big enough? Take another look. The fault may be not so much a lack of space as under-utilization of what is there. Many a family as large as yours lives comfortably in less space than your house probably includes, in an efficiently arranged compact apartment in an American or European city.

If your house has an attic, that is probably the best way to go for more space. Roof and floor framing and weather protection are already there and paid for. All that an attic usually needs to become both good looking and useful is a combination of home improvements of the kind to which this book is devoted—plus improved access and a generous application of insulation. Conversion of a typically depressing and underused attic is shown in the next chapter.

Unlike attics, garages are seldom unused space. But they may be worth far more when they house people than when they shelter cars or junk. You may be able to gain time as well as space by making over a dismal garage into an apartment, as shown in the pair of before-and-after photographs. Such a conversion can mean almost instant house-expansion, and the family transportation can sit outside until you have leisure to build a new garage or the simple carport that may be all that's needed.

A basement, if it has no moisture problem that cannot be defeated, is another good way to go for added living space.

Most often this will take the form of a family room, and that's what our basement-improvement photograph in this chapter shows as does the picture-story that constitutes the next chapter.

Sometimes a house has plenty of room, yet somehow functions badly. One symptom is quarreling among children, something that can usually be mitigated if not ended by improving their quarters in respect to privacy. Easing the chores—and improving the disposition—of the woman of the house often is dependent upon giving her a more efficient kitchen, ideas for which occupy a section of this book. When that's not the answer, what is presented here as a "clutter room" may be.

What a clutter room does is take clutter out of the house by grouping and isolating some important and messy functions. Roughly speaking, these are the household chores a woman does that are not related to food preparation.

A clutter room should be a major consideration in any house being built or improved, one home-equipment editor has said, describing it as "a new kind of all-purpose, do-everything room."

Just what is a clutter room? It's a laundry designed with the sink, storage cabinets, washer, dryer, and ironing board all within a few steps of each other. It's a sewing center, complete with a table large enough to lay out patterns and a sewing machine that is left up at all times.

A clutter room is a woman's home office—a place to pay bills, make a list, write a letter. It can be a studio—a place to paint a picture, write a poem, or wrap a birthday present. It can be a place to arrange flowers or install a pottery wheel or kiln. Usually a clutter room is also a playroom where a mother can keep an eye on youngsters while she does her chores.

A clutter room doesn't need to be kept in apple-pie order. This is one of its greatest virtues. If a neighbor happens to drop in while the laundry is being folded, its owner simply walks out of her clutter room and closes the door, leaving her work out until she is ready to resume it. A half-finished painting need not be stowed away and, perhaps, never finished because it is too much trouble to get all the materials out again.

In reorganizing your house to include a clutter room you'll find these considerations to be of primary importance: noise control, lighting, ease of maintenance, and an attractive appearance.

The noise problem—the sounds of active children combined with the din of several appliances running at once—calls for the use of effective acoustical materials. For the room shown in the photograph, designers at the Armstrong Cork Company chose

Cramped though it may look, even a small garage contains ample space for creation of a studio apartment or suite. Such an addition, because of the privacy it offers, is especially appropriate for a relative or a grown child or a high-schooler in need of a degree of independence. Ceiling is acoustical tile, floor is vinyl tile, walls are prefinished woodgrain Masonite Royalcote paneling installed over furring mounted on the old cinder-block walls.

A dingy basement transformed into a bright new living area like this constitutes a major home-improvement indeed. Floor is vinyl-asbestos tile in a veined-marble pattern with feature strips in three colors. Acoustical ceiling has metal box beams in a woodgrain finish to harmonize with the generous use of natural wood trim and built-ins.

Toys, sewing machine in mid-use, ironing board not stowed away—all the things that would be clutter in other rooms look neat enough here. This "clutter room" for the woman of the house splits into laundry, sewing center, home office. Acoustical panels of ceiling soak up noise, while its luminous panels provide even, glare-free light. Floor is vinyl-asbestos.

This addition to a typical twelve-year-old "rambler" will do the most with the least. As a new family room it will relieve pressure of daytime activities on the limited bedroom space, while supplementing a living room become too small to carry its load. Big window to go into wall framing at left will look onto a new patio. Opening in fore-ground is for fireplace.

a box-beam suspended ceiling with 2′ x 4′ acoustical ceiling panels. These panels can soak up as much as 70 percent of the sound waves striking the ceiling surface, making the room quieter and more comfortable.

Lighting is extremely important since the housewife will spend much of her time at the sewing table, the ironing board, or working at her desk. Bright, glare-free illumination is needed. The ceiling can provide the answer. Translucent luminous ceiling panels, incorporated into the grid system directly beneath fluorescent fixtures over each major work area, provide an even, softly diffused light. Details of building such a ceiling are found in an earlier chapter.

Vinyl-asbestos tile was selected by the designers for the floor of the clutter room for several reasons. Vinyl-asbestos tile is available in a wide variety of designs and colors, including many with embossed effects that are designed to complement the current interest in natural home furnishings. Other factors helped swing the decision—low cost, easy maintenance, and the fact that this tile can be installed by the do-it-yourselfer with some adhesive, a paintbrush, and a pair of household scissors.

To turn an ordinary small laundry into a pleasant and efficient clutter room, replace space-eating appliances with more compact ones. A most notable instance of this is the space-gain that is produced when a bulky automatic washer and clothes dryer are replaced by a "Skinny Minnie."

That's the name by which the manufacturer, Frigidaire, has been known to refer to a novel vertical washer-plus-dryer that became available in 1970.

Although Skinny requires only a single electrical connection for washer and dryer, she is not a combination in the ordinary way. She's more a Siamese twin—a washer and a dryer joined into a one-piece vertical unit, so that washing and drying can go on independently at the same time.

Front-to-back depth of the new device is the usual 26″ but the width is just two feet—compared to the five feet and sometimes more of width used by most pairs of laundry appliances.

The difference is enough to multiply the usefulness of a small room.

The photographs show how space for a larger hobby bench and sink were produced by introduction of Skinny into a laundry room having barely 40 square feet of floor space. The washer and dryer used previously had alone consumed more than one fourth of the area. With the space required for their operation, they took up more than half of it.

But not every home has an attic or basement or garage that is convenient to expand into and not every house has space that can be converted into a clutter room. There may be no answer but selling out and moving—or adding to the structure.

When home-improvement needs reach this level, it is time to stop and look hard at two considerations, one subjective and personal and the other purely economic.

The first is this: Do you like the house and, especially, its location? If the place suits you in most respects other than size, and you plan to live in it for a long time to come, then you can't go wrong by expanding it to fit your needs.

If you don't plan to stay in the house for many years, you should consider whether the addition you have in mind will add proportionately to the value of the house—in a buyer's eye and dollars. You're making a dubious investment if, for instance, the neighborhood is in transition to commercial and the house will be torn down in a few years anyway. It is also true that in many neighborhoods there is a maximum amount a house can be sold for, and improving one beyond this level won't increase the figure substantially.

If you are going to do much or all of the work yourself, you need not figure these things quite so sharply. Since you will probably be adding several dollars of value for each dollar of investment, you have a big margin of safety. And, within the limits

By adding a family room owners of this house were able to remedy a serious lack—that of a fireplace—in the existing house. View here is from the direction of the old living room with the window to the new patio at the right. The vaulted ceiling with widely spaced beams was made possible by use of very thick plywood (called 2.4.1) usually employed to build floors, where it serves as both subfloor and underlayment and can be placed on spans of 4'.

Here the view is across the new patio and through the sliding glass doors into the new family room. The patio has an inexpensive and highly durable concrete-slab floor made attractive by use of exposed aggregate. The redwood grids of the floor make pouring it easier and also add to the design while minimizing cracking.

If your living room is too small, consider adding an auxiliary living space instead of trying to expand the existing room. Whether the addition is a family room, a library, a study, or—as here —a music room, this may be a far more effective solution and it can also solve sloping-lot problems by permitting a change of level.

541

The new living room with emphasis on music and reading has its roof and ceiling at a lower level (and its floor as well), giving an attractive play of angles and perspectives. Four-step difference in levels corresponds to slope of lot.

Here you look through the old living room to its new auxiliary. For harmony the common wall between these rooms was done over in redwood paneling of the same kind used for the new area.

If your home needs an expansion of its indoor living space, it very likely has equal need of more outdoor space. One answer is to expand as was done here by adding a large redwood deck.

suggested in the preceding paragraph, appraisals of home values generally give more weight to square footage than to any other single factor.

What and where to add to the structure of your house will depend, naturally, on the layout of the house and the space available on the lot, as well as on what your family needs. But there are a couple of money-saving principles that apply generally.

One is that the least expensive way to add space is in the form of room that does not require a lot of expense for what contractors call "mechanicals"—that is, plumbing, wiring, and heating. A bedroom or family room, for instance, involves relatively few mechanicals, but a kitchen, bathroom, or laundry room requires substantial outlays for them.

The second is that the room you need may not be the wisest one to add.

If, for example, what your house needs most is a separate dining room, you may do best to convert your living room to dining and add a spacious new living room. This double play can have the advantage of putting the dining room near the kitchen while placing the living room where it need carry no through traffic; and it means that those fresh new walls and all will be where you want them most.

Similarly, an additional bedroom is what most houses need more than anything else. But as you increase the number of bed-

The first attempt to turn this small laundry into a clutter room, with facilities for pursuing a hobby as well as washing clothes, was a limited success. Bench space at left is too crowded by washer and dryer and there is no possibility of putting in a needed sink.

The laundry room was created in the first place by closing off the end of a passageway. Half its 8-foot width was walled with Filon translucent plastic in a frame of black-stained pine. A matching door on a sliding track completes the inclosure. But the laundry appliances, each about 30" wide, nearly fill the tiny room.

rooms in a house you are likely to find the living room becoming more inadequate in size than ever. Consider the feasibility of converting the living room to sleeping while adding the kind of living room you really need.

The photographs show an addition to a house in which the bedrooms were overcrowded by a growing family that found their space insufficient for a mixture of sleeping, study, and hobby activities. A better answer than an added bedroom was found in attaching a new family room to take all but sleeping functions away from the bedrooms, leaving them quite adequate as they stood.

Photo left

The old washer and dryer are out and Skinny Minnie is in. The lower part of this new development from Frigidaire Division of General Motors is an automatic washer and the upper part is an electric clothes dryer. Functions are independent except for sharing electrical connections and the control panel placed safely at the top.

Photo right

Looking past Skinny you see the space gained by the replacement. Peg Board, prepainted in a cheery shade of yellow, forms a shield over the plumbing. There is plenty of space now for a sink to be used for hobbies and laundry as well.

60

Convert a Basement

A new floor and woodgrain paneled walls providing an unusual assortment of nearly invisible built-ins are the main elements of this space-gaining home improvement

"Less is more," said the great architect of simplicity, Mies van der Rohe.

One thing this means is that the less furniture and conspicuous built-ins a room contains the more spacious it seems and the better it functions.

Storage facilities camouflaged within economical hardboard wall paneling are the more-in-less feature of this home improvement that added a whole new living and recreation area to a suburban home. The principles involved are valid everywhere, of course, but they are especially applicable to major wall-paneling jobs.

To create a new room, in basement or elsewhere, you should usually begin by finishing the ceiling and installing any needed lighting and other wiring. Then frame the walls and add furring to existing ones. Furring seen at left here is for the special storage arrangement shown in the next two pictures. Your floor may be vinyl asbestos (in long, narrow "plank" tile here) or, for a quite similar effect, the seamless process described in an earlier chapter.

A two-section ping-pong table is hidden behind this wall. The hardboard panel (Masonite Royalcote in Honeytone Cherry woodgrain) is grasped by means of a finger pull of a kind sold for sliding pocket doors. The panel sits in a shallow groove at the bottom, a deeper groove at the ceiling, just like a typical sliding door. When the panel is lifted it slips further into top slot and comes free of the bottom one.

Back side of hardboard panel-door is reinforced with wood strips for stiffness. This is one of three panels that are lift-outs for access to floor-to-ceiling shallow storage space. As seen here and in the first photograph, this wall has been made approximately 8" thick to provide ample space for this specialized storage need. Card table is another of the items that this kind of space is well adapted for.

The high, narrow windows commonly found in basements are a problem usually best solved by giving them added importance. Here the visual size of the window is at least tripled by louvered shutters that also permit storing table-tennis paddles out of sight. The framed lift-out panel to the left is for access to an electric switch.

Laundry equipment and a small electric range become accessible when louvered doors are pushed aside. A matching louvered room divider at right conceals the furnace for the house. Other desirable storage features included in this much-for-little home improvement are a cedar-lined closet for out-of-season clothes and an adjacent broom closet.

Now the electric range—used for cooking when the owners entertain—and the laundry appliances have vanished behind the louvered doors. Portable television set at left rests on steel shelving in the workshop behind. When it is removed for use elsewhere, the opening is hidden from view by slipping in a rectangle of the cherry-grained hardboard paneling.

61

Expanding Into an Attic

**If you've an attic with headroom it's a valuable asset:
a weathertight shell awaiting only lining—and generous
insulation—to become the answer to your space problem**

An attic snuggles right under the roof, the part of a house that
lets in the most heat in summer and loses the most in winter if
uninsulated. Turning attic space into pleasant living quarters hinges
on insulating it thoroughly.

The usual thing, for permanent effectiveness with low cost,
is fiberglass with foil backing. Apply half- or full-thick bats between the studs of any sidewall, full-thick or heavier (or two
layers) between framing to which the ceiling will be applied. Which
thickness to use depends on climate—but don't forget that heat of
summer is as important a consideration as cold of winter.

If you put tie boards across between rafters to make an
area of flat ceiling, insulation should go just above the ceiling. The
uninsulated space between ceiling and roof peak can then be
ventilated to carry off moisture and, in summer, accumulated heat
from the sun.

The simple, budget-level conversion you see in the photographs was done by a family to meet a common kind of space
crisis. A house already well-filled by the parents and three daughters quickly became overcrowded as a son was born and grew
beyond nursery stage.

The decision was to provide new quarters for the two
daughters of most compatible ages. There was no place to go
but up, into an attic that looked most discouraging but was quickly
found to have what it takes—space.

After providing a safe stairway (and don't overlook the possibility of a spiral one in tackling an acute problem), first attention in converting an attic should be to structural strength. Floor joists may need greater strength and stiffness. Light and ventilation may be provided by windows, as was done in this case, or by skylight.

After floor joists had been strengthened and subflooring installed, sidewalls were framed to provide continuous storage space along both sides of the new room. When space is salvaged in this way, no headroom problem is created. Such space can be divided between relatively inaccessible parts for dead storage of bulky things and handy shelves.

Built-ins are especially important in rooms where space is limited: they not only accomplish more for the space they use, but also blend with the room to produce the uncluttered feel that is the secret of spaciousness without space. This is especially true when you build them of the same material used for the walls—here a woodgrained hardboard.

Here you see the other end of the room, with the same window treatment but no window seat. Plywood subflooring, which can be seen in some of the photographs, has the advantage over lumber of taking many kinds of finish floor materials without need of underlayment. Ozite carpeting designed to take the abuse of a room like this can be laid directly.

62

Masonry Methods Indoors

For some solid and durable home improvements use rock—in such special forms as slate, volcanic veneer slabs, and pebbles or exposed aggregate in concrete

To bring an air of solidity and permanence to a house, there's nothing like rock used in an appropriate area. And since rock is essentially an outdoor material it is a prime choice for places that must fight off fire, water, and hard wear.

SLATE is a special form of rock in such broad, thin slabs that it can be used for a floor or for a small part of one, without its thickness making it a literal stumbling block. In an entryway it is unaffected by scuffing feet and puddles of water. As a hearth it shrugs off the heat of spilled embers and the blows of dropped logs.

In the photograph you see an entryway built where horizontal winds off the Pacific blow water and sand against a sliding door. Since this small area of slate was added to take the brunt of abuse, there has been no problem of maintenance or of damage to more vulnerable flooring materials.

When doing an area as small as this one—or any typical entry or hearth—it is feasible to choose only the most suitable pieces from the pile of slate in the supply yard. Choose mostly pieces having at least one or two straight-cut edges so that these can form the perimeter without trimming. Slabs of nearly uniform thickness will be easiest to handle and will take the least adhesive.

Lay out your pieces to cover the desired area and to fit together as well as possible. Try for gaps of about half an inch. Where pieces overlap, mark for trimming by scratching with any pointed tool.

Borrow a slate cutter from your dealer if possible, or bring the marked pieces back to him for trimming. Simplest of all is to lay out the pieces right in the dealer's yard and bring them home all trimmed and ready to lay.

For an entryway or hearth where minimum thickness is important, use waterproof ceramic-tile adhesive. Spread it thickly, adding more adhesive wherever necessary to bring a piece of slate to level.

If there's no objection to an extra half-inch or so of height, you can lay your slate in mortar. Buy a sack of the dry-mix kind, the most convenient type for any small job. Make your mix about the consistency of peanut butter. Press the slate pieces well down

Photo left

To solve problems of wear and damage from fire and water, substitute everlasting slate for more vulnerable materials. Installation here was made with ceramic-tile cement, grouted with dry-mix mortar.

Photo right

To mark slate pieces for cutting, arrange them as efficiently as possible on the area to be covered. Keep joints generally to less than 1" and scratch-mark at overlaps. Trim with a slate cutter.

When slate is installed with tile adhesive, grout must be added separately. This is dry-mix mortar, sold in sacks and small boxes, mixed with water to pouring consistency.

into the mortar, testing them all for a consistent level with a long level or a straight-edged board. By trimming off with a putty knife and filling in where necessary you can bring the mortar between the slabs of slate to a level with the slate. Clean up spilled mortar as well as you can as soon as you can.

When setting slate in tile adhesive, wait a day and then grout by filling the spaces with cement mortar.

After a day, during which the grout should be kept damp, do a final cleaning (with water, and steel-wool pads if necessary) and apply slate dressing. Or polish with paste wax.

PEBBLE CONCRETE. Producing quite a different effect, pebble concrete is a rival of slate for an entryway, a hearth, or a porch. But since it must be applied 2″ to 4″ thick, it won't fit in everywhere.

For a pebbled surface, pour concrete within a form in the usual way and immediately after leveling it with a long strike-off board strew flat pebbles over its surface. Press and trowel them in level, wait a little while, then gently hose off the surface to reveal them.

For an exposed-aggregate surface, again pour concrete in the usual way. Strike it off level and float it or steel-trowel it lightly at once. After it begins to set, hose off the surface with a fine spray to reveal the gravel or stones used in mixing it.

Exposed-aggregate concrete, especially suitable for fireplace hearths and porches and patios, is shown here in an especially imaginative interior use. It is combined with cork-tile squares and unpaved plant pockets.

The kind of surface you get with this process naturally depends upon what variety of stone was used in making the concrete. Smooth stones, such as river-run, will produce a surface that is more attractive and smoother underfoot than you will get with crushed gravel aggregate, which has sharp edges. Many transit-mixed-concrete dealers will use a smooth aggregate if you explain your purpose when ordering.

VOLCANIC ROCK. But suppose the place where you want the ruggedness of stone is not a floor but a wall—perhaps one of which a fireplace is a part. Building one that looks as massive as you like is no longer a multi-ton backbreaker of a job.

Just apply a facing of lightweight volcanic rock over any

concrete-block or even wood-frame wall. This volcanic rock, long popular in the West, is now available coast to coast.

Medium-weight varieties of naturally thin stone will ordinarily call for wire ties set into the mortar of the base wall. However, when the ultralight volcanic stone called Featherock is used, no ties are needed. So it can easily be applied to existing walls.

For veneering, this volcanic rock is sliced to make it thin. The most economical type is sawed on both sides to a thickness of 1¾". A type called Bold Face is sawed on only one side and varies in thickness from about 2" to 5". In both kinds the pieces range in width from about 4" to 12". It takes only about 6 pounds of the veneer to cover a square foot of wall when the thinner type is used, or about 10 pounds of the Bold Face. Colors are varying light and dark gray and tan.

Big appeal of a stone-veneer job to the amateur mason is that so little skill is required. Irregularities in the block wall will be hidden by the stone facing. If unusual strength is needed, it is easily obtained by using thicker blocks or by reinforcing them with steel and concrete in the hollows.

Any stone veneer can be applied to a block wall containing ties by use of a single mortar application, as shown in the photographs.

A suitable mortar is made by mixing 1 part portland cement to 3 parts plaster sand and ⅜ part hydrated lime. This is called Type S and is easy to work with. Most types of stonework will be much handsomer if the mortar is colored by adding lampblack or black oxide.

One secret of easy stone work is this incredibly light volcanic rock from California, now available nationally. The young lady holds a hunk of Featherock, which averages one-fifth the weight of granite.

Where a very light veneer, such as Featherock, is used no ties are needed and any sound existing wall will serve as the base.

This ultralight volcanic veneer can be applied directly to a clean, unpainted masonry wall, in a bed of ½″ to ¾″ Type S mortar. The stone units are then pressed into place. Whether you will then point around the units with additional mortar depends purely upon which way the joints look better to you.

A better method of application, however, is this three-step process:

1. Apply a scratch coat of mortar about ½″ thick, troweling it on firmly. Scratch it after it has begun to harden to roughen the surface. Allow to cure for at least forty-eight hours.

2. Cover the scratch coat with a ½″ mortar bed. Do just enough area for each stone, so it won't harden before you press the unit into place.

3. Butter the back of each veneer unit with the same mortar and press it firmly into the mortar bed.

With some types of wall, there will have to be one preliminary step. Over painted concrete, first apply stucco wire. Over stucco or wood siding, first cover with building paper and metal lath. Over open wood studs spaced 16″ on center, first cover with building paper and metal reinforcement as for exterior plaster application.

In each of these cases, then proceed with the three steps outlined above.

And the volcanic rock formed ages ago in the Sierra Nevada of California will be beautifully at home on your walls wherever you live.

The last of our four solutions to masonry problems tackles one of the opposite kind: the existing concrete floor you want to get rid of.

Garages, basements, and patios are favorite targets of families that need more living space but don't want to move or build an addition. A frequent drawback to remodeling these areas is the cold concrete floor, frequently cracked and oily, unsuitable as a base for decorative floor coverings.

An easy way to overcome the concrete floor problem in remodeling has been worked out by the American Plywood Association, using Styrofoam panels and plywood underlayment to provide a warm, resilient floor.

The first step is to lay out a grid of plywood nailing strips as thick as the Styrofoam panels. The strips are squared and nailed to the concrete on 4′ centers, with crosspieces on 8′ centers offset 4′ in alternate rows for strength.

Metal ties may be placed at 6″ intervals in mortar joints while laying a block wall as a base for medium-weight stone veneer. Since ties are not needed with ultralight types of veneer, Featherock may be applied to an existing block or frame wall.

Whether fastened directly to block wall or laid in mortar over a scratch coat, each unit should have its back buttered with mortar like this and pressed into place.

Press and tap each stone unit as you go along so that mortar is squeezed out into the joint. Rake and brush the mortar after it has become stiff.

An adhesive that doubles as a vapor barrier is troweled on the concrete between the nailing strips, and the Styrofoam panels are laid in place. The adhesive should be a kind, such as unfilled asphalt, that doesn't attack Styrofoam.

It is best to do this part of the job a row at a time to avoid walking on the uncovered plastic panels and crushing them.

The same vapor-barrier-adhesive then is troweled over strips and Styrofoam in areas slightly larger than the plywood underlayment panel. While working, use one panel to kneel on to avoid crushing the plastic. After covering the floor in this way, use ordinary wallboard joint adhesive to fill hammer dents and the joints between panels.

Sand the filled areas and the floor is ready to be covered. Over plywood underlayment any floor covering may be used.

560

You need not allow its cold or cracked concrete floor to prevent your turning a basement or garage into comfortable living space. Cement Styrofoam slabs between 2" x 4" framing to form an insulating vapor barrier, then make a new floor.

Since plywood is a suitable base for resilient flooring, in sheets or tiles, or for carpeting, you are free to finish your new floor as you like. Note the use of a spiral stairway in this attractive home improvement.

63

Add a Deck For Outdoor Living

For an end to that cramped feeling extend the living space of your home with a deck built of wood

To add a deck is to gain a room. And a dollar spent in this way will provide as much new area as five or ten used inside. A wood deck can extend your space for lounging or recreation or dining; it can be a garden displaying plants in containers; it can serve for private sunning or public entertaining.

A deck is economical because it doesn't require walls, ceiling, roofing, wiring, and expensive furniture. For the home-owner who is unsure of his ability to tackle the more complicated aspects of remodeling, building a deck is often a good first step in major updating. It can be done without creating the inconvenience of noise and sawdust inside the house. And since deck carpentry is rough it doesn't require a cabinetmaker's skill.

Planning your deck should begin with a visit to your local building-inspection department to learn what you can or cannot do. Codes vary from one city or county to another. Furthermore, a building department can be helpful in supplying information on what will work best for your climate, topography, and structure.

To make your deck planning as simple as possible, start with two principles:

A deck is an extension of a house.

A deck is for fun.

A deck as generous and as private and protected as this one vastly expands the house of which it becomes a part. Dark-stained framing of windbreak panels contrasts sharply with fillers and with light tan of water-repellent-treated decking of clear all-heart redwood 2″ x 4″s.

WHERE TO BUILD IT. Try to place your deck where it will extend the living parts of your house. Direct entrance to living or dining room is ideal, of course. Nearness to kitchen is often helpful, too, and this may be easiest to arrange.

If your house, like many these days, has a sliding glass door between living or dining area and the outdoors, this may be the natural spot for the deck. If you don't have this kind of access to the outdoors, you may find it worthwhile to provide it. Replacing a section of wall or ordinary windows with a glass slider is by no means major surgery, and sliding glass doors are surprisingly inexpensive now. By all means pay the small extra cost of buying one equipped with safety glass. Many building codes now require this.

Properly locating your deck to use house walls for protection can easily double its usefulness. Depending on your climate, you may need protection from wind or sun or both. Privacy from neighbors or passersby may be just as important.

You should find many ideas for accomplishing these things exemplified in the decks shown in this chapter. The chapter that follows show step-by-step the art of building a typical wood deck and also how to erect a windbreak, a very useful addition in many deck situations.

A deck's for fun and beauty. What kind depends on the location of the house and the family that will use it. For two adults a deck may bring in a view from outdoors or create a view with its own garden and plants in containers. Space for dining, reading, lounging, and sunbathing are the deck requirements for most adults. Consider the possibility of adding more than one deck to fit a number of specialized needs.

Most homeowners will use a deck for entertaining. Area required will depend upon scale and time of entertaining. Will the deck be needed in the daytime only, or for evenings as well? This is largely a matter of climate. Areas where evenings are consistently chilly or buggy need deck space for sunshine hours alone.

If yours is a family with small children, consider building a deck large and safe enough to provide play space reasonably separated from adult activities.

In deciding the size and shape of your deck, allow space for some of these possibilities: dining table and chairs; easy chairs and chaise longue; hammock; pad for sunbathing; table tennis or other game; outdoor cooking equipment; plants in containers.

Keep in mind the importance of a safety railing, especially when the deck is high off the ground. This need can be met by an ordinary railing or by one that is also a bench that will cut down on the need for furniture.

The less of the outdoors you own the more you need a deck to make maximum use of limited space. Zigzag pattern of the boards in this one is nicely echoed in the shape of the raised portion that serves for seating and for displaying plants.

Decks can add unity as well as utility. Connected twin decks pull various living areas of this house together while providing for separation of functions. The design is by Dave Swarthout Associates.

LOW-LEVEL DECKS. From the point of view of construction, decks are of two main types—low level and high level.

If your lot is flat and your house site close to the ground, yours can be a low-level deck, not much higher than a patio. It may even be so low as to require neither posts under it nor safety railing around it.

A low-level deck of wood is pleasanter than a paved patio to the touch of the foot on either a hot or a cold day. It won't give off excessive heat from sun, doesn't reflect glare, can be formal enough for a dress-up party or informal enough for a barbecue.

Appropriately detailed, it will go well with a house of any design.

A typical low-level deck will consist of decking 2″ x 4″s nailed to joists spaced about 3′ apart. The joists should rest on concrete piers or on concrete blocks, preferably supported by pads or piers of poured concrete. The piers should extend down to solid soil or rock; and local conditions may require that they go below the frost line.

HIGH-LEVEL DECKS. If your site slopes or the floor level of your house is well above grade, you should regard your deck as high level. A deck even a foot or two above the ground will require some kind of safety barrier along edges where there are no steps. And any deck much higher than this will usually need supporting posts differing only in length from those of a very high deck.

A broad step can ease the transition from house floor to a deck at a much lower level.

A high deck will usually need a supporting member attached to the house. This often can be omitted from low-level decks, which may not be tied to the house at all. Such a support can be a timber, such as a 2″ x 12″, spiked to the house framing or anchor-bolted to the foundation. A 2″ x 4″ nailed to it forms a ledger on which one end of each joist rests. The joists should then be toenailed to ledger and timber.

And don't forget that wood may decay at any point where

Fully walled and indoor-outdoor carpeted, a deck like this comes within a roof of being truly a room . . . making the presence of a good-sized tree impressive.

it touches the ground or can accumulate moisture. For this reason it is well to use a preservative, even on such woods as redwood, cypress, or cedar heartwood that are comparatively resistant to decay.

Reasonable protection can be achieved (and this may be quite adequate in a dry or snowless area) by brushing on creosote. It is also possible to purchase lumber that has been treated with a solution of pentachlorophenol, an effective preservative under most conditions. There are also resin sealers, copper naphthenate, and a commercially available pentachlorophenol solution, any of which you can brush on or soak into lumber that will be exposed

Photo left

If your house is built on more than one level it may need decks to match. Here each level of the lower floor has its own deck, as does the second story. When decking is laid solid, some slope for drainage should be provided.

Photo right

If your lot slopes so that an end of your deck is more than a step above grade, there's the place to put a safety railing. Dual-purpose seating-railing serves well enough when dropoff is moderate.

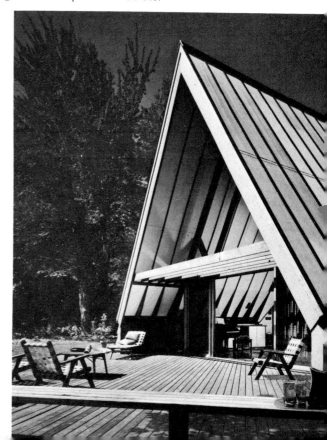

to decay conditions. Your lumber dealer can tell you what is recommended for the area in which you are building your deck.

In typical deck construction the joists are supported near their far ends by a beam. It, in turn, is held up by posts resting on piers. These posts may come at the extreme ends of the beam, but usually they are placed a foot or so in, to reduce the span between them. Likewise, if the joists cantilever a foot or so beyond the beam, they too will be stiffer because of the shortened spans.

Safety railings. High-level decks need safety railings. Strength is the first consideration. It is easily met, since uprights of 2″ x 4″ lumber are adequate if no more than 5′ apart. However, if young children will use your deck, spacing should be reduced to perhaps 8″. Or several horizontal members may be added.

A railing can be a decorative as well as a safety feature. Parts, or all of it, can be painted or stained. Translucent plastic panels can be inserted to add strength, light, privacy and color, or the railing can be made solid or designed to provide support for flowers and vines. A railing that is a suncatcher and windbreak—and colorfully decorative as well—is shown in the next chapter.

Benches. You will get a great deal for a small added investment if you surround your deck with a built-in bench.

Such a bench makes an effective safety railing that adults —even elderly people—cannot fall over and children or pets cannot squeeze through. It adds privacy and can be designed so plants in pots can safely edge the outer rim. It eliminates the need for most seating furniture. Movable chairs and benches may be more expensive and take more space. A surrounding bench will do more than anything else to make your deck look truly hospitable and comfortable.

LUMBER. If your deck is to be painted, and repainted when necessary, any good construction lumber will do. Douglas fir and other members of the pine family are a good choice as are redwood, spruce, hemlock, incense cedar, or red cedar. All-heart redwood is a superior, decay-resistant grade. Redwood will weather to silvery gray without paint or stain.

For supporting members, an economical grade redwood is construction heart. Grades containing sapwood should be avoided since their creamy-white streaks are as subject as any other lumber to decay.

In purchasing wood your choice will be determined not only by appearance and use but also by what is available in your climate at a cost you can afford.

A deck in the form of a platform on which the house sits is often called an engawa. This one's not wide but it provides useful outdoor living space as well as a far more welcoming entry than the ordinary porch.

You may wish to use rough lumber for the posts, beams, and joists, and possibly for railing members. Use a surfaced type, however, for the decking itself and for any built-in seating. One joy of a wood deck compared with a paved patio is that it is springy underfoot. Splinters in rough lumber put an end to barefoot pleasure and may reduce the usefulness of the deck for children.

Since knots limit the span of your decking material and detract from the appearance of the job, you may prefer a better grade for the deck floor. Clear all-heart redwood, for example, will take a 3′ span nicely. If you must exceed that span, or if you are using a lumber grade containing occasional knots, you should

For a sun-trapping, wind-shielded deck, an ideal location is one protected by the house on three sides. Here additional protection and total privacy are obtained by running a fence of translucent plastic along fourth side.

go to 2″ x 6″ instead. Even wider lumber is sometimes used for decks, but the result is usually less attractive and the danger of cupping from dampness is increased. For very long spans, use 2″ x 3″ or 2″ x 4″ lumber on edge.

Leave narrow expansion spaces, not to exceed ¼″, between decking. Small spacer blocks or shims between boards will make it easier to line up the boards, insure correct spacing, and provide an attractive surface pattern on the deck. Or you can use nails as temporary spacers, as shown in the next chapter.

NAILS. Ordinary nails will rust and make streaks. Use galvanized nails (and be sure they are the hot-dipped type, rough to the touch) for the structural parts of the job.

Galvanized nails will do for applying the decking, too, but they involve one risk. The zinc on the heads may be chipped off by the hammer permitting them to rust and streak like plain steel nails. You can avoid this danger by using aluminum nails. Hardened aluminum alloy ones, such as Hy-Tensil, are easiest to drive successfully.

For nailing 2″ decking, 16d nails are about right. Use two nails at each bearing for 2″ x 4″s and three nails with 2″ x 6″ lumber. Drive them at a slight angle and you'll increase their holding power.

FINISH. If you're using lumber lacking built-in weather resistance, painting your deck like your house will give it good protection.

If you want a clear finish, you can use a polyurethane varnish, the kind sold in marine supply outlets. Or you might want to try one of the clear epoxy resin materials sold in lumberyards. Some of these products are expensive but far more durable than ordinary varnishes.

Stains especially formulated for decks give good results. Cabot makes a decking stain, with an alkyd resin base, that comes in shades of red, brown, and gray and may be used with any kind of lumber. Decking stains are far easier to maintain than ordinary paint or varnish.

No finish at all is often the best treatment. Redwood, for example, may darken in streaks but eventually will settle down to a weathered gray. If you're in a hurry, treat it with a commercial bleach or use a gray bleaching stain.

If you prefer to keep something closer to the original red-

For a house on a lake or one with an ocean in its back yard—as is the case with this Palm Beach home—here's a spectacular idea. Edward D. Stone, Jr., designed this one of redwood with brick steps leading down from a patio.

Seating built into railings adds to the hospitable feeling of this redwood deck. Decking 2″ x 4″s are spaced to drain. A canvas canopy protects one end, while the other is left exposed to the sun.

wood color, use a water repellent. Put on two coats. Brush in thoroughly. Don't spray. Redwood treated this way will slowly lighten in color to a light buckskin tan and then slowly turn soft gray. Water repellents also come in a variety of pigmented types to produce almost any color effect you might want.

A lazy man's rule for finishing redwood used outdoors, especially for decks, is avoid varnish or any other clear coating. It really doesn't need it, so you're making yourself both extra expense and maintenance.

Among the vast variety of stains and paints available today, many are chemically quite different from anything you may have used before. They often do not combine satisfactorily nor can you use one on top of another. It wouldn't be a bad idea to keep a note in your files on the kind and brand used, so you won't find yourself in trouble a few years hence when the deck needs refinishing.

A deck can be a bonus springing from such a home-improvement project as the rebuilding of this dingy back porch. Good way to give a bedroom access to such a deck is by putting a long casement window or sliding door where an ordinary window stood before.

There's never a shortage of seating on a deck whose railing is a bench as well. Pictures and captions in the next chapter cover how to build working railings of this kind as well as decks of 2" x 4" lumber like this.

64

How to Build Decks and Windbreaks

With only rough carpentry required, these are among the easiest of major home-improvement jobs, yet they yield a lot of comfort for their cost

All by itself a deck can make the difference between an ordinary, stodgy, cramped, and not quite livable house—and one that offers both comfort and distinction. Where the preceding chapter was devoted to convincing you of this by offering some stunning examples, the pictures that follow are intended primarily to show you the fundamentals of building a deck of your own.

Deck construction is an excellent topic to finish a book that began so many pages back with the contention that improving your home is one of the greatest avocations in the world. Consider these aspects:

When you build a deck you work out in the open air.

Since no two decks are alike, you exercise your ingenuity in creating one best suited to your house.

For every dollar you spend on the materials for it you can expect to increase the value of your home by several dollars at least.

It's a permanent improvement that you can actively enjoy. And admire. And get compliments on.

And on top of all that, it's fun to do.

Typical construction details for both high- and low-level decks are given in this drawing, which also shows how to combine a wood deck with a brick terrace or porch. Although this house was already well-decked, the owners saw a need for more outdoor living space. The deck salvages area otherwise lost to daily use due to its slope.

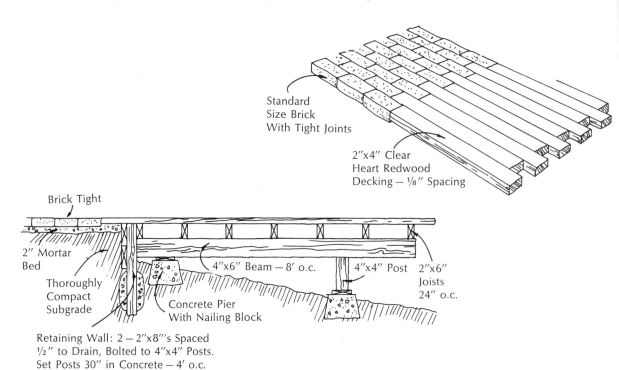

Standard
Size Brick
With Tight Joints

2"x4" Clear
Heart Redwood
Decking — 1/8" Spacing

Brick Tight

2" Mortar
Bed

Thoroughly
Compact
Subgrade

Concrete Pier
With Nailing Block

4"x6" Beam — 8' o.c.

4"x4" Post

2"x6"
Joists
24" o.c.

Retaining Wall: 2 — 2"x8"'s Spaced
1/2" to Drain, Bolted to 4"x4" Posts.
Set Posts 30" in Concrete — 4' o.c.

Built by the authors as part of a California cabin, this high-level deck represents something close to a minimum in cost and effort. Because of the wide span between girders, decking is 2" x 4"s on edge. Skeletal railing can easily be added to if necessary for safety of small children. Rigging overhead is to take canvas sunshade during the brief part of the year that need is felt.

The cabin deck and the one that is shown in the series of pictures that follow both require anchoring at the ground—as do most high decks. One method, shown at A, uses a metal post anchor, or strap, cast in a pier poured in place. B is a version of the method actually used on these jobs: wood nailing block as part of either a precast or a site-poured pier. Drift-pin method, C, is a good choice when the underside of the deck will be in open view.

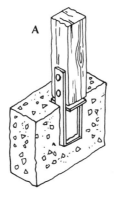

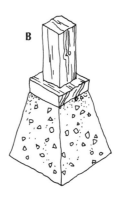

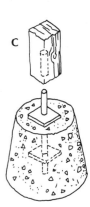

A   B   C

This compact deck was built by the authors to add usable outdoor space to their house on a tiny and sharply sloping city lot. Since the corner seen here is all of 10′ above the ground, guard railing is essential. The photographs that follow show the steps in construction of the deck.

HOW TO BUILD THE COMPACT DECK

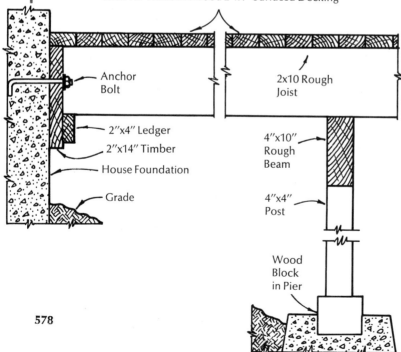

Clear All-Heart Redwood 2″x4″ Surfaced Decking

Anchor Bolt

2x10 Rough Joist

2″x4″ Ledger

2″x14″ Timber

House Foundation

Grade

4″x10″ Rough Beam

4″x4″ Post

Wood Block in Pier

Diagram shows how joists rest on a 2″ x 4″ nailed to a plank bolted to the foundation of the house. At the end away from the house the joists are held up by a beam resting on posts.

578

1. First step in actual construction of the deck is providing support at the house end. Here a timber is bolted to the concrete foundation. With wood construction it would have been spiked to the framing. This plank has been preservative-treated for insurance against rot.

2. Each 4" x 4" post is spiked to a block of decay-resistant wood set into a concrete pier. This may be a precast pier from the lumberyard, resting on a poured-concrete base; or, as here, it may be a large block of concrete poured in place.

3.

4.

3. If any posts are to be set directly into the ground, they should be pressure-treated lumber or be given a treatment with wood preservative. Much better than just painting it on is pouring preservative into a plastic bag in which the post rests. Thus thorough soaking can be provided even while construction goes on.

4. Here is the framing completed. Joists rest on 2″ x 4″ ledger at house and on post-supported beam at far end. Temporary braces seen at far right steady the framing during construction. A few decking 2″ x 4″s are laid out to provide a temporary platform to kneel on while nailing joists.

5. Nail on the decking, using two 16d galvanized or hardened aluminum nails at each bearing (three or more nails if your decking is wider than 4"). Space between 2" x 4"s should be no more than ¼", to bar spike heels. For minimum spacing, using a nail.

6. The safety railing needed around a high-level deck is more attractively, more usefully, and almost as easily provided by combining it with seating. Construction details for this simple and economical railing-bench are shown in the accompanying diagram.

5.

6.

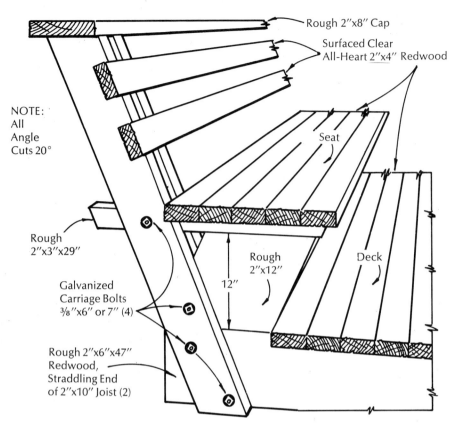

Rough 2"x8" Cap

Surfaced Clear
All-Heart 2"x4" Redwood

NOTE:
All
Angle
Cuts 20°

Seat

Rough
2"x3"x29"

Rough
2"x12"

Deck

12"

Galvanized
Carriage Bolts
3/8"x6" or 7" (4)

Rough 2"x6"x47"
Redwood,
Straddling End
of 2"x10" Joist (2)

7. With the exception of deck and seat 2" x 4"s, where splintering must be considered, all the redwood lumber used to build this deck is rough. Besides contributing to rustic effect, rough construction lumber is wider and thicker than the surfaced kind of same nominal dimensions, hence provides greater strength and stiffness.

8. Near side of deck gets neither railing nor bench. Because it is close to a neighboring house, it will be completed with a privacy fence of translucent plastic that serves also as a windbreak. The photographs and drawings show how to build a windbreak-fence adaptable to any deck or patio.

Fencing in your deck or patio for wind-protection and privacy makes it seem far bigger as well. This colorful barrier is made of red, white and yellow translucent Filon plastic framed in redwood 2" x 4"'s prestained to match the house.

Each framing 2″ x 4″ has one or two saw kerfs ⅝″ deep plowed into it and is then stained before assembly. Framing is designed so that openings are 1″ smaller in each direction than the plastic sheets they are to take.

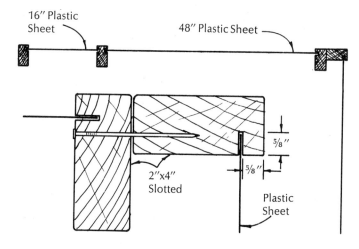

Build up the framing, slipping in the plastic sheets as you go. An interesting alternate construction method is building a frame of 1" x 4" surfaced or rough lumber, fastening the Filon to the face of it with waterproof panel adhesive, then nailing on a second layer of 1" x 4". This is a version of the method shown in an earlier chapter for building sliding sandwich doors.

Your Workshop For Home Improvement

How to choose and organize the tools and shop that make home-improvement easy, enjoyable, and economical

Building a good workshop and equipping it for efficiency is a home improvement that leads to other home improvements. A great many of the things this book is about can be accomplished by any householder if he has a good workshop as a basis.

And since home improvements can come out of your workshop at a rate that equals many hundreds—even thousands—of dollars a year in savings, any reasonable tool purchase is an excellent investment. If you use the tool, that is.

Some people are not so much tool users as tool collectors. Theirs is an interesting hobby, perhaps, but hardly the productive and economical one we're talking about.

If you fall into the habit of buying a new tool every time you tackle a job, you won't save money by doing the work yourself. You may be money ahead by hiring a professional to do the job. Then you won't need to store the unnecessary tools you purchased.

Most projects outlined in this book require only hand tools, but almost any job can be made easier with the right power tool.

For special projects and one-time jobs the best solution is to rent tools from one of the many agencies that stock all types of equipment. They're listed in the yellow pages of your phone book, and the dealer is prepared to give you a short demonstration on how to use the tool properly. Renting first, buying later, gives you a chance to try a tool and find out whether it is worthwhile investing your own money and shop space in it.

The tool cabinet shown in the photographs is a simply constructed means of keeping your hand tools clean and out of sight, yet ready for use in a second. As the pictures show, it neatly stows the minimum tools every household needs, yet provides space for just about everything that may be added later. And it does this in a space of less than 4" deep.

Hang this tool panel on a wall, add a wooden bench or table to which a vise may be clamped, and you have an efficient home workshop.

These are the materials you will need to make it:

Thirty lineal feet of standard 1" x 2" lumber, such as pine or redwood.

One panel of ¼" hardboard (Masonite), 3' x 4'.

34½" of ¾" or ⅝" continuous hinge with screws.

One 1" flat hook and assorted steel hooks and cup hooks for hanging tools.

Glue, 6d finishing nails, 3d box nails.

Here are the steps in building it.

1. Cut four 24" lengths and four 34½" lengths of 1" x 2". Plane two of the longer pieces slightly to take the hinge, marking them with Xs to indicate the set-in edge. With glue and nails, assemble into two frames 24" x 36".

2. Cut two 22½" lengths of 1" x 2". Bore assorted holes in one to fit your present (and expected future) supply of bits, screwdrivers, nail sets, and chisels. Slot the second piece to handle files, hammers, hand drill, and the like.

3. Glue and nail these two strips into one of the frames in the positions shown in the photograph. Distances from inside bottom of frame are 6" and 21".

4. Steel hooks inserted into the top of the frame will hang such tools as bit brace and planes.

5. Cut two more 22½" lengths of 1" x 2". Notch and slot for saws and squares. Fit these to your own tools, making notches generous. Glue and nail in these strips in positions that fit your tools best.

6. With glue and nails, cover each frame with half the sheet of hardboard. Hardboard goes onto the side of the frame *not* marked X. Paint the underside of the hardboard white first if you wish.

7. Do this with the two frames sitting side-by-side as you see them in the photograph of the opened cabinet.

8. Add a flat hook to keep the cabinet closed and a nail on one outer edge for hanging up a yardstick. Put a pair of heavy

Home workshops in the several houses the authors have built over the years have been the starting point for nearly every kind of home improvement described in this book.

Model shop shows how yours might occupy space off, or in, garage or carport. When a shop is small, a wide doorway is important so that work can spread into the neighboring space when necessary. Glass used this way should be safety type; or translucent plastic could take its place.

Add a tool cabinet like this to a workbench with vise (and preferably drawers as well) and you have a functioning hand-tool workshop. Details on building one are given in this chapter.

Tool cabinet closes neatly against the wall, exposing chalkboard-painted surface useful for messages, jottings, and design sketches.

shelf hangers on the back for hanging the cabinet on the wall. Give the front two coats of green chalkboard paint. And your tool cabinet is ready to use.

VALUE OF CLAMPS. In addition to the assortment of hand tools you see in the picture of the tool cabinet, you'll need a decent collection of clamps.

Aside from such chores as gluing, for which clamps are often indispensable, a clamp can serve as a third hand when you need a helper and there's nobody around. What's more, a clamp doesn't grouse or say "Wait a minute" or "I'm busy," as people do when called away from their own activities.

Clamps are not expensive. You can buy them new, or add to your collection whenever some retired do-it-yourselfer has a shop sale. There's nothing much that can go wrong with them, no concealed wear or danger that you're buying a lemon, as there can be with a tool that has intricate mechanical parts.

Clamps (especially the versatile, inexpensive C-clamps) are among the home-improver's most useful helpers. Here one temporarily suspends a post until concrete for a porch is poured around a steel pin in its bottom end.

Photo left

Such things as concrete form boards and wall framing for paneling jobs can be first assembled with clamps. Then leveling and making straight or plumb can be completed and checked before nailing.

Photo right

Clamps made of wood are less likely then metal ones to mar the face of a sheet of paneling while holding it for edge sanding.

For an instance of the value of a clamp. Suppose you have a plank, a hefty 20′ 2″ x 10″, to lift and nail across the ends of some rafters. How can you hold up one end while you climb a ladder, shift the board to exact position and nail the other end?

Two people and two ladders make an answer, but there's a better one. Use a C-clamp to fasten a scrap of wood to the underside of one rafter. Let it stick out far enough to form a ledge on which one end of the plank can rest while you lift the other and nail it.

Suppose you have to cut a number of wooden parts all the same length, using a radial saw. You can make a stop by nailing a block to the saw table or bench top, or . . . That's right, you can save time by *clamping* the block instead.

While remodeling a room you have to cut off some metal parts. You could carry them to your shop, where you have a vise.

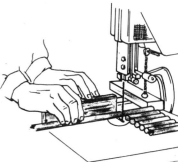

But you save yourself a walk by clamping each piece against a wall stud while you cut it.

(If the metal is thin, clamp it between bits of hardboard and cut the sandwich. Cuts faster, comes out smoother.)

Perhaps you have some things to push apart—a pair of overly close wall studs, say. Or you want to spread a cabinet apart from the inside; or to exert pressure between a cupboard and a countertop below that you are covering with flexible roll material. There's a special clamp (it's Adjustable Clamp Company's No. 56) you can put together backwards to do just these things.

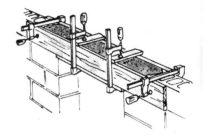

Are you working with concrete block? You can make a quickly reusable form for lintels. Clamp two boards across the opening, use two more clamps to hold a bottom in it.

A single clamp is usually enough to hold two or more pieces of wood together for tracing a pattern or for simultaneous cutting or sanding.

If you have a buried timber or a post to pry out of the ground, try putting a heavy C-clamp on it. That will give you something to pry against or fasten a chain or rope to.

When marking screw holes for an overhead closet-door track, use a C-clamp to keep the track from slipping. Sometimes you can just clamp the track into place and then drill the holes and sink the screws without taking it down.

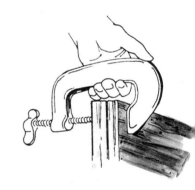

In any kind of framing while building or improving a wall to take paneling, try clamping parts and then checking position before nailing. That's easier than pulling out your mistakes with a claw hammer.

To knock a stubborn post or stud into place, put pull on it with a bar clamp or a pipe clamp while you swing a hammer or maul.

Paneling a room or a house with plywood or hardboard involves a lot of awkward carrying. You can handle large, heavy sheet materials, or several thin sheets at a time, by using a pair of C-clamps as handles. Unless you can turn the good faces of the sheets inward, protect them with scraps under the jaws of the clamps.

To force tongue-and-groove paneling or flooring boards into place, clamp a block to the framing and use it to pry against with a pry bar. Or, when possible, pull the boards together with a bar clamp. Use a narrow tongued scrap on the grooved side (and a grooved scrap on the tongued side) to protect the work from damage.

When a home improvement project requires concrete work, speed the building of forms by clamping boards into approximate position first. Then check the level, tap into place, and nail.

To fit a badly cupped board into a dado, first draw and hold it straight with a big bar clamp and a length of 2″ x 4″.

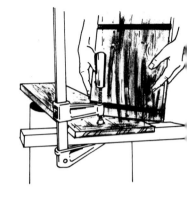

Clamp your miter box to your workbench for easier sawing. When using it on the job, clamp it to a sawhorse.

Do you need a temporary prop to hold up a beam while you measure and perhaps cut the permanent post? There's no need to cut one. Use a clamp to splice two shorter scraps and you can adjust them to precisely the length you need.

It's difficult to sand curved strips to shape without a jig. Yet you often need to make several identical ones for a built-in. Clamp a pointed stick to the disk-sander table so that the inner edge of the work rides against it.

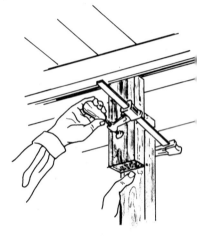

Power tools—a small electric drill at least—are part of most households these electrified days. Since anyone planning important home improvements will want to acquire additional tools, here is a rundown on all the types that may belong in a home shop.

In addition to general tips for choosing each kind of tool, you'll find information on judging condition and suitability of used equipment. Since the first buyer takes the big depreciation, there are great savings in acquiring your more costly tools secondhand. And if you need them only temporarily, there is a good probability you will be able to resell them at a loss that is only a small fraction the cost of renting.

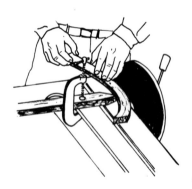

Buying a drill press, saw, lathe, or whatever is like shopping for a car. Just looking at the paint job and poking blindly at the innards is not enough. There are certain rather specific things you need to know in order to tell a sound bargain from a shiny lemon.

There are a few general points too. The first is the name of the maker. Is he known for good tools? Is he still in business? (There's nothing more annoying than owning an orphaned tool with a broken-down bearing that can't be duplicated.)

Note whether the tool is of the manufacturer's first-quality line or something designed for light home use. The latter may do you very well, but you want to know what you're getting when you begin to talk price.

Don't overlook accessories, especially when buying second-hand. The seller of used equipment is likely to have accumulated a good many of these at considerable cost. A used drill press offered at the original retail price may be a bargain if such items as a set of drills and a mortising attachment are thrown in. An 8″

dado head and a few blades may cost as much as a medium-priced table saw.

DRILL PRESS. First question is suitability. Is it a rugged enough model for the kind and amount of work you have in mind? Is it big enough—in distance from center of chuck to column? (This is how the "size" of a drill press is measured. A small, home model such as the 11¾" will drill a hole in a center of any circle up to 11¾" diameter.) Is the spindle travel long enough for your purposes? It is likely to vary from 4" down to 2" or less.

When you have answered these questions, you are ready to check condition if it's a used machine you're considering.

1. Is there lateral play between the quill and the headstock casting? Just run the quill down and then try to move it back and forth with your hand. If there is noticeable play, better just slip quietly away with your wallet still in your pocket.

2. If the drill press has a tapered shank spindle (rather than Jacobs chuck spindle), is the taper undamaged? To check, push a new drill shank by hand into the spindle. If it fits tightly, the spindle taper is all right.

3. If there is a chuck, is it still accurate? Put a new drill into the chuck, and turn the spindle by hand. If the chuck is good, the drill won't wobble. If it does wobble, you'll have to buy a new chuck.

4. Are the pulleys worn or cracked? If there are shiny spots on the bottom of the pulley Vs, add a couple of dollars for replacement to the price asked for the drill press.

5. Any cracked castings? These will have to be replaced, and they're expensive.

6. How does it run? This, of course, is the big test and if you have to buy without making it you are taking a big gamble. The best you can do in that case is to turn the spindle by hand. It should turn freely, without the gritty feeling or sound that indicates bad bearings.

If the machine is set up to run, turn it on and listen. Excessive noise suggests that the bearing housing castings are worn and the machine is of little value.

Put it through its paces as far as possible—drilling holes, of course, and using what accessories are at hand.

JIGSAW. Suitability here is a matter of size, of quality, of condition—and especially of how you expect to use it. If you don't have a band saw, and don't expect to get one, you may need a pretty heavy jigsaw, one that will do some of the work that properly calls for a band saw.

1. With used equipment: Try to move both upper and lower operating shafts from side to side. If there is play, try to find out whether the shafts travel in bushings or in castings. This is important because worn bushings are fairly easy to replace while worn castings are likely to cost more than the machine is worth.

2. Check the drive shaft in the same way. Lateral play indicates worn bearings or castings.

3. If you can, turn on the machine and listen. Noisy operation indicates worn parts.

WOOD LATHE. Begin by asking whether the lathe was built to do the kind of work you need it for. If it has an 8″ swing and you need a 12″, it is hardly a bargain for you at any price.

Same goes for distance between centers. The 24″ size may do you nicely, but not if you want to turn table legs. And if you contemplate making some kinds of furnishings, even 30″ centers may not be enough. In that case, investigate whether a bed extension can be bought.

Next, check condition:

1. Look first at the threads on both ends of the spindle. If these are worn or damaged, add replacement cost to the asking price of the lathe.

2. Check the spindle for lateral play by trying to move it back and forth. If bearings or bearing housings are badly worn you won't be able to do accurate work.

3. If you may want to use attachments for turning metals or plastics, make sure the bed hasn't been nicked or gouged. This could prevent your using the required attachments.

4. Are any accessories included? Various chucks and arbors are worth having and may cost anywhere from $1 to $10 each. Wood-turning chisels cost $1 to $2 apiece.

BAND SAW. Size is measured in depth of throat, 12″ from blade to throat being a typical size. If you expect to work thick stock or do resawing you'll want to know the maximum cut capacity— 4″, 6″, or, on the big floor models, 12″ or more.

1. Try to wiggle the upper and lower wheels. If you can, the bearings are worn and it may become impossible to keep the blade on.

2. Are the wheels in balance? To check this, take off the wheel guards and spin each wheel several times. If the same part of the wheel ends up at the bottom on several spins, the wheel is probably out of balance. The machine is likely to vibrate so

much that it would spoil the accuracy of your work—to say nothing of taking most of the pleasure out of it.

3. If you can turn on the saw, let it run a bit, listening for uneven sounds. Watch to see if the blade can be adjusted to run near the center of both wheels—a necessary thing.

MULTIPLE TOOL. If you are eagle-eying a secondhand Shopsmith, or one of the new flexible-use radial saws, or any other multipurpose tool, you'll need some of the tricks listed here, plus a few special ones.

1. Even if it is not set up to run, you can put it through its changes to see how easily it converts from one tool to another. Watch for damage to bars or rods that might prevent a quick shift.

2. Look for external signs of neglect—cracks, mars, and rust.

3. Most important is condition of the bearings and power-transmitting assemblies. About the only way to check these easily and surely is by running the machine under power. Your ear will tell you more about the condition of the machine in thirty seconds than your eye could in an hour.

4. Put a saw blade or sanding disc on the spindle to find out if it runs true. You can check this by holding a piece of wood against the disc or blade as it revolves. If it does not maintain even contact as it revolves, either the blade or disc is out of alignment—or the spindle is. Switch to another blade or disc. If the misalignment still shows up, you can figure that the trouble is in the spindle—a fairly costly replacement on most tools.

5. Check suitability of the combination tool much as you would with single-purpose tools. Is the depth of cut adequate for your sawing operations? As a drill press, is there enough distance from column to chuck? Is the spindle travel as long as you'll need?

CIRCULAR SAW. Decide first if this one is big enough for you. "Big" has three meanings here: depth of cut, horsepower of motor, area of table.

If you're going to build houses with it, you'll likely prefer a 10″ or 12″ saw with plenty of table and at least a ¾-horsepower motor. But for most home-workshop jobs an 8″ saw will have enough depth and a ½-horsepower motor will power it.

Now for the details:

1. Is the saw table cracked or warped? Check it with a straightedge. If it is damaged or off-flat, you don't want the machine—unless a replacement is available at a reasonable price. A look at the underside of the table will tell you how well it was

built; heavy ribbing is more important than thickness in giving strength.

2. Examine rip fence and miter gauge. Adjust the fence to see how easy it is to use. Is the miter gauge accurate, and can it be adjusted to accuracy if it is not?

3. Inspect such metal parts as the trunnions, watching closely for inconspicuous cracks. Trunnions can be replaced but you want to figure their cost into the price you are paying.

4. Work the controls that tip the saw arbor or table. They should work freely—or they'll be a nuisance, and you may be in for trouble.

5. And, of course, actually use the saw if power is available. If there is any hidden damage, your ear is likely to find it for you.

6. Look for lateral play in the spindle. Such play usually indicates worn bearings.

7. A loose pulley on the end of the spindle, or a scored spindle shaft, is evidence that you're probably going to have to buy a new spindle.

JOINTER. Any well-made jointer in good condition will do its main job—producing true flat edges, the kind you need when gluing up stock. But if you want it for other things, you'll have to examine it with these in mind. A good jointer is handy for beveling, chamfering, rabbeting, and for surfacing lumber. A jointer is not a thickness planer, but you can make a 6″ model do a pretty good job of surfacing stock up to 12″ wide.

With the question of size settled, look at the adjustments. Individual adjustment of both tables will permit such operations as spot chamfering. Sealed-for-life ball bearings are important—they'll save you a lot of trouble.

1. Work the various knobs that control the tables, to see that everything operates smoothly.

2. Use the fence adjustments. They should loosen easily and lock tightly. A jointer fence that creeps out of square or moves under pressure can ruin a lot of lumber before you discover it. And the fewer the knobs needed to control these adjustments, the handier and more trouble-free the machine is likely to be.

3. If the jointer is used, try the spindle for lateral play. If you can wiggle it up and down or from side to side, the bearing housings may be worn beyond the point where accurate work is possible.

4. Use a straightedge to check for warping of the table. You might about as well abandon any jointer with a bowed table.

Bring both tables to a level and check diagonally from corner to corner, both ways.

5. Search for broken castings. Small ones can usually be replaced at minor cost—but be sure replacements are to be had before you buy the tool.

6. More than likely, the knives will need sharpening. Can they be sharpened and then locked again *safely* in the head? Or should you add the price of new ones to the cost?

7. Try removing the screws that hold the blades in the head. If a screw won't come out, it's probably broken or about to break. Removing a broken screw can be quite an operation and there's little use buying yourself grief like that.

SANDERS. The question of suitability to your particular needs hinges mostly on whether or not you will own more than one kind of sander. If, for instance, you will have a disk sander available (or if it comes in combination with a belt sander) you won't ask the belt model to do any tricky operations. You'll use the latter mostly for sanding surfaces and edges of lumber.

But if you expect the belt finishing machine to do also the work commonly done with a disk, then it must have the proper table, one that will tilt within an adequate range. Accuracy is important.

1. On the belt machine, examine the drums for cracks. If you can run the machine, see if it tracks properly. A sanding belt that won't stay in position as it runs often indicates a shaft or spindle that has been bent.

2. Excess vibration in running is another sign that some part is out of true.

3. You can best check a disk sander (or the sanding disk on a belt sander or other tool) by running it. Listen for vibration. Let some object rest on the table while the machine is running; bad vibration will make the object hop around. At best, such a machine is no fun to use.

4. With a portable belt or jitter sander, design is the first consideration. Will the sander work close to an edge? Will it get into corners? For some jobs, these are prime questions, but if you intend it merely to take down table tops they make little difference.

5. In many portable belt sanders, condition of the guides will tell you a good deal. Open the machine up and inspect the surfaces against which the edge of the belt may bear in running. If the machine tracks badly, these may be cut—and so may the housing. With any machine having a motor built in, the condition

of that motor is probably the major factor. We'll discuss that a bit in a minute.

SHAPER. By the time you get into a tool like this, you probably know about what you want it to do. But there are a few points about condition to remember.

1. Look first at the spindle threads to be sure they are not damaged.

2. Check the spindle for lateral play. If you can move it at all from left to right, it's a good guess that bearings or bearing housings are badly worn. The machine will need a repair job before it will cut accurately.

3. Try all the controls to see that they are functioning.

4. Wind up with the usual operating test, if power is available. And, in any case, examine closely for cracked castings, cracked or out-of-true table, and the like.

MOTORS. In many tools, the motor is the important thing. This applies especially to portable drills, disk sanders, and grinders—where there are few moving parts outside the motor itself. It applies pretty much, too, to portable sanders, flexible-shaft setups, and radial saws.

Unfortunately it is not often feasible under buying conditions to tear down a motor sufficiently to examine it. You have to rely to a considerable degree on external clues.

1. Power is the first question. If you are offered an 8″ circular saw equipped with a ¼-horse motor, you might as well figure on replacing it. Check the power given on the nameplate and compare it if possible with the recommendations of the maker of the tool. Remember that these are figured for average conditions: if you are doing heavy work, you may need more power. Usually recommended are these horsepowers, the smaller figure applying to smaller tools or fairly light work, the larger figure to heavy work:

> 8″ circular saw, ½ or ¾ h.p.
> 10″ circular saw, ¾ or 1 h.p.
> 4½″ jointer, ½ or ¾ h.p.
> band saw, ⅓ or ½ h.p.
> belt and disk sander, ⅓ or ½ h.p.
> lathe, ⅓ or ½ h.p.
> 18″ jig saw, ¼ or ⅓ h.p.
> 24″ jig saw, ⅓ or ½ h.p.
> drill press, ⅓ or ½ h.p.

2. Read the name plate to be sure that the motor will work on your current, which is probably 115-volt, 50 or 60 cycle, single-phase. A three-phase motor is cheaper, but you probably can't use it.

3. Some kinds of trouble show up on the outside. Inspect for broken or cracked mounting or end plates, bent shafts, or burned lead wires.

4. Test for bearing trouble by trying to move the shaft up and down; any movement indicates worn bearings. Turn the shaft by hand: if it does not turn freely, you can suspect bad bearings, a bent shaft, or improperly assembled motor.

5. Availability of winding leads to permit reversing the motor is another desirable thing, though not always needed.

6. *After* completing the tests above, plug in the motor and turn it on. It should start briskly, come up to full speed quickly, and if it is a repulsion-induction type, there may be a distinct click as the starting switch cuts out the starting winding. The motor should run without much heating up. Signs of internal trouble: slow starting, slow running, smoke, noise.

7. Give it a smell test. Any off-smell suggests partially burned windings or a previously damaged motor.

8. If the motor refuses to start until you set it off by turning the shaft by hand it probably has a dirty or burned-out starting switch, burned out starting windings or capacitor.

9. Excessive sparking says that the commutator needs turning down and the mica separators should be undercut. This job costs only a few dollars, so it is not necessarily a fatal defect. But there is the risk that it may already have been done to the motor so many times that there is little copper left. It's usually hard to tell about this matter without removing one end bell from the motor.

Hard-headed checking of your prospective tool purchases against these standards is one way to be pretty sure you are getting your money's worth. An inaccurate, balky, or worn-out tool is no bargain at any price.

Sources of Information

PART I—IMPROVE YOUR FLOORS

E. L. Bruce Co. Memphis, Tenn. 38101	Plank, strip flooring, self-stick parquet flooring
Ozite Corporation 1755 Butterfield Road Libertyville, Ill. 60048	Indoor-outdoor carpet, self-stick carpet squares, Pride 'N Joy nylon shag self-stick tiles
Armstrong Cork Co. Lancaster, Pa. 17604	Resilient floor tile, indoor-outdoor carpet, wide seamless sheet vinyl
Congoleum Co. Kearny, N. J. 07032	Shinyl vinyl
The Flecto Co. Box 30 Oakland, California 96604	Seamless plastic flooring
Dur-A-Flex, Inc. 269 Franklin Ave. Hartford, Conn. 06114	Seamless plastic flooring

PART II—IMPROVE YOUR WALLS

Masonite Corp. 29 North Wacker Drive Chicago, Ill. 60606	Peg Board, Royalcote decorative paneling
Weyerhaeuser Co. Tacoma, Wash. 98401	Paneling

602

Georgia-Pacific Corp. P. O. Box 311 Portland, Ore. 97207	Hardboard, plywood, redwood
Marsh Wall Products Division of Masonite Corp. Dover, Ohio 44622	Marlite paneling
Evans Products Co. 1121 S.W. Salmon St. Portland, Ore. 97208	Rough boards, paneling
U. S. Plywood Corp. 777 Third Ave., New York, N. Y. 10017	Panel adhesive, plywood
California Redwood Assn. 617 Montgomery St. San Francisco, Calif. 94111	Information on working with redwood
Simpson Timber Co. 2000 Washington Bldg. Seattle, Wash. 98101	Redwood boards, redwood plywood
West. Wood Prodts. Assn. Yeon Bldg. Portland, Ore. 97204	Information on using lumber from the western pine region
Samuel Cabot, Inc. 246 Summer St. Boston, Mass. 02210	Stain Wax and other finishes for wood and concrete
United Wallpaper Co. 3101 South Kedzie Ave. Chicago, Ill. 60623	Flocked papers
Wallpaper Council, Inc. 969 Third Ave. New York, N. Y. 10022	Wallcovering information
Cole Custom Foils 70 Pike St. Seattle, Wash. 98101	Foil wallcovering
Birge Co. P. O. Box 27 Buffalo, N. Y. 14240	Scrubbable flocks

Grasscloth Unlimited
966 Mission St.
San Francisco, Calif.

Cloth wallcovering

Armstrong Cork Co.
Lancaster, Pa. 17604

Suspended ceiling

Am-Finn Sauna
Haddon Avenue & Line St.
Camden, N. J. 08103

Polyurethane Lite Beams
and wall paneling

PART III—MODERNIZE YOUR DOORS

Filon Corp.
12333 S. Van Ness Ave.
Hawthorne, Calif. 90250

Translucent fiberglass-
reinforced plastic sheets,
flat and corrugated

Samuel Cabot, Inc.
246 Summer St.
Boston, Mass. 02210

Paint, stain, Stain Wax

Pinecrest Inc.
2710 Nicollet Ave.
Minneapolis, Minn. 55408

Dividers, decorative doors,
plastic panels, imported
entryway items

Cardenas Division,
Architectural Designs, Inc.
2132 Pacific Ave.,
Tacoma, Wash. 98402

Custom plastic doors,
dividers

St. Louis Crafts, Inc.
15 W. Moody Ave.
St. Louis, Mo. 63119

Coppertone foil

Acme Appliance Mfg. Co.
P. O. Box 9807
Cleveland, Ohio 44142
P. O. Box 575
Monrovia, Calif. 91016

Sliding door hardware

A. E. Moore Co.
Waupaca, Wisc. 54981

Moore-O-Matic garage-
door opener

Filon Corp.
12333 S. Van Ness Ave.
Hawthorne, Calif. 90250

Designer carvings

Presto-Matic Lock Co., Inc.
8228 W. 47 St.
Lyons, Ill. 60534

Pushbutton door lock

Simplex Lock Corp.   Door hardware, including
150 Broadway   combination locksets
New York, N. Y. 10038

Kwikset   Door hardware, locks
516 E. Santa Ana St.
Anaheim, Calif. 92803

PART IV—WINDOWS AND SKYLIGHTS

Libbey-Owens-Ford Glass   Windows, Mirropane
  Co.
Toledo, Ohio
Mirror Division—
Brackenridge, Pa. 15014

Ventarama Skylight Corp.   Skylights
174 Main St.
Port Washington, N. Y.
  11050

Filon Corp.   Fiberglass-plastic panels
12333 Van Ness Ave.
Hawthorne, Calif. 90250

PART V—BATHROOM MODERNIZING

Eljer Plumbingware Div.   Triangular toilet, corner
Wallace-Murray Corp.   fixtures, designer
3 Gateway Center   bathrooms
Pittsburgh, Pa. 15222

Milwaukee Faucets, Inc.   Adjusto shower and tub
301 E. Reservoir Ave.   fillers, mixing valve
Milwaukee, Wisc. 53212   and shower hardware

Delta Faucet Co.   Dial faucets, single
Division of Masco Corp.   handle faucets
Greensburg, Ind. 47240

Arvin Industries, Inc.   "Tuck-In" heater
Columbus, Ind. 47201

Kohler Co.   Wall-hung toilets, fixtures
Kohler, Wisc. 53044   for above-floor roughing-in

Wade Inc.   Steel hangers for wall-
2021 N. 25th Ave.   hung toilets
Franklin Park, Ill. 60131

Jacuzzi Research, Inc. 1440 San Pablo Ave. Berkeley, Calif. 94702	Whirlpool Bath
American Standard 40 West 40th St. New York, N. Y. 10018	Ultrabath, Spectra 70 bath
Fiat Metal Mfg. Co. 3419 Fowler St. Los Angeles, Calif. 90063	Shower cabinets, fittings
American Bidet Co. 2094 Rosecrans Ave. Gardena, Calif. 90249	American Bidet
Speakman Co. Wilmington, Del. 19899	Colortemp faucet, Anystream self-cleaning shower head
NuTone Madison & Red Bank Rds. Cincinnati, Ohio 45227	Heater-Light-Ventilator
T&S Brass & Bronze Works 128 Magnolia Ave. Westbury, N. Y. 11590	Shower Queen handspray
Alsons Products Corp. Somerset, Mich. 49281	Personal showers
Davis Steel Products Co. Rm. 516 219 West Seventh St. Los Angeles, Calif. 90014	Davisteel in-a-wall scale
Formica Corp. 4614 Spring Grove Ave. Cincinnati, Ohio 45232	Panel system 202
The Swan Corp. 721 Olive St. St. Louis, Mo. 63101	Tubwall fiberglass liner
Kinkead Industries Inc. Showerfold Div. 5860 N. Pulaski Rd. Chicago, Ill. 60646	Showerfold tub enclosure
Dur-A-Flex 269 Franklin Ave. Hartford, Conn. 06114	Seamless plastic shower material

Viking Sauna Co.   Solo door for mini-sauna
909 Park Avenue
San Jose, Calif. 95150

Symtrol Valve Company   Temptrol '76 non-scald
445 C Street   shower valve
Boston, Mass. 02210

PART VI—TOWARD A BETTER KITCHEN

Ozite   Kitchen carpet, self-stick
1755 Butterfield Rd.   carpet tiles
Libertyville, Ill. 60048

Armstrong Cork Co.   Kitchen carpet, tiles
Lancaster, Pa. 17604

Masonite Corp.   Kitchen mural
29 Wacker Drive
Chicago, Ill. 60606

Formica Corp.   Plastic laminates
4614 Spring Grove Ave.
Cincinnati, Ohio 45232

The Flecto Co.   Flecto Seamless,
Box 30   pour-on plastic for counters
Oakland, California 94604

Dur-A-Flex   Pour-on plastic for counters
269 Franklin Ave.
Hartford, Conn. 06114

The Castolite Co.   Castoglas for table surfaces
Woodstock, Ill. 60098

NuTone   Power center for built-in
Madison & Red Bank Rds.   mixer-blender, ice crusher,
Cincinnati, Ohio 45227   juicer, etc.

Swanson Inc.   Hide-A-Way toaster, can opener
607 S. Washington St.   Kitchen Kaddy for paper goods
Owosso, Mich. 48867

Hobart Mfg. Co.   Super Hot Instant faucet,
Troy, Ohio 45373   dishwasher-sink combination

Fram Corp.   Water filter
General Products Division
Henderson, N. C. 27536

PART VII—IMPROVE YOUR HOME SYSTEMS

Intermatic Time Controls
International Register Co.
4700 West Montrose Ave.
Chicago, Ill. 60641

Time controls, switches,
appliance timers

Edco International Corp.
19302 Grand River
Detroit, Mich.

Delayed action switches

Paragon Electric Co.
1600 Twelfth St.
Two Rivers, Wisc. 54241

Time switches

Kirsch Company
309 North Prospect St.
Sturgis, Mich. 49091

Electrac traverse rod

Ramic Products Inc.
San Francisco, Calif. 94107

Time switches

Slater Electric, Inc.
45 Sea Cliff Ave.
Glen Cove, N. Y. 11542

Newly styled switches
and outlets

Leviton Mfg. Co., Inc.
236 Greenpoint Ave.
Brooklyn, N.Y. 11222

Full-range dimmer
and other switches
and receptacles

Sonus Corporation
15 Strathmore Road
Natick, Mass. 01760

Whistle Switch, Sonuswitch,
Pool Sitter

A. E. Moore Company, Inc.
Waupaca, Wisc. 54981

Moore-O-Matic garage-door
opener

Rasmussen Iron Works
12028 E. Philadelphia St.
Whittier, Calif. 90601

Automatic pilot for gas
fireplace, remote control
wall switch for fireplace

Filon Corp.
12333 S. Van Ness Ave.
Hawthorne, Calif.

Luminous ceilings

NuTone
Madison & Red Bank Rds.
Cincinnati, Ohio 45227

Music-intercom systems

PART VIII—BUILT-INS AND STORAGE

Swanson Inc.
607 S. Washington St.
Owosso, Mich. 48867

Hanging desk

Western Wood Pdts.
Yeon Bldg.
Portland, Oreg. 97204

Plans for Caravan
Storage Wall

Dorfile Mfg. Co.
1131 S.E. Umatilla St.
Portland, Oregon 97202

Lustra shelf system,
hanging desk

Meilink Steel Safe Co.
P. O. Box 2567
Toledo, Ohio 43606

Hercules home safe

Mosler Safe Co.
350 Fifth Ave.
New York, N.Y. 10016

Mosler home safe

Nor-Gee Corp.
4093 Walden Ave.
Lancaster, N.Y.

Nor-Gee between-studs
wall safe

George C. Brown & Co.,
    Inc.
Greensboro, N. C.

Cedar boards for closet
lining

Giles & Kendall Co.
P. O. Box 188
Huntsville, Ala. 35804

Cedarline paneling

PART IX—ADD A FIREPLACE

Acorn Fireplaces, Inc.
174 Main St.
Port Washington, N. Y.
    11050

Steel fireplaces

Vega Industries Inc.
Syracuse, N. Y. 13205

Zero-clearance fireplace,
Heatilator circulator core

Condon-King Co.
5611 208th S.W.
Lynnwood, Wash. 98036

Firehood, Machester-Pierce,
Aztec fireplaces

Fire Drum 172 Clara St. San Francisco, Calif. 94107	Steel fireplaces
The Majestic Co. Huntington, Ind. 46750	Gasilator, Majestic Thulman electric fireplace
Malm Metal Products P. O. Box 1479 Santa Rosa, Calif. 95404	Carousel, other steel fireplaces (also handled by Sears Roebuck Co., either stores or catalog)
Strawberry Bank Craftsmen Box 475 Little Compton, R. I. 02837	FirePot
Washington Stove Works P. O. Box 687 Everett, Wash. 98201	Olympic Franklin heaters, iron stoves
William Wallace Co. Belmont, Calif. 94002	Metalbestos all-fuel prefabricated chimney and fittings
Canterbury Enterprises 6523 Hollywood Blvd. Los Angeles, Calif. 90028	Dial-A-Flame log lighter
Rasmussen Iron Works Inc. 12028 E. Philadelphia St. Whittier, Calif. 90601	Gas logs, automatic fireplace lighter
FM Products 467 Harmony Lane San Jose, Calif. 95111	Heat-Master circulator fireplace liner
Northwest Tube & Metal Fabricators P. O. Box 02214 Portland, Ore. 97202	Enameled-metal prefab fireplaces

PART X—HOW TO ADD LIVING SPACE and APPENDIX A—YOUR HOME WORKSHOP

Armstrong Cork Co. Lancaster, Pa. 17604	Suspended-ceiling systems, Excelon vinyl-asbestos tile
Masonite Corp. 29 North Wacker Drive Chicago, Ill. 60606	Royalcote woodgrained hardboard and panel adhesive

American Plywood Assn. Tacoma, Wash. 98401	Information on plywood for subfloors
California Redwood Assn. 617 Montgomery St. San Francisco, Calif. 94111	Information on building redwood decks
West. Wood Prodts. Assn. Yeon Bldg. Portland, Ore. 97204	Information on building wood decks
Samuel Cabot, Inc. 246 Summer St. Boston, Mass. 02210	Decking stains
Filon Corp. 333 S. Van Ness Ave. Hawthorne, Calif. 90250	Translucent plastic for windbreaks and fences
Adjustable Clamp Co. 417 N. Ashland Ave. Chicago, Ill. 60622	Steel and wood clamps
Cincinnati Tool Co. 2018 Waverly St. Cincinnati, Ohio 45212	Woodworking and metal- working clamps

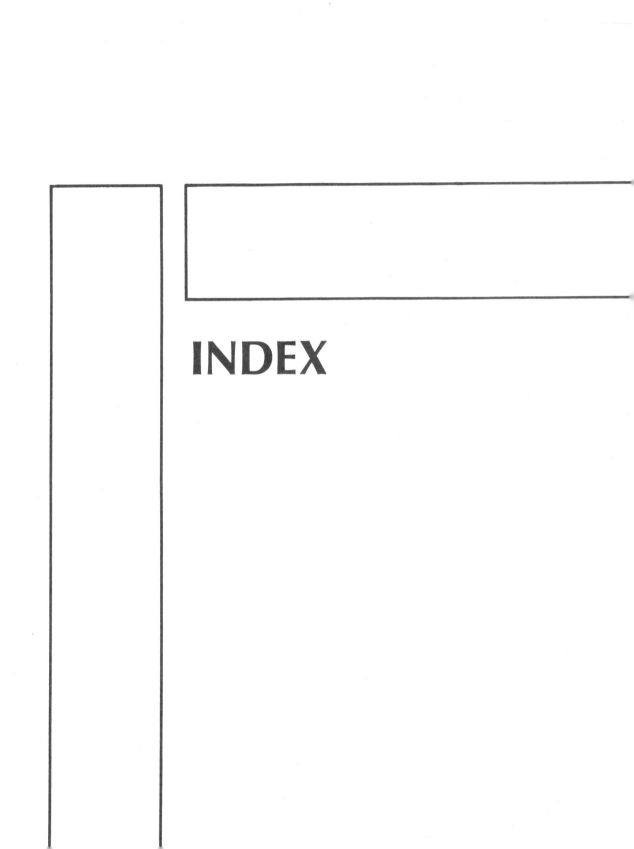

INDEX

Index

T _____

U _____